The Free State of Jones

and

The Echo of the Black Horn

The Free State of Jones
and
The Echo of the Black Horn

TWO SIDES OF THE LIFE AND ACTIVITIES OF CAPTAIN NEWT KNIGHT

THOMAS JEFFERSON KNIGHT AND ETHEL KNIGHT

Foreword by Jim Kelly

Racehorse Publishing

The Life and Activites of Captain Newton Knight originally published in 1935
The Echo of the Black Horn originally published in 1951 by Parthenon Press

First Racehorse Publishing edition 2016

Racehorse Publishing books may be purchased in bulk at special discounts for sales promotion, corporate gifts, fund-raising, or educational purposes. Special editions can also be created to specifications. For details, contact the Special Sales Department, Skyhorse Publishing, 307 West 36th Street, 11th Floor, New York, NY 10018 or info@skyhorsepublishing.com.

Racehorse Publishing™ is a pending trademark of Skyhorse Publishing, Inc.®, a Delaware corporation.

Visit our website at www.skyhorsepublishing.com.

10 9 8 7 6 5 4 3 2 1

Library of Congress Cataloging-in-Publication Data is available on file.

Cover artwork: Shutterstock

Print ISBN: 978-1-944686-95-6
Ebook ISBN: 978-1-944686-96-3

Printed in the United States of America

Table of Contents

FOREWORD   vii

PART ONE
The Free State of Jones by Thomas Jefferson Knight

Thomas Jefferson Knight's Story of His Father, Newton Knight   3
An Intimate Sketch of the Activities of Newton Knight and "Free
     State of Jones County"   13
South's Strangest 'Army' Revealed   73

PART TWO
The Echo of the Black Horn by Ethel Knight

PREFACE   91
CHAPTER 1. The Echo of the Black Horn   95
CHAPTER 2. The Sale of Rachel   102
CHAPTER 3. The New Slaves   119
CHAPTER 4. The Secession Convention   127
CHAPTER 5. The Volunteers of Mississippi   132
CHAPTER 6. The Deserter   142
CHAPTER 7. Organization   151
CHAPTER 8. Men of the Organization   176
CHAPTER 9. Bold Ventures   191
CHAPTER 10. The Sadness of War   205
CHAPTER 11. The Avengers of Ben Knight   218

CHAPTER 12. Preparation   228

CHAPTER 13. Captain Knight's Strategy   241

CHAPTER 14. Many Fronts   256

CHAPTER 15. The Captain's Decision   269

CHAPTER 16. December Battles   280

CHAPTER 17. The Last Year of the War   296

CHAPTER 18. The Carpetbag Rule of Jones County   302

CHAPTER 19. Reconstruction   311

CHAPTER 20. Discord   325

CHAPTER 21. The Unhappiness of Serena   333

CHAPTER 22. Shunned by Society   341

CHAPTER 23. Molly's Marriage   347

CHAPTER 24. Tom's Marriage   368

CHAPTER 25. The Captain's Last Days   381

Foreword

The remarkable story of Newton Knight is an American classic. After studying Newton Knight off and on for the past ten years I see Newt's experience resonates today more than ever. He was just 150 years ahead of his time. Newt is one of those rare individuals who took a stand for what he believed was right then lived his truth for the whole world to see. He was so comfortable in his skin that he seemed to live without fear. In one of his only interviews, at ninety-one, Newt observed, "You know, There's lots of ways I'd ruther die than be scared to death."[1]

Just as the war divided Jones County into warring factions, these two books offer competing accounts of who Newton Knight was. Thomas Jefferson Knight published the first biography of his father, *The Life and of Activities of Captain Newton Knight and His Company and the Free State of Jones County* in 1934. Tom was seventy-four years old and he gets a few dates mixed up and confuses names like Maury with Lowry. Tom was Newt's son with his first wife Serena. Tom relates stories his father told him and testimonies from people in the community. He portrays Newt as the good shepherd who loved children.

Tom knew his father to be a devout man who never drank, cussed, or used tobacco. Newt was also an avenging angel known for protecting the poor women and children against the tyranny of Confederate abuse. Tom writes that his father saved some black children from their white master who was trying to keep them in bondage after the war was over.

---

1 *New Orleans Item*, March 20, 1921.

After the war, Tom talks about Newt going to Jackson a lot on business. We know this is true also because Newton Knight was on the winning side of the war at first, and he held several key governmental and military appointments that would have required him to travel by rail to Jackson.

On the first page of his text Tom inserted an odd story about a young Newt killing a black boy and how his mother changed the date of his birth to protect him from being charged with murder (which was almost impossible). I believe Tom invented this story to demonstrate that his father was on the right side of the race issue. Tom never once mentions that Newton entered into a common law marriage with his wartime ally, a former slave woman named Rachel with whom he fathered many children. Tom's book also contains the rare Meigs Frost's interview with Newton .

The second book, *The Echo of the Black Horn* was published by Newton's grandniece Ethel Knight in 1951. Ethel was a very smart, independent woman, whose dark eyes seemed to look right through you. She dropped a bombshell when she introduced Rachel in her book. Although she used Rachel's character to denigrate Newt, Ethel's book was the only public acknowledgement of Newton's love for Rachel and their family together. Ethel alternately attacks Newt and Rachel with all of the racial venom she can muster because they had crossed one of the most taboo boundaries of white supremacy by mixing the blood of the races. Ethel seems to have a love-hate relationship with Newt, and she chronicles his skill as a military leader, his defense of the poor women and children during the war, and his alliance with blacks during the war and after.

When Mississippi's slaveocracy led the state into war in 1861 they had made one of the most colossal mistakes in American history. Historian James Silver wrote, "At least three generations of Southerners have paid a terrible price for the erratic behavior of their Confederate ancestors."[2] One of the cherished tenets of the Lost Cause apologists was the idea

---

2 James W. Silver, *Confederate Morale and Church Propaganda* (Tuscaloosa: Confederate Publishing, 1957).

that white Southerners were united in a noble war against overwhelming odds. The truth is the Confederacy was so divided against itself that it collapsed from within. Class antagonisms between small farmers and wealthy planters flared during the secession crisis, then exploded as the war dragged on. However, the yeoman farmers and cattle herders of Jones County had little use for a war over a "state's right" to maintain the institution of slavery. Realizing it was a rich man's war and a poor man's fight, thousands of men deserted the Confederate service in 1863. In Jones County Newton Knight became the leader of a pro-American, anti-Confederate rebellion that was one of many hammer blows from within the heart of the Confederacy that helped bring about its collapse.

Confederate President Jefferson Davis knew of the Knight Company men. Davis was informed in March of 1864 that the deserters in Jones County were "in open rebellion, defiant at the outset, proclaiming themselves 'Southern Yankees', and resolved to resist by force of arms all effort to capture them."[3] A week later another letter from the Pine Woods warned Confederate Secretary of War James Seddon that the Jones County deserters have "raised the United States Flag over the Courthouse in Jones County."[4] One Confederate force, almost one thousand strong had just invaded Jones County with "200 cavalrymen, a battalion of sharpshooters, and a section of horse artillery." Another Confederate detachment of nearly one thousand men led by Colonel Robert Lowry quickly followed. Lowry hanged nine or ten of the Knight Company men, including one or two who were just boys. Both raids were unsuccessful, and the Knight Company remained. Since the Confederates could not defeat Newt in battle they changed the names of the county and town.

Tom and Ethel's books also contain the 1865 petition to change the name of Jones County to Davis County in honor of Confederate

---

3 Lt. Gen'l Polk to Jefferson Davis, March 21, 1864, Official Records, 32 (3), 662-63.

4 W. Wirt Thomson, to James Seddon, March 29, 1864, Official Records, 32 (3), 711-12.

President Jefferson Davis and the name of the county seat (Ellisville) to that of Leesburg, to honor Robert E. Lee. This way Jones County's

> past history and name may be obliterated and buried so deep that the hand of time may never resurrect it, but by chance posterity should learn that there was a Jones county and the black part of its history. We would ask (not egotistically) that this petition, together with the names of those annexed, may be recorded in the journals of both Houses, that their mind (posterity) may be disabused of any participation on our part of any of its dark deeds, and in duty bound will ever pray.

Approximately one hundred people signed this petition. However, in 1866, Jones County Unionists petitioned to have the names changed back to Jones County and Ellisville. Approximately 233 names are on this petition.

Mississippi is now the last state to fly the Confederate battle flag and the governor recently proclaimed April as Confederate Heritage Month. Confederate Heritage has long been a misguided refrain of those whose perceptions were misinformed by "Lost Cause" mythology. After the war, white Southern politicians and ex-Confederates, including Jefferson Davis, set about sanitizing the memory of the war by glossing over the fact that the Confederates had committed treason to protect slavery. Unfortunately this falsified history was adopted into many American history textbooks and became the accepted version of events in the popular mind.

The upcoming release of the major motion picture *The Free State of Jones* has generated great interest in who Newton Knight was and what he was fighting for. There is no doubt that Newton Knight acted on principle as he fought for truth, justice, and the American way. One hundred and fifty years later he can rest in peace knowing that he was on the right side of history when many were not. He is buried on his old farm beside Rachel in their family cemetery. The inscription on his tombstone reads: "He Lived For Others."

Jim Kelly
May 2016

Part One

The Free State of Jones

Thomas Jefferson Knight's Story of His Father, Newton Knight

Naturally, the history, or story, of the Newt Knight Company, should begin with a short sketch of the man who was known to many in this section of Mississippi as the "Great Chieftain." This sketch is given by Thomas Jefferson Knight, son of the leader, as follows:

I will try to write a sketch of the life of Newton Knight, and I want to say that I will not be able to give it in full, as I would like to do, but will state the facts as I know them.

His father was Albert Knight, and his grandfather was Jacky Knight. His mother's name was Mason Rainey, and in some way that I have not learned, was a Griffin. She was raised an orphan by Jacky Knight. My father, Newton Knight, had eleven brothers and two sisters, the latter named Kisey and Martha. His brothers were: the eldest John, then Tom, Reuben, William, James, Albert, Jesse, Sill, Leonard, Frank, and Tailor was the youngest. My father was born on November 10, 1830, though the family records show it was 1833. His mother changed the record after he shot a negro boy to get him out of being punished in court. He was the eighth of the twelve boys, and was raised a poor farmer boy, making his living farming, also building houses for his neighbors. In those days they would go out in the woods, cut their logs and haul them up. Then they would split those logs and ask in a few hands and put the logs up. Then my father would hew them down on the inside, and when it was finished, they would call it a fine house.

Newton Knight's father died while he was yet a boy, and he did not get the benefits of any schools as schools were scarce in those days. Poor boys and girls were reared without an education. I have been told by those who knew him that he was a quiet and peaceful boy, being liked by all of his boy associates. They looked upon him as being a leader among them. He believed in peace, and was never known to be rough and rowdy, as some boys were. He was never known to have any trouble with anyone after he shot the negro boy. He was strictly business and did not believe in any kind of foolishness. When he was nineteen years old, he was married to my mother, who was Serena Turner, daughter of John Turner; her mother was a Duckworth, and as well as I can remember they were both reared in Jones County, Mississippi. After they married, my father purchased some land in Jasper County, Mississippi, about one mile from the Jones County line, about three or four miles north of where Soso is now located. He built a log house on this land, and he and Mother moved into it and went to work clearing the land for a farm, and they farmed there for some time, and three of their children were born there.

At about the time the war was declared between the North and the South, their home was burned and everything they had in the home was destroyed; so they moved back into Jones County, near where my father's mother lived, on a creek, near Old Hebron, a mile or two east of the Reddoch Ferry on Leaf River.

After war was declared, the Confederate States passed a conscription law, taking all men from eighteen years up to thirty-five, and in this they took my father and carried him off with lots of other good citizens who had voted to stay with the Union and would not enlist to go and fight the Union, and when they took my father, he told them he would go with them since he had to go, but he would not fight the Union.

So during the war and after the war, my father won a great name. He was considered one of the bravest and best men that ever lived. He was a kind-hearted man, and he was a man of good judgment, and was looked upon as being the leader in his community in matters of schools and other local affairs. Newt Knight was called on to lead in all these matters, though he had no education. My mother taught him to read and write after they were married, which was all the education he had. Yet with all that, he was looked upon as being a very smart man.

Following the surrender, he was appointed Provost Marshal and this gave him the power of Brigadier-General, with authority to call out troops of the United States Infantry to put down any riots or any other troubles which he could not stop. He served for several years during these reconstruction days, and people came to confer with him from many sections of the state, asking assistance in their troubles. I remember seeing an old negro man and his wife come crying one day to see my father and to get his assistance in effecting the release of his boy, who had belonged to Mr. Tom Mayfield. When the negroes were freed, they wanted to leave, and Mr. Mayfield refused to allow the boy to go. My father made arrangements for the boy's release, and the old couple left rejoicing and thanking him for his kindness. So, the next day Mr. Mayfield came to see my father. He wanted to keep the boy as he was raised on his place and he felt he had the right to keep him. But my father told him that as long as the negroes were slaves he had the right to keep him, but since they had been freed he had no further right to hold the negroes or their boy. Mr. Mayfield went away very much disappointed. I only mention this instance of settling a slave matter, though there were many more. Newt Knight was also appointed Federal Revenue Collector and handled the affairs of this office for some time. He had a great deal of government business to attend to, and was often in Jackson for three or four weeks, and I remember his account of an experience which befell him when five or six men attempted to catch and kill him at Newton, Mississippi.

My father had gone to Newton to catch a train, and while he was waiting he heard two men talking. One of them told the other that "that is Newt Knight; let's go and get some more men and take him out and kill him." My father waited until they had gone away. Then he went out to the cotton platform and arranged the bales so that he could hide behind them. Here he waited until the train pulled in. The men returned and stood very near him, so that he overheard them talking among themselves and telling how they wished they could kill him. When the train arrived, he slipped from beneath the cotton and caught it just as it was pulling out, but he overheard one of the men saying that "if we don't catch him now, we will wait for him and get him on his return trip."

Newt Knight told the governor of his experience at Newton, and the governor said: "We will trick them when you go back." When his business was concluded the governor gave him a good pistol and told him to buy a good double-barreled shotgun, and for him to shave off his beard and have his hair cut, and he would guarantee him that he would make the return trip in good shape. He had his long beard and his hair cut according to the governor's instructions, and when he stepped from the train at Newton with his new gun shining no one seemed to know him neither did they ask any questions. So, when he arrived at home, we children did not know him.

When my father went to Jackson or other places after that he carried his gun and was never bothered. He said he learned that it was best to go prepared for trouble and never wait until he got into it and it was too late. When he went to church he carried only his pistol, though he was a very quiet and peaceful man and never had any trouble with his neighbors. They looked upon him as a great man and a leading citizen.

I remember an occurrence when I was about twelve years old. My father and all other people for several miles around made occasional trips to Shubuta, Mississippi, to market their chickens, wool, and other kinds of produce which they had for sale in the springtime when my father, who was a poor man, needed supplies. It required six days to make the trip, going and coming. On this occasion he took me with him, and we rode behind a team of oxen. We would travel all day until late in the afternoon we would come to some big hollow that ran up near the road. Here we would stop and turn the yolk of oxen loose in the hollow, where I would keep after them until about dark. Then I would tie them up until just before daylight next morning, when I would turn them loose again, and in an hour or two they would be filled up again, so we would drive on.

So, it happened that one morning after we had left Shubuta the day before, we were traveling back towards home, and it was about ten o'clock, I suppose, when, as my father walked along beside his oxen, we saw a man riding a horse and coming in our direction. Father knew this man, but the man did not know him. Father said it was Babe Eaton and he was considered a very bad man. Eaton rode up to Father and pulled out of his saddle-bags the biggest pistol I had ever seen. He cursed and asked Father if he could dance. Father said, "yes, a little, sometimes." The man cursed again and told Father to go at it; he wanted to see if he could. So, Father danced some for him, so Mr. Eaton laughed heartily and said that was fine. He then put his pistol back into his saddle pocket. Father laughed a little and said "that would do to take a drink on, wouldn't it?" "Yes," said Mr. Eaton, "bring out your jug." Father stepped back to the end of his wagon which had a covered bow-frame on it, and instead of pulling out a jug he pulled his double-barreled shotgun out and aimed it at Mr. Eaton, asking him if he ever danced. The man said "No, but I guess I will have to try." "Yes," Father said, "dance or I will shoot you off your horse." Mr. Eaton very politely alighted from his horse and began to dance, jumping and skipping around until he was very hot and almost dead, and at last Father said to him, "that will do now, Mr. Eaton; when you get back home, tell your folks that you met Newt Knight today."

Mr. Eaton said to Father, "I thank you, Uncle Newton, I did not know it was you." He had married one of my father's nieces, but did not know him, although he had heard of him many times, and he was now learning who Newt Knight was. This incident has been told a great many times as a joke, but it was an actual occurrence. My father was a good, easygoing, kindly spoken man and would do anything for his neighbors. He was a shoemaker. I have known him to make shoes all day and into the night for his neighbors, and any time they needed assistance he was always ready to help. I have known people to come from miles away to get his advice on business or other matters. Some people were never able to understand how he could have been that sort of man when he had such a wide reputation over this part of the

South as being such a dangerous man. A few years ago, when this country went into the Great War, a great many young men went to him for advice as to what they should do. He told them invariably that his advice was for them if they were drafted to go ahead as good citizens and do their duty, as it was not like the Civil War.

Newt Knight was a man who believed in peace, in obeying the law of our country, and when the law for dipping cattle was enacted to eradicate the cattle tick, they dug a dipping vat about one-half mile from his place, and he assisted them in digging the vat. When it was finished and the people around about were notified to dip their cattle, some were opposed to it, and they sent a man to my father, asking him to meet them at the vat on the following night, when they would hold prayer meeting and blow up the vat. He said, "Boys, that is wrong; don't do that. I will never go into anything like that." And I want to say that his old friends never did go back on him as long as they lived. They always spoke well of him as being a great man. I remember carrying one of his old friends, Mr. Jim Thigpen, to see him about a year before he died. They had not seen each other for about fifty years. My father hired him to teach a school for our community when I was a small boy. So, when Mr. Thigpen wanted me to take him over to see my father, both were old white-headed men. I will never forget when I drove my car up to my father's home, Father recognized Mr. Thigpen and said to him, "Get out, Jim, and come in. I'm awful glad to see you." Mr. Thigpen got out of the car and grabbed my father around the neck and they hugged and patted each other for some little bit, crying and laughing at the same time. It made me shed tears to see these old tottering heads meet and be so happy to see each other. We stayed with Father until after dinner. My sister prepared a good dinner which we enjoyed very much. I sat and listened to those two old men talk about their adventures which they had in their young days and about the Civil War, and it was very interesting. As we went back to Laurel, where we both lived, Mr. Thigpen told me he thought as much of my father as he did of any of his brothers, having known him for more than seventy years, knowing him to be honest and reliable in all his dealings with other people.

Several years after the war, according to a story my father told, two men came to him one day when he was in Ellisville doing some trading at J. P. Myers' Store. They pretended to be great friends to him and were mighty glad to see him and soon began to talk about the war times. They told him how he was talked about as being the bravest man that ever lived, and about how easily he could fool the cavalry and get away from them. At last they proposed to him that he take his gun and go with them to the swamp and get into a thick place of bushes and show them how he would shoot his enemies, so that they might make some pictures while he was in the act of shooting. So, they pretended to be his best friends, and he agreed to go with them. However, just before they reached the place in the swamp, something seemed to tell him that he had better watch these men, as they might be luring him into the swamp to kill him. He said to himself that he would go with them but that he would keep his eyes open.

When they reached the spot selected by the men—a very thick place of bushes and undergrowth—here they had him back himself into the undergrowth with just a small opening for making the pictures. Here he posed for them with his gun in firing position, and the pictures were taken. Then one of the men stepped toward him and suggested that he hand him his gun and show him how he used to get away from the cavalry. My father said: "No, I'll give my gun to no man, but I will give you both barrels of what is in it if you don't leave here and do it now!" They left him in a considerable hurry. Instead of showing them how he got away he showed them how to get away and he returned to the store and completed his trading. My father said he never saw those men anymore—if he did, he did not know them. He returned home, and he said he did not go into the swamps to have his picture made anymore. He told his children, "Never allow any man to hug and pat you, for he is likely to be pretending to be your friend when he really intends to do you harm and deceive you."

Just a few days ago I was told by a friend of mine that he heard a lady tell his wife that she knew old Newt Knight, that he was the meanest man she ever saw; said she knew of him killing lots of men after the war. I want to say the lady must have been dreaming. In best respect to this lady I want her to point out just one man he killed and leave the others off. I have known him all my life. I ought to know him, as he raised me, and if he ever killed any men after the war I sure would have known something about it. So such false accusations are why I am writing this book. I know and there are hundreds of others who know there was not a more peaceable man to be found than my father. He stayed at home attending to his own business unless he had business away from home, then he would return back just as soon as he could. He was never known to go about over the settlement stirring up trouble trying to attend to other people's business. He always said he had no time to try to attend to other men's business, that he had plenty to do to attend to his own business. The lady must have meant during the war when he killed those men she told about. So in all of my recollection of him I never knew of but one man he tried to hurt and he was somewhere near seventy years old then. It took place at Sunday School near his home. There was one man in the settlement who got mad with my younger brother about some hogs, and as my brother was fixing to move off in a few days he wanted to whip my brother before he left, so he got his brother-in-law and one more man so those three men plotted how they would get him off from home so they could get the advantage of him. After learning of he and his family going to the Sunday School they went and laid for him at the schoolhouse. My father was there too. And just as they closed their Sunday School it just so happened that I rode my horse up to the yard and got off of him and they came out of the house. I spoke a few words to my brother about his moving. So the man who was mad with my brother said to him, "I want to talk to you a minute." He spoke kindly to him. I never had the least idea of him raising a fuss with him. So they walked off from the yard and he squatted down on a pine limb. About the second word he said he began cussing my brother so my brother turned to walk off from him. The man jumped up and grabbed that limb he was on and hit my brother and he fell. We all thought he was killed. We all went running to where they were and as soon as I got there I jerked the limb out of this man's hand and threw it off to one side. Then I began working on him with my fist. So about that time his brother-in-law got a hold on me and then as my father was old he was the last man to get there so just as he came trotting up to where we were the third man picked up one of his feet and kicked my father with the toe of his shoe on his shin-bone and he peeled the skin off about 8 inches. So my father never said a word to anyone but made a hit with his knife at that man's neck vein. The doctor said he only missed it about one-eighth of an inch. So that ended the fight. The cut man had to have a doctor to stop the blood. So my father said it looked to him like it was a free-for-all fight and he was old and had been crippled up and he just did not feel like being kicked about by anyone and especially by a big young man. He said he would learn him that it was Newt Knight he was kicking. So my father put him in bed for thirty days or more. So we all got into court about the fight. It was all settled in Justice Court except my father's case, and he waived his right to the grand jury. So those three men, determining to have him put in the penitentiary, got three true bills against him as though he was some great murderer or some great outlaw. So when his case came up in court I was there and those three men swore some of the hardest things I ever heard, trying to send him to the penitentiary. So my father's lawyer had him plead guilty to the charge of attempt of murder so the judge opposed the other two indictments. After the judge heard those three men make their statements he asked my father to stand up. I thought he wanted all the people in the court room to see him. So he began talking to him, telling him what a serious charge he was charged with. "Now, Mr. Knight, you are an old man and I have been told by some of the best old citizens of this county that you have been one of the best and quietest citizens ever since the war that can be found in Jasper County or anywhere else. So as you was out at Sunday School trying to serve your God and as it seemed those three men were strolling around hunting trouble and found it, I am going to make it just as light as I can. Twenty-five dollars, and if you have not the money you can make bond with the sheriff for twenty-five dollars. You can go home and send it to him," said the judge. So I, the writer, made the bond and all went home. I want to say I sure was sorry this thing happened. Those three men were some of my best friends and neighbors, so after it was all over we just forgot the past, and I am glad to say we were still friends and neighbors just as we had been. So I would not have written this if the lady had not told what she did about my father.

My father was a Primitive Baptist. He joined at Zora Church, about three miles southeast of Ellisville, Mississippi, about 1885 or '86 don't remember just when. So when he died he was trusting in God of all power, both in heaven and on earth, who rules and super-rules all things according to his own will and purpose.

An Intimate Sketch of Activities of Newton Knight and "Free State of Jones County"

(As Told by His Son, Thomas Jefferson Knight, of Laurel, Miss.)

In presenting this brief historical review of the life of Newton Knight and the circumstances of his unusual position and stand in the time of the American Civil War (1861–65), I do not wish to stir up confusion, nor to mislead anyone as to the facts. The facts are what I want you to know.

There have been many histories, biographies, write-ups, and stories of our state and nation and of various sections of both. Mississippi has come in for her share of these writings; yet in it all, the story of the life and activities of Newton Knight and the so-called "Free State of Jones County" has been largely overlooked.

There are said to be two sides to all questions, and since much has been said and written in a general way about these events, I am asking my friends to allow me the same privilege, that I may give "the other side" as it was.

The following is a list of the company of United States Infantry organized and equipped at Salls Battery, Jones County, Mississippi, on the 13th day of Oct., A.D., 1863, and commanded by Captain

Newton Knight, until the 10th day of September, 1865. The names of the company:

Captain Newton Knight, 1st Lieut., J. J. Collins, 2nd Lieut., W. W. Sumrall, 1st Serg.,; Sim Collins, Second Serg., W. P. Turnbow, First Corp., Alphus Knight, Second Corp., S. T. Owens.

Privates:

Tapley Bynum, P. N. Bynum, Montgomery Blackwell, J. W. Blackwell, J. M. Collins, B. F. Collins, M. C. Collins, K. J. Collins, M. M. Coats, S. C. Colman, B. F. Cawley, James Ewlen, J. M. Gunter, Tucker Gregg, B. H. Hinton, John Hogan, J. W. Hatchhorn, G. M. Hatchhorn, W. B. Jones, M. W. Kerven, S. W. Kerven, J. M. Knight, T. F. Knight, H. C. Knight, B. F. Knight, C. F. Prince, Laze Mathews, Ausbery McDaniel, Daniel Reddoch, J. J. Valentine, Patrick Valentine, M. B. Talentinie, Elija Welborn, Terrell Welborn, Younger Welborn, W. Y. Welborn, R. J. Welch, T. T. Welch, W. M. Welch, H. R. Welch, N. V. Whitehead, G. J. Whitehead, D. W. Whitehead, James Yates, Thomas Yates, Joseph Youghn, Mose Richardson, R. H. Valentine, Tom Colman, Dickey Knight, Levy Prints, Dave Prints, John Jones, Green Hoskins, Berry Jordan, Jeff Lee, Marge Michel, Jack Smith, Jesse Smith, Jack Arnol, Jim Blackledge, Allen Blackledge, Jim Tiner, Drew Gilbert, Archy Walter, J. L. Walters, Guss Lambert, Blake Lambert, Enoch Davis, Math Davis, Tom Flint, Colvan Reeves, R. C. Reeves. When enlisted: Oct. 13th, 1863.

This is a copy of the muster roll of the officers and privates as shown in said muster roll of Captain Knight, in the organizing of said company.

These are the ones who enlisted after organization: Tom Holoman, Jim Holoman, Giles Loftin, Elisha Wade, Daniel Wade, Scott Bush, Mose Walters, John Willis Musgrove, Bill Holifield, Bill Cranford, Bill Elzey, B. F. Dykes, D. Prigen, Jack Holifield.

Those are all the names I have. There were more but I haven't got them.

These are the names of men of the Newton Knight Company who were killed and those who were captured and carried off: Tapley Bynum, killed on picket at his home near Tallahoma Creek, January 10, 1864. P. M. Bynum, cut off by Lowry Company, re-enlisted at New Orleans in Colonel Tisdale's regiment. J. M. Collins, captured on picket by Lowry Infantry, April 25, 1864. B. F. Collins, captured April 25, 1864. M. C. Collins, captured April 25, 1864. M. M. Coats, captured April 25, 1864. S. C. Coleman, run down by dogs and hung April 15, 1864. R. J. Collins, cut off by Lowry Company, April 25, 1864, re-enlisted in Captain Wolfe's company, New Orleans, La. James Ewlen, captured in Jasper County by Lowry Company on picket, April 25, 1864. J. M. Gunter, captured in battle near Leaf River in Jones County, hung by Lowry Company Dec. 28, 1864. Tucker Gregg, shot and killed on picket in Covington County, Miss., Lowry Company April 11, 1864. B. H. Hinton, captured by Lowry Company on picket April 16, 1864. W. B. Jones, cut off by Lowry Company and re-enlisted in Captain Wolfe's company, Colonel Tisdale's regiment. M. W. Kirven, wounded in battle in Perry County, Miss., Dec. 10, 1864. B. F. Knight, run down by hounds and hung April 15, 1864, by Lowry Company. Lazarus Mathews, captured April 20, 1864, by Lowry Company. Daniel Reddoch, killed on picket by Lowry Company, April 15, 1864. J. J. Valentine, captured by Lowry Company April 25, 1864. Patrick Valentine and M. B. Valentine, captured April 25, 1864. Elijah Welborn, cut off by Lowry Company April 25, 1864, enlisted in Captain Wolfe's company, New Orleans, La. T. T. Welch, captured April 25, 1864. W. M. Welch, captured April 25, 1864. H. K. Welch, captured April 25, 1864. Younger Welborn, captured April 25, 1864. W. Y. Welborn, captured April 25, 1864, Lowry Company, N. V. Whitehead, killed on picket in Covington County, Miss., by rebels, April 18, 1864. T. J. Whitehead, run down by dogs and hung, April 16, 1864, by Lowry Company. D. W. Whitehead, run down by dogs and hung by Lowry Company, April 16, 1864. Thomas Yates, run down by dogs and hung by Lowry Company, April 16, 1864. Moses Richardson, wounded in battle on Tallahala Creek near Ellisville, Miss., by rebels, December 24, 1864. R. H. Valentine, captured April 25, 1864, near Knight's Mill, on picket by

Colonel Lowrey Company. Seventeen were captured and carried off, and I have been told some of these escaped and came back.

According to my father's old muster roll, here are the battles that were fought by him and his company:

The first battle was at Salesbattery, Jones County, Mississippi, near Smith's Store, October 13, 1863.

Two, battles at Levi Valentine's old field, on November 1, 1863.

Three, battles at Curry Creek, in Covington County, November 1, 1863.

Four, battles at Tallahala Creek, near Ellisville, December 24, 1863.

Five, battles at Rocky Creek, near Ellisville, April 26, 1864.

Six, battles at Reddoch's Ferry. Seven, battles at Big Creek Church. Eight, battles at Cohay Creek in Covington County, April 15, 1864.

Nine, battles at Hebron Lodge. Ten, battles at Knight's Mill, April, 1864. Eleven, small skirmishes on picket near Knight's Mill, April 16, 1864. Twelve, captured a lot of rebel prisoners near Reddoch's Ferry, Jones County, said to have belonged to Forrest's cavalry, twenty-one in number. These were paroled in November, 1864.

Thirteen, battles at Big Creek, December 28, 1864. Fourteen, battles at Gunter's near Leaf River, December 28, 1864. Fifteen, skirmishes January 10, 1865, at Salesbattery. In the last fight, J. M. Valentine was wounded by Miller's cavalry; S. G. Owens was wounded by Captain Gillis's company; J. M. Gunter, killed by Captain Gillis's company; Tucker Gregg, killed by Colonel Lowry's company near Cohay Creek.

These battles are the ones my father would write down on his muster roll, which he kept throughout the war.

One of the strange things about my father's activities was that he would never tell anyone how many men they killed or wounded. All he would ever tell us was that when they were in battle they killed everyone they could. "It was to kill or be killed," he would say, "so we did the best we could. We got lots of them, and for some cause they bothered us very little in the last year of the war."

* * * *

As there has been so much said and written about the Free State of Jones County, and about Newton Knight and the company he helped to organize during the Civil War, and as there have been some facts and lots of erroneous statements concerning the same, I feel that it is my duty to try to write the facts about him and his company. As I am the only son of said Newt Knight, I can say that his company was composed of the very best citizens of Jones and Jasper counties; and I mean the BEST.

Therefore, in writing this statement, or account, there is no intention or purpose on my part to insinuate against the good name of anyone or anyone's people.

Just the facts—that is my only aim. I wish to show the people who have accused my father and his Company of being bushwhackers, jay-hawks, and deserters, lying out and keeping out of the Confederate army, that those accusations are false.

The truth is, my father never joined the regular army of either side. In the first place, Jones County never seceded from the Union, as some claim. The people held an election to see whether they would secede or not. So one Mr. J. D. Powell was the candidate for delegate to the convention. He favored remaining with the Union. Mr. J. M. Bayliss was the candidate of the secessionists. Powell received about 376 out of 400 votes and Bayliss 24 votes; so it can be seen how Jones County stood with regard to secession.

Therefore, when Mr. Powell went to the convention at Jackson, and after all of the counties had voted to secede, except Jones County, he reversed his vote and left his party and joined with the secession party. So the union party had no representative after Mr. Powell left them. Jones County still stood 375 for the Union and when Mr. Powell turned over with Bayliss, it gave them 25 for seceding.

This situation prevailed until the war was declared between the North and the South, and the Southern states passed a conscription law, which was to take all over eighteen years old and up to thirty-five years old. I learn that, by conscripting and some enlisting, three compa-nies were organized, and that some help was given in raising four more companies in Jasper and Covington counties.

In this way my father was caught in the conscription, and a great many more citizens were carried along with him, off to war.

As my father had voted to stay with the Union, he told the officers he would not fight the Union but would go and wait on the sick and wounded soldiers. He was, therefore, placed in the Seventh Mississippi Battalion, as hospital orderly.

He went and did his duty as every good man should do. Everyone who knew him liked him. He was very kind to the soldiers in his care.

When the Southern States passed the "20-negro law," so that a man having twenty negroes or more could stop fighting and go home, and if he had forty negroes he could get a brother out if he wished to, one Mr. Jasper Collins went to my father, they being good friends, and told him that he had quit, as it was a "rich man's war and a poor man's fight." He said he was going home. It happened that my father had just received a letter from my mother stating that the Confederate cavalry had come to her home, and that one of the men had caught her horse out of the barn, placed the saddle upon it, and got on the horse, and cursed and abused her as she cried and begged that he leave her the much-needed animal. It was several miles to the nearest mill and there were several children to be fed.

This was too much for my father, so he went to his captain and asked for a furlough, and he and Jasper Collins came back home. They found that the Confederate army had been all through Jones County, destroying everything they could. They would go into a poor woman's home where they had cloth in the loom, trying to make clothing for their little children while their husbands were off in the war, and they would take the cloth and many other valuables.

When my father and Mr. Collins learned how the defenseless women and children and old men were being mistreated, they decided, as they had never joined the Confederate army, they had the right to quit when they so desired.

And it was not very long before a great many of the Confederate soldiers from this county and other counties left the army and came home, following the 20-negro law. They decided that if they had to fight, they would fight at home, trying to protect their families and their property.

Thus it was not long before the Confederates sent raiders into Jones County to capture those men who had come home and failed to return to their commands.

The result was that my father and Mr. Jasper Collins, and many other citizens (whom I may name later in this narrative), after realizing the fact that Jones County, almost 100 percent for the Union, was in for a fight, decided among themselves to organize a company of their own to fight for their rights and the freedom of Jones County.

These citizens came together with an obligation binding themselves to each other to fight for these rights and for each other to the last man; never to surrender to the Confederate States until the last man was killed, or until the war ended. The obligation was somewhat in this order: "As it has become necessary for us to organize a company of men to fight for our rights, for which we live, and to protect our families and also our property; Therefore, be it resolved that we select a captain and two lieutenants." Newton Knight was elected as captain, Jasper Collins first lieutenant; W. W. Sumrall, second lieutenant; J. M. Valentine, first sergeant; Simeon Collins, second sergeant; Alphus Knight, first corporal; S. Y. Owens, second corporal.

These went before Mr. Vince Collins, he being a Justice of the Peace, and here they took oath of their various offices.

The next day they met, and Captain Knight gave his company instructions. A part of these instructions were that they were not to destroy or tear down property or anything that belonged to their enemies, treat them kindly just as long as they permitted such treatment; they were not to shoot to kill anyone except to protect their own lives or those of the company or families of same.

The men were then instructed upon an agreed password, so that all might be recognized at night by sentries, etc. One of these passwords was: "I am the Red, White and Blue." And the guard or sentry would say: "I am a friend to you. Come up to camp and be recognized."

The company had several camping places, and where cavalry was in other parts of the county, these members of the company would work around in one another's cornfields in crop time, and they maintained watches. Many of these men had horns which they blew as signals which each and every member of the company understood.

My father, Captain Knight, had a solid black horn. It was the only black horn I ever saw and it had a different sound from any of the other horns, so that when he received any news about the cavalry coming in, he would go to a certain place with which all were familiar and blow his horn, and soon the other members of his company would gather around him for orders.

The company did not remain together and under orders except when Captain Knight or some of the scouts were looking for the cavalry to come in. But I want to tell you that sometimes they got mixed up and things got hot in those days. Sometimes the cavalry got Captain Knight's company on the run, and sometimes Knight's company had the cavalry on the run.

Before I go further into this narrative, I wish to say here that I am proud of the fact that none of the men who went into the Confederate army ever came back with any of the cavalry to destroy the property and cause distress among the poor people. I learned that it was a Company from the State of Louisiana Cavalry that came through Jones County destroying property, commanded by a Colonel Lowry who it seems had no mercy on the people here in Jones County. They were mighty rough on the boys they caught in Jones County. They caught one of my father's brothers and one Mr. Whitehead and hung both of them. Lowry thought it was my father and had them hung without a cause. So he got things stirred up here in Jones County, and Newt Knight and his company got busy and made it too hot for them. After carrying those two men they had hung to our house and placing them on the floor, they all left for Ellisville, Mississippi, and stayed there the remainder of the day and all that night. Captain Knight and his company got word the Lowry company was coming back over where they caught the two men the day before. He and his company went to Rocky

Creek where the cavalry was to cross and hid themselves by the side of the banks of the creek and it wasn't long after they got orders how to shoot and had got comfortably located, until Lowry and Company came along at a gallop, seemingly in high spirits. They were talking in a high tone of voice, seemingly having a good time in pursuit of Captain Knight and his company. All at once and to the surprise of Lowry and his company, Captain Knight and his company rose up out of the creek and began shooting at Lowry and his men, then the leaders of Lowry's company began falling off of their horses, dead or wounded. The rest of the cavalry that was behind turned their horses back toward Ellisville. One of the cavalrymen said several years afterwards talking about the war that he "picked his horse up with his spurs and flew back to Ellisville." He said he had never been frightened so bad in all his life. There was about fifty cavalry in their company and Newt Knight's company, I have been told by my mother, killed and wounded fifteen men and killed three horses in that battle at Rocky Creek. That wound up their work for that day. They had revenge for the way the cavalry had done them the day before.

Things seemed to be quiet for a few days until they got their dead buried. They went to other parts of the state and recruited their forces, and then came back. As I have stated, they had several camping places, and I remember hearing my father tell about camping one night, in the fork of the branch called Panther Branch, near the Jasper County line about three miles north of Soso. Where the two branches came together was very boggy and nobody could get through there except those who knew the place. They had out a watchman on the little path that led down into the forks of the branch. Just after breakfast the watchman came running to the camps saying the cavalry and their dogs were coming right down into the camps after them and sure enough the cavalry had them completely surrounded. There was a road that crossed the branch about one half mile from where they were camped. They began to ask Captain Knight what they must do to be saved. There were only about ten of Knight's company present, so they knew they could not stand much chance to fight fifty or sixty cavalry. The dogs were coming barking on the trail of the watchman. Some of them began to say "My God, what can we do?" Captain Knight told them to follow him, he would help them to safety, God being their leader. "Let's go. We will have to get out of here and try to get over into Etahoma swamp." This was about one mile across hills and hollows, and they had to cross the road that led across the big branch. The cavalry thought that Knight's company would come down the branch, and they had the road completely blocked. They were sure they would get all of them, but Captain Knight told his men to follow him, so they crossed one prong of the branch and went up a hollow and crossed the road upon the hill. Captain Knight gave his men orders if anyone saw any cavalry not to shoot until instructed. As they came out of the branch they saw a cavalryman drop down behind a big log. He did not say anything to them. They made it safe across the road and the dogs were in behind them. By the time the dogs got to the road and the cavalry got together Knight's men were just about to the swamp. The dogs and cavalry kept coming on. They hiked out across the woods about two miles over into Clear Creek swamp and crossed the creek on logs. As the last man crossed he sprinkled some parched red pepper on the logs. When the dogs got there they stopped. It seems they did not like that red pepper. They began to cough and sneeze and turned back. That was the end of that hunt.

Next day the cavalry was out pretending to hunt Captain Knight's company and about fifteen of the cavalry rode up to a lady's house and asked her where her husband was. He being one of Captain Knight's company, she told him she did not know where he was. He replied, "Yes, you do know. Tell us where he is." "I told you the truth, I do not know," she said, "but Sir, I can find out for you in a few minutes." She turned and walked to the side of her house and took down a blowing horn that was hung up on a peg and blew it one time. Right down a big hollow below the house there was a horn answered and just over on the hill beyond there another horn blew, and another and another. Five or six horns answered her. The leader of the cavalry said, "My God, we will all be killed in less than 15 minutes." I tell you they left NOW. They were not slow getting away. They never did come back to ask her any more questions about her husband but left and went to another part of the county.

Things were quiet for a few days but in about one week they came back and as part of Knight's company was camping in the forks of Horse Creek near Service they started another hunt with their dogs, on one prong of the branch that runs out where Soso is now. They started down to the branch with some on one side and others on the other side. They went on down near Knight's camp, the captain being out at Sallie Dulancy's house, getting some cooking done. When he heard horses running he looked out and saw the cavalry coming. He had to go a path through the field to the spring near their camp, and go about 200 yards through the field. As soon as he started the cavalry began shooting at him, but he made it back to the camp. They shot his shotbag strap in two and two holes in his hat, and three holes shot through his coat. A few minutes after he got to the camps one Mr. McGilbery and his dogs came right on down to the spring. He could not come any further on his horse but the dogs kept right on to the camps, so Knight's company began killing dogs. Mr. McGilbery, sitting on his horse said, "You quit killing my dogs." One of Knight's company men stepped up to a big oak tree and laid his rifle upside of the tree and shot McGilbery off of his horse. Some of the boys went up to him where he was laying on the ground. He begged them not to shoot any more. He asked them to give him some water before he died. One of Knight's army raised him up and another one dipped up some water and give him. They laid him down and one of the boys stuck his finger in the bullet hole where his brains were running out. They carried him to a house nearby where he died that night. The rest of his company formed a line and marched away and left him in the hands of Knight's company. They did not make any further attempt to go to battle with Captain Knight and his army. On that occasion they had lost their leader and a number of their dogs and thought it safer for them to travel on until a better day. Knight and his company were well-trained soldiers and were well fixed with supplies and ammunition and knew the country, and the places to camp, so they whipped Lowry and his company on every occasion and won every battle.

On one occasion Captain Knight said the supplies began to get scarce, and about that time he learned there were big supplies of corn sent by the government to Paulding, Jasper County, Mississippi. So he and his company got up six wagons and went to Paulding. About fifteen of his boys went to guard the wagons and supplies. As soon as they got to Paulding Captain Knight went to the saloon keeper who at that time kept whiskey to sell and told him not to let his men have any whiskey that if he did he would shoot him. He did not want his men to get drunk because they might raise trouble up there. He then went to the man in charge of the store and asked him to let his men have some supplies. The man said he had no orders to let his men have anything. Knight asked him to open the door and he replied that he had no orders to open the door. So Captain Knight called to one of his men to bring him an axe out of the wagon, which he did, and Captain Knight took the axe and walked around to the side of the house and began to chop him out a door. The keeper of the store hollered out, "Don't do that, Captain Knight, I will open the door for you." Captain Knight replied, "I asked you to open the door but you said you had no order to open up so you need not bother yourself. I will soon have a door open around here." He kept on chopping, and soon had a hole chopped in the house. He told one of his men to drive the wagon around there, then to load it. So he loaded his wagon. They kept on driving up the other wagons and loading them until all six wagons were loaded. He said there was some Irish families that lived there at Paulding. They came to Captain Knight and told him that they were out of bread to eat for their families. He told them to get all they wanted. They did not want to go to the war and fight, so they would not let them have any supplies to eat. So my father kept his men there until the Irish people got all the corn they wanted, then my father, Captain Knight, bid them good-bye and bade the Lord to bless them. So they left for Jones County, and made the trip without any trouble. There they distributed corn out to all who needed it. They hardly ever ran short on ammunition, or supplies either. They would learn of wagons loaded with supplies coming through the county, and they would watch for them, and when they came upon them they would stop the driver and get as much as they needed. Then they would tell them to go on. In that way and in the spring and summertime by making a crop they got by. There were lots of good women who would cook for them. They felt like it was their duty to cook or do all they could, as Knight's company was protecting them and their property, and they helped them in other ways. The cavalry had lots of dogs that would trail Knight's men and run them to their camp and if the cavalry could catch a few of them away from the company they would run them down and catch them and hang them. But if they could outrun the dogs and cavalry by going through branches and swamps until they could get to the company they were safe.

The rebels would not follow them into the company's camps. I suppose they thought it would not be healthy to go where there was so much powder and buckshot, ready and awaiting them. The ladies were sorry for those poor hungry dogs, so they would feed them, and naturally they would eat anything they gave them and they would eat so much of the good grub the ladies would give them that they would go off and die. They used a great quantity of powdered red pepper, mixed with other ingredients, so it would make the dogs so hot they would die. They soon got rid of all the dogs. Captain Knight's company wasn't bothered but very little more with the dogs then. The cavalry said it would be best to keep their dogs, to catch the runaway negroes. On another occasion my father said his cousin, Alpheus Knight, was to get married on a certain night in Christmas week and there was a certain woman in the settlement that didn't like my father's company of men. So she wrote a note to the rebels' cavalry at Ellisville and delivered it to them. Captain Knight got word of her sending the note. At the time there wasn't more than ten of Knight's company together there, so my father told his cousin to go ahead and get married that he and the rest of them would be there on watch for the rebels. My father started about dark down to the river at the crossing to guard the crossing. Some of them said to him, "Captain, you will get mighty cold down there in the swamp." He said no, he would not that God always lit up a fire into a man's heart to keep him warm when he was doing the right thing. He went on to the river and walked up and down the river about 1 to 2 mile above the crossing then back down below the crossing then back. He said he kept up walking all night. It was awful dark and lonesome down there, and about sun-up he heard a rattling of chains up at the crossing. So he slipped up near enough to see them. It was about one hundred cavalry crossing the river on the ferry boat. He had to go about 1 to 2 mile to where Alpheus Knight and his bride was but he said he made that 1 to 2 mile pretty fast. He got in the house and they said, "You are just in time for breakfast." He said, "You got lots of good eating but I have no appetite. There is a fight coming." They kept on urging him to eat, so he said, "I will eat some pie and cake and drink a cup of coffee, but come on, we got to get out of here, there is about one hundred Confederates marching toward this house now." So they got their guns and he and his cousin and other of my father's men went another direction and were to meet at another point nearby. He and Alpheus and his wife and two other women started down through an old bay place and struck an old field. About the time they got 200 yards from the house they heard the horses running and the ladies began to get frightened and one lady had a baby in her arms carrying it, so she said, "I can't carry this baby and keep up with you." My father said to her, "I will carry your baby." He took the baby and she said, "Captain, I will carry your gun." "No," said he, "no one carries my gun but myself." The noise they heard was some colts running out. About the time they were getting over their scare they heard another noise and it was twenty of the cavalry coming ahead of the other cavalry. Just as soon as they saw my father and his little bunch with him they began shooting their guns to let the other cavalry know they had found them. My father told the lady, "Here is your baby." The little fellow hung on to him when the guns began to fire. My father being a tall man he squatted down so the lady could reach her baby easily. Then he told his cousin not to shoot until he shot one barrel of his gun; then for him to shoot one barrel of his gun. Then he would shoot the other barrel of his gun; then for him to shoot the other barrel of his gun. As he looked around there was a big man, a captain, coming right straight toward him. My father raised his gun and said, "O Lord, direct this load of buck shot."

So he popped down and the man fell off of his horse and Alpheus shot. Off went another man. Then father shot again and killed another man. Then Alpheus shot his other barrel and off went another man. The others ran back to the other part of their company. Just about the time my father raised his gun he hollered out as loud as he could: "Attention, battalion! Rally on the right! Forward, march! Fall in line! Attention! Rally to the right. Face forward! Attention! Forward march, and make ready for battle." I tell you the truth, at that time there was no battle line. There was nobody there but Captain Knight and Alpheus and the three ladies, and the ladies had no guns. But the cavalry must have thought that the whole place around there was covered with men ready for battle. So you see God always helps the ones that are in the right. My father said they went on after loading their guns and wasn't bothered by the cavalry anymore that day. Mrs. Martha Knight, an aunt of mine that married my father's youngest brother, told me just a few days ago that she was one of the women that was with my father and Alpheus Knight at the time of the skirmish. She said she saw the cavalry fall off their horses, dead, when Captain Knight and Alpheus were shooting them. She told me they killed four men and one big gray horse in the skirmish. She said that she never would forget that sight as long as she lived. She told me after the cavalry got up their dead men and left, Alpheus and my father came back and skinned that horse and carried the hide to the swamp where they had a hole dug out in a big log where they tanned leather. They tanned that horse hide and my father would make shoes for the poor women and children to wear in the wintertime. She told me that she and other neighbor women would watch while he made shoes. She said she wore a pair of shoes he made out of that horse hide and they lasted a long time. She also told me that she did not know what would have become of the poor little children and women here in Jones County had it not been for Captain Knight and his company. She said that God must have sent him here to care for and protect the poor women and their little children. She said that he was a great man. Never did hear him swear an oath. He always meant business. When he was to do anything he did it in a nice, smooth way.

On one occasion there was a young negro man lived in the settlement. They did not know just who he belonged to but he got to slipping around the white women's houses after dark and was run off several times so they told my father about it and they gave him orders to stop his way of doing. He kept on, so in a few days he went down to a little creek fishing. That negro is still fishing; or at last he never came back. The people never were bothered anymore with that negro.

I remember my mother telling about a man named Morgan, who married my father's sister. It seems that he was a bad man. He would keep the Confederates' cavalry posted about my father and his company. He made himself mighty busy attending to other people's business. He also lived in our home with mother and we three little boys, and mother said nearly every time I went to the table to eat that man would bounce on me and whip me just because he could and wanted to show off smart. So my mother got tired of it and told my father. So father went to him and asked him to move out of his house, and he did not want to hear of him whipping his children anymore, but he didn't try to get out, and he didn't quit whipping us children. So one night, after supper, he was sitting by the fire rocking his baby. His wife was sitting by him and someone poked a gun into the window and shot his brains out. My aunt grabbed the baby out of his arms and he fell out of the chair dead, so we never were whipped any more by him and he never told the cavalry any more news about Newt Knight and his company. Times ran on quietly for a while and Captain Knight got word that Colonel Lowry's company was making another raid with his cavalry coming through Jones County. The cavalry had before tried to get some of the people to give them a dance so my father's company fixed up a dance, for Lowry's men to have a good time, with Mr. Levy Valentine, who was too old to go to the war. They wanted Captain Knight to make it up with Mrs. Valentine and the girls to let them know the night they was to give them the dance, so Knight's company would be there too; also agreed that just as soon as the first gun was shot, all of them were to run out at the back door to keep from being shot themselves. So everything being ready, Lowry and his company came around and asked them again to let them have the dance. They set a certain night for them to have the dance, and they agreed to be back on time. They got my father and his company word the night it was to be, so Knight's company got themselves ready. They were little late; just in time to get in the fight. The cavalry was there on time and they were having a big time. They brought a negro fiddler to play for the dance. They had out guards watching for them while the rest were in the house carrying on the dance. While they were in a big way all at once Captain Knight and part of his company walked up on the guards that were out watching and the guards began to shoot at them.

Knight's company began to return fire so they had a hot little battle. The women went out at the back door and the cavalry came out on front, shooting. That ended the dance. After the shooting stopped, Knight's company reloaded their guns, the cavalry got on their horse and left and never asked for any more dances. They left, one of their men hot dead and one died next day. Mr. Malton Valentine told me he and his sister carried the two in an ox wagon to Ellisville the next day after the battle was over. Knight lost one of his men, John Parker, who was killed in the battle. No one else was hurt during the fight. Another time the cavalry made a hunt on Dry Creek east of where Laurel is now and as Knight's company wasn't looking for cavalry to come in the settlement at that time, they were scattered. Some of them were on or near Leaf River, others in other parts of the county. The cavalry caught four of Knight's company on Dry Creek and carried them up near Errata and started to hang all four of them. Then they found a white feather in the hat band of one named Mitchell. The captain said to Colonel Lowrey, "Don't hang the man that has the white feather in his hat band; it may mean something." So they hung Jack Smith and Jessie Smith and Jack Arnal, and they carried Mitchell to Ellisville. After questioning him for a long time they hung him too. There were a few more of the boys with those four but they got away and made it back to Knight's company and told the rest of the company what the cavalry had done. So Captain Knight got his company together and made a march over the hills, hollows, swamps, and creeks to Errata hoping to get there before the cavalry left. They felt like exchanging a few shots with them, but they had left with Mitchell for Ellisville where they hung him. Knight's company kept together close around Ellisville, hoping to catch the cavalry out of Ellisville, but the cavalry stayed some time waiting for Knight's company to scatter out before they left Ellisville. Some of the Knight Company wanted to go right on into Ellisville, after them. My father told them it would not do as they would have all the advantage of them and there was about five of the cavalry to one of his men, so they disbanded but kept close watch. The cavalry slipped across Tallahala Creek and went upon the east side back up on Dry Creek, hoping to catch some more of the men. They asked a lady where her husband was. She told them she did not know. She knew if they caught him they would hang him. So she denied knowing where he was. She got her blowing horn and blew it one time. That was to let him and others know that the cavalry was there. Her husband was then in a big briar patch near the house. As soon as she blew the horn the cavalry started out with their dogs in another direction from the briar patch. As soon as they got out of sight she and two other women went to the briar patch and told her husband the cavalry was after him with their dogs. So he and the three women started out. They didn't go far before they came to a field. The man climbed the fence and went through the field and the women went around the fence. It wasn't very long after they separated at the fence until they heard the dogs barking. The cavalry had made a circle around the house and the dogs struck the trail of those three women. So here they came right on to the fence and they kept right on trail of the women and ran them down, so the cavalry never knew about her husband in the briar patch. He got away all right and the cavalry left for other parts of the county. They were bothered but very little after that. They would come around some times and catch up some of the boys not old enough to be carried to the regular army, and some of the old men, and keep them in their company and question them pretty hard, trying to make them tell about my father's company and where they were. There was a strange thing that happened several different times. Every time the Knight Company learned that Lowry's bunch was coming into Jones County, he would get busy and get his company together in order to give Lowry's cavalry a nice reception of powder and buck shot. They would get word somehow, I suppose someone would tell them and they would go the other way. The cavalry kept posted about Knight's company and when they would learn of them being scattered they would go after them but never would go up to Knight's company to have a sure enough battle. They would go some other way. I remember hearing my father tell about some trouble his men had with the cavalry on Tallahala Creek, about seven miles north of Ellisville, just below Laurel and near Mrs. Sallie Parker's place, near the swamp. She was a widow and a mighty good woman. She would cook for my father's company, and they had a camping place near her house. So one evening the cavalry came and began shooting into them, and in a few minutes the guns were firing all around the place. My father said that they had a real battle there for a few minutes. The cavalry seemed to think it was getting to be too much for them, so they left with some wounded cavalrymen. He never learned just how many there were, but they left one or two wounded men and one dead. He got three of his men wounded, John Valentine shot in the leg, Mr. Whitehead hit on the heel, and Moses Richards was shot on one leg. As soon as they could they fixed up three litters out of some blankets and carried them to Salbaty camp near where Soso, Mississippi, is now, about eight miles. As soon as they got there they stretched up a tent to keep those wounded men in. Then they put a man on a horse and sent him to Ellisville after a doctor, and when he told the doctor what he wanted him to do the doctor says "I can't go." The man says "you will have to go or take what will follow you." The doctor decided that he would rather go and administer to the wounded men than to be shot, so he went. The men left word for Lowry's cavalry to come too, told them they would be found at Salbaty camp in the forks of Horse Creek Swamp about two miles east of where Soso is now, near old Aunt Sallie Dulacy's place. Those cavalrymen showed those wounded men very fine respect. They never carried them anything to eat or to drink, but the doctor kept on going to see them and administered to the wounds until they got well.

He treated them awfully nice. Someone asked Colonel Lowry why he and his men, who numbered about one hundred, did not go and make a charge on that camp where Knight and his company were camped. He told them that it would take several hundred men more than he had to go in that swamp where Captain Knight and his company was camped and take them. Colonel Lowry said he was not afraid of the swamp but that he was afraid of them old shot guns that they had there in their camps, and the way they used them. Those men in Knight's company sure knew how to shoot them guns, believe me. So there was a long time they had no trouble. Those wounded men got well and got out of the camps and were able to go on duty again. They never were bothered while they were in camps.

Mr. Reeves told me a good joke he got on the cavalry. Said he and a negro boy were picking pears in the field at Aunt Sallie Parker's place on Tallahala Creek near the Captain Knight camp just back of her field when the cavalry, looked to him like about one hundred, came up to the fence where he was picking pears and asked him if he had seen any of Newt Knight's company down there anywhere, Reeves said to them: "Do you see that fence down yonder?" "Yes," they replied. "Well, there is two men in every corner of that fence ready to shoot." The captain of the cavalry said, "Boys, we better be leaving from here." He said they sure left too, and that quick. He told me him and the negro boy took a big laugh, to see how bad they scared them cavalry. He said he could not recollect them ever coming back to see about Knight and his company. If they did he never saw them anymore. The cavalry had been going to Aunt Sallie Parker's place, taking her chickens and her hogs, and her corn, and at one time they took an old horse that wasn't any good, almost dead, and carried it into her lot and caught out her good horse and took it, and left her their old deadhead horse. But after my father and his company got to camping there in the swamp near her home they quit coming around her place. The cavalry was camping at an old gin house near Ellisville, and Knight and his company got around them one night and killed one man and wounded two others. So they moved their camping place up to Jim Knight water mill, about sixteen miles northwest of Ellisville, on the Raleigh and Ellisville road, and it was there they caught two of Knight's men and hung them to a big limb that reached over the road. They were Sill Colman and Tom Yates. They went to Mr. Parker's house and Joe Gunter being there in the house, they shot and killed him. Captain Knight would get in a little boat that Jim Knight had there in his mill pond and after dark he would paddle it around to a little island in the pond near where the cavalry was camping. He would lie in there and listen to them talk about how they would like to catch Captain Knight and he was in about fifty steps of them. He could hear them plotting how to catch him, and when he got all their plans to get him, he would get in the boat and go back to his company and tell them. The cavalry fixed up to go down where my father lived on a little creek called Mason Creek, one morning. They started down there and Captain Knight knew their plans, so my father got part of his men in a thick place in the swamp near my father's house. It wasn't very long until they came and surrounded the place believing that my father was there in that swamp. He was there and he wasn't by himself. Two of his brothers were there and several other men of his company. As the cavalry were slipping in on them, one of the cavalry saw Uncle Albert and Uncle Jessie saw the cavalryman raise his gun to shoot his brother, Albert, so Uncle Jessie threw up his gun and pop down at the cavalryman. He fell dead on the spot, but his gun went off as he fell. His bullet went astray in the air, so that started the shooting. There was about fifteen or twenty shots fired there in that little place just about 2 or 3 acres square, and under the excitement one of the cavalrymen was running trying to get out of there. He made it out and just as he got out he looked back and saw a man coming running trying to get out too. He, thinking it was Captain Knight after him threw up his gun and shot the man. But it was not Captain Knight. It was one of his own company's men that he shot. He was so frightened he never took time to see who it was. They soon got to their horses. All of them except six left that place. It seems like they didn't like that place very much. They left in a right smart hurry. They did not take time to pick up their dead men, but left them for the people around there to get them up and bury them. So their plans they had made the night before to catch Captain Knight didn't work out just as they had planned it would. Captain Knight was on the little island in the mill pond the night before and heard their plans how they would catch him the next day. So they didn't like to get into a big crowd and they left for some other place. As I have stated before, if they could catch a few of the men that belonged to Knight's company they would treat them without mercy. Lonnie Flynt told me his grandfather Flynt, who was a good man and a fine citizen, who was drafted into the Confederate army said he didn't know how long he stayed with them but some time in 1863 he received a letter from his family back at home saying that his wife was sick and wanted him to come home. He showed the letter to his captain and asked him for a furlough to come home. The captain of his company granted him a furlough to come home to see his sick wife, and while he was at home the Confederate States passed that 20-negro law. He had no negroes to fight for, so he had decided if the man that had the negroes could stay at home he would stop too. So it wasn't very long until the cavalry was after him. One morning he took his gun and fishing pole and went down to the creek called Big Creek, near where he lived, trying to keep out of the way of the cavalry. But somehow they slipped up on him before he knew it. He grabbed his gun and threw it into the creek. They asked him what he was doing there and why he hadn't gone back to the army. He told them that he was aiming to start back tomorrow morning; that his folks had been sick and had just got able for him to go back. So they put a rope around his neck and led him out of the swamp, to hang him. He told them to send to the house after his wife and mother; that he would prove by them that he was telling the truth, and that he was going back the next day. So they sent after them and just before they got to him they had the knot tied around his neck, and if they had not got there just when they did they would have hung him. They begged so hard for them to give him a chance to go back that they took the rope off Rim and turned him loose. After they left him he studied over how they had treated him and decided that he would never go back, so he had been trying to locate my father's company. The next day he found them and joined the Newt Knight Company, and stayed with them until they surrendered. The cavalry made it back to Ellisville, to their old camping place. One morning they started up Tallahala Creek and went on up near old Aunt Sallie Parker's place. Knight's company had its camping place near her home in the swamp. The cavalry left their horses and took their dogs and went on up near Knight's camp. Only part of Knight's company was there. Some of them were fishing; others were out at Aunt Sallie's getting some cooking done, and the cavalry caught two of those who were off from the rest of them, handcuffed them, and tied a rope on them, intending to carry them out. Knight's company heard them and went to them, and as soon as they saw the cavalry they began to shoot into them and the cavalry turned back on Knight's men. They say it was a sure enough battle for some time, and while they were shooting at Knight's men, one of the men that they had hand-cuffed slipped his hand out of the cuff, so both got in the creek and swam across and got away from them. Knight's men stepped across the creek and kept making it so hot for the cavalry that they decided to make it back to the rest of their company at Ellisville. Captain Knight's company followed them about three miles down the swamp, shooting at them every time they could get in sight of them. Not a man of Knight's company got killed or hurt in the battle, so the cavalry left Ellisville for a few days, for other parts of the country. Knight's company would scatter out, some in one place and some in another place watching and protecting their families and property, so before long they got to Ellisville and someone went and told them that there was a few of Knight's company at their camp up at Aunt Sallie Parker's place whom he thought would be easy to catch. So they got their dogs and hit out for the camp. They rode their horses up near the camp, and got off, aiming to shut right up on them. But instead of them being asleep they were watching and saw them coming in on them. As there was so many more of the cavalry than there was of them they decided to try to get away, so they lit out running up the swamp to where there was a foot log. They all got there and began crossing and all got across except Warren Walters. He fell off the foot log into the creek and got wet. He said, "Damn if I run any further." So he crawled out on the bank and got in some bushes and Meg Walters was the last man to cross the foot log. He had some ground red pepper with him and he sprinkled the log with pepper. When the dogs ran up to the log and got a sniff of the pepper they were through. Warren Walters, sitting over on the other side of the creek where he had crawled out of the water, fired on the dogs and killed two of them, so the boys went on about their business and the cavalry went back disappointed. Everything got quiet for a few days and my father decided while things were quiet he would leave the company, and go home, which was about six miles from the camp, and see his family. He had been walking for some time and got in about two miles of his home going down through the piney woods. He got down close to the head of a little branch when all at once he heard the noise of horses running. He stopped and looked back and there were about ten or twelve cavalry coming right on after him. He just knew his time was up. He said he knew it would not do to run. All at once it came to him to blow his horn three shorts and began to holler, "Here they are boys. Fall into line, boys," as long as he could and at the same time he shot into them with both barrels of his gun. The cavalry turned their horses and left him right there by himself. Just as soon as they got out of his sight it came his time to run. Believe me he ran about one mile as fast as he ever ran in his life. He ran until he reached a little swamp, where he stopped and loaded his gun and went on to the house and stayed a while with his family. He then went back to his company. He sure had something to tell the men when he got back to the camps. I tell you the truth, he never left the boys by himself any more as long as the war lasted. He never learned whether he wounded any of the cavalry or not. He sure was glad when they got out of his sight. He was almost sure his time was up. He knew if they caught him they would hang him, without giving him time to say the Lord's prayer, but it seemed to him that something told him not to run, so he stood still and saw the power of the Lord demonstrated in his favor. He felt that it was God's power that delivered him from the enemy, the ones that were trying to take his life.

I remember a circumstance that my father told me, and the people mixed up on it. Some say different but my father told me when he sent Jasper Collins to Memphis, Tennessee, to get his company into the Union army they sent him to Vicksburg to see a certain officer and the commanding officer sent a small company to admit them into the regular Union army, but just before they reached us the Confederate soldiers waylaid them at Rocky Creek near Ellisville, in Jones County. They shot into them and killed one man and wounded two more, and they surrendered to the rebels and were carried back to Jackson, Mississippi. Some say they were to tear up the railroads at Waynesboro, Mississippi. That may be true but they were aiming on getting my father's company mustered into their company, and failed to reach them in time to get help through my father's company. After failing to get mustered into the regular Union army, my father decided to send a courier to New Orleans to get a recruiting officer there to come and recruit them into the Union army. The commanding officer ordered a recruiting office here to Jones County, but he also failed to reach Jones County. My father and his company determined more than ever to fight the Confederate cavalry just as long as there were men left of them to fight. As the war went on the boys would leave the Confederate army and come back to Jones County and join Newt Knight's company. I remember hearing my father say that one Mr. Scott Bush had been with the cavalry for quite a while; he did not know just how long, but he decided to quit the Southern cavalry and join the Newt Knight Company. One day they stopped to eat their dinner down in the little creek swamp near his home and he thought it would be a good time to play the trick on them. He told them he would go to the house and take dinner with the folks, and they said to him, "All right, go ahead," and told him where they were going. Told him if they left before he got back for him to come on. They left before he got back and as he was by himself he thought now was his time to leave them. He decided to fool them, which he did. He took his knife and cut one of his fingers and rubbed some of the blood on his saddle and shot a hole through his hat and left his horse with the saddle on him. He went to Knight's company and joined them and stayed with them until the war ended. The cavalry sent two men back to see what had become of him. They found the horse and saw the blood on the saddle and his hat on the ground with a hole through it. They took the horse back to the company, and they decided that Knight's men had captured him and carried him to their camps.

Mr. Scott Bush worked his trick on them pretty slick. The cavalry was busy hunting Captain Knight's men. If they found two or three of them off from Knight's company, they would treat them rough without showing them any mercy. I learned of one of the Knight men, Mr. Tap Bynum, whose wife was sick in bed with a little baby. He thought he would go and see them, so he left and went to his home to see how his wife was getting along. He had not been there but a short time when he heard a noise out at the gate and stepped to the door to see what it was. There was a big bunch of cavalrymen rode up to the yard fence and as he stepped out of his house they shot him down and killed him in his own yard, without any warning at all, his wife being in the bed sick, not able to get up. That was the way the cavalry treated men in Jones County. They seemed to be busy most all the time doing such stunts, but it seemed like they did not want to get with Captain Knight and his company. They did not love them and never did care anything for them, but they thought it would look better on their part to stay away from Newt Knight and his company. The truth is they didn't want to get in contact with them old double-barreled shotguns. My father said on one occasion a doctor was attending a wounded Confederate cavalry. He found fourteen rifle balls that Knight's company had shot into him. The doctor said Knight's company must have been fine shooters to hit a man fourteen times with a rifle, but the truth is, they run rifle balls in bullet molds and loaded their shotguns with them. They would put fifteen or eighteen balls in one barrel and when they turned them barrels loose on the cavalry there was something doing. That is why they never charged Knight and his company at their camps. They knew that they had 36 bullets to each double barreled gun, and them heavy charged with powder behind them. It seems that they kept posted where

Knight's company was, and it seems like they would take great delight in destroying what Knight's men had at home. One Calvin Walters told me that he had two brothers in Newt Knight's company and he well remembered one event. The cavalry rode up into the lane at their home and began to get off their horses and began hitching their horses. There were lots of little shade trees in the lane and they would hitch two horses to every tree. There was the most men he ever saw. There must have been five hundred horses or more. He said, "I will tell you the truth them men went to our corn crib and toted out corn to feed them horses. It was a sight to see how they wasted our corn. I remember going out there the next morning with a larger brother of mine. He got up four or five barrels of corn where they had just wasted it, and the horses had just tromped over and left it.

"It was awful to see how they had wasted our corn, and that wasn't all. They caught nearly all mother's chickens and killed them and cleaned them in the lane. Mother heard them catching her chickens, but she was afraid to go out and say anything to them. She said that she wished that Newt Knight and his men could have known that they was here destroying our stuff that we had worked so hard for but there was no way to get them word. They were over near Leaf River, in the west part of Jones County, and we lived on the east side of Tallahala creek, two miles east of where Laurel is now."

He also told me that was not all they did; that they went to their smokehouse and got lots of their meat and sliced it up and left big chunks of it in the lane, wollered up in the dirt. Our corn and meat was all we had to live on and they wasted practically half of it that night. Just about the time they were fixing to leave that morning, one of the cavalry went out to the lot and was putting a bridle on the best mare we had. Mrs. Walters happened to be up and saw him when he caught the mare and she ran out there and grabbed her up a fence rail and knocked him down with it. He fell loose from her mare and then she took her mare and put her back into the stable. She then turned back on the cavalryman with another fence rail, and told him that she would kill him if he didn't get out of her lot and let her mare alone. He took her at her word and left, so all the cavalry left after they had destroyed a great portion of her stuff.

I was talking to Mrs. Courtney a few days ago, who is living with her son-in-law, Warren Tucker, five miles south of Laurel. She is ninety-seven years old but it seems she has the best recollection I ever saw for a person her age. She is the oldest one I ever talked to who knew all about the Civil War and what happened in Jones County. She told me lots of things that were done during the war; things that my father had told me about before he died. She said she knew my father and saw him lots of times during the Civil War. She said he and his company was considered good men. She told me that if it had not been for such men as Newt Knight, Jasper Collins, and Bill Sumrall, and lots of other good men of Jones County that left the Confederate army and came home and organized a company here to protect their families and property and us poor women and children in Jones County whose husbands were conscripted and carried off to the war; forced to go and leave us without anything to go upon. We were forced to go through cold, rain, heat, trying to make something to eat and wear. We had to go rain or shine in order to keep our children from suffering. She said that she plowed and hoed many a day when she did not feel able to go, trying to make an honest living.

She told me that she was plowing one day and some cavalry came up to the fence where she was plowing and said to her, "Where is that man that has been plowing there?" She said to him, "There has been no man plowing here." He said to her, "You are a liar; tell me where he is." She said, "Sir, I have told you the truth." The cavalry got off his horse and climbed over the fence and began walking across where she had plowed, looking for men's tracks, to see whether it was men's tracks or not who had been plowing there. She said to them, "Does them tracks look like men's tracks?" "No" he said, "I guess they are your tracks." They got out of the field and on their horses and left.

She told me that the women would have to work all day in the field and at night they would wash their clothes and hang them out to dry so they could get to work soon the next morning. Sometimes the cavalry would come along where they was hung out to dry and carry them off with them, and leave them without clothes to wear. That was why such men as Newt Knight, Jasper Collins, and Bill Sumrall and other good men stayed in Jones County, to see that the cavalry did not take everything we made to feed ourselves and our children on. Believe me, they would take anything they could lay their hands on. It was hard that our husbands had to be sent to the war to fight, and that the cavalry was allowed to take and destroy what we poor women and children worked for to live on while our folks were gone to the army. I remember on one occasion she said she and several women went up to Jasper County, to where Mr. Lindsey lived. He ran a gin. We told him we had no clothes for our children to wear and had no cotton to make clothes out of. He sent an old negro woman down in Jones County and told us to come up there and he would give us some cotton to make us some clothes for us and our children to wear. We got up a wagon and a yoke of oxen, and one of our neighbors had a boy large enough to drive. We went up to Mr. Lindsey's place and he gave all of us women 12 pounds of lint cotton each and gave us all one peck of cotton seed each. We thanked him for his kindness, and left for home back in Jones County. Us poor women and children suffered terribly during the war, but I want to tell you when Newt Knight and his company got organized in Jones County, things changed. The Lord must have sent them here to help us poor women, which they did. There was very little damage done us by the cavalry after Newt Knight and his company got started in after them.

There are some people who think hard of my father and his men that helped him organize the company. Some people called them deserters, bushwackers, and all kinds of bad names. Some of the best citizens of Jones County that knew my father, say that he could never have done a better thing than he did when he and his men came back home and started a company of their own. I don't understand that they deserted from the army of either side. They never joined any army of their own free will but were conscripted and carried off against their will and forced into the Confederate army.

While they were there they did their duty the best they could until the states passed that law that was called the 20-negro law. The law was, as I understand it, and as my father understood it, if a man had twenty negroes or more he was excused from army service and could go home. My father and all of his men came home and went into the organization called the Newt Knight Company. They were all poor men. They had no negroes to fight for, but the most of them had a dear wife and little children that needed their protection at home.

They came home and did their duty here at home in Jones County. It is true they killed lots of cavalrymen, but they were forced to do that or be killed by the cavalrymen, or to just surrender what property and effects they had to them, to be wasted, and to let the good women and children of this county suffer. You who have said hard things about Newt Knight and his company, take this home to yourself. Just suppose you were a poor man and had a dear wife and some little children at home you loved above everything else in this world. How would you like to have been snatched up and carried off from them, who needed your companionship and protection at all times: having to leave them at the mercy of what ever happened to them, and the children hungry and half naked, and asking their mother where their daddy is and if he is coming back? That isn't all; the mothers worked almost day and night to keep them from starving to death, while their daddy was in the army. It was awful cruel to have to stand out and see the cavalry come into their homes and take their knives and cut the cloth out of the hand looms, where they had spun the thread out of cotton that they had carded with cards at night after a hard day's work in the field, and dyed and sized it and warped it and threaded the old hand loom and then wove the cloth to make clothes for their children to wear; then to see them come and cut it out and carry it off with them for their own use. Think of this before you say hard things about Newt Knight and his company, and ask yourself if any red-blooded man could stand for such conduct and not resent it.

And that was not all; they destroyed their property, and would kill their cows and hogs and chickens and eat them. And that was not all they would do; they would take their corn that they raised and feed their horses and waste it, leaving the women and children without bread to eat, and lots of other things they would do that is too numerous to mention. You people who speak hard things about Newt Knight and his company, just consider that if you had a family that was treated that way, what would you do? I am persuaded that you would do as Captain Knight and his company did and furthermore, you would repent of the hard words you have said about Newt Knight and his company.

Now I want to tell you a few things about Jasper Collins, my father's first lieutenant in his company. I want to say that Mr. Jasper Collins was considered one of the best citizens of Jones County. He was well posted in business matters; he read lots and kept well posted on various matters that would come up. In fact, he was an honorable gentlemen. He had other brothers who were all fine men. They all lived in Jones County. Mr. Jasper Collins, who was the son of Stacy Collins, was raised by Christian parents and honorable citizens of Jones County. He was looked upon as a great man. He was carried off from his family into the Confederate army, and while there in the army he did his duty as a soldier should do. When he learned of the 20-negro law that was passed by the Confederate States he went to his captain, being a good friend of his, and told him that he was through with the war. Told him "Here is my gun; I don't intend to shoot another gun here." The captain said to him, "Jasper Collins, that will never do. Don't you know they will kill you?" "No, I don't know that. They will have to catch me first, before they kill me." He shook hands with his captain and bid him goodbye. The captain said, "Jasper, I hate to see you leave us. I hope you will get through safe."

Mr. Collins got through safely and went where my father was and told him that he had quit the Confederate army, and that he was going home. My father had just received a letter from my mother, stating to him how the cavalry had come to her house and caught out her horse and got on him and cursed her and abused her for everything he could think of. My father said, "I am quitting, too, Jasper." My father went to his captain and got a furlough to come home. He got his furlough and left for home. He made it all right and found the people had been treated awful bad here in Jones County, which I have already stated. He decided to organize a company of their own. They appointed Jasper Collins as first lieutenant. He was a close friend of my father, and when there was a fight on he was right there with my father. He was considered a brave man and he made a good officer. He was a man that did his whole duty as an officer, and as a citizen he was of the best. He lived after the war to raise nine children, five girls and four boys. They were all raised to be first-class citizens, and were honored by the people that knew them. The four boys grew up to be honorable men. Some of them have been honored with different kinds of offices in Jones County and have served the people well. If you wanted any information they would take pleasure in telling or showing you what you wanted to know.

I will tell you a few things about the second lieutenant, which was W. W. Sumrall. Lots of people in Jones County remember him today as Uncle Bill Sumrall. Lots of people knew him to be the second lieutenant of the Newt Knight Company. He served his company well. He never got scared and ran out of a fight. He stayed right on the front and did his part in fighting the cavalry, and did his part of the shooting. He was considered one of the bravest men in the Knight Company. My father said he could trust him and his first lieutenant. They never left him but stayed with him in the hardest fights with the cavalry. He lived to raise nine children, four boys and five girls, which he raised to be law-abiding citizens of Jones County, and as the people know the Sumralls to be among the best citizens of Jones County. W. W. Sumrall was a quiet businessman. He was a sawmill man and a farmer; he also ran a gin in cotton-ginning time for several years. He ran his sawmill a long time and in his business transactions always gave his neighbors a square deal. In all of his dealings he was liked by all that knew him. I would like to mention something about all the men that composed the Newt Knight Company but have not the space to do so. I will say, as my father told me, all of them were the best of citizens; all of them were citizens of Jones County and ready to do their duty to the best of their ability for their families and their neighbors and their families. My father told me that all the men that joined his company were brave men, and would come right up to the front and fight and stay right in line with him. I have heard him say it made him feel good to know his men would fight and die by him for the cause they were fighting for and the interest they had in Jones County. He said he was never afraid to go into a fight when all the company was with him. He knew they would win; it made no difference with him how many cavalry were in the fight on the other side. All of the men who joined his company stayed with him until the war was ended, except those that were killed or captured by the cavalry, except some that enlisted into his company and got into a fight, and when the guns began to fire they would slip out and go to New Orleans and join the Union army in order to do guard duty as they called it. My father said they were good men but they did not like the smell of gun powder, and the roaring of the guns, while in battle. In other words, they felt that they would be safer in New Orleans. My father said that he did not blame them for going off and leaving their dear wife and babies back here without their protection. He said he supposed they thought he and his company would protect them while they were gone, and they did. I tell you the truth, he said after his company got busy and killed all the dogs and some cavalrymen that was going about destroying what the poor women had made for themselves and children to live off of, after so long a time they thought it best to stop destroying what didn't belong to them. The cavalry would not know just where my father and his men were. They got afraid to bother those good women's stuff anymore for when they would ride up to one of their houses and ask for her husband she would tell them she did not know where he was but she could find out where he was in a few minutes if they had time to wait. She would get her blowing horn and give it one long blow and you could hear other horns blowing in almost every direction answering her. My father said they did not like to hear them horns blowing. The sound of the horn made the cavalry think there was trouble not far off, and they thought it would be best for them to ride on, not to be taking up very much time around those ladies' houses where they had horns. The last fight they had was at the camp they call Salbatry, in the fork of the little creek called Horse Creek, on a little island between Soso and Servis on the G. S. I. Railroad. This was long before the road was built through that place. One man told me that he helped to clear the right-of-way through that old camp and he and others cut out lots of shot out of those trees that was shot into them during that war. Father said that the cavalry and a company of infantry they had, made it up to capture him and his company, by surrounding the little island. They had it arranged mighty nice and if it had not been just as it was, they might have killed all of us. But as it happened he had a friend in the infantry that slipped off from his company and came and told him all about how they had their plans fixed. The cavalry was to ride down to the big spring near our camps, and the infantry was to come up the swamp and surround our camp. The orders were for the cavalry to begin shooting into our camp, Knight's company would go for the cavalry in front of them, then the infantry was to crowd on them on both sides in the camp. It was awfully thick around the camp. They thought if they could get right in on them it would frighten them so bad they would surrender and they would have a great name for capturing Newt Knight and his company. Just as soon as his friend left he got busy. He got all of his company there with him and they made everything ready for a sure enough fight. The infantry was to come the next morning. My father divided his company into three parts just about the time they began to look for them to come. The first lieutenant, to-wit, Jasper Collins, took his men on the right side. W. W. Sumrall, second lieutenant, took his men on the left side. Newt Knight took his men out in front to face the cavalry. It was understood with the infantry that the cavalry would come in front of the camp and was to give them plenty of time to slip up close to the camp on the back of their camp. The cavalry rode up to the spring and began shooting in toward the camp at long range. They knew they would not hit anyone but they thought that Knight's company would turn all their attention toward them and give the infantry all the chance that they wanted to get right in their camp on them before they knew it, but it did not work out as they thought. As soon as the infantry started to run into where they intended to catch them, they met a surprise when Jasper Collins and men began shooting on one side of the line and W. W. Sumrall and his men shooting at them on the other side. The infantry decided that it wasn't best for them to stay in that swamp and try to catch Newt Knight and his company where there was so much gun shooting and buckshot flying all around them. They said one to another we better get out of this swamp before some of us get killed if we follow orders and try to capture Newt Knight and his men. They slipped out just as quick as they could. They never shot a gun. It was so thick in the swamp and there was only a few of the infantry that got where they could see them, and they hid themselves behind trees to keep from getting killed. The cavalry kept on shooting toward the camp for quite a while until the guns stopped shooting in the camp, they not knowing what had happened. My father said his men never shot a gun on the front line. They were waiting for the cavalry to get off their horses and come on them but not knowing how things were they all left and went back to Ellisville, and after learning how it turned out they were badly disappointed. Father said they gave it up as a bad job. They never bothered them any more after that day. Father said they did not kill anyone that day but crippled three or four of the infantry. They were able to get back to their camp at Ellisville. The infantry hiked it next day for Waynesboro except those that were wounded. They stayed in camp with the cavalry until they got well.

Mr. George Valentine told me just a few days ago that Morge Valentine and his brother and another man, a good friend to my father, that Morge and Josh Hinton and Jim Gunter went where an old man Gunter lived and caught out three of the old man's horses and rode them off and they hadn't been gone very long before they rode into a company of cavalry, and the cavalry began shooting at them and Hinton and Gunter jumped off of their horses and ran through the thick bushes and got away, but they hit Morge Valentine in one of his shoulders and they caught him and carried him over on Tallahala swamp, and it was getting late in the evening, nearly dark, and decided to hang him. They put a rope around his neck fixing to hang him. While they were fixing to hang him, it was close to the edge of the creek, he got a chance and slipped down into the water and swam across to the other side of the creek. They shot at him several times as he was getting into the swamp but their shots failed to stop him. He kept going down the creek and as soon as they could get across, and as soon as they could get their dogs across they struck his track. He had swum back on the other side. He swam the creek five times and foiled the dogs, and the cavalry left him and went back. They supposed he was drowned in the creek with the rope on his neck and one shoulder broke. He wasn't drowned. He got out of the swamp though it was dark and went to Aunt Sallie Parker's. That night she let him have her horse to ride over to where my father was at Salbatty camp. She sent a negro boy with him to bring the horse back. As soon as he got there my father began to doctor him and kept him there in the camp, and when he got able to go he carried him to his house until he got well. Feeling a little uneasy that the cavalry might find him, he dug a big pit in the back yard and covered it and kept him in there until he was able to go home. My father did the doctoring to him until he got well. They say he never left my father anymore. They stayed together until the war ended. On another time the cavalry found Med Coats away from Knight's company, and ran him all day with the dogs. This was before they had killed their dogs, and they were riding their horses, about ten of them. He would go through the swamp, and across the creek two or three times trying to get away from them. The dogs kept on his trail until late that evening, he being tired and almost given out he thought he never wanted to kill anyone, saw it was to kill or get killed. He went just as far as he could go; he placed himself in some bushes and got ready to shoot. A few minutes after he sat down, the dogs were still trailing him, he saw one of the cavalry coming straight toward him. He had his head bowed over in front coming under some limbs and brush. He thought now was his time to shoot so he popped down at him and he fell off his horse dead. He saw he had killed him. He did not like to stay around dead folks. He was tired but he walked on away from him pretty fast, for some distance but kept looking back to see if any one of the cavalrymen was following him. They never came any further following him. He supposed they thought he had gotten to Newt Knight's company, and as they did not like Newt Knight and his company they would go back to their company. When Coats got to the camp where the rest of the company was he was very tired and given out. After resting a while he began to tell about his race he had with a bunch of cavalry and their dogs, how far they ran him. Some of the boys wished they could have known it and dropped in with him. He wished so too but there was no way to let them know. He kept running trying to get away from them without being caught and hung. He said he could see no way for him to escape being hung by them. He had run from them until he had given up all hopes. He had shot one man as before stated, and he supposed the other cavalry was not far behind him coming on after him. He never saw but one man. Tell you the truth, he never stayed to see if there was any more coming. He had business on down the swamp. This was on March the 25th, 1864.

There was another little company of men that organized themselves into a little company and struck their camps two miles above Myrick, in Jones County, for the purpose of protecting their families and property during the war. Said company was composed of Jack Arnold, Gus Lambert, Drew Gilbert, Albert Blackledge, Jack Smith, Jeff Lee, Tom Holoman, R. C. Reeves, Mose Walters, Warren Walters, Blake Lamber, Jim Tiner, Jim Blackledge, Jess Smith, Morgan Mitchel, Jim Lee, Calven Reeves, W. T. Temple, Dan Pitts, and others. Their camp was in behind a big bluff on Mill Creek, in the edge of the swamp. The Walters brothers who live near the place tell me it was a fine place for a camp of that kind. It was thick swamp on each side and a big heavy dam and a big pond of water out in front, and near the water was a big hole under the bluff large enough to accommodate seventy-five or a hundred men. They would stay in there during cold and rainy weather. They also had a place fixed up in there to cook and eat and sleep. Everything was kept in fine shape. I have been told that Lowry's company never did try to get into their camp where those men were and it was well they didn't. It was so arranged that a few men could have killed a whole company of cavalry as fast as they could get to them. These men did not stay in camp all the time. When they knew the cavalry was in other parts of the country they would help their wives work in the field to help them make bread to eat. They would have out pickets in different places to give notice by the certain alarm to blow their horn which would go from house to house of the approach of the enemy but that failed to work at all times like they wanted it to. Lowry's company would slip in the settlement in the night time. Early in the morning they would divide out. By so doing they caught a few of those men on picket before they could give the alarm and hung them. After that they decided that they were not strong enough to fight large companies of men. They disbanded, some of them went to the Union army. The most of them joined Newt Knight's company and stayed with them to help protect their families and their interests in Jones County, who were trying to live here under almost unbearable burdens. They needed our protection at all times. You will see in other parts of this book how they were treated while their husbands were in the war. My father said when those men over in the eastern part of Jones County came over and joined his company, and after getting lined up with us in good shape they put a stop to Colonel Lowry's company destroying the people's property here in Jones County. The first thing they did was to kill all of Lowry's dogs that they had run down our men and hung them with. My mother told me they went to killing dogs in every way they could and the women helped them by poisoning them, old hungry dogs that would eat anything you gave them to eat. She said "Believe me, we women got lots of them that way." They were great soldiers. They learned how to kill dogs without a gun. It wasn't long until Lowry's company had no dogs to run our men with. Lowry and his men could not smell the tracks of Newt Knight's men enough to track them, Lowry and his men being a little skittish of them were afraid to get close enough to them to smell their tracks but as soon as they got rid of Lowry's dogs they had the advantage of them and it wasn't long until Newt Knight Company had Colonel Lowry Company going the other way. For revenge Colonel Lowry Company would catch up old men and young boys and keep them away from home all day and sometimes all night. They would put them in pens. Called it their bull pen and questioned them sharply, threatening to hang them if they didn't tell them all they knew about Newt Knight and his company. Mr. W. B. Temples told me they caught him one day and hung him three times that day. That is they had a rope around his neck and the other end of the rope over a limb. They would draw him up then they would let him down and they would question him again but he would refuse. W. B. Temples told me the third time they hung him up Captain Gillis stopped them or they might kill him but told him to run. He said he lit out running and they shot four or five times, and believe me it like to have scared him to death. He was only twelve years old. Brother Richard Blackledge told me during that war he was a small boy and had to go to mill to get their corn ground. One day he was by himself he was riding along the road, and just before he got to the mill he rode up into Colonel Lowry's camps where they were camped beside the road. They stopped him and asked him where he was going. He told them to mill to get his corn ground. They told him to go on. He supposed they saw he was scared of them. He went on to mill and got his corn ground. As there was no other way for him to go back home except to go back by them where they were camped. As he was riding by their camps they saw him, and one big man caught his horse by the bridle and stopped him, and said to him you must get down off of your horse and stay all night with us. If you go on you will be killed. They took the meal and saddle off of his horse and tied the horse to a tree and then took him in the camps, and said to him we want you to tell us all you know about Newt Knight and his company. He said he told them he had heard of Newt Knight but he didn't know him or that he ever saw him. They said he is a bad man. He will kill you if he gets in gunshot of you. You had better watch out for him. My father, being an old man and uneasy about the boy thinking that something had happened to him he walked up the road thinking that he would meet the boy unless something bad had happened to him. He kept walking until he reached the Lowry camps and there he found the boy with his horse tied up to a tree. He asked them what did that mean keeping his boy there and not letting him go home. They told his father they were afraid that Newt Knight's company might be coming this way and the boy might get killed. He told them that he knew Newt Knight and lots of his company, and that he never knew any of them catching up boys and old men, and keeping them away from home. His father asked them to let his boy loose so he could go on home. They replied to him we will let you both go in the morning. They kept us both all night and our folks did not know where we were. Lowry and his men were cruel to the old men, women, and children in Jones County during the war. They caused us to suffer many hardships that they could have avoided.

There was a man that lived in Ellisville named Mr. McLemore. He seemed to be a leader for Lowry, and his company would ride around in the county looking up the people's fat cattle and hogs and would let one man by the name of Fairchild and another man by the name of Kilgore know about them. Those two men were left here to get up supplies for the Confederate soldiers. But they would keep Lowry and his men posted as to where they would find Knight and his company. They got to be so busy giving information about Knight and his company that Knight and his company got tired of him making himself a news-toter from them to Lowry's company and they ordered him to stop. But he kept on carrying news. One night my father said he and two of his men went to McLemore's house. They climbed the fence instead of opening the gate for fear the gate would make a noise and McLemore would suspect something and run. All three of them eased up to his window, and one of the three men shot him and he died. They intended to stop him from spying out what little liberty they had, and they did. They sent him word to leave their business alone. He told them that he knew his business and expected to attend to it. It was not long until his business was wound up.

During the year of the war, 1865, the cavalry quit destroying the people's property in Jones County and they stopped trying to catch any of Newt Knight's company. It seems like that Colonel Lowry disliked Captain Knight and his company and of course they quit visiting them. It seems that Colonel Lowry and his company were not trained soldiers and did not know the lay of Jones County as Knight and his company did. They could not have any success in catching Knight's men except when they caught them off from their company, one or two in a place. Colonel Lowry found a place just above Big Creek Church in Jones County, an old field. I am told they met there once a week, he and his men, to drill. I am told they had lots of fun there drilling. I have been told that after Knight's company killed all the dogs that Colonel Lowry could get, or had, to run Knight's men with, they thought it best to play safe. Colonel Lowry passed the word to Knight and his company: "We will not bother you all any more if you will let us alone." Knight and his company were good citizens. They did not want to kill anyone except in protection of their rights and property. Knowing the country as they did they could have killed every one of them. Colonel Lowry learned that they could not capture Knight and his company, as they knew every road, swamp, creek, and foot log to cross on, that it was impossible to capture them. Knight's company was organized of good citizens of Jones County—such men as Jasper Collins, W. W. Sumrall, Warren Walters, Meg Walters, and other good men that lived and died in Jones County. My father said his men wanted to see Colonel Lowry's men drill and on one occasion they found out that they were going to drill on a certain day. Knight and his men went to where they were to drill and scattered out in the swamp a distance apart with their blowing horns. They knew that Colonel Lowry's men were scared of the sound of the horn. After they got to drilling one of Knight's men blew his horn. Another answered him, and another horn blew and they kept on blowing their horns until all of them had blown. Knight had it understood with his men that if they started toward any of them that all of his men were to circle in around them and capture all of them. My father told me that they caught the direction the horns were blowing and they left their drilling place to go where their horses were hitched and mounted them and left for Ellisville. Believe me, it caused a sad feeling on them to hear a horn blow for they knew what it meant. They dreaded the sound of a horn and the odor of gun powder, of which Knight and his company carried both, and they knew it. Another time we went to see them drill and we got in an old wash-out place where they could not see us, and we saw them drill. There were seventy-five of us. We could have given them trouble, but we went to see them drill. They got through drilling and went to where their horses were hitched, mounted them and rode off. There was one man who had trouble getting his bridle loose, and the rest had left him. He was slow about starting. Knight's men thought they would have some fun and they shot five or six times in a different direction from where he was. Believe me, his bridle came loose from the tree where it was tied. He mounted his horse and believe me, you could almost have rolled marbles on his coat-tail behind him, he ran so fast. That horse went down the road in full speed. Knight's men did not go there to do them any harm, but they had lots of fun seeing that man get his horse loose so quickly after the guns fired and seeing him getting away so fast. If Colonel Lowry's men ever went back to that place to drill after that time we never heard it. My information is they never did.

As I understand, Colonel Lowry and his company were sent here to do what they were ordered to by the officers of the Confederate army. They were citizens of the Confederate States, and good men. They were only on duty, sent here to pick up men who had left the Confederate army, and send them back for duty. They were Confederate soldiers, and called the cavalry. Newt Knight and his company was at one time in the Confederate army and served the Confederates States well as soldiers. Newt Knight, Jasper Collins, and W. W. Sumrall, being citizens of Jones County, Mississippi, which county was located in a Confederate state, came home to visit their families and seeing how their families were being treated and how their property was going to waste and their children being bare for clothes and hungry for food to eat, they felt their first duty was to take care of them, they being poor people and having no negroes to fight for, they organized a little company called the Newt Knight Company in order to protect their interests as before stated. It was unfortunate for them that they had to fight their own people. They were not deserters, as some people think they were. They only fought as they saw it for their own interest and their families. They felt like they fought a good fight and saved many a woman and child from starving. There was no hard feeling after the war between

Newt Knight and Colonel Lowry. Each of them was performing a duty that they thought was right and honest as citizens. Colonel Lowry and Captain Newt Knight met in Jackson, Mississippi, after the war ended and shook hands with each other and congratulated each other for their generalship during the War Between the States and Colonel Lowry extended to Newt Knight his congratulations saying, "You are a soldier that will fight, and seeing the war is over let us forget the past and be friends." They again shook hands goodbye, with love toward each other. He said some of his men did things he didn't approve of and were not responsible for.

Some people claimed that when J. D. Powell left his party that sent him to Jackson to stay with the union party, he left his party with 375 votes asking that Jones County stay with the Union. They claimed that he was their representative, but when he got to Jackson he left his 375 votes and went with Baylis, who only got 24 votes as representative to secede. The 375 men who sent Powell, and lots of others, claim that Jones County never seceded from the union. I suppose when the state seceded from the union it carried Jones County with it. Be it as it may, I am no judge and can't say, but will leave it with the reader to say. As Mr. Goode Montgomery says in his history of Jones County, there is room for it to be debated on. Yet I will leave it for the reader to decide for himself.

Now a few lines concerning the Free State of Jones County. As my father told me, and several old men have told me the same thing, when the State of Mississippi seceded from the union, Jones County stood 375 votes for the union and 25 votes to secede. The majority always rules. Jones County never seceded from the union. L. R. Collins was right when he wrote the New Orleans States that Jones County never seceded from the Confederate government. In the first place they never joined the Confederate States. They considered themselves free from Confederate States and was a free state of their own. They call it the Free State of Jones County. They never tried to confiscate any property, nor ever conscripted anyone into their company, but they let things be just as they were and as most of the people in Jones County at that time favored the Newt Knight and Collins Company, they would help them in various ways. In fact they were Knight's and Collins's friends, and they stayed with them until the war ended. After the war was over those secessions came back home. They found that the good people who stayed in Jones County to protect its interests on behalf of them and their families had named it the Free State of Jones County. The secession party decided to try to have its name changed. They sent a petition of 106 of their party to Jackson, Mississippi, to the representative to get it changed. Here are the names of some of the petitioners, as follows:

J. M. Bayliss, W. M. Bayliss, Hugh Gellender, J. W. Grayson, Henry Gardner, J. E. Walters, R. Jenkins, Charles Williams, Angus McGilvery, M. W. Slaten, Danuel McArthur, Enoch Walters, W. M. Wood. Willis Windham, Robert Windham, John McKnight, B. C. Ducksworth, W. H. Turner, R. Safford, A. Simmons, W. Duckworth, Edmond Dossett, Abner Dossett, H. D. Dossett, John Byruns, W. M. Byruns, W. M. Byruns Sr., S. H. Smith, J. A. Fairchilds, Willis Dickson, Henry Parker, E. M. Duvall, W. W. Shows, W. B. Shows, W. J. Shows, J. L. Shows, J. P. Shows, John Ferguson, A. B. Jordan, W. M. Grayson, John Walters, James Cooper, Hiram Cooper, Allon Smith, D. C. Smith, John Smith, M. F. Smith, J. Y. Gardner, D. Melvin, M. A. Melvin, James Melvin, Robert Jordan, P. C. Jordan, J. G. Williams, Bradford Shows, A. Gaddie, F. M. McDaniel, C. C. McDaniel, George Davis, John Ferguson, Jr., M. Ferguson, B. F. Barrett, Jeff Musgrove, Robert Cooper, T. C. Bryant, Ruben Creel, J. B. Reeves, Sam Trest, R. C. Trest, N. Y. McGill, A. G. Welborn, E. C. Welborn, W. M. Gore, A. P. McGill, Daniel McGill, James McGill, James Gaskin, J. H. Overstreet, James Gunter, R. J. Craven, Arch Patterson, Berry Smith, W. M. Temples, Elliot Stewart, Sam Walters, John W. Harvy, Allen Gunter, Thomas Walters, W. M. Dement, Eligh Powell, Robert Fairchild, A. T. Dossett, Sam Prince, W. M. P. Tisdale, Elijah Tisdale, West Tisdale, J. A. Tisdale, John Overstreet, A. N. Drennan, Simpson Bruce, S. N. McManus.

These petitioners sent a petition to the House of Representatives of the State of Mississippi to have the name of the Free State of Jones

County changed to the name of Jeff Davis County in honor of their Confederate president, and they got the name of Ellisville changed to Leesburg in honor of General Lee. All business was transacted in those names for about two years. The union party did not like that name. By the help of one V. A. Collins, in the Constitutional Convention of 1868, they got the new names changed back to the old name of Jones County, and Leesburg back to the name of Ellisville. The people, seeing the condition the war had left them in, all parties agreed to lay down their differences and be friends. They went to work to that end. Jones County at that time was considered the poorest county in the state but today it ranks third in being the wealthiest county in the state.

Sometimes both parties would bring out a candidate for county and state office so most of the time the Democratic Party would beat the Republican Party. They would manage in a way to get their man ahead. I remember on one occasion I was in Smith County at Taylorsville, Miss., on election day. There were two men running for board of supervisor, one Democrat, the other Republican. I was there about all day. The Democrat tickets was there when I got there but the Republican tickets never got there until after two o'clock that afternoon, so all the Republican's friends had about gone home, supposing there would be no Republican tickets come there that day. So the Democrats got their man elected, and as I remember that was the last Republican ever to run for an office in Smith County. So the last man that run as a Republican in Jasper County for office was waylaid and shot and killed. So that stopped the Republican Party in Jasper County. So far as I remember Jones County is considered straight out a Democrat Party and they have never had a Republican Party run for office as I ever knew of.

Now, as I have been asked the question, "What became of the union party here in Jones County after the war ended," the best information I have on that question is: After the war there seemed to be the secession party and the union party. After some time the two parties changed their names. The secession party called themselves Democrats, after the order of Democracy, and the union party was called the radical party. I heard one old gentleman say that the slave negro said "dem rascals was dem old dead democrats that was resurrected." He could not think of radical and called them rascals. They changed their names to the Independent Party. Back in those days after the war ended the people had a different rule they were governed by. In their elections their voting places were several miles apart and those people who had negroes would take them to the voting place on election day. When they got there a white man would walk up to where the voting place was and get him a handful of the tickets. He would take those negroes off to some place and sit down. He would begin to make out their tickets. The negro did not know how to vote. He had to let his boss vote him. Both parties would vote the negro. The democrats had more negros than the radicals. The democrats always got their men elected. As time went on the radicals decided they had the wrong name. They changed theirs to the Independent Party. By this time the colored man had learned to vote. He learned that he had been voting for the wrong party—learned that he was voting against the party that freed him from being a slave. They went to voting for the Independents, and as time went on the Independents changed their name to the Republican Party. On the platform of Thomas Jefferson, the founder of our great Democracy, which both parties claimed to be governed by, there were some that did not like either party. They organized a third party called the Populists Party. It seems they didn't get very far, and as I remember, they changed their name to the Socialist Party. We still have three parties and in the South the Republican Party is divided into two parties. The old line party is called the black and tan party. Others called themselves the progressive or lily white Republicans. They don't believe in sending negroes to sit in council with the white people in the national convention. As I see it I may be wrong, but just as soon as the Republicans give the lily white delegates seats in convention the people will see that the Southern people will be better represented and will get more votes here in the South. I hope that I haven't hurt the feelings of anyone. Let us come to a better understanding of each other and try to work with and for each other in building up our great and glorious nation called America.

So my father said when the war ended peace was declared and we all disbanded and laid down our guns and tried to forget the past and do all we could to live peaceful with all men as far as possible. He also said that what he and his company did he felt like they did no wrong as they were forced into the war and also forced to organize themselves a company to protect themselves and their loved ones; also to fight for the principle for which they stood for and what they voted for, so they had the same right as the opposite side did to vote as they thought best. My father's company was poor men, had no negroes to fight for though they were all good citizens as Mississippi afforded.

Back in the dark day of our state in Jones County where the people were divided over the rebellion of the states and the strife grew so strong until a great many deserted the Confederate army and lay out in the woods and this act was declared to be sufficient for capital punishment, the army sent men into Jones County to force those who were lying out back to the army. When they made their appearance fights began to occur and men were killed. At that time there were two citizens left at home to gather supplies for the army. They would gather up beef cattle and hogs to send the army. Now on the east side of Bogahoma Creek swamp was a fine stock range and these two food gatherers found out that there were lots of hogs and cattle in this swamp; so one man named William Fairchilds and one named Nat Kilgore went to the house where one of the hog-owners lived and told his wife to tell her husband to shut up for them as they did not want to have to gather them up, "but if we do have to gather them up and we happen to find him while hunting the hogs we will shoot him as quick as we would an old buck." So the husband and his crowd was near the place at the time they were doing the talking. So when the husband and his crowd got the news they drew straws to see who would do the killing of these two men, and the lot fell on two young men. They went and placed themselves behind a big clay root in which they cut two holes to shoot through right near the road that the two men that had left the threats would come on their way back to Ellisville. But there was one man in the crowd who did not have any faith in these boys for the job, so he took a stand by the road in another place and when the men came along both boys shot, but both missed and when they passed the other man he gave them both barrels and killed both. This occurred about ten miles northeast of Ellisville, Miss.

Mrs. Neda Owens, the widow of Sy Owens, told me just a few days ago how the cavalry shot her husband in battle near Leaf River or about the Gunter old place. He was second corporal in the Newt Knight Company. On Dec. 28, 1864, Captain Gilless's company ran into the Knight Company at Gunter place. She said they had a sure battle for a few minutes there. It seemed to her that Captain Gilless got the advantage of the boys. Only a few of the company was there. Her husband was shot three times or was hit by three shots. They had broken one of his shoulders and one of his legs and another ball went through his body. They ran up to him and he was trying his best to shoot them and he was shot so badly one of the cavalrymen started to shoot him again. The captain gave orders not to shoot him anymore. "A man who's got the grit he's got, I sure won't see him shot anymore." So they took him to his home and got a doctor to dress his wounds for him. The doctor kept waiting on him until he got well, then he went back to his company.

G. M. Gunter was caught and hung during the battle. The rest of the boys made their getaway. None of Captain Gilless's men were killed but several got wounded.

The eighth battle they had was on Ocahay Creek about 2 miles west of the Reddoch's Ferry on Leaf River in Covington County where Colonel Lowry's company ran into part of Knight's company. Mother told me that was where Tucker Gregg got killed and one more of their company was wounded and they killed two of Lowry's company and wounded two others. The ninth battle was fought at or near Hebron Lodge, same as the old Masonic Lodge near where we lived in the swamp on Mason Creek near our house. Mr. Dan Pitts, who being one of the oldest men now living in Jones County is generally called Uncle Dan Pitts, tells me that he was in the Civil War. He lived over on Boguehoma Creek when the war was declared between the North and the South, and as he did not want to be conscripted and carried off into the Confederate army he and lots of other good citizens went to New Orleans and joined Colonel Tisdale's regiment and did guard duty until the war ended. He said he personally knew lots of Newt Knight's company and they were all as good honest citizens as could be found anywhere and as to them organizing their company to protect their families and their property they did no more than they were forced to do, and it had come to be their duty and as good citizens they never destroyed any of their enemies' property or mistreated them only as they were forced to do. Mr. Pitts is eighty-eight years old if I mistake not and is well known as being honest and truthful and what he says can be relied on as the truth; in fact he is a Christian gentleman.

TESTIMONIALS

I hereby state what I know about Newt Knight and his company. There were no better men to be found than they were and as I see it there seem to be three causes why they left the Confederate armies and came home. In the first place they voted to stay with the union and when they were conscripted and put into the Confederate armies they were forced to fight against the principle of what they stood for. Second cause was when they passed that twenty negro law, they saw it was a rich man war and a poor man fight and as it was they were using the poor men to protect the rich man and his negroes. The third cause was the most of them had families that needed their protection, as Colonel Lowry's company was destroying what the poor people had here, and I understand they organized a union company aiming on being mustered into the United States Infantry. But after making two unsuccessful efforts to get mustered into the United States Infantry they remained loyal to the principle of what they believed was right.

Yours truly,

W. B. (BUD) TEMPLES.

Here is another man who says he was born and raised in the settlement where Newt Knight lived. And as a neighbor there was none better. He was a great man and was one of the leading citizens of our country and when he and lots of other good citizens were forced to come back home to protect their family and were forced to organize a company he was chosen captain of the company and he served them with perfect satisfaction and after the war was ended he was appointed Provo Marshall. He had lots of business to attend to. I have known him to go to Jackson, Mississippi, and stay up there two and sometimes three weeks at a time, attending to business. He was very quiet and peaceable. I never knew of him having any trouble after the war except one time; then it was forced on him. He was near seventy years old at the time it happened. He was a man who stood firm for the union. He voted for the union and fought for the union and died a union. I submit this for your consideration.

GEORGE VALENTINE.

I am authorized by Loranzy Clark to say that he knew Newt Knight and lots of his company during the Civil War, and some of them before the war. They were good law-abiding citizens and thought they did their duty when they were forced to come home and to protect their family as Lowry Company was destroying their family property. He says he would have done as they did if it had been him; he also said that he knew Newt Knight to be a man who strictly attended to his own business and was a union man. He was always firm in the principles of the union, he lived and died a union man.

TO WHOM IT MAY CONCERN

I hereby state that I personally knew Newt Knight and his company. There were no better men to be found; in fact they were all good, honest citizens and as I see it they were forced to come back home to stop Lowry Company from destroying what little the poor people had here to live on. So as to Newt Knight, he was a great man; he was very quiet and peaceable; he was strictly a union man, he lived and died a union.

Yours for better times,

GEORGE ELZEY.

Now in closing this little book I want to say I have done my best to give you the facts as far as I have written that would be interesting, but being unable to get all the facts about it I shall have to pass it by for this time, but I am hoping to get out a new addition to this little book in a year or two. I will have more time, if it is the Lord's will. I know there are some names of my father's company I have left, I am sorry to say, though I am still trying to get them, and lots of other things that would be interesting to know, while they were roaming through the swamps, piney woods, in the rain, hot, or cold sleet, or snow they had to go in, in order to protect their loved ones. Now, friends, I have tried to write this so as not to hurt anyone's feelings. Now to you who differ with me what I have written, consider that you don't know it all, neither do I, but have written what my father and mother told me and two or three others of the oldest people now living in Jones County—one especially who is in her ninety-ninth year. She tells lots of those things that took place during that war. If she is still living she will tell you what she told me. I have five men's testimony, as good citizens as ever lived in Jones County. If you don't believe what I have written, ask them.

Your friends, I hope, with best wishes to all,

T. J. KNIGHT.

* * * *

Now as I have decided to write a little more to be added to the little book of Captain Newt Knight and his company during the Civil War of 1861 to 1865. So it seems after the war went on for 3 years they, the 375 men that voted to stay with the Union, became afraid that the South that voted to secede from the North was going to win the war. So they did not want to be put under a slave government. They believed in a free government, equal rights to all people, rich or poor. It should not make any difference who they were. So as my father told us the 375 men that voted to stay with the Union about 250 of them met together with the understanding they would come together and bind themselves together and constitute a Free State of Jones. So now this is the way my father said the Free State of Jones County, so much talked about, came about by those 250 citizens of Jones County, of the 375 men that voted to stay with the Union. So they met in May if I am not mistaken, 1864, to organize and to select someone to write up the Constitution of the Free State as they called it. So they selected Mr. Riles Collins to write the Constitution, then proceeded to select their officers as follows: Captain Newt Knight, governor; Jasper Collins, lieutenant governor; Bill Sumrall, sheriff; Meg Walters, deputy sheriff; Ned Coats, land surveyor; Marge Valentine, board supervisor; Alpheus Knight, supervisor; Will Welch, supervisor; Orsberry McDaniel, tax assessor; Jim Blackledge, tax collector; Sim Collins, justice of the peace.

So time went on until Mr. Collins got the Constitution written up as he had promised and turned it over to Captain Newt Knight and as my father said, sometime had passed before he got the write-up so at that time it looked like the North was about to win the war, so they waited for some time to see whether it would be necessary to go any further with our work. So my father said it was just a short while before the South gave up and stopped the war. So it left them where they were before the war started with in the free United States they had everything, only to go and take the oath of office.

Now I have told you how the people made soap and how they would save their old scraps of meat and meat skins and spoiled meat. They would be particular and save every piece. Everything was so scarce and; they would keep this grease and scraps of meat. They would call it soap grease, and the way they would do: they would plant some gourd seed in the spring of the year and raise them some gourds and they had a funny idea about planting their seed. They would fix the ground like they was going to plant watermelons, then they would take the seed and go out where they had the ground prepared and if they wanted big, flat, round gourds they would sit down flat on the ground and plant their seed. So when the seed came up and the vine began to make young gourds they would watch the young gourd and keep it on level ground and when the gourd got grown and dry they would take them and put them under the house or some dry place and after they got good and dry they would begin to clean them by first taking a fine-tooth hand saw and being particular to keep the gourd level and when the top is sawed off the top will make a lid to fit the top to keep the dust and trash out. They would saw off enough so they could get their hand in the top so they could clean the inside. They would have to put water in the gourd and soak it for several days and so when they wanted to use the gourd to put their lard in after they killed their hogs in the winter they would pick out the best gourds and clean them which would take longer as they would have to keep soaking until they got all the gourd taste out of the gourd. So at that time as I remember there were no such things as tin cans or tin dippers. The people used gourd dippers and they raised their gourd dippers. They would plant their seed by a fence or someplace where the vine could run up on something and there were some foolish people who believed if you wanted a long-neck gourd they would stretch their arm straight out, but if you wanted a crooked-neck gourd you would crook your arm and drop the seed so you would make the kind you wanted. I have raised gourds but never tried the old fogey way as I never believed in such foolish ideas.

So now 'way back after the Civil War there was no big farming done around in our settlement. There was no such thing as commercial fertilizer. The people would make their corn and peas and potatoes, also plant some peanuts to fatten their hogs. They raised their hogs in the woods until in the fall of the year when the acorns and beech mass began to fall, then the people would take their hogs to the swamps. They would go about once a week, call them up and feed them a little corn to keep tame so they would not go wild. They did not raise very large hogs. Sometimes they would get them some guinea hogs. They didn't get large but were easily fattened. They would make lard out of their guinea hogs. They called some of their other hogs rake straw. I suppose they got their name by the way they do in the winter as they were raised in the woods, when it turned cold they began to rake straw with one of their forefeet; when they got a small pile raked up they would open their mouth, get a mouthful of straw, tote it to their bed until they would make them a big bed and before a snow came (it seemed like they would know it was going to come a snow) they would begin raking and toting straw, piling it up until they would have a big bed. While I was a boy I would watch them hogs make their beds and when people saw those hogs toting straw they would say it was going to snow, and after seeing the hogs preparing for snow some people would prepare for the snow by getting up their pine wood ready for the snow. It hardly ever failed.

During the war there was but very little farming being done here in Jones County. The men were conscripted and carried and put in the war so the men's wives had to do the farming and take care of their children. So it was not much they made but by the help of the Lord they made it through to the end of the war. After the war ended it left lots of the people in bad condition. Some had no homes to go to and my father especially had nothing but my mother and three little children, no home. As I have stated before, their home got burned just before the war started. Had no stock, the Southern cavalry took our horse during the war, so it left my father in bad circumstances but he was not the only one. There were lots of good people left in the same condition. I can remember it was hard times. My father would manage to get corn meal and mother would sift the meal, parch the bran and boil the bran and use it for coffee. Believe me, it was good. There was no way to buy coffee in those days, only a few people were able to buy coffee and flour. After a few years the people began to build up so in the spring of the year the women folks would raise a few chickens and some few would raise a few sheep and after shearing time someone in the settlement would agree to go to town, which was Shubuta, which was 40 some odd miles. So the day before they started to town the neighbors would bring in their produce with a list of groceries they wanted. As time went on business got better and sometimes the merchants would credit a few big farmers. One of the sorriest men in our community borrowed a team which was wagon and four yoke of oxen, went to Shubuta about March; went to Mr. Greenhood, told him he wanted some help to make a crop. He told Mr. Greenhood he owned a big farm and had plenty of help. "Well," Mr. Greenhood said, "Mr. Blank, about what will you need?" "Well, first thing I want one dozen weeding hoes and two barrels of flour, 50 pounds of meat, 50 pounds of lard, 50 pounds of sugar, 20 pounds of coffee, and a few other things." "All right." So they loaded him up and he rolled out for home. It took one week to make the trip, so he made it home all right and in about one month some other man went to town from our settlement. When Mr. Greenhood learned he was from the settlement where the big farmer lived he wanted to know how the big farmer was getting along with his crop; told him who he was; why that man's got no farm, he's got nothing but a wife and two or three children. So that made it hard on some other farmers until the merchant sent a man from Shubuta out to our community to find out about the people, so he went back with the names of good and reliable farmers. The people did lots of trading there until they built the Southern Railroad through here.

My father did his trading with Mr. Weems, was treated nice and Mr. Weems moved here in Ellisville and helped build the little town up. My father still traded with Mr. Weems until he went out of business. About that time Mr. J. P. Myer located here in Ellisville so my father went to trading with Mr. J. P. Myer. He was a great friend of my father and helped him in many ways.

The people usually talk about hard times. They don't know anything about hard times like some of those old people that were raised just after the war was ended. They had no money and the few old clothes they could get they had to wear until the husband could go out in the woods, cut down some oaks, generally black jack or post oak, which they claim was the strongest. They cut the logs up and piled them, then burned them. When the logs were all burned they would wait until the ashes got cold then they would take a box, take up the ashes, take them to the house where they had a place fixed to put them. They called it a hopper. They would make a trough, then would stand some boards in that trough flared at the top so it would hold the ashes. Then they would pour water on the ashes several times a day, not much at a time, until the ashes got good and wet. Then the water would begin to drip through. They would catch the water, call it lye. When they got enough they put it in a wash pot, then they would begin to boil that lye. So it happened sometimes when they didn't have enough old meat scraps or grease to get the lye to thicken they would have to send over to some neighbor's house and get some old meat skins to boil in the lye so it would thicken up and make soap. Meat was so scarce those days that when a hog died in the settlement if it had any fat about it they would dress it and cook it up and make soap grease out of it if they could get it before it began to stink. So now it wasn't all the people here in Jones County had to live so hard, it was those people that the Southern cavalry robbed and destroyed what they had during the war. So the God of Heaven blessed them to endure all those hard times. God blessed them to build up and to have homes again and to enjoy life as others do, although it was through the mercies of a God of all power that they were blessed and hard work which enabled them to own their home and to raise their little children about half naked.

I very well remember the time when the only clothes we wore were longtail shirts. That was all we had, hot or cold. After a few years it so pleased the Lord to bless my parents and enable them to get along better. My father made my mother a loom so she would weave cloth and made us long pants to wear. I remember the first pants I wore. I thought I would soon be a man. They called me a little man and that made me feel lots bigger than I was. About the time that I was ten years old my father and his neighbors got together and hired a school teacher to teach us children. As I remember there were about ten or twelve children who went to school. Money was so scarce until the people could not send all their children. They had no free school in those days so they had to pay the teacher. As well as I remember they paid $10 a month and boarded him. They would not have but two-month term for a while. After a year or two times got better. They would then have three months a year.

Some have asked me how my father came to lose his standing with the people. It was in this way. After times got better the people decided to build them a schoolhouse. They met together and divided the distance between them and built the house, then they called on my father to see and hire them a teacher to teach the school, so he did as he was always called on to do, take the lead in all business that came up in the settlement. So he hired a man to teach the school and the day was set to begin. The teacher and the children met at the house and there was a negro family of two women that had several children. They sent their children too, thinking as part of the men was coming around their home having lots of fun with those two negro women. As soon as the negro children came in the teacher dismissed the school, told them he had come there to teach a white school. So the people had the negro children stop. It made those negro women mad and they stopped those men coming around having such a big time with them. So they got mad with my father about it and blamed him with the women stopping them having so much fun but my father had nothing to do with it. As those negro women owned their home and ran their business in that way to suit themselves it was not all the people that fell out with my father. It was those that were running around after those women. My father had lots of good friends that stuck to him as long as they lived. It was for his kind and helpful deeds he did for them that they never forgot.

COMPOSED BY NEWT KNIGHT

I rise one morning with the rising sun.
    I thought I of my rusty gun.
I thought I would have a little fun
    Way down in old Catoomer.

I call to Bob, "Go catch out Jack"
    While I put on my hunting sack
And in that sack a little snack
    For me to eat way down in old Catoomer.

Neither did I or Bob forget
    To put in plenty of powder and shot.
I jump on Jack and rode him in a trot
    Way down in old Catoomer.

I travel on 'til about noon
    And on a limb I spied a coon
I up with my gun and give him a clew
    And down to the ground I brought him.

Come listen a while, it's to my song
    I'll tell you now, it won't take long
About Young James a liar grave
    Who did lie at graduate.

It was on a political day
    When I and James, we had our fray.
I said to him in a unfriendly way,
    "You better make your get-away."

He bucked his horse, he gagged him thru
    He put him on straight duty too.

He thought his horse run of the sorriest
  Until he met old General Forrest.

Old General Forrest unto him did say
  In a unfriendly way
We've gained the victory we do call
  And run away and left it all.

General Van Dorn was a warrior too.
  He was superiored by General Lee.
Gen. Van Dorn and Gen. Price too
  Both lost their ranks when they met of Gen. Grant.

THE BOY SOLDIER
By a Lady of Savannah

He is acting o'er the battle,
    With his cap and feather gay,
Singing out his soldier prattle,
    In a mockish manly way—
With the boldest, bravest footstep,
    Treading firmly up and down,
And his banner waving softly,
    O'er his boyish locks of brown.

And I sit beside him sewing,
    With a busy heart and hand,
For the gallant soldiers going
    To the far-off distant land—
And I gaze upon my jewel,
    In his baby spirit bold,
My little blue-eyed soldier,
    Just a second summer old.

Still a deep, deep well of feeling
    In my mother's heart is stirred,
And the tears come softly stealing
    At each imitative word!
There's a struggle in my bosom,
    For I love my darling boy—
He's the gladness of my spirit,
    He's the sunlight of my joy!
Yet I think upon my country,
    And my spirit groweth bold—
O! I wish my blue-eyed soldier
    Were but twenty summers old!

SOUTH'S STRANGEST 'ARMY' REVEALED BY CHIEF[1]

Newt Knight, Aged Leader, Speaks After Fifty Years

By Meigs O. Frost

Far up in the heart of Jasper County, Mississippi, amidst a forest of pine and oak where winding woodland paths lead through a tangle of thick underbrush, lives a man now nearing his ninety-second year. Volumes have been written around him. Testimony of men now living, of men long dead, has been taken for and against him. Frugal of speech, he has gone his way through the years, careless of what men said of him in the outside world into which he ventures rarely. In simplicity primeval he has lived, as in primeval simplicity he will die.

That man is Newton Knight, captain throughout the Civil War of the famous Knight's Company that ranged Jasper County and "The Free State of Jones" as the neighboring Jones County is christened in some histories.

"Uncle Newt" Knight here for the first time in all the years breaks silence to tell his story in *The Item*. As he recounts the tale, it is an epic of the Civil War. About him, he says, were banded men who, owning no slaves, believing in the Union of Abraham Lincoln, hoped either to fight through the Confederate cordon and join the Federal forces, or hoped that the Yankee ranks would fight through to them.

As others in Jones and Jasper County, staunch Confederates through-out the war, tell the tale, Newt Knight's Company was composed of "bushwhacking deserters" from the armies of the Confederate States.

More than half a century has passed since men in this part of Missis-sippi bore arms for the Lost Cause. Their sons and their sons' sons since then have fought overseas for the United States of America.

Yet beneath the surface in Jones and Jasper counties still rankles the feeling that Uncle Newt Knight's Company engendered when from 1862 to the end of the Civil War it defied the armed forces of the

---

1 The following narrative was taken from *The New Orleans Item* March 20, 1921.

Confederacy and remained unconquered, though surrounded by Confederate armies from start to finish.

Whether Knight's Company was a band of men whose loyalty to the Union was beyond their loyalty to the South; whether it was a band of Confederate deserters who simply "hid out" in the brush to avoid army service—those are questions that will be debated in Jones and Jasper counties of Mississippi when the headstone of the last combatant has been long overgrown with moss.

But here and now enters Newton Knight into the Court of Public Opinion with his tale—a story that he told to me in the ninety-first year of his age, speaking with a mind apparently as unclouded and keen as that of one five decades younger than he.

And as he tells his story, simply and clearly, one sees a band of men numbering never more than 125, against whom the Confederacy sent cavalry and infantry and bloodhounds; a band to which the Union commander at New Orleans sent four hundred rifles that the Confederates captured; a band that would have been mustered into the Union service with formal recruiting oath, had not the Confederates by stratagem captured the Union soldiery that the Federal commander at Vicksburg sent out into Jasper County when Newt Knight's couriers at last by stealth broke through the gray line of sentinels and won their way with his message to the blue lines of the invader.

Only seven of that company remain. (Original copy not readable here) And he, their commander, is the only surviving officer.

"Well all die guerrillas, I reckon," he mourned. "Never could break through the rebels to jine the Union army. They neveh did break through to jine us. Th' Johnny Rebs busted up the party they sent to swear us in. Always was inofficial. Well, I reckon it don't make much difference, now, anyhow."

"You won't get old Uncle Newt to talk much," said the old-timers at Laurel, Miss., as I sought preliminary facts before motoring out to interview that aged chieftain. "He never would say anything about the old days."

"Watch out you don't come back with a charge of birdshot in your legs," warned others, smilingly. "If Uncle Newt ain't feelin' right—."

＊ ＊ ＊ ＊

"There's Uncle Newt's place," pointed out my guide, as the automobile jolted up the clay road and topped the crest of a hill.

Low and weather-beaten the house stood against a background of pine and oak and thick-growing underbrush. The great brick chimney filled all of one side. To the rear stood an ancient log-house, mud-chinked, with sloping roof of hand-split shingles. A neat picket-fence, also hand-split, surrounded the place.

A hound yelped shrilly as the motor grew silent. We climbed out, stamping chilled feet. The January morning air was keen.

Forms loomed in the low doorway—a woman in blue calico; a man in blue denim.

"Uncle Newt home?" called the guide.

"No, suh. He's oveh at th' otheh place, 'bout three miles off," spoke the woman in blue calico. "Comin' heah sometime today, I reckon."

"Let's go over and meet him," I suggested. "Make it by flivver?"

"Reckon not," said the man in overalls. "Nothin' but a country path through th' woods."

"Which way?"

"Oveh yonder, past that naked pine."

Past the white skeleton of a lightning-blasted pine we made our way by the winding forest path. Arid as we headed down the steep hill, the bushes at the foot parted. A tall form emerged.

"Lord, that's luck," said the guide. "It's Uncle Newt himself."

Draw your own picture of a ninety-one-year-old veteran climbing a steep hill by a narrow path through thick-woven underbrush, at the end of a three-mile tramp. It won't be the site that greeted my eyes.

The shoulders of the tall, gaunt form that mounted the hill were a trifle stooped. At that, not much more than many a city desk stoop in men half his age. From heavy boots up a dark suit of homespun my eyes traveled, and stopped just below the great hat of light-colored felt— "white hats" they call them on the Texas range. For the face beneath that wide hat-brim would arrest attention anywhere.

A mighty beak of a nose jutted out like a promontory. The jaw was seen through a sparse white beard. The white hair, uncut for years, hung about the shoulders. But the eyes held you longest. They were that cold, clear gray-blue eye of the killer now vanishing from the West. They looked clear through you. And by some peculiarity of control, hawk-like, the lower lids never moved.

That trick, or power, has stood Uncle Newt Knight in good stead, as he told later. Even today, on peaceful mission, it was a bit uncanny. In fighting times—well!

My guide presented me with the customary formula.

"Glad to see you, sir," said Uncle Newt, shaking hands. His grip still had power. His hands were oddly full and muscular; not shrunken with his great age.

"Come on up to the house," said Uncle Newt. "I'm feelin' right peart this morning, but I reckon a little fire would feel good, don't you?"

"He used to have the biggest, longest teeth you ever saw," murmured my guide, as Uncle Newt climbed the steps and entered the house. "Big, heavy-set man, quick as a cat on his feet. Just a fightin' fool when he got started."

Into the plain match-boarded living room of the house we went, where oak logs were roaring in the whitewashed fireplace.

"Draw up a cheer and make yourself comfortable," said Uncle Newt, cordially.

"Now, sir" spoke up our ninety-one-year-old host, "what is it you want me to tell you?"

"Uncle Newt," said I, "there's a lot of stories going 'round about you and your company in the Civil War. Nobody seems to have your own story of it, yet. And folks say you were pretty busy out here in Jones and Jasper counties for awhile. Suppose you tell it to us just the way you remember it."

"Well, I remember a right smart of it," conceded Uncle Newt.

"Memory still good as your eyes?" I asked. He was without glasses.

Memory All Right

"Better," said he, promptly. "My memory's all right. 'Bout my eyes; I've worn out three-four pair spectacles. Don't think much of 'em. Quit 'em. I can see enough to shoot a bird on the wing or a rabbit on the run yet. That's good enough for me."

"He can shoot 'em that way," spoke up his grand-daughter. "Keeps us supplied with birds and rabbits all the time. His memory—well, you ought to hear the old songs he sings us."

Uncle Newt smiled at that.

"Voice aint as good as it might be," said he. "But I remember lots of the old songs yet."

We urged him to sing us a tune and, by George, he did. Straight through from first to last verse the old voice carried the ancient tune of an ancient English ballad.

And then, spurred by occasional questions, he launched into his story.

"They used to call Jones County, Mississippi, the Free State of Jones," said he. "That started a lot of stories about the county. There's one story that after Jones County seceded from the Union she seceded from the Confederacy and started up a Free State of Jones. That ain't so. Fact is, Jones County never seceded from the Union into the Confederacy. Her delegate seceded. When the Southern states was all taking a vote on whether to secede, we took the vote in Jones County, too. There was only about four hundred folks in Jones County then. All but about seven of them voted to stay in the union. But the Jones County delegate went up to the state convention at Jackson, and he voted to secede with the rest of the county delegates. He didn't come back to Jones County for awhile. It would a been kinder onhealthy for him, I reckon.

"Well, we'd voted again secession, but the state voted to secede. Then next thing we knew they were conscripting us. The rebels passed a law conscripting everybody between eighteen and thirty-five. They just come around with a squad of soldiers 'n' took you.

"I didn't want to fight. I told 'em I'd help nurse sick soldiers if they wanted. They put me in the Seventh Mississippi Battalion as hospital orderly. I went around giving the sick soldiers blue mass and calomel and castor oil and quinine. That was about all the medicine we had then. It got shorter later.

"Then the rebels passed the twenty-negro law, up there at Richmond, Virginia, the capital. That law said that any white man owning twenty niggers or more didn't need to fight. He could go home 'n' raise crops.

"Jasper Cellins was a close friend of mine. When he heard about that law, he was in camp, in the Confederate army. He threw down his gun and started home.

"'This law,' he says to me, 'makes it a rich man's war and a poor man's fight. I'm through.'

"Well, I felt the same way about it. So I started back home. I felt like if they had a right to conscript me when I didn't want to fight the Union, I had a right to quit when I got ready.

"There was about fifty or sixty of us out here in Jones and Jasper counties. Later there was about 125 of us. Never any more.

"We knew we were completely surrounded by the rebels. But we knew every trail in the woods.

"So we stayed out in the woods minding our own business, until the Confederate army began sending raiders after us with bloodhounds. Then we saw we had to fight. So we organized this company and the boys elected me captain. They elected Jasper Collins first lieutenant and W. W. Sumrall second lieutenant."

Uncle Newt rocked back and forth meditatively and gazed into the fireplace where the oak logs were crackling.

"Yes, sir," said he, "there was right smart trouble then. We were pretty quiet for awhile. We figured out that the rebels were too strong for us just then to fight our way through to jine up with the union forces. And we thought that we'd wait until the Federals fought their way down closer to us or we got stronger.

Battle With Rebels

"But the rebels started to build a fire under us. I remember the night Alpheus Knight was married up near Soso. That wedding ended up in a battle. Not that I ain't heard—" and the old man smiled with quaint humor—"that lots of other weddings end up battles, too.

"Only this was a right smart battle. You see, there was one woman living near who didn't like us. She got word of Alpheus Knight's wedding. He was a cousin of mine. And she told her nigger cook: 'Gal, you take this message and don't you stop to eat or sleep until you've delivered it to the Confederate soldiers by Ellisville.' But some folks that were friendly to me, they sent word about it.

"Well, Alpheus, he got married all right. It was a right cold night, just durin' Christmas week. I told 'em to go ahead and celebrate the weddin,' 'n' I'd keep watch. There was only less'n a dozen of us there. We kept scattered a lot, so the rebels couldn't trail us so easy.

"'You'll freeze to death,' they told me, when I started out to watch the nearest crossin' on the river.

"'The Lord lights a fire in a man to keep him warm when he's workin' for a good cause,' I told 'em, and I started out. I walked up and down the bank, about half a mile each way. It was deathly still in the woods. Then just after daylight I heard a chain rattle on a flat [flatboat]. I knew it was the rebels crossing the river. I could hear their horses' hooves. Then I caught sight of 'em. They was about one hundred of 'em stomping on that flat. I had about a half-mile to go to the house where Alpheus and his bride were with the rest of us who went to the wedding. I made that half-mile right fast.

Carries Baby and Rifle

"When I got to the house the lady had a big breakfast laid out.

"'You're just in time,' she told me. 'Sit down and eat.'

"'I've got no appetite,' I said. 'There's a fight coming.' They urged me to eat. Finally I ate a little piece of pie and drank some hot coffee.

"'Come on,' I said. 'We've got to get out of here. There's about a hundred Confederates marchin' on this house.'

"Well, we all packed up and started. There were some ladies there. One of 'em had a baby in her arms.

"'I can't carry this baby so fast,' she said. So I took the baby.

"'I'll carry your gun,' she said, when I took the baby.

"'No, madam, you won't,' I said. 'Nobody carries my gun but me.'

"We hadn't gone two hundred yards from the house, when I heard a clatter of hoofs.

"'Here they come!' I yelled. But it was only a passel of critters roamin' wild. Some colts out in the brush. We all felt easier—and then all of a sudden there were guns going off all over the place.

"About twenty of the Confederates had ridden up behind those wild critters. The minute they saw us they opened fire.

"That baby clung tighter than ever to me when the guns went off. 'Here, ma'am, take yo' baby!' I told the mother. I had to scrunch down so she could get it. She was a sort of low-built woman. But she got it.

"I swung 'round to look at the Confederates. There was a captain riding straight at me. A big man, with his head set sort of cross-ways on his shoulders. I can see him yet.

"I raised my gun.

"'Lord God, direct this load,' I prayed, and I fired.

"He tumbled out of his saddle. I looked around the place. We were outnumbered. So I jumped into the brush, and I yelled as loud as ever I could!

"'Attention! Battalion! Rally on the right! Forward!'

"There wasn't no more battalion than a rabbit. But there was thick woods all around, and the rebels must have thought there was an army in them. They reined in their horses, anyway, and dashed back to the main body. That gave us a chance to get away."

Again old Uncle Newt lapsed into silence.

"Any of your men wounded?" I asked.

"Yes, a few."

"Wounded yourself?"

"No—but they did their best. They shot off my hat and powder horn. All we had was muzzle loader shotguns mostly. They had these new repeatin' rifles."

"Shotguns?"

"Good Ol' Guns"

"Oh yes. We got pretty good results, though. I heard one doctor say we must be right smart shooters to hit one man fourteen times with rifle bullets. I didn't tell him we used to use 'bout eighteen rifle bullets to the barrel, loadin' those ol' percussion cap shotguns. Good ol' guns. Here's mine."

And Uncle Newt brought down from its wooden pegs an ancient weapon. Oiled wood and polished steel were as immaculate as when it came from the hands of the worker more than a half century before. It was a double-barreled twelve gauge shotgun, muzzle-loading, with twin hammers and nipples for the percussion caps, and a slender polished wooden ramrod down beneath the barrels.

"Sal's a good ol' gal," grinned Uncle Newt as he fondled the weapon, brought it lightly to balance at his shoulder and aimed at an imaginary bird flying high.

"How'd your company get its powder and lead?" I asked.

"Off the Johnny Rebs, mostly," grinned Uncle Newt. "We got word once of a Confederate wagon goin' through Jones County. There warn't many of us, but we scouted up on 'em and got 'em surrounded. The boys all had big drive horns. They were the horns used in rounding up stock, summoning the men folks from the fields, driving cattle, etc. Well, there'd be a big blast up in the woods, to one side. Then another on the other side. Then another in front and one in back. Those drivers must have thought we had an army in the woods. Then when we came a-shootin,' they cut and run.

"We got a lot of powder that time, and some lead and a lot of subtler stuff. But we never had much trouble about ammunition. There was a lot of powder and lead in the country stores when the war started. And one widder near us had a piece of lead, about 50 pounds. One of my men was courtin' her daughter, so of course she gave us what we needed. Th' ol' hen flutters when you come 'round the lone chick, you know." And Uncle Newt grinned.

"Didn't you capture a Confederate commissariat base up near Paulding?" I asked, mindful of one exploit of which I had heard in Laurel.

"Shucks, that warn't much of a job," said Uncle Newt. "Yes, I took the boys up there to Paulding. There was a guard of Confederates over the building. The supplies was all corn. They made out I took right smart other stuff. But it was all corn. I just walked up to the saloon man there and told him I'd shoot him if he gave the boys any whisky before we got the stuff loaded. He didn't give 'em any.

"I remember there was some Irish families there at Paulding. They were pretty bad off. They didn't want to fight, and the Confederates wouldn't give 'em or sell 'em anything. I gave 'em all the corn they said they wanted. Then we took the rest back to our headquarters in the woods."

"Ever run short on food?"

"Lord, no," said Uncle Newt. "There were plenty of deer and wild turkeys in the woods, and lots of our friends kept hogs and other stock. We had right smart of friends about Jones and Jasper counties, you know. They helped us a lot. The women were fine.

"I was tellin' you about the time we scared the Confederates in that wagon train by usin' the big drive-horns. Well, there was one lady I remember, all alone in her house. Some Confederate cavalry, four or five of 'em, rode up to her one day and asked her where her son was. He was one of my company.

"'I don't know where he is,' she told 'em.

"'Yes, you know,' they told her. 'Now tell us where he is.'

"'Well,' says she, 'I told you the truth. I don't know where he is. But I can find out.'

"She took up a big drive-horn and went out on the gallery and blew it. Pretty soon somebody answered with another blast up on the hillside in the brush. Then another blast came from another point. I guess there were 'bout a dozen answers to that horn.

"That Confederate leader looked at his men.

"'Boys, I guess we'd better get out of here,' he said. And they sure got.

"Do you know," mused Uncle Newt with a whimsical grin on his face, "there's lots of ways I'd rather die than be scared to death."

Women Helped

Silence again for a few minutes while the ancient splint rocker creaked.

"Yes, those ladies sure helped us a lot. I recollect when Forrest's cavalry came a-raidin' after us. They had forty-four bloodhounds after us, those boys and General Robert Lowry's men. But forty-two of them hounds just naturally died. They'd get hongry and some of the ladies, friends of ours, would feed 'em. And they'd die. Strange, wasn't it?"

A grin of almost school-boyish mischief lit up the rugged old face.

"Them dogs certain had a hard time of it. Some of 'em died of lead poisoning, too. And then we'd scatter red pepper on the trails, and polecat musk and other things a hound-dog loves."

He grinned again.

"I'm told that General Lowry caught some of your men," said I.

Lightning-like that grin vanished. In its place flashed a look of bitterness that showed the fires of half a century ago were not all dead, cold ashes.

"He was rough beyond reason," said old Newt Knight, with sudden curious absence of country dialect in his speech. "He hanged some of my company he had no right to hang."

"There's a story current in Laurel that while Lowry was running for governor of Mississippi he never came into Jones or Jasper counties. That he wouldn't want to meet you."

Uncle Newt Knight's face remained granite-hard.

"I don't know about that," said he. "But I do know that I never saw Lowry, knowingly."

And I remembered the words of Goode Montgomery, former mayor of Laurel, who had known First Lieutenant Jasper Collins of Knight's company, now dead these ten years.

"Collins told me," said Montgomery, "that he'd get up on the coldest night he ever saw to kill Lowry if he knew he was passing through Jones County."

The clear old voice broke into my thoughts.

"You was asking were we short on supplies," said Uncle Newt. "We were all-fired short on tobacco. Didn't bother me. I didn't use it. But it sure bothered some of the boys. I remember one feller in my company. He got some fine navy sweet plug on one raid we was on. There was one youngster was almost a-dyin' for a sweet chew. He'd fixed up some chewin' of part tobacco 'n' part bark—bitter'n gall. 'N' he begged this man for some of his sweet navy plug to mix with his bitter stuff.

"Well, the' ol' feller was cantankerous. He wouldn't give up any. He said if he shared with one he'd have to share with all. So he wouldn't share with any.

Got Sweet Chew

"We was a-campin' by the river one day, a-castin' lead in bullet-molds. This fellar who had the sweet tobacco took out a big chew he'd just cut, 'n' stuck it on the end of a pine branch while he went down to the river to get a drink of water. The youngster was right thar. I saw him slip out his old, bitter chew, pop the sweet one into his mouth, 'n' stick the bitter one on the pine branch. Th' ol' stingy cuss came back. He reached for his chew.

"'Holl on,' said the youngster. 'That's my chew.'

"'The h—— it is,' said the old feller, and put it in his mouth. It made him almighty sick, it was that bitter. When he came to, he jumped at the young feller.

"'I'll whop you to death,' he yelled. And he meant it.

"I had to step atween 'em, 'n' tell th' ol' feller that the youngster was right. He'd told him it wasn't his chew. But that shows you how men get when they can't get tobacco."

"How many fights did you have with the Confederate forces?" I asked him. "And how many men did you lose?"

Uncle Newt thought for a moment.

"There was a lot of skirmishin' that you couldn't properly call battles," said he. "But we all had sixteen sizable fights that I remember, and we lost eleven men. I never kept track of how many wounded. I used to treat their gunshot wounds myself. There were a number of them."

"Many close shaves yourself?"

Uncle Newt smiled cryptically.

"One or two," said he. "I remember once when a big fellow was coming at me, and my gun-hammer spring wouldn't work. It was a home-made spring I fixed after the first one broke. He pretty nearly got me."

That was all he would tell of that encounter.

Then—"There was once," he smiled, "when a fellow who was afraid to come out in the open and fight me paid another man to come up and whop me. This fellow who was paid for the job came up, wavin' a bottle of whisky and inviting me to have a drink. I didn't drink. He kept waving that bottle around my head. I knew he was looking for an opening to smash me. I kept watchin' him. I was ready the first move he made. Then he says: 'Great God, Newt Knight, don't you never wink your eyes?' 'Not when I'm looking at your sort of cattle,' I told him. He judged it warn't a good day for fighting, I reckon. Anyway, he quit."

And as he spoke, with those chill, blue-gray eyes staring, Uncle Newt illustrated how his head had followed the motion of that whisky bottle. Ninety-one years old!

But about some details Uncle Newt had naught to say. He lapsed into silence, to speak later on some trivial matter, when asked about the current story that his command had executed at Ellisville a Baptist preacher reputed to have told the Confederates one of his hiding places.

"We never did have any luck," he said, "in connecting up with the Union army. I sent Jasper Collins to Memphis as a courier to the Union commander to get us all regularly recruited in the Union army. They sent him to Vicksburg to see General Hudson or Huddleston, or something like that. Then the Federals sent a company to recruit us. That company was waylaid by some Confederates near Rocky Creek. It surrendered.

"Then I sent a courier to the Federal commander at New Orleans. He sent up four hundred rifles. The Confederates captured them. We just naturally never did connect up with the Union officers and get enlisted regularly. So when the war was over, we just disbanded and went about our business."

"How many of the company are living today?" I asked.

"All I know is seven," said he. "I keep my old muster rolls out here in the woods in one of my places. Whenever I hear that one of the boys has died, I mark him off on the rolls. Who are the ones left? I'm not tellin' that. No use namin' a lot of names and getting people worked up again. When this last war with Germany came along, I called all my folks together and told 'em to do the right thing and get into it. The Civil War's over long ago. No use stirring up that old quarrel this late day, is there?"

There was cordial farewell; cordial invitation to "drop in again."

Gift of Peanuts

At a sign from old Uncle Newt, one of the folks on the place brought out a sack of peanuts from the log store-house. It was pressed upon us with courtly hospitality—all the gift Uncle Newt had to offer.

As we drove away, the gnarled old figure stood erect by the hand-hewn picket fence, waving good-bye.

* * * *

Records of the Mississippi Historical Society bear out in many details Newton Knight's story. I am indebted for them to Judge Stone Deavours and to W. S. Welsh of Meridian, as I am indebted to Sheriff W. E. Welsh of Jones County, former Mayor Goode Montgomery of Meridian, Mrs. McWhorter Beers of Meridian, historian of the D. A. R., now writing a history of Jones County, and W. L. Pryor of the First National Bank of Meridian, for many of the local stories current about the Knight Company.

Jones County, named after John Paul Jones, was in 1861 almost a unit against secession. Its citizens elected J. D. Powell, anti-secessionist candidate, to the Secession Convention at Jackson, by a heavy majority, only twenty-four votes being recorded for J. M. Baylis, the secessionist candidate. But when the test came, Powell voted for secession. He was hanged in effigy in Jones County, and abused so violently that he did not return within its borders for a long time.

Nevertheless, Jones County responded loyally to the Confederacy's call for troops. From her scanty population she recruited three full companies of infantry and furnished a great part of four more on her borders, jointly with Jasper, Covington, and Wayne counties. They served the Confederate States throughout the war.

Federals Ambushed

When a party of Federal troops set forth from near Brookhaven to destroy the Mobile and Ohio Railroad about Waynesboro, Lieutenant W. M. Wilson of the 43rd Tennessee Infantry was sent to intercept the force. He started with a handful of men. Covington and Jones counties reinforced him with men too old for regular service and with boys too young. By strategy he outwitted and ambushed the Federal band who outnumbered him greatly, killed one, wounded several, and bluffed them into a surrender at Rocky Creek near Ellisville. This is the Union force that Newt Knight says was sent to muster his company into Federal service.

Part Two

The Echo of the Black Horn

Dedicated to the memory of the
Noble Confederates
who lived and died for
Jones County

Preface

Jones County, Mississippi, has probably occupied the national spotlight more often than any other county in any other state of the Union.

Surprising? No. Why? That is the question that is asked by those who are not acquainted with the early history of this wonderful section of the South. The answer is disunity. Disunity of what? Disunity of whom? Where? and When? are the questions that come popping from every direction.

When disunity rears its ugly head, elements foreign and unwelcome creep in to belittle the efforts of the majority to uphold the good name of the county; where the people adhere strictly to the old traditions of the South; where there is still class distinction, and racial segregation.

Does segregation contribute to disunity? No. All races in Jones County share equal rights, but not social equality. Under disunity comes betrayal of public trust, Treachery, Greed, Deceit, Crooked politics, Hypocrisy, and the inclination of a certain few to live, not by the written law, but according to the trend of opinion. Through these are admitted the communistic elements that would seek to tear down the good reputation of Jones County.

Criminal tendencies of aliens, reputedly Jones Countians, which have led to acts of violence and hate, have been flashed in screaming headlines by newspapers over the nation, and this peaceable prosperous county comes in for unjust, unfair, and disgraceful publicity, ridiculed as "The Free State of Jones."

Fiction writers, with itching palm, which has too often been greased by these same elements outside the realm of Jones County, have helped to heap undue criticism upon this land and its people that are deserving of the highest respect and praise, for having pre-served the principles of Democracy, despite all obstacles and outside interference.

Occupancy of disunity began here almost 150 years ago, coming in along with the land seekers early in the nineteenth century.

The people all over the nation were reminded of that fact when Mis-sissippi's fair and impartial judicial system was attacked by Northern publications featuring "The Davis Knight Case," which came up at the December 1948 term of the Circuit Court for the First Judicial District of Jones County, which indictment was for violating section 459 of the Mississippi Code of 1942, which is our miscegenation statute and pro-hibits the marriage "of a negro or mulatto, or person having one eighth or more negro blood with a white person." The indictment charged that Davis Knight had, on the 18th day of April 1946, contracted a marriage with Junie Lee Spradley, a white female.

The case was continued from time to time until it came on for trial at the December 1948 term of the Circuit Court in Ellisville, the indict-ment having been returned at that place for the reason that the parties secured a license and contracted a ceremonial marriage, performed by J. M. Powell, the mayor of Ellisville, at that place.

The defense of Davis Knight was purely factual. The only witness testifying for the state, who even made a pretense of knowing anything about it was Tom Knight, son of Captain Newton Knight, the "gover-nor" of "The Free State of Jones County." He testified in a general way that Rachel, the great-grandmother of Davis Knight was a negro, but never did say positively that she was a full-blood negro, it being obvious that no man having due regard for the truth could so swear, and this especially after a lapse of sixty years. It is obvious that in order to sustain a conviction against Davis Knight the proof must first have shown that Rachel was a negro of pure blood, for if she were not, he would, by the same ratio, be that much less than one-eighth negro.

The Hon. Quitman Ross of Laurel, Mississippi, was the attorney for the defense. His statement of the facts is herewith quoted:

"At the time of the trial I held in my hand and offered in evidence a marriage license issued in Jasper County to the parents and the grandparents of Davis Knight, each of which showed the contracting parties to be white persons.

"I also had in my hand and offered in evidence the honorable discharge of Davis Knight from the United States Navy, which showed that he was inducted at Camp Shelby, Mississippi, from Jasper County as a white person, and served and was discharged as a white person. All of this proof was excluded by the court, and the jury found the defendant to be guilty of the crime charged, and the court imposed a sentence of five years imprisonment in the State Penitentiary.

"Immediately upon the announcement of a conviction, newspapers all over the world took the matter up, not on a factual basis, but on the basis that all persons should be free to marry whomever they choose. Because of this extraordinary publicity I was besieged with telephone calls, letters, and all sorts of gratuitous advice from almost every state in the Union, and at least three European countries. Various domestic organizations having to do with the Negro race sought to inject themselves into the matter but their offers of assistance were courteously and firmly declined, and the case proceeded to our Supreme Court in the usual manner. Several errors were assigned in that court, but the only one the court found necessary to deal with was the contention that the verdict was against the overwhelming weight of the evidence, and accordingly the conviction was reversed in an opinion rendered by Associate Justice Montgomery, and recorded at page 747, Southern Reporter, second series.

"The State having introduced all the proof at hand, and this having been found by our Supreme Court to be insufficient for a conviction, the case was nol-prossed at the December, 1949, term of the Court. Thus ended the celebrated case of the State of Mississippi vs. Davis Knight."

But the curious cannot be satisfied, and the quest for more information goes on by many people outside the South, who would use that information against us, once they can obtain and distort the facts into wicked propaganda.

Who was Captain Newton Knight? He has been portrayed as a great character, a man who died a martyr to the Union cause.

Who was Rachel? The answer is truthfully given. All the information contained in this book is a matter of record, or is taken from the "bill of sale" of slave purchases, old letters from old trunks, land deeds and other documents, and the pieced together remnants of old grave markers dug from old cemeteries over Jones County.

CHAPTER I

The Echo of the Black Horn

There is a broad and beautiful country that stretches for miles and miles through Smith, Jasper, Jones, and Covington counties. Beginning as a little springhead trickle up in Scott County above Smith is the River Leaf. Passing along the foot of the famous Sullivan's Hollow, and gaining in width and depth and swiftness as it flows southward toward the "Great Water" that the Indians spoke of long before the badmen inhabited the hollow. The water shed of this little unpretentious river is the fertile uplands that are known as the hills of Sullivan's Hollow, from which source much of the silt is washed into the stream and deposited over the valley below. On the opposite side of this valley lie the hills and hollows of Jasper and Jones counties, including "the No Man's Land" of Captain Newton Knight.

These counties comprise approximately three thousand square miles. Of all these Covington was the first organized, the 5th day of January 1819, and named for Leonard Covington. Prior to that time all this area was known as Mississippi Territory East of Pearl River.

An old survey is recorded, 1810, 1811, which vividly describes this "District of Mississippi." No names are given to the small streams, but they are beautifully described, as to width and depth, and the notation is made that many cannot be forded. The beauty of the trees and vegetation and the type of soil, the valuation of the land is given. Example: "Two dollar quality; three dollar quality" (per acre). The magnolia is mentioned as "a sweet flowering bay" and other flowering trees and shrubs are described. Detail is given in describing the timber, as a big hickory, a hollow beech, crooked sassafras, big white oak, tall pines, etc., throughout the account, and the springheads and campsites along the route are so beautifully described, it is not a strain upon the imagination to visualize this paradise of the pioneers. For indeed, it must have appeared so with its unlimited possibilities; to the hunter, or a man with his eye on trapping, it could not be surpassed for wild game of every kind was abundant. To the farmer, this country was waiting with a wealth of soil richness to produce his crops. The springs were flowing from hillsides, beginning streams for power, for livestock, for fish for his table, in an enviable climate with a long growing season, with just enough cold weather to kill off the insects in winter.

At one time Covington County's line joined Perry County on the south and included a great part of Jones County and that part that is now Jefferson Davis County. Later in 1826, January 24, a slice was taken from Wayne County and added to the cast portion of Covington, and that area, containing 696 square miles became Jones County, so named for John Paul Jones.

Forrest County was made up in the same manner from a part of Perry County, and the south part of Covington, Lauderdale, Jasper, and Smith counties were organized the same year, 1833, and it was not until 1906 that Jefferson Davis County was organized, cutting the area of the original Covington down to 410 square miles.

This territory is a part of the Mount Dexter Treaty Grant, 1805, the Choctaw Cession from which resulted all of Covington, Wayne, Green, Madison, Lawrence, Pike, Perry, Jones, Lincoln, Lamar, Forrest, Jeff Davis, and Walthall counties.

After the white man came, many Indians chose to remain, and were indeed friends in need, as they assisted the early settlers in many ways. Especially were they helpful in holding off hostilities, and many things they taught their new neighbors about the simple way of life in a wilderness.

One of the choice delicacies was a concoction that the Indians taught the settlers to prepare for the children. It was parched corn, pestled to a powder in a pestle stone, and to this was added sugar and roasted nuts.

From them we learned the secret of making beautiful shades of dye from the bark of trees, the purple from the sweetgum, the soft grays from the willow, and the browns from walnut. They also taught many things about the tricks of trapping, of catching fish, and the tricks that "medicine men" could work upon the human body by the use of herbs, barks, and plants.

Many old Indian remedies are still used by the negroes in this section. May apple is still used in a spring tonic, and a mess o' poke salad is a spring must to dispel spring fever. The alder is still used for a tea to break out the hives on young babies. Red oak "oose" which is the liquid boiled from the bark of the tree is wonderful combined with red clay for a sprained knee or ankle. Jerusalem Oak cut into beads and strung on a string and placed about a child's neck is still a good teething remedy, so the old negroes say. The mistletoe has a use other than to shelter a Yuletide kiss. No better medicine is found than the delicate berries and tender twigs of this parasite to treat a sick cow, after the birth of a calf.

Ages back the Indians had noticed that does, after hiding their young, would wander into the bogs and nibble the mistletoe that grew low on the branches of black gum. Swamp cattle feed very much like deer, and their natural instincts prompt them to seek out and eat that which was by nature provided for them.

The Choctaw Nation was divided into many tribes and there were many important chieftains among them, some so distinguished that they have become historical figures, while others remain obscure traditions. One of these seldom mentioned in the accounts of the early settlement were the Mingoes, a tribe of friendly Indians that inhabited the region in Jones County along Leaf River. From these people are descended our friends Abba-ha-ha-hubbee and East-tubbee. It was among these Indians that the first white settlement east of Pearl River in the Mississippi Territory was established.

The first four families to locate here following the first of the ten Choctaw treaties, which treaty provided only for unmolested wagon train passage into the territory, were Knight, Welch, Robertson, and Ducksworth. Soon after them came the families of Wade, Foxworth, Reddoch, Rogers, Speed, Graves, Pickering, Brumfield, Hatten, Pemberly, Magee, and others of the old aristocracy, bringing in slaves and finery from an older civilization. And, as has always been the custom, new developments bring in a flood of people. The notoriety of this beautiful new country brought in a rush of newcomers. Many other pioneers were poor, without lands or money, and others were simply adventurers and vagabonds.

After the passage of the Harrison Land Law, 1800, the laboring class migrating southward could obtain lands by making one-fourth down payment and the balance in three more annual payments. There were other means of acquiring land without too much trouble or money as land offices were set up and homesteads were granted. There was much dispute and conflict about these lands, as treaty grants and territories were placed in the hands of land commissioners who were not always honest. Much land was illegally sold, and the proceeds pocketed by the unscrupulous commissioners.

There are records on file which show that these men were brought up for trial for misappropriating properties, and demand was made for the return of the monies received in such transactions, but there is no record of a conviction. Illegal land sales made a certain few rich, and their descendants have inherited the spoils taken from this part of Mississippi soon after it was relinquished by the Indians.

This first white settlement in Jones County was along the east side of Leaf River, all of the high ridge between the river and Mason Creek, and extending down the river below the Welch Landing. There is no record as to how part of this land was acquired from the Mingoes, but legend has it that the early Knight came first offering gifts, and it was he who made a trade with the Indians to live among them, and in exchange for a flint knife he was given a tract of land, with permission to clear fields and build houses. The other three families were likewise accepted, and there was never discord among them. The only trouble was, the chief was always on hand to receive another gift, and there was the problem of having to divide the very scarce necessities. Once the giving was begun, there was no stopping.

These early trades between white man and Indian, followed much later by the crookedness in the land offices has caused land trouble in Mississippi since, and by rights, many people do not own the land on which they pay taxes!

As these early settlers were Christian people, their first requirement was a place to worship, and since they were not all of the same faith, there being three denominations among the four families, they were faced with the problem of establishing a church satisfactory to all. So they came together, asking Divine Guidance in planning for their spiritual needs. The result of such wisdom was the establishment of the Union Church, which was a church for the worship of one God. With the formation of a union, denominationalism was cast aside, and one Christian church was built for all the people in the territory that became Jones County.

With the coming of other settlers, the church grew and became more the center of community activity. This first building also served as a Masonic Hall, and was used as such until the execution of the following deed:

JONES COUNTY, STATE OF MISSISSIPPI

This indenture made and entered into by law between Albert Knight and Mason Knight of the one part and the officers and members of the Hebron Lodge No. 200 of the other part, all of the County of Jones and the State of Mississippi, in consideration of the sum of five dollars to us in hand paid. The receipt of which is hereby acknowledged witnesseth that whereas, Albert Knight and Mason Knight of the first part hath this day given, granted, bargained, sold and conveyed, and by these presents do hereby give, grant, bargain, sell and convey and confirm unto the said institution, Hebron Lodge No. 200 all that certain parcel or tract of land lying and being in the aforesaid county and state, more particular known and described as follows, To Wit:

Commencing at a suitable distance northeast of the Masonic Hall (or Union Church) turning west 100 yards, thence south 100 yards, thence east 100 yards, thence north 100 yards to the beginning, as to place the said Masonic Hall at or near the center of the said designated tract of land to have and to hold unto the said Hebron Lodge No. 200 against the claim of ourselves, our heirs, executors, administrators and assigns, and we will further warrant and defend the claim or claims of any other person or persons whomsoever, either inlaw or equity, unto the said Hebron Lodge No. 200 its officers and members of legal representative, or assigns for ever. Given under our hands and seals this the 27th day of August A.D. 1859.

ALBERT KNIGHT (*seal*)

MASON KNIGHT (*seal*)

The Old Union Church was at the time of the conveyance of the above deed in a state of dilapidation, having been hastily and crudely built out of square hewn logs, and it was now time, with the expansion of the settlement, and the increased wealth of the community to build a nice church. Since some of the people were of Baptist belief, a church across the river in Covington County (Leaf River Church) and the people of the settlements of Big Creek and Cracker's Neck had established the Big Creek Church and combined school, and the members of Methodist belief had established the Bethel Church down below, and across the river, the new church which was built along with the new Lodge became Methodist, and was called Mount Olive Church. This combined structure was built with the Hall occupying the upper story, and the school and church the lower floor. It was also built of hewn timber and was large enough to accommodate large congregations, including the negroes, as they too were accepted as members, and were welcomed as Christian brothers and sisters into the church.

On the old Mount Olive Church roll, which is as often spoken of as old Hebron, are the names of the colored members along with the names of the white members, although they were not social equals.

There were enough benches reserved for these members, who remembered their places and kept them, never daring, or for that matter, never thinking of such a thing as sitting beside a white member.

Segregation was the rule and always will be the rule as long as one Southerner descended from the old South lives, and as long as the teachings of the old Christian colored race are remembered by their descendants there will be no danger of a Mongrel race, as purity of race is the primary objective of segregation. Adherence to tradition is a tendency almost as strong as heredity, and environment does not create drastic change.

When Mount Olive's meeting day called for dinner on the ground, the colored sisters helped the white sisters to "put out the dinner," and heaped plates of food for the children and the menfolks. After this service more of the same kind of food was taken from baskets and spread for the negroes who gathered to themselves under the trees where they could eat to their full capacity. After much eating, laughing, and talking the colored sisters packed leftovers back into the baskets to carry back to the quarters for their supper. Those were the happy days never to be forgotten.

The afternoon service was opened with both races joining in the song service. The singing and praying was immensely enjoyed by the colored members, and it is their descendants who are today holding the South in unity and peace. To them goes the credit for the love and respect the two separate races have for each other, as a segregated people.

CHAPTER 2

The Sale of Rachel

It was the second week in April 1856.

The fresh was a little late in coming, so the logs had been snaked up to the dry banks of Old Leaf to wait. All was ready for the spring rains; all ready and waiting. The sap had risen weeks before, and the wind kept up a continuous howl from out of the southwest.

During a lull in the wind, the chirping of birds filled the air. Occasionally a rain-crow or a mourning dove, which was the omen of corn planting time, would sound a plaintive note, which would be blended in and lost among the chirpings of many other birds. The bluejays, the wrens, the red cardinals, and the black birds kept up a chatter, not unpleasant to the ear, as they pivoted with the swaying of the boughs of the full-budded trees. A wild turkey sounded a mating call from the top of a rail fence. Then the old gander, in annoyance and defiance, raised his voice in a shrill challenge from inside the freshly plowed enclosure.

Already goose nests were in the making in the fence jams and along the ditch banks. Already the garden sass was right for eating, and up in the hills on higher ground, corn was up and shining green from one end of the rows to the other. But the lowlands would be flooded as soon as the wind ceased, so there was no hurry about planting.

Spring was late this year anyway, as there had been an early Easter, from which follows changeable weather. But considering the golden buds, the size of the red oak leaves, the red of the maple, the green of the willow, it was definitely here, making the woods fragrant with that certain unmistakable sweetness of the yellow jasmine, honeysuckle, and that earthy invigorating odor peculiar to spring. Away from the swamps and in the pastures, the johnny-jump-ups, violets, cowslip, and buttercups' delicate scent was mingled with the pungent odor of last year's corn stalks and brush heaps burning in the clearing. The blue smoke settled, then rose and scattered with the rise of the wind.

Night came, and all was still except the croaking of the frogs. In the far distance the thunder rumbled, and a faint glow of faraway lightning was discernible low in the south and west.

The rains came. For days and nights it poured, until all the creeks and springhead branches had spilled over their banks in a mad rush to the river.

The workmen rapidly bunched the logs into bundles to be drifted down stream. Long straight yellow pine, some measuring 150 feet in length, for this was the virgin timber, for which, much later, Mississippi was to become famous. At the time of this launching, such trees were thought to be bringing in a big price if they sold for fifty or seventy-five cents. But the big cypress and this fine pine timber that completely covered the land except whereever a small farm or larger acreage had been carved out of the wilderness was of no value except for the use of the settlers to build houses, barns, rail fences for the patches, pickets for yard fences and palings for gardens and orchards, since there was no market except small scale for turpentine, and the square timber which brought a tremendous price delivered to Moss Point for ship building.

The square timber was the cuts from choice trees, hewed smoothly on all sides to make it square, some fifty or sixty feet in length. Usually a broad axe was the implement used for hewing. The finished pieces were placed, edges together, and yoked; that is a binder was fashioned by boring holes with an auger into each end of a gum pole, fastening together both ends of the square timber, making a raft which was equipped with a propeller type oar arrangement, about center, to make guiding easier, and side oars for steering this huge raft clear of obstacles in the river.

Hired labor at thirty cents a day, from among the people who were not slave owners or land holders, brought their oxen to move the timber, but the slaves were the ones who did most of the work of cutting and hewing. The patience of these faithful black people was equal to the endurance of the oxen. No hurry, no rush. Endless toil accompanied by song.

These square timber rafts provided a means of transportation down the river, and at least one raft in each half dozen was fitted out as a makeshift kitchen.

The whites and blacks toil side by side, singing and shouting in high glee. "She's a risin' Boys," rings the glad cry. The foam is still coming down, and the muddy water is eddying out into the low places and lagoons. More and more rafts are launched, as the sweating men work rapidly cutting loose the holds, and the timber goes slowly down, lightly as a drifting straw, towards its destination. Some of the trees are cut to be drifted down to a saw mill below where old Bouie runs into Leaf, later to be hauled back over land as fine lumber for a plantation mansion.

Men, women, and children, including slaves are on the high bluff overlooking the river, to watch the ever-new spectacle of the timber launching. On this particular morning there were an unusually large number of people on hand, for watching the river this flood time was for a purpose.

The oldest man in the settlement was about to take a trip down by raft. He had come to inspect the river conditions, with the intention of leaving the next day. He was old John Knight. There he sat proudly on a frisky horse (he loved frisky horses), waving to neighbors. A man of wide reputation, spoken of as an Indian fighter, back when all this vast timbered acreage was known as Mississippi Territory, back when the settlements along the Gulf Coast, along the Mississippi, and the eastern settlements along the Alabama line were the only sections inhabited by the white man. He had helped General Jackson cut the Monroe Road into New Orleans and was a veteran of the War of 1812. Quite a commotion his preparation for a trip was causing for he was too old for a risky trip by raft with the river tricky at flood stage. There was much to be taken into consideration, the possibility of hitting a snag, a log jam, or the "ghosts of a drowned tribe" which would surely upset the raft.

His aged wife sat beside him on her gentle mare. Her blue bonnet framed her face, youthful despite her eighty years, although wisps of white hair showed beneath the bonnet; hair as white as his, which hung in soft curls to his shoulders.

A young male slave cantered up from the rear on an old raw-boned nag. He dismounted, letting her pick at will while he ran around and seized the reins of both mounts. "Me take yo bridles an' hole you hosses, whilst you git down an see de rivah," he offered, respectfully. "Mought be when Marst John see how she bialin' up an' a whirlin' 'roun,' he back out." He lowered his voice in a fearful whispered tone, and apparently to himself, he whispered, "Mought be, you neber come back! Mought be de raf' sink an' yo' sho drown." There was no reply. The master, if he heard, paid no attention.

Several men approached the old man on the subject of his proposed journey and to them he replied, "Pshaw! Older men than I have gone about 'tending to business. Why! I can throw any man in the crowd, right now," he grinned.

"Oh, I didn't mean to insinuate that you are at all old," sensing the touchy spot, the friend replied, apologetically. "It is just that the trip back over land will not be so pleasant. With the rainy season, the trail will be a mud-hole, and with the streams still swollen, which they'll be, the crossings will be tedious, the journey long and tiresome." "Pshaw! Just a four or five day, not more'n a week's trip," snorted the old man. "I've changed my plans. It's Augusta where I am to meet my friends and transact my business. Not Moss Point where I a few days back talked about going. And besides, I never cross my bridges till I get to them, as the saying goes," he smiled.

"The letter said that the horse traders would be there by the time of my arrival, and there will be a lot of fun, so I expect to ride back on a friskier animal than this," he said, stroking the white blaze of the unsuspecting animal's face, whereupon he reared, snatching the bridle reins out of the darkey's hand, as he was so busy listening to the conversation he had forgotten his duty for the moment. There was not a word of reproach to the slave, but the old man, with thumb and forefinger thumped the ear of the careless one. That ear thumping brought a sting very like that of a wasp, and the negro bounded off in pursuit of the runaway horse, with both hands clasped over his ears. That brought a big laugh to the onlookers, which the wife of the prankster brought to silence by the sudden exclamation, "Land Sakes, John, a body would think it a matter of life and death, the way you talk about this river trip! Why don't you give it up, seeing as how all your friends are agin it? Business can wait till summer when the crops are laid by, and by then you'll have more time."

"Business can indeed wait, but not my promise. I have always been a man of my word. When I tell a man I will meet him in a certain place at a given time, then on that day and hour, I will be there, unless hindered by Divine Providence. My reputation to that effect precedes me whereever I go, and many a time I have profited by it." That statement was a fact, for this man had set the example of truth and honesty before his family and his slaves, and he had experienced the pride that comes from having well fulfilled a duty. He had as carefully reared his slaves as he had his own children, and they were of a class above many of those owned by the poorer white people. It was the custom for slaves to pattern after their owners in morals and manners, and with slave Jim's effective disciplinary measures, the Knight negroes were a learned and respectable people.

But old Jim had about played out. He lay now under a great live oak, reclining on its naked roots, where long ago the sandy soil had washed away, leaving them bare and gnarled. As gnarled as old Jim, whose white head, contrasting with his black skin, made his old wrinkled face appear blacker still, his sunken eyes, faded and pale, even bigger. But those old eyes saw it all, never missed a thing. He was able only to give orders to the other slaves and assist with the pickaninnies in the quarters, and sometimes play with the grandchildren of his master. Great tales he could tell the children, for he had accompanied his master to this wilderness from North Carolina, and he loved to tell tales of Indians, "haints" and adventures of his childhood in Carolina, for his daughter.

Just now he was busy teaching Carolina's yearling how to play with a goose feather which had been dipped in molasses. He had taught many a baby to take the feather by the quill with one hand, and with the other arrange the plumage into shapes which would stay in that position, stuck together by the syrup, until the child decided to rearrange and lick his fingers. But this stubborn child of Carolina's! He thought only about eating for he was trying to cram the feather, fist and all into his mouth!

"You got to set on de san' Black Chile," said Jim, rudely dumping the baby on the ground. "Here come some white chillurn, an' I'se no mo' time to fool wid you. Crawl on ober to whar you mammy," commanded Jim, motioning the child towards Carolina, where she stood with a group of other women, black and white, engrossed in conversation with her mistress.

But the children did not stop under the oak with old Jim, for they had come flying to their elders with news of interest. This was proving to be the biggest fresh in several years, and the livestock was in danger of becoming lost in the rising floodwaters. The word that danger was upon them, broke up the carefree party. The negroes were hustled off ahead to herd up the stock and drive them up into the hills for the duration.

Such a thing as a stock law was unheard of in that day, and every man's stock was allowed to run at large, provided they were all marked. Every stock owner had his own particular "mark" which was a cutting in the ear of the animal, a hole, a split, or a fork, or perhaps a combining of all three. Salt licks were put out for the cattle, sheep, and goats near the home range so that they would not go entirely astray and be picked up by the county ranger. The hogs were called up occasionally, and a little corn shelled down to them, in order that they might not forget the scent of man, and become so wild they could not be called up at killing time.

Any family could go at any time provided they had a "claim" in the woods and kill meat for his table, although the meat was never firm and sweet until after the swine had fattened on the pine mass, the beech mass, and the acorns that were plentiful in the fall of the year.

The goats "used" in the swamp in the winter and early spring where the buds grew abundantly along the river, but they were deathly afraid of the water. Whenever there was backwater in the lowland, many were marooned on the higher knolls, safe and dry, but the wailing and bleating the mothers would do would start the kids crying like children in distress, when it seemed that all escape was cut off by the rising floodwaters. Then they had to be boated out along with the young pigs, for there was not only the danger of drowning but the danger from wild animals, also forced out by the waters over the swamps. The bears and panthers ate the young of all domestic animals, and were a danger to humans as well.

Even a ferocious Bull dog was no match for a panther, and quite frequently a pack of hunting hounds would come in, all torn and bloody from an encounter with one of these beasts of prey.

The negroes would stand wide eyed with horror when someone came in with a story that such a creature was stalking the neighborhood, and when dark came, to be sure, no slave was caught away from the quarter.

The young men enjoyed the excitement of a flood and were ready for an emergency. Out of cuts of birch, or cypress, they fashioned dugouts with paddles made with the adz. These boats were rowed into the backwater to rescue animals, and even neighbors who lived in Cracker's Neck settlement where the flatlands were overflowed. Great pleasure was had when the young ladies became frightened and were forced to cling tightly to the youthful boatmen, who always pretended that there was imminent danger of the dugout becoming upset. In that sly way, a good neck hugging repaid for all the trouble and long hours wielding the adz getting ready for just such a pleasant calamity.

Morning came with all the stock herded up on the high knolls, and the horses saddled and waiting at the hitching post outside the front gate at the Knight plantation. A little ways from the house the water stood in the lowlands. The trail to the Reddoch landing was covered by the backwater, muddy and swirling, but the opening between the great trees, hanging with silvery Spanish moss, clearly marked the path.

The master led the way, his horse never hesitating to swim where the water was deep, nor failing to smoothly let down to find bottom in the shallows. The other horses took courage from the leader and plunged in, churning the yellow water into a golden spray. The riders bringing up the rear were negroes, silent, resenting the frightening journey, but never complaining.

The trip down to Augusta was uneventful, except greater care had to be exercised for there were more drift afloat than had ever before accompanied a launching. There were strange formations of dead wood, taking fantastic shape and color, vegetation and foam, looking like strange monsters ahead, fence rails, washed from the fences of bottom land fields were scattered and tossed by the raging waters. Occasionally the carcass of a drowned animal drifted down, over which two or three hungry buzzards dropped and soared, and dropped again to peck a bite.

Augusta was a busy little town for it boasted two stores, a blacksmith shop, a cotton gin, the United States Land Office, post office, warehouses, and to one side, apart from the main section of the business district stood the ancient courthouse, a mute reminder that here law and justice prevailed.

Ah! Justice, that noble word! Beside the courthouse stood the jail built by the hands of many slave people. Many, many black, sore, and torn hands had moulded the brick by hand, from the chalky clay brought from the river's bluff. And some remain, indestructible by time and weather, having been cemented by an old Egyptian process of adding sugar to the mortar of a smoother more adherent type of clay. (Souvenir hunters have hacked away most of the remainder, as this was the place where the leader of the Copeland Clan was hung, along with Edd Savage, a minister turned bandit.)

At a remote distance stood the gallows, out in an opening, where all would have the opportunity to witness a hanging, and be forewarned. All executions were public, and the people came from miles around by horseback, by ox wagon, and carriage, bringing children, in order that their young might be impressed with that air of gloom, awe, sorrow, and despair that hovered over the settlement, as some poor condemned victim approached and mounted the gallows to give his life as payment for some crime or offense against society.

However death was preferable to life in prison, and lucky was the person to escape the deplorable condition of the incarcerated who existed in the unlighted, poorly ventilated dungeon, crawling with vermin, and filled with the stench of body refuse. There were no such things as baths, or privies, or convenience of any kind. The food provided was bread and water, so a long-term sentence was usually terminated early by the Grim Reaper, who came mercifully to relieve the suffering of pellagra and consumption.

Fronting the beautiful river, up on the high bluff above the landing, was the inn, shaded by rows of sycamores and fragrant cedars. Here, in sharp contrast, was a place of lodging that provided fine foods and good wines for the many guests that stopped on their way to and from the coast, as this was the only sizable town north of Mobile.

The trading season always brought visitors who did a lot of buying from the competitive stores. Each merchant tried to procure merchandise of unusual kind and quality in order to stimulate trade. Each tried to create some excitement of interest in an effort to draw customers from the other. When one managed to get the horse traders to headquarter at his establishment, the other, not to be outdone, invited the slave trader to stop at his place.

The horse trader was acceptable, but not the slave trader, so instead of an attraction, this unwise merchant lost the lady customers, who came to buy cambric and bright calico, pins, needles, ribbons, and hard candy, called "sugar hards." The very mention of the slave trader was enough to cause whispers among the women, and the children were not allowed to go near.

Even the dogs slunk away from such a repulsive person, possibly because he was uncouth and boisterous, and possibly because he had a habit of cracking the leatherthonged whip which he carried.

There was a law against slave beating, but that law was ignored by such men who would stoop low enough to obtain filthy money by traffic in human life. The slave trader was a social outcast because of the rumors circulated as to the crimes he was guilty of; the crime of separating families, which was one of the most undesirable sides of slavery. Next to selling off a child from its mother was the fact that traders subjected the women to lives of horror, as prostitutes for measly sums, which was usually spent for debauchery. From this type of men sprang the first Mulattoes. In many instances, the females were bred, unwillingly, like beasts. Although it has been stoutly denied, many Southerners made a business of raising slaves for sale, but that was a touchy subject, and the general public was led to believe that the only purpose of contacting such vile characters was for the purpose of obtaining more labor for the fields, as the cotton industry continued to grow.

The international slave trade was outlawed in 1808, and after twelve more years, as it continued to be a practice regardless of the law, another law was passed that made the act punishable as piracy, and a conviction carried a stiff sentence. But the right to buy and sell and swap in the United States, and to transport them from one slave state to another, was not illegal. The upper South had a surplus of slaves, whereas the Gulf South was in need of more labor, so there was extensive buying and selling at the time the South was enjoying its greatest prosperity. Into the lower South poured 120,000 negroes from the State of Virginia alone in the year 1836. Georgia sent almost as many to be distributed over Alabama, Mississippi, Louisiana, and the territory west.

However, many Southern families would no more think of selling off their slaves, and breaking up families, than they would think of selling off their own children, for such was considered sin, and a slave was not looked upon as other tangible property but as a human, with conscience and soul, and was so treated by their good Christian masters.

However this good characteristic of the big-hearted slave owner caused many to become slave poor. The race reproduced rapidly, marriage not being a prerequisite to parenthood. Although the master taught them that Christian marriage was essential, the progeny of the unmarried were just as acceptable (he could do just as much work) if the mother acknowledged the wrong in a public confession.

Most of the slaves were deeply religious and attended every religious service. These loved their white folks and were in turn loved by them, as members of families, even an affection similar to blood relationship was not uncommon between master and slave.

The negroes expressed their joy and contentment by singing and shouting. Dancing was a favorite pastime in the quarters, and there was seldom one who worried, for in return for his labor, the master stood between him and responsibility. He had no cause for worry because his food was the same as that served to the master; he was clothed with the good coarse cloth of the loom, which the white mistress had taught the women to make, and there was warmth and comfort in the cabins where the slave born were taught to follow their elders in respect and obedience.

But sometimes even the best master would be forced to sell off a slave for an objectionable reason. Some slaves were undesirable and refused to submit to discipline, and others were not trustworthy. These made up the largest group to be sold along with the numbers of good slaves "sold down south" for a profit. Many of the objectionable reasons were never mentioned, such as rape, and in many instances where a slave woman became a mistress of a white man, which was the only way of breaking off the liaison: sell the woman off and send her out of the country!

Such a practice was horrible, since these unfortunate people were victims of circumstance, treated without any consideration whatsoever.

Once in the hands of a trader, they were herded together like cattle, in stockades, old warehouses, and even jails, without regard to sex. Frequently, they were marched overland, shackled together with leather thongs which cut and bruised the wrists.

The bigger cities, New Orleans and Mobile, had auction blocks, where the final bid was the accepted price, but the transient slave trader availed himself of every opportunity to sell along the route, at the wharves and villages where planters congregated.

The price of slaves varied with the economic conditions of the times, the price of cotton which was a controlling factor. For instance, in 1818 the price of cotton was thirty-two cents per pound, and in 1820 it fell to eighteen cents, thereby cutting the South's buying power, so following a rise in the price of cotton, came a rise in the price of slaves. They were always much cheaper just after a panic, and the trader met with great competition, so he had to resort to unscrupulous and fraudulent means to dispose of his human property. Just as a horse trader, he learned to cover up the defects of the human body. Just as the horse trader resorted to purchase of gay tassels, new bridle, all decorated with shining brads, and a handsome saddle to help sell an outlaw horse, by giving him an attractive appearance, the slave dealer bought bright calico and gay headdress for the females, and the males were decked out with red bandannas about their necks. While the horse trader was busy currying and clipping and brushing the coats of his animals, the slave trader was busy grooming his "property" for the impending sale, clipping out mats, killing louse on the heads, and scrubbing and cleaning the sun-roughened skin with sweet oil.

The preparation for both sales was complete that fair April day when old John Knight arrived in Augusta.

The horses were sleek and glistening in the corral across the muddy street. Several men were observing them as the trader ran them around for inspection. There was laughing and joking as different animals were "mouthed," and bets were staked on races. Everyone was in a good humor, and soon old John Knight was mounting a beautiful white-stockinged sorrel mare.

It seemed that the store sponsoring the improvised horse corral was getting all the attention of the traders, curious and loafers. But just as Knight was mounting his new mare, a terrible commotion began across the street.

The slave sale was beginning. The bearded slave trader was cracking his whip and renting the air with profanity. A baby was screaming as if in pain. People were craning their necks, while others were hurrying away from the scene of pathos and grief. Often slave women fell prostrate in a faint, or went into hysterics, and screamed like savages when they were sold away from their young. Others plodded slowly toward the auction block, with a show of emotion, preferring to impress the prospective purchasers with their quiet and gentle manner. While even others were stoic and silent, stone-faced, heedless of their surroundings.

The store was a hewn log structure with a high platform the full length across the front of the building, with steps at each end. The steps were two blocks, about a foot and a half high, the other higher by about the same measure, cut from a big heart tree, and fastened to the side of these were skinned poles to be used as handrails.

Two husky negroes rolled away to the side a barrel of cider to make room for the display of human flesh.

First up was a big black male. He raised his big black bare arm, and the greased muscles glistened in the sun, as he wiped the drops of sweat from his forehead. He was straight and strong, not a blemish to mar his youth. Surely he was not an objectionable slave; his manner was meek and his face was not hard. A buyer spoke to him, and he turned in that direction, attempting to speak but no word would come, but by mumbles and sounds and motions he made it understood that he was not able to speak English. After a bit of bickering he was sold, and the new owner counted out the money to pay for his new servant.

The next was a little slow in approaching the steps. The whip cracked menacingly above her head, as she paused to deposit a bundle on the ground. It was a baby whose face was completely concealed by an old cloth. The screaming recommenced, as the child fought off the covering.

The onlookers were amazed. The child was white and appeared to be about a year old, small and puny for its age, with delicate features not at all like a negro. The mother clutched it to her bosom, while tears streamed down her face.

"Get going, get going!" shouted the slave trader. "Don't have all day to waste with a young'un. I should a' thrown it in the creek back there like I started to." He cracked the whip again, barely missing her face, as the plaited thongs' ending zinged above her. "Get on up, you slut," he snarled.

The baby could not be quieted. The girl steadied herself by the handrail as she hurried to take her place on the platform. She was trembling from head to toe, and she shivered as one going through an ague, so reluctant was she to be sold away from the pitiful crying bundle lying on the ground. She was an unusual Mulatto, almost beautiful standing there with her tear filled blue-green eyes, which color is characteristic of a mixed-blood. Her hair was not covered by a head scarf, as was the custom, for hers hung down to her waist in waves of shining chestnut, which was only a shade darker than her smooth face and plump young body. She was a mere child, it was plain to see, as she stood there, oblivious to the jeers and sneers of the onlookers. Hers was a breaking heart, for surely the babe would be sold separately.

The gifts of new raiment brought happiness to these people who needed such a little to give them joy, but this woman showed no appreciation of the gay apparel which adorned her. There was no radiation or happiness expressed in the face of this girl. The purple, green, and gold triangle of silk, which the trader had draped about her frail shoulders, ill concealing her busts, as the wind whipped it about, was intended to create the impression of a seductress, as men had been known to pay a fabulous price for such an attractive one, but he had failed to achieve that effect. Instead, she was bowed in grief and shame, seeming to realize that she was improperly clad, with only the drape and a full bright skirt for raiment.

An aged Negress, leaning on a bent cane hobbled up, and lifted the child, and proceeded to give it some goat milk out of a gourd. The flies were swarming over it, and on second look, the old crone discovered that several had fallen in and were swimming around, but she deftly ran her free hand down into the gourd and scooped the offenders out. Then she forced the infant to drink.

"Make me an offer! What am I bid for this wench?" boomed the trader. There was no offer. There was silence as the girl continued to weep.

The man on the white-stockinged mare sat thoughtfully for a moment, watching the pitiful girl, then he broke the hush with, "Why don't you offer the two of'em for one price?" The trader considered, then replied, "The young'un is of little value, sick, and a she, and a too white mixed, but this woman has possibilities." He strutted to and fro across the length of the platform, spat his ambere forcefully on the ground, and laughed loudly, showing his yellow stained teeth. "Without the young'un she will sell high to the smart man who needs women for the brothels and saloons in the new west." He sighed, "If only I had her out there!" He turned and spat again, and in doing so, he missed the murderous expression on the girl's face. When he turned again to her, her smouldering eyes, very like polished green glass were staring at the gallows down the street. She was silently preferring death by hanging to being sold away from her child.

"Throw in the child, and I'll give five hundred," said the old man, starting the bids. "Oh, no! Can't take that," replied the seller. "Each is worth that."

"But you just said yourself, that the brat is sick, and the woman appears to be one of little use," answered old John, "but I'll give you six hundred for them both."

"Oh, no," replied the trader, "gimme seven, and I'll put up the next one."

"No other bid? Going once, going twice, going three times, and sold!"

Knight dismounted and was in the act of lifting his money sack from the finely engraved saddle bag, when a friendly voice asked, "Now aren't you one to tell the news around that you are slave-poor, and now I catch you buying again?" It was his neighbor Hatten who had walked up unobserved, and placed his hand on the old gentleman's shoulder. "They tell me that you give away to relatives any number of slaves they might wish, and now—already with too many mouths to feed, you're at it again," the friend reprimanded him.

"But somebody had to buy that wretched thing and her brat, to get them out of the hands of that rascal, and it might as well be me."

"Ah, your better judgment is overruled by your old big heart!" exclaimed Mr. Hatten.

"Yeah, I know I don't need any more, for the more you have, the more you're likely to lose, with the abolitionists aspreadin' propaganda, and aspreadin' hate among the niggers. We are going to be in for it if this all keeps up," answered Knight.

He was removing his coat, exposing a fine brown velvet waistcoat, of English make, over a well-fitting blue shirt, which revealed wetness of perspiration over the gusset under each arm. He handed his coat to the slave girl, who had gathered up her child and was standing by to receive his orders, for now they "belonged" to him.

"Here, Wench, you are not clothed in decent garb. Put on this coat to cover your disgraceful nakedness." Upon sudden thought, he exclaimed, "But, wait a minute! I plumb forgot to ask your name."

"Rachel," she answered meekly.

"And the babe?"

"Georgianne," she whispered in a small voice.

Hatten and Knight were so engrossed in their conversation, they were not paying attention to what was going on a few paces from them. Now that the purchase was concluded, they ignored the loud voice and the crack of the whip.

"Master, Master!" Rachel cried, falling on her knees, and clutching his trouser leg. "Look, look!" she screamed in bitter anguish, pointing towards the platform.

A tiny black child was scrambling and tugging in an effort to gain the platform, a little girl, about three years old, was up for sale.

"My child, my little Rosette, my baby is being sold away from me! Please, Master," she begged. "She will be big enough to work. Buy her too." Her tears were again flowing freely, and unheeded.

"Why, what does this mean?" asked the man in surprise. "I have, out of sympathy for you, just bought one small worthless brat, and now, why, that cannot be yours also."

"But she is mine, my first one, my little Rosette," cried Rachel.

"But you cannot be the mother of a family? You are only a child yourself. . . ."

"But they are mine, my own flesh and blood," wept Rachel.

Already the gentlemen were approaching the platform, very amused at the little banjo-bellied, spindle-legged waif, who was accepting the situation in calm bewilderment. She rolled her big eyes, and scratched her kinky head, and tugged at the old sack which half covered her little black body as a makeshift dress.

After a little bickering, Rosette also belonged to Knight, and a happy family, united by the sympathies of an old man, set out on the overland trail for Jones County. A family that were to shape the destiny of a strange people, a people doomed to lives of bitterness and unhappiness.

Rachel became Rachel Knight, black Rosette became Rosette Knight, small white Georgianne became Georgianne Knight, and the unborn child, which Rachel was carrying, became Jeff Knight, because they belonged to the Knight family.

CHAPTER 3

The New Slaves

A small fire lay smouldering on the hearth in Jim's cabin, although the night was warm and sultry. Through the open doorway, the old voice of the head of the house drifted out into the stillness.

"That's old Jim, either praying or reading the Bible," explained the master, as he stopped at a respectful distance with the new arrivals, that he was escorting in to old Jim. After listening a second, he knew that it was scripture reading, as the splash, splashing of the churn dasher became audible to his ear. Another sound came from inside the cabin, but not the sound of voices. There was a rhythmical tearing sound, as if someone was gently but firmly rending into shreds a piece of old linen; the sound of Carolina's cotton cards, as she pulled the wiry teeth of the cards through the cotton. The change in the rhythm was the sudden swift backward motion, as she deftly fashioned the carded tufts into rolls for the spinning wheel.

The old voice droned on, and the newcomers advanced forward preparing to step upon the threshold, when there came a sharp detonation of the snapping together of the opened pages of the book. Jim had finished. The churning was finished, for the time being. The carding ceased.

None of the slaves could remember of a time when they had not been called into the "family altar," as that was the custom of the good people. Big, little, old, and young were instructed to kneel while old Jim prayed. Nothing could interrupt these lengthy prayers, so all became as comfortable as possible, on both knees, with elbows propped on the seats of the cowhide bottomed chairs. Perhaps the reason Jim was so unmindful of the discomfort of the others, his own old knees were protected by the thickness of the sheep skin rug on which he knelt.

The outsiders stopped again, and the tired travel-weary man seated himself on the edge of the gallery.

Rachel looked in on the scene in astonishment. The light glistened on the old darkey's black bald pate, rimmed with a white ring of wool, which looked very like one of the playful pickaninnies had snitched it from the pile of Carolina's cotton rolls and draped it turban-wise around his head.

There were fifteen or twenty persons kneeling there, but all were not listening to Jim's prayer. Out of the corners of their eyes, many cast furtive glances out the open door to where the strange pale woman stood, bathed in the light of the full moon. It seemed that old Jim would never finish and let them up to satisfy their curiosity. When he did finally finish, all leaped to their feet in a glad cry, for there entering the doorway ahead of the stranger was their beloved master.

"Uncle Jim, a new slave woman, and her family," explained the master. "This is Rachel." Jim bowed stiffly from the waist, but he did not utter one word of greeting. None of the others could find anything to say. The silence was embarrassing.

Rachel gave an exploring look around, and observed the big eyes, filled with awe, big mouths open in surprise and wonder, as this was to them a strange sight. Many questions were darting through their minds, but they could not ask. Was this a white woman? Beside them with their black skins and short kinky hair, which was whitened by the cotton fuzz settled upon them, she appeared to be. But then white women were not sold as slaves to live among negroes in their quarters. Excitement and curiosity caused these simple people to forget their manners.

"Now, Carolina, this woman is tired and hungry, and the little ones have taggered out. Until we can find a place for her, she is to stay with you and Jim in this cabin. Feed them, and bed them down," instructed the master.

"Yes, sir," replied Carolina. Rachel was not welcome, but there was no protest.

"Where are the others? Abed?" "Oh, no sir, dey is still havin' pray'r, I go see. I spec dey is," answered a young buck, who was anxious to relieve such a situation, and also to be the first to spread the news further among the negroes that a strange white female had come to live with them.

"Oh, no, never mind, just wondered what you've all been doing since I've been gone. No stock lost in the flood?" he asked.

A lantern was lighted by a young negro, who kneeling on the hearth, lighted a broomstraw by poking the end to a red coal.

"Les all go see de new hosses," he said starting at a rush out the door. All the males followed, racing toward the hitching post at the entrance.

It was not comfortable to be left in the company of this stranger who sat down before the fire, tight-lipped and sullen. The other women eased out and left, one by one, until only Carolina and old Jim were alone with Rachel and the children. Conversation was hard to make. There was not much said, until after the sleeping black child had been aroused and fed, and the tension began to wear between the two women.

Jim usually had ready conversation and many wise remarks, but he too was over-awed by this strange green-eyed person, who did not "belong." So he pretended to be busy with punching up the fire. Now and then he would shake his old head sadly without a word, as he watched the woman and baby eat the roasted sweet potatoes which Carolina raked from the ashes.

"We'll hav' mo' grub t'morrow," she promised by way of conversation. There was no comment.

Finally, "Whar youall frum?" asked Jim.

"Geo'gie," answered the stranger. No words added. A lapse of silence. Then Jim ventured, "You got a husbin'?" There was no reply. The woman shook her head. Old Jim also shook his head, and rolled his eyes in Carolina's direction, as if to say, "I thought so." Another embarrassing silence. Then, "He daid?" There was no answer.

Carolina tactfully turned Jim's questioning aside with an offer to fix the babies to bed for the night. She decided to offer conversation of her own as none was forthcoming from her imposing guest.

Aside to the stranger, she whispered, "I'se in fambly way." For an answer Rachel gave her a friendly understanding smile.

"I'se carryin' dis chile fer Mis' 'lizbeth," Carolina confided proudly, placing her hands tenderly across her enlarged abdomen. "Ever year I has a chile, an' long fo' he born, I knows who's to be de one he's to 'blong to, 'cause ole Marst John want two for each ob he fambly frum me, and soon as dey weaned, I'se happy to see dem go. Doe sometimes dey gits up a argument ober my chillun, an' to settle it fair, Marst John won't let neider one uv de argufiers hav' him. Den we jes keeps him here on de plan'a'shun wid us all."

Rachel did not answer, or express any of her own sentiment. She shrugged her shoulders in disgust, and stood up, ready to lie down with the babies.

Soon there were sound snores coming from the bed over in the back corner of the room, where Carolina had invited her to sleep the first night in the quarters.

Old Jim held down the corner by the fireplace, continuing to punch the fire occasionally. Carolina hitched up her chair closer to his in order that they might talk in low tones about this thing the good master had done to them.

"Dat's a no good sum'p'n, dat's what. A mixed-blood. Dey'll be trouble acomin' up fum dis. You mark my words," prophesied the old man. "Now, what did he do dat fer?" Carolina shook her head, but old Jim spoke his mind without fear of the woman's hearing, the gourd-sawing sounds reassuring him that the sleeper was not playing 'possum.

"Huh! She think she bettern' us. De way she draw up her shoulders, and shiver lack, jes lack a rabbit ware arunning ober de groun' whars to be her grave. Huh! When you wuz a tryin' to talk wid 'er. No good! Dat's what. No good! Huh!"

"Well, dat's maybe why he lef her here wid us," replied Carolina. "Maybe dat's why he didn' take her on down to Aunt Sis' house, an' leave her wid dem. He knowed you'd pray an' preach, an' preach an' pray bout her sins," said the granddaughter.

"An' dat I will. Mo'nin' come I go down an' hav' ole Missus turn to de place in de good Book, whar it say, 'No mixin' up and a whole lot mo'', an' I'll read it ever night fore pray'r til she see she got ta do sum'p'n," promised old Jim.

Morning found Jim up early, slowly plodding up the path to the big house. Under his arm he carried a book, which had its old backs carefully covered by a piece of faded blue brocade, hand-stitched along the edges with a coarse piece of homespun thread, exactly like that with which the bone buttons were sewn on the coat which he wore.

Jim had, in his younger days worn the full uniform which his master had discarded from the War of 1812, but now the breeches were replaced by a pair from the hand loom of his granddaughter, of coarse dyed homespun. But the coat was still perfectly good, faded a little, until it was no longer bluish-gray, but was grayish-black. The white bands crossing upon the breast were no longer white but were a shade lighter than the material of the coat, which came together with a tight closing at the waist, securely fastened by a bright square nail. Of course, there were a few moth holes, and the tails, or skirts, and the sleeves were frayed at the edges, but there was still plenty of warmth left in it for a morning when Jim was on the dewey path, before the sun had time to up and warm his old bones. The distance was less than a quarter of a mile, but by the time the decrepit one entered the gate, the dew-dampened soil picked up along the path had dried to a dust which covered his bare calloused old feet, turning them into the same shade of gray as the coloring of his coat.

He stood before the doorway of the kitchen, bowing, old misshapen, sweat-stiffened hat in his hand, as he awaited the mistress to come in answer to his summons.

The master came instead. Good mornings were exchanged, and Jim was welcomed in. He was invited to sit beside the fire, but the offer was declined, and he stood resting his hand on the back of the chair, twirling his old hat with the other hand, hesitant to bring up the subject of his visit.

"Not on your way to preach, this morning, Jim?" asked the master, noticing the familiar book under his arm, and grinning broadly.

"No suh," began Jim, fumbling with the book's covering. "I fetched it along fer de Missus to turn me down de coan'er uv some special pages I needs to read." "Oh, I see," replied his master, "but the mistress is sick abed this morning, and will not be up."

"I knowed it! I knowed it!" cried old Jim. "I could feel it in my very bones! Las' night when dat pale yaller woman wuz a rollin' dem eyes, an' a lookin' lak a witch, I knowed she gwin a bring us bad luck!" Once started, Jim kept pouring out his opinion of the new woman to his master. "No good can come frum nothin', an' dat's what she is, a no good mix-up. An' you know, dis mo'nin' she 'low she war'n't no nigger much atall. She say she part Injun, an' her Pa a white man, an' dat chile is white as you," continued the exasperated negro, without fear of offending by the comparison.

"Well, whatever she is, she is my slave, and you will have to help me to manage her, Jim," replied the master, humoring his old servant.

"Dat I will. I'se gonna rain fire an' brimstone down on her haid, out'n dis book," declared Jim, shaking the book to add emphasis to his statement. "Dat's what I wants to find, whar dat piece say fer ever thing to stay de same as is, widout no mixin' up."

"Oh, you mean about cattle and such—," and before the reply was finished, Jim put in, "an' bout 'dultry, an' witches an' all dat, and a heap mo'."

Soon Jim was back on the path with passages from the Book of Exodus, Deuteronomy, and Leviticus turned down. So many times he had heard these passages read, he needed only to find the place, and then he read to suit himself, not being able to actually read more than a few simple words, but that was enough to suffice, as he knew most of the rest "by heart," and his people always got the kind of lecture they needed.

His favorite sermon was taken from the nineteenth chapter of Leviticus.

21—"Ye shall keep my statutes. Thou shalt not let thy cattle gender with a diverse kind; thou shalt not sow thy field with mingled seed; neither shall a garment of linen and woolen come upon thee.

22—And whosoever lieth carnally with a bondwoman, betrothed to an husband, and not at all redeemed, nor freedom given her, she shall be scourged; they shall not be put to death, because she was not free.

23—And he shall bring his trespass offering unto the Lord."

But instead of helping the unfortunate woman, Jim's frank statements regarding his opinion of mixed people drove Rachel into seclusion. And soon there was open antagonism existing between them, with the pale one delighting in doing the things forbidden by the righteous one, especially delighting in informing the old negro that the child which she would bear would also be white.

"Huh! If'n hits a sin to mix up stock, den how much mo' hit mus' be a sin to mix up peoples," reasoned old Jim. "Here dis woman say she don't know what all she is, an' she don't wanna 'soshate wid us all, an' here she lives, all by her sef in a cabin, cause she ain't got no place. De white folks won't have er, an' she don' want de niggers, an' dey don' want her, so dare!" he spread his black hands, palms upward, in dismay. "Dat proves hits a sin fer de races to mix up. De good Lo'd sho didn't aim to hav' no sech colors, er he'd a made he sef a in-be-twixt color to start wid."

All his people nodded agreement. Their views were entirely in accord with Uncle Jim's, and with this new woman, they were ill at ease. So for a long time, Rachel was left out of the heart of things, for she did not "belong," but the white folks in the big house were very pleased with their new possession, as Rachel was extraordinarily intelligent and industrious, and was anxious to please. Soon she became the favorite household help.

"C'lamity sho to fall on dis house," predicted Jim. "Dat woman is a witch. She's de one whats havin' to do wid so many deaths in our fambly ob white folks. 'Fore she come here wid dem conjure powers, all our folks wuz happy, an' now dey dyin' lak flies in a pile. Soon de graveyard yander at dem big walnuts won't be big 'nough to hole us all."

Jim was honest in his belief that the green-eyed Mulatto was partly responsible for the deaths in the Knight family. Many of the old ones died that same year, and by the end of the Civil War, which was then brewing, all of the first family by that name were buried beneath the walnuts.

CHAPTER 4

The Secession Convention

April 12, 1861, was the date Sumter was fired upon, starting the four years war between the states. Earlier than Ellisville's interest was manifested in the conflict, many Southerners had volunteered and were already fighting on distant battlefronts against the Yankee armies.

It must be remembered that this was still frontier country, and modes of travel slow, and communications difficult, or almost impossible. In fact, there was mail service only once or twice a month delivered to these post offices in this part of the South. The only local newspaper was from Paulding, printed there at the county seat in Jasper County, *The Eastern Clarion* was the publication, so news was always late in reaching its destination.

This side of Shubuta there was no railroad, so the mail was relayed by horse rider to Ellisville, and from there it was delivered to the old Pinion place on Big Creek, the old post office in Cracker's Neck, which was later removed to the Hilbun Place, Old Hebron, Reddoch, and Williamsburg. But despite this the people were pretty well informed of events abroad, as magazines and newspapers were brought in from other sections. Especially were there numerous publications and pamphlets put out by the Northern Abolitionist movement.

So much discussion kept under way, heated arguments took place among men wherever they were assembled, and especially about the question of secession. At that time, people did not pay too much attention to the importance of voting, since there was no necessity of great political interest. At one time there was only one vote cast in an election from the Pinion Box up on Big Creek, a thickly settled neighborhood.

The County Board of Police practically took over every phase of county government. As a matter of fact, the old Police Court was still in effect, and this board had the power to grant privilege license to engage in business, the power of levying and collecting taxes, the appointment of land commissioners, appointment of overseers of the poor, sick, and destitute, overseers of public roads, and even the power to grant an immigrant nationalization papers was vested in the Board. In every other respect it was very like our present Board of Supervisors. Other than the probate judge, the judges of other courts and the sheriff, there were no other county offices of importance.

The secession argument intensified in heat until the Police Board called a mass meeting in Ellisville, where a straw vote was cast as to how the majority stood as to secession. There was a great number for remaining with the Union. The continued arguments resulted in the severance of friendly relations between members of the Board, as those preferring to leave the Union and cast in with the other seceding states wished to open the meeting with the invitation of all those preferring to join the Confederacy to come up and join that day.

One V. A. Collins was at that time president of the Board of Police in Jones County, and he was bitterly opposed to fighting for the Confederacy, since he believed that the war was waged solely in defense of slavery, and that the men who owned the most slaves were those who stood to profit from the spoils of war. At that time, it looked as if the South would gain the victory.

Across the desk sat a member of the board, a quiet mannered Southern gentleman, whose name was Willis Windham. Although he was a slave holder he was not offended by the antagonistic views of his associate, since he believed with the same strong conviction that the South was in the right, and Mississippi should secede along with the other Southern states, not in protection of her slaves but because he saw that in reality the North was trying to force us to trade at home rather than with England. The Northern manufacturers, by the imposition of higher prices on merchandise stood to profit tremendously by Southern trade. England was supplying the South with cheaper and better quality goods than could be purchased within the United States, and at the same time, was taking our raw cotton. Thus, the South was becoming richer and richer until this section became the envy of the nation, and other nations as well.

Mr. Windham vehemently declared that slavery was the excuse for war, but that excuse was so flimsy one could plainly see it was "the oil to be poured on the fire" once kindled, since even our great Thomas Jefferson was opposed to slavery, and the slave question was not, at this time, any more bitter.

There were boos and shouts from the throng of men before Mr. Windham's argument was concluded, and all those wishing to secede walked out of the meeting.

Being of the gentry, Mr. Windham was reluctant to engage in nose bloodying or the commonness of vulgar language, but he was the type of man, once aroused, who would as freely and nonchalantly as "taking a drink of water," kill another. But on this occasion he was unarmed, so he gracefully swallowed the insults of his adversaries and strode from the courthouse.

It will be observed that his name appears on the roll of volunteers from Covington County, Williamsburg.

The Board of Police vacancy was not fulfilled after Windham's walkout (there was no official resignation), so the Collins faction was very much in control, and as there was no conscription law, at the time, as has been charged, those choosing to remain out of the army did so, while the ranks of the Gray increased by volunteers, who were willing and ready to give their all for the cause of the Confederacy.

There was no recruiting service thrown open to Jones Countians by resolution of a Board of Police, due to the dissension at Ellisville. After the meeting had broken up in such a disorderly manner, those preferring to remain with the Union got together and cast a vote among themselves. That is the so often debated "straw vote," which required a representative to the Secession Convention. This vote was not the result of an issue to be settled by ballot presented to the people in the usual manner. Even if there were 375 votes, as has repeatedly been asserted, against secession, cast in the absence of members, whose presence would have been required to make such an act legal, there remained 905 citizens for secession, as there were 1,280 families here at that time.

There were two representatives from the county, Baylis and Powell, just as there were from the time of the adoption of the State's Constitution, and the fact that the majority of the opposition chose Powell to represent their petition, he has since been called the "Anti-Secessionist Candidate."

No doubt this group of people were led to believe that Mr. Powell would cast a vote against secession upon their request. (Politics have always been politics, regardless of promises.) There was much "hush mouth," and it was hard to tell exactly how one stood on the question, and in this case, the people made a mistake for J. D. Powell was a staunch Confederate, and was very much in favor of seceding.

J. M. Baylis was the "secessionist candidate," according to the way in which the people friendly to the anti-secessionist move described him, because he openly expressed his views.

Baylis and Powell were close friends, and together they attended the convention, and were accompanied to Jackson by Willis Windham, whose influence was very probably, in a measure, responsible for Powell casting his vote for secession despite the fact that he was pledged to vote to remain with the Union.

Not in Jones County alone was there dissension and contention, but the people all over the State of Mississippi were much perturbed, and heated arguments took place as to whether we owed it to our nation to remain united, or whether, as a people united by a common interest, to stand firm in the protection of our rights, and protect our property and homes against invasion of a people determined to tear down a civilization for which our ancestors had braved the fevers, the hardships, and the trials of a wilderness to build a land of happiness and prosperity.

Governor Pettus called a special session of the legislature which session provided for the Secession Convention. Senator L. Q. C. Lamar offered the resolution which provided for the drawing of the Ordinance of Secession, and Mississippi was on January 9 promptly taken out of the Union, by a vote of 84 to 14.

When news of the legislature's action reached Jones County, there was high feeling, bordering on violence, carrying with it the threat to tar and feather Representative Powell, because he in the opinion of this small group had betrayed their confidence.

The streets of Ellisville were filled with riders, wagons, and oxen when about twenty-five men swarmed on the town in protest, as if a show of any kind could alter the state's ruling.

There was cursing and drinking, and tobacco chewing around big bon fires that night when the men met to discuss the type of vengeance to be inflicted upon the person of the traitor.

The next morning light broke upon a figure hanging to a scaffold; a man's dummy with a big placard hanging across the bosom, which read: "Powell, the Anti-Secessionist Candidate."

CHAPTER 5

The Volunteers of Mississippi

During the horse era before the Civil War, equine terms were applied superfluously to individuals and events.

Life in the South centered about the horse, as he was the means of transportation, the pride and joy of the young. Here there was horse worship, horse talk, and the nicest gift short of jewels that one could give, was a fine horse. A gift almost equal in value to a slave! It was a custom for young men to present their ladyloves with a beautiful animal, so it is not unnatural that such terms came into popular usage.

Bastardy was almost unheard of, and was certainly one of the unmentionable subjects, but occasionally the term "wood's colt" was applied to an illegitimate, in a stealthy inaudible whisper. Even "wood's colt" was a disgraceful term for a lady to use in that day!

"Hold your horses" meant to control one's temper. An act of impatience was described as "pawin' the ground," and a man with pugnacious inclinations was said to be "a rearin' an' snortin' to go." A swollen stream was described as being "on a hoss."

So, with the heat of war, hot-blooded Southern youth, surging with patriotism, were "rearin' an' snortin' to go." One of these was a young gentleman by the name of McLemore, who like a fiery stallion, "raised his heels." His comrades dubbed him "Ole Raisin' Heels" McLemore, and on the old volunteer roll of Covington County that epithet precedes his name! That title fitted the young handsome captain like a glove, for he was "rearin'" and ready to give his life for the Confederacy.

Since there were no recruiting facilities at Ellisville, it was an inconvenience, and a little disgraceful for the patriots of Jones County to be compelled to ride over the trails west, to Leaf River, cross over into Covington County, and be inducted into the army at Williamsburg. So Captain McLemore set up a recruiting station, not in Ellisville, but up on Big Creek, in an old log house, which stood out in an old forsaken flat field, untended, and near where Big Creek Church now stands.

That is why that place became a battle site. Its location interfered with the progress of anti-Confederates.

Men streamed over the trails, riding in groups, singly, on oxcarts, and many men walked to this little Jones County recruiting station on the edge of a wilderness, to offer their all.

Records were regrettably destroyed in Ellisville's courthouse fire, which gave the names and enlistments of these gallant men who joined the ranks of the Gray.

Later on, another station was established in Ellisville, despite opposition, and from there, three more companies were organized.

Willis Windham came back, after enlisting at Williamsburg, to help organize the "Ellisville Invincibles."

Homes were thrown open to the officers, and at Ellisville, the old Deason home was converted into a boarding house for the officers of the Confederate cavalry. And McLemore, being one of them, took up his abode in this house.

Jones Countians had joined their friends across the river in Covington when they met to throw in their lot in defense of the South. There were 198 men who came from far and near, not because they believed in war, and not because they wanted to hold the negro in bondage, but in defense of their rights.

The following is taken from the original record:

Proceedings had and done at a special term of the Police Court of Covington County, in the State of Mississippi, begun and held according to law, at the Court House in the town of Williamsburg, on the second Monday, it being the 10th day of February, 1862, A.D.

Be it remembered that on the 10th day of February, 1862, there was filed the following list of names of persons volunteered in the services of their country, to wit:

H. R. McLaurin, Captain

W. B. Dykes*

H. C. Dykes*

Archa McDonald

A. B. Short

J. V. Eaton

G. W. Burkhalter*

Edwin Burkhalter

Alford Burkhalter

Wm. Bullock

W. F. Leggett

J. C. Stewart

H. H. Dunn

Albert Swor

W. M. Burkhalter

J. R. Baugh

W. B. V. Watts

W. J. Lott

Joseph Yawn

J. Yates

B. F. Robertson*

G. W. Robertson*

J. B. Reed

Wm. Thames

A. McKenzie*

Norman McInnis

G. F. Whitehead*

G. F. Applewhite

H. Smith

L. McGrew

W. W. Williamson

J. D. Patterson

R. W. Sherrord

B. L. Henagan

H. R. McLaurin

M. Smith

Jo Chain

Robert Powell*

Wm. Ogle

T. H. Craft

Wm. Black*

Noll Whitehead*

J. Hill*

A. Knight (Alpheus)*

Dan Knight

L. Knight*

F. Knight*

D. H. McLeod

G. Burkhalter*

George Whitehead

James Welch

J. H. Loflin

M. J. Mitchell*

A. J. Mitchell*

Cadar Mitchell

Benjamin Blackwell

B. C. Blackwell

John Dewitt

Dr. Dewitt

C. L. Rodgers

J. Rodgers

D. W. Whitehead

Frank Williamson

Willis Lott

J. G. Hathorn

Witham Hathorn

G. W. Patterson

John Walker

A. J. Robertson*

J. W. Scarber

D. M. Strickland

G. W. Lott

"YANKEE TERRORS"
Capt. Wadkins

D. J. Ducksworth

B. Duckworth*

L. Bunket

W. S. Mathews

Charley Burkhalter

COMPANY UNKNOWN
Capt. J. M. Norman
COAST GUARDS

Franklin Burkhalter

Benton Taylor

Tayton Bullock

Judson Robertson*

J. B. Bridges

G. B. Yawn

J. H. Yawn

R. J. Magee

W. L. Strahan

Calvin Lott

Willis Windham*

Amos Graves

J. R. Bullock

John Pope

R. Williams

J. J. Byrd

V. L. Terrell

Richard Williamson

W. J. Eaton

W. M. Coulter

B. J. Leggett

Thomas Thames

R. S. Bullock

James Williamson

Alex McGrew

A. R. Graves*

Andrew Bird

W. J. Draughn

James Laird

Willis Barnes

W. P. Rastus

"Raisin' Heels"

    McLemore, Captain*

Daniel Patten

Ethridge Watts, Capt.

Jeff Davis Sharp

"Shootin' Captain" Pope

T. Bryant

T. J. Davis

Jessie Bryant

Mat Whitehead

"COVINGTON RANGERS"

J. T. Fairly, Captain

Frank Dyass

C. L. McDonald

Calvin Hood*

George McRaney

C. P. E. Carter*

Robert McRaney

A. W. Harper

Henry Walker

J. F. Fairly

Jackson McRaney

Peter Fairly

Washington Leggett

Alex Fairly

W. J. A. Eaton

Neil McInnis

Thomas Davis

J. V. McInnis

C. Graham

H. McInnis

C. C. Storz

R. M. McInnis

Elam Hathorn

Wm. Rutlidge

Faten Failor

L. W. Gray

Jacob Craft

J. L. Reddoch*

Nedon Blount

J. C. Copelin

C. Storz

Jackson Dyass

Daniel Walker

A. J. Carter*

M. Harrard

Wm. McPhail

Calvin McNeill

D. B. Smith

Arch Short

J. Beavers

Marvin Smith

Wm. Holloway

Frank Polk

W. C. Holloway

Peyton Rodgers

Jno. Holloway

Wesley Rustin, Jr.

W. W. Self*

Wiley Russell

E. Pfeifer

Albert Turnage

W. Williams

Peyton Turnage

C. Lee

Preston Turnage

J. T. Lee

V. Garner

C. M. Reddoch*

Jeff Garner

C. Robertson*

H. C. Holloway   G. A. Loflin

S. J. Williams   Stephen Foles

W. J. Williams

J. D. Terrell   T. L. J. Carraway

Duncan McRaney   John McRaney

It will be noted from the distinguishing stars, that a number of the volunteers from Williamsburg were Jones rather than Covington County citizens.

With the turmoil of war, men rushed from their homes, and were immediately inducted, and were soon serving in various branches of the service.

One of the volunteers, whose enlistment is not obtainable, the record having been destroyed at Ellisville, was a young husband and father whose name was Newton Knight.

His story is here told, for the first time, truthfully, with nothing withheld.

Knight was leaving for the duration (how long that would be no one had any idea, but it couldn't last long). He took with him the best horse in the corral for his personal use. He petted the horses, and loitered around awhile, before mounting to ride away.

He worked his mouth and grinned, as he stroked the white blaze of the fine saddle mare that belonged to his wife.

He took another look into the harness house, for no reason at all, and there before him was the side saddle that his wife had ridden upon many a time as they were traveling from one settlement to another, attending social "to dos," and distant meetings. He touched the polished leather lovingly. He had not noticed it before, but every article about the place that belonged to them had in some manner become a dear possession.

The gap was let down by his brother-in-law, a handsome man whose name was Morgan. And Newt, as he was called, led his animal out in preparation to leaving.

Morgan was the neighborhood Smithy, and he was not going, not until it was to be seen if his services were not more in demand at home, as someone had to stay behind, to keep the plows sharpened and the horses shod in the absence of the menfolks. It was decided that Morgan should remain.

Women were left, heavy with child, or with tiny bundles in arms, and many with several little ones clinging to their skirts. Such was the case at Newt's house. His wife had two small children and twin babies, little boys, but that did not alter her husband's resolution for he was known to be one of the most trustworthy and also one of the bravest men in Jones County, and his services were needed abroad, and he knew that Serena was capable of taking care of herself.

Most women of that day could fire a gun, and many could shoot as well as men, so his wife was not left without protection.

Besides that, Newt had made arrangements with his brother-in-law, Morgan, and his sister, Martha, who was expecting a child, to live in his house during the period of his absence. They would be a help to Serena with the children, and they would not be alone.

So, fearlessly, he rode away from his family, to do his part as a soldier in Gray. There was no worry for him, for he knew that his home was in good hands. He knew that his faithful young wife would be anxiously awaiting his return.

After the South was organized and men were fighting to hold strategic points against enemy invasion, it was decided that the Confederate forces would be strengthened by offering financial inducement to get more recruits. So the first offer was a sixty-day furlough at the end of the first year, and a fifty-dollar bonus.

The Southern armies were supplied by men who fought, not for money, but in defense of the Southern way of life. But the North in an effort to dissuade men who could be swayed by price, raised the offer from the South's fifty dollars to an even hundred dollars, in an attempt to gain Union troops from Southern territory.

Then again, in 1863, the Union raised the bonus to $302.00, and to veterans who would re-enlist, the sum of $402.00. So price did become a factor in Union enlistment.

Many honorable men from Covington and Jones, and other nearby counties, joined Tisdale's regiment stationed in New Orleans. And since then, there has been no reflection on the good name of any man who did openly join the Union forces, as every man in the South has always been free to express his opinions.

But there were many men in Jones County, and other counties as well, that were not concerned, and it mattered little to them, on which side was the winner, but even so, the first year of the war saw 35,000 Mississippians under arms, and before the close of the war, there were 85,000 men from this most importantly located Southern state, on which ground were fought the hardest battles in the history of the nation.

Among the volunteers who were ready to throw down their lives for their white friends were faithful slaves, who hated the Yankees as much as did the Johnny Rebs. Contrary to general belief, Southern negroes did the Confederacy great service, and although it is said that no slaves were taken into the army, below is a copy of an old record of an ex-slave, who was born Willis Edmund because his mother, at the time of his birth "belonged" to a white Edmund family. Later he became Willis *Dixon*, because he was owned by the Dixon family, and his descendants are so named Dixon, Jones County, Mississippi.

"Willis Dixon (colored) Confederate soldier born Nov. 3, 1842. Deceased Civil War Veteran. He served as Private, Co. H. 136, U.S.C. Volunteer Infantry. He enlisted May 1, 1865, and was discharged Jan. 4, 1866. His number: x c—897-748. He also bore the name Willis *Edmund*, age 21 years, born in Madison County, Miss., Enrolled at Macon, Ga., for a period of three years, and was mustered in to the service July 15, at Atlanta, Ga., and was honorably discharged with his company, as a private Jan. 4, 1866, at Augusta, Ga."

Oak Grove Baptist Church stands on a red washed-off hill in Jones County. It is a place of worship of the negro settlement, south of Center Ridge. Beside it is the cemetery, hoed clean, and swept often by brush-brooms. None other than negro are buried here. There are mounds on which are placed sea shell by the bereaved. On other graves are broken glass vases, and old figurines and ornaments and broken china. Some are heaped with white sand and small pebbles. Many had once a headboard of wood, sharpened to a point at the top, that has long ago rotted away, and fallen down into the caved-in edges of the graves. A crooked oak limb marks the head of one grave. Among this varied array stands a plain simple Confederate marker. The inscription reads:

ANSE WADE

PRIVATE 814 PIONEER INF.

DIED AUG. 23, 1920

Actually, the colored people of the South are as proud of those of their race, who stood with the Confederacy, as are the white people of their gallant ancestors, and here and there throughout Dixie are to be found graves of noble gentlemen of the colored race, whose sacrifices were not in vain. Their deeds live on in the memory of this present generation, and their descendants, through them, have attained "class distinction," and are not thought of as a "race," but a people.

Another veteran of the Civil War, who fought on the side of the Confederacy, is Ellisville's Isom Benson, for whom Benson School (Colored) is named. Uncle Isom has contributed greatly to negro advancement in this section, educationally and spiritually. He is the man who built two churches south of Ellisville, a Methodist church for himself and other believers of that faith, and a Baptist church for his wife, as she preferred to retain membership in the church of her earlier belief.

Uncle Isom did not volunteer from Jones County, as he lived at that time in Lawrence County, where he was adopted into the family of Benson, as his mother was a slave woman. But he was not for sale, and was, in reality, not a slave for he was the son of an Indian.

The young men of the Benson household who were soldiers were Fate and Doyt, both volunteers. Young Fate soon returned home with one leg and along early in 1864 Young Doyt decided to come home to get married. Not wishing to leave the army for the necessary length of time as he felt that his services were so sorely needed at the front, he fell upon the plan of sending a man in his place. That was entirely permissible, and was in many instances done, when one wished to remain away from duty for a period of time. So he went into the kitchen where

Emalin's half-breed was eating his supper, and asked him if he would like to go to the front and give two weeks service.

Young Isom was thrilled over the prospect of going in his friend's place, and stood proudly, while the young soldier fitted on him his own uniform, and placed in his hands his own weapons. Thus, Isom Benson became Doyt Benson, and marched straight to the battlefront, using that name.

By the time the two weeks were up, Isom was doing some fast fighting and was so filled with this new adventure that he was happy to learn that the real Doyt Benson was sick and would not be able to return. But before long, the sweet became bitter in his mouth, and Isom's spirit was laid low. The fighting became more furious with the Union's effort to gain more Tennessee ground, and without warning, Isom was struck in the hip and thigh, but he did not fall. He spun around in a daze, trying to wipe the heavy smoke from his eyes. All the men were the same color, smoke-blackened, and grimy, and he thought it was smoke that blinded and choked him, as he stumbled over the bodies of fallen comrades.

"Don't step on me," moaned wounded men, as they wallowed in their own blood. Isom stepped carefully, then stumbled blindly on, wading through blood for a hundred yards, before he fell unconscious.

However, he partially recovered from the injury, and lived to limp in and stack arms at Jackson, Mississippi.

It was not until after Jones County was recovering from the war that Benson came to Ellisville, with the railroad company that built the first railroad in Jones County, and through Ellisville. That was in 1881, when the first train whistled down the track, creating more excitement than did Amos Anderson's new buggy, when the whole town turned out to see him drive in from Waynesboro, a few years before.

There had, before this, been carriages, but not buggies in Jones County.

NOTE: Benson Story related by Isom Benson.

CHAPTER 6

The Deserter

Soon after Serena Turner and Newton Knight were married, they moved into their new home which he had built up above the northern boundary of Jones in Jasper County, in a sparsely settled section.

Just before the beginning of the war, that house was destroyed by fire and they moved back to his birth place on Mason Creek.

Serena was better satisfied now, since she was back in the more thickly settled neighborhood in Jones County. She had been very much alone, with only a few scattered Indians and a few scattered white families, where there were no modern schools or churches, and to her, it seemed that she had been deposited miles from civilization.

She and her family were finding happiness living in this old house that had been vacated by her father-in-law, years before, after he had acquired more lands, and more slaves, and had constructed a new and elaborate mansion, of fine timbers, with plastered inside walls, for his present home. (Old relics, remnants of fine imported silk, table linens, and velvet prove that Captain Knight came from a home of culture and refinement.)

But the first house of Albert Knight and Mason Knight was a one-room structure built early in the eighteenth century of square-hewed logs, with a drop-roof gallery across the length of the front. The kitchen was built away from the house and connected by a sheltered walkway to a side room, also a bedroom that was built to the big living room, as that was the favored style of building of that day.

The place was quiet and was sheltered by great oaks, and back of the house, even against the very back steps, flowed Mason, clear and cold. This creek was handy for bathing the children, for washing the clothes, and for refrigeration, which was the only way these people knew of to keep their milk and butter fresh and sweet in summer.

Crocks of milk were weighted with a stone atop the cover to keep them from floating, and the swift water whirled around the container, as it flowed southward, keeping the contents cool and refreshing.

Nearby was this newer home of Albert Knight, a house large and accommodating, where there had before the war lived a family of eleven boys and two girls. Now all the sons were in service, except the three youngest who were not old enough to join. The youngest was Taylor, a lad of fifteen, who took over the responsibility of managing his aged and sick old father's plantation.

There was no occasion for many battles to be fought on Jones County soil because at the time there were no railroads or vital supply lines. And Jones County's volunteers were dispatched to other more strategic areas that did not enjoy this quiet isolation. By being more a part of the country that could rally to the demands of the Southern armies, our people could work without molestation.

Jones County's sheep were shorn too close for comfort, but the resourceful Rebels kept them huddled for warmth under protecting shelters in cold weather and in their eagerness to obtain more wool, shearing knew no season. The good women carded and spun the wool and knitted it into sox and mufflers for our fighting men. The maimed and old men, unable to serve, would then gather together these supplies and, accompanied by boys too young to fight, would go to the supply depot at Meridian. Usually about three yoke of steers made up the wagon teams, and often several wagons would be piled high, loaded with delicacies, plain food, warm clothing, and letters and headed for the trip, which took two weeks in good weather.

More letters left Jones County in this way than by the regular mails. The soldiers looked forward for the messages that would give them news of the happenings back home. The news was not always good news. There was one fellow who received letters that upset him to the extent that he went to his captain seeking leave to return home and see for himself just what was going on.

Serena wrote to Newt that a group of Confederate cavalrymen had ridden up to her house and had led off her fine saddle mare, leaving an old worn-out horse in place of hers, without consulting her about exchanging. In the same letter, she further stated that she thought that the brother-in-law Morgan had had something to do with it, or at least had some knowledge, as he was overly friendly with the strangers, had kept them overnight, and had shod their horses for them before they left.

Soon another letter came, announcing the birth of Martha's child. This letter paid Morgan compliments as a good husband and father.

Newt felt better.

Before long other letters reached Newt from other sources, informing him that there was "talk" about Morgan and Serena.

At about that same time another letter arrived from Serena, saying that Martha was becoming unreasonable and jealous of her and the handsome smithy, and there was discord existing in the household.

These letters lowered Newt's morale, and he became morose and was filled with misgivings. His imagination grew with every detail as he turned them over in his mind, and he wondered if there were not more going on than had ever been mentioned in the letters. He remembered Morgan as a dandy, having a way with women, and he knew that Serena was young and pretty, and was deprived of masculine society. The thoughts drove him wild with jealousy. Finally he could bear it no longer, and set out across the great distance that separated him from his family.

Arriving unexpectedly, Newt hitched his horse in a thicket near the creek, where there would be no danger of it being seen, as he would have the advantage of sneaking up on his own house. The little voice inside him whispered, "That's a cowardly thing to do," but he paid it no mind, as he had, back there in the army, made up his mind that would be the way to see, for sure, sneak up under cover of darkness, and watch to see what was going on between his own wife and the husband of his sister. He crept up to the window unobserved and watched and listened. He saw at once that the handsome smithy had assumed the place as head of the house. He believed that he saw Serena "wrapped around his finger," happy to have him in this role. He saw that Morgan even had the audacity to spank his little children for offenses too insignificant for notice, and he saw that his sister had stepped into the role of "neglected wife," or he imagined that was the reason that her eyes were large and lustreless, deep set in her pale face. He had forgotten that Martha's child was young, and she had not had time to regain her color and strength. He knew that all was not well, and it was a temptation to refrain from walking in and venting this rage that was beginning to swell within him, leaving him a little weak and shaken. All this he saw from the darkness outside, which gave him cover to approach without his making his presence known.

The next day, he had his horse concealed further from the premises, and he lay on the sunny hillside and rested from his journey, but he could not sleep. He had plans for the next night. He would watch again and see what he could see.

That night just after night, Serena, Morgan, and the children were at the table in the kitchen eating their evening meal.

Newt crept up to the back of the house and concealed himself in the shadow of a fig tree that grew against the building. He had full view through the open window where he saw Morgan spank his little boy at the table. His first impulse was to shoot, but he restrained himself and lowered his shotgun where he had hastily thrown it to his shoulder, taking aim on the unsuspecting man at the table. He would have liked to have killed him then, but he did not have any proof of what he wished to know, so he waited, keeping his hiding place secret.

After the meal was finished, the group returned to the big room to keep the young child while Martha departed to the kitchen to eat her supper and wash the dishes. Each night, the same thing occurred, and each night the figure of a stealthy Confederate soldier crept around the house, from the hiding place beneath the fig tree to the one in the chimney corner, where he could watch Morgan and Serena alone together, while Martha was in the kitchen. He noted the gaiety and brightness of his wife, the pleasantness of the companionship that existed between them, and his suspicions overwhelmed his better judgment. Now, after several nights of watching, he felt sure that his wife was in love with another man.

Coming to that conclusion, he strode boldly in and confronted them.

Morgan sprang to his feet in surprise.

Serena was struck dumb by the suddenness of the appearance of her husband whom she thought was miles away serving the Confederacy. She rushed to throw her arms about him, but he roughly cast her aside. Without ceremony or salutation, Newt ordered his brother-in-law out of the house. "Get out, and take your folks with you, or I'll kill you," he said, looking Morgan straight in the eye. His lips were moving and twitching with this terrible emotion.

Martha ran from the kitchen, and placed her hands on her brother's arms, demanding that he tell her something. Newt did not answer. Morgan did not speak, and Serena whimpered like a kicked puppy. Neither did Morgan make an effort to leave the house. Both men glared at each other. "I'll give you time to get out," said Newt, and he darted out the door, reluctant to murder the man in his own house. He kept walking into the night, walking to try to conquer this demon that interfered with his plan, this unseen something that grasped his trigger finger when he should have pulled the trigger. In his heart he knew that it was wrong to kill, but he knew that this was a life that he must take; the life of a snake. So, out there alone with the night wind blowing through the trees, and cooling his hot brow, he had time to think. Newt was capable of thinking when not subjected to such emotional strain.

No one knew that he was in the vicinity, so he walked back to his house and tricked Morgan into believing that the outburst was a sham, that he had pulled a big joke on them. Together, they all had a hearty laugh, and Newt was back home, the same as he ever was, enjoying his family, but biding his time.

Each day he put off killing Morgan. He watched each day for an opportunity to kill him "accidentally." He followed him to the blacksmith shop, and loitering there around the busy man, whose face glowed before the bellows, whose long-lashed eyes were reddened by the heat, as he worked, he could not muster the courage to shoot him, so he pretended to rest on the rough-hewn puncheoned bench under the tree, and enjoy the musical ringing of the anvil. Although this "thing" within him shut out all consciousness of sound and time, and that still small voice inside him kept whispering, "Tomorrow, wait until tomorrow," and another day was gone, and night was near again, with his wife's lover still living.

Doggedly, Newt followed his brother-in-law back to the house where the subject of Newt's leave came up. To the chagrin of Morgan, Newt announced that he was over-staying his leave.

Morgan had a "feeling" that Newt meant to kill him, because little things, the look in these strange eyes, that constant following, as a cat stalking its prey, filled Morgan with a dread premonition of evil that kept him awake nights, and the loss of sleep was telling on his nerves. He kept remembering about the incident on the night of Newt's arrival, and he was not altogether sure that it was a prank. He wished with all his heart that Newt would return to the army, and now that he knew that there were other plans, he persuaded him to leave at once.

"You can't remain without leave," reminded Morgan. "The cavalry is near, and soon the word will be spread that you have deserted," said the brother-in-law threateningly.

"But no one knows that I am here," replied Newt, "except my family, and surely no one of them would betray me." Morgan was led unwittingly, further into conversation, and finally in his over-anxiousness to have Newt gone, he confided that he was in contact with the cavalry at all times, and he hinted that if he were asked he would be obliged to tell that Newt was absent without leave.

The last remark was enough to drive Newt insane with fury and jealousy, but his countenance gave no hint of his emotion, and to the relief of Morgan, he announced that he would be leaving that night for the army.

After Knight had been gone from the house long enough to be well on his journey, Morgan lifted his child from the cradle where it had awakened and was crying. He sat with his back turned towards the open window, the window through which Newt had watched night after night.

Relieved with Newt, and his strange ways, departed, he rocked to and fro, quieting the infant. It became quiet and still, asleep, but Morgan kept rocking.

Serena sat nearby, knitting, and although she heard no noise, she was aware of another presence, as she glanced quickly toward the open window. She could not cry out in time to warn Morgan of his impending fate. She was speechless with horror. There stood her husband, his face fully revealed in the light from the window. His mouth was working and twitching spasmodically, his teeth were sunken into his lower lip, which at that instant was released, and his mouth sprang open. His eyes were great opaque holes in his head, and that expression made a lasting impression on poor Serena's tortured mind.

There was a terrible blast from the old musket, and Morgan fell face forward, with the back of his head blown off.

The sleeping child was almost crushed to death beneath his sprawled body. Bits of his brain were scattered over the room and stuck to the furniture, and tiny fragments clung to the design of the counterpane, and the red chain-stitching on the pillow shams on the bed. His life-blood oozed out, and puddled on the floor, wetting the baby's garments before Martha and Serena could regain presence of mind, and pull it clear of its dead father.

Newt did not re-enter the house. No word was spoken. He had no excuse to offer. He walked away from the scene of his crime and went to his father's house.

Old Albert was grieved already by the loss of his sons to the armed service, yet he was proud of them. He lay upon his bed of affliction and read the letters that came to him occasionally from the front.

He was overjoyed when he heard the footsteps of his son as he entered the house, but that joy faded with the first look that he gave him. This person was so unlike the son who had gone away to war. This was a man crestfallen and unhappy. The father knew that something had happened to cause such a change.

Newt did not wait to be questioned. He told what he had done. In order to spare Serena and Martha the humiliation, he did not tell why he killed Morgan, but he did tell his father the following: "I came home to kill him, because he was a snake in the grass. I had to kill him because I had a right. He thought I was a deserter, and he was fixin' to turn me in." But his old father knew the reason, though he would not mention it.

"I am a deserter!" exclaimed Newt. "Before now I had intended to go back to the army; now I shall stay at home."

"But, Son, you must go back. You can't stay out of the army, and you can't escape the penalty for slaying Morgan in cold blood," counseled the old man. "Why don't you go in to Ellisville and give up to the Sheriff?"

"I'll never give up, and I'll never be caught," declared Newt. "Catching comes before hanging, and they'll never catch me alive."

"My son, my son, my pore son," wailed the old man wringing his hands. "You don't know what you're doing!" He dropped weakly back upon his pillows.

"I can get Jess and Albert to join me, and I will not be alone. We will put up a fight before we are hung," said Newt.

"Oh, but you can't escape! You will be hung! You can't desert the army, the penalty is death and disgrace!" cried the old man.

Newt slammed the door upon his words and was gone. That was the last time he was to hear his father's voice.

News of the murder reached Ellisville soon and was spread over the settlement, and the sheriff and his deputy were scouring the woods in search of the fugitive. There were no young men, or able-bodied, left from which to organize a posse, so there was not much danger of Newt being apprehended, unless he were seen and his whereabouts disclosed.

But he knew that law-abiding old men would report him if he did not keep out of sight, so he knew not to come near his own home or the home of his father. He took to the woods with the intention of sneaking out and slipping into the slave quarters to be fed, when there was no danger. He knew that he could trust the negroes. With this in mind, he set out, a hunted man, a fugitive from justice, and a traitor to his country.

CHAPTER 7

Organization

A long-haired, bearded man with strange furtive eyes emerged from the tall cat-tails that bordered the lagoon near Horse Shoe Lake.

The marshy ground had dried and cracked in the summer's sun, where cattle paths led through the tall grass to the water's edge, where thirsty animals could escape the heat and flies by wading in and standing in the murky shallows.

The bearded one struck one of these paths and headed for the Old Flat that lay along the Porter-Welch trail. This heavily timbered flat was known as "no man's land," and for a hideout, no place could equal it, for one had to be familiar with the swamps not to become lost in them among the tiny lakes and dense forest growth.

At that time, most of the people preferred the hill land above the streams and springhead hollows, as crops were surer where there was drainage in wet years, and it was not until after the Civil War that much swamp land was in cultivation. In the nearby settlement of Cracker's Neck, most of the people were poor, as the soil was crawfishy and unfertile as compared with other sections of the county. But even so, there were several families that owned slaves, and even the poor in Jones County, unless newly married and just beginning, or a newcomer with debts, owned from three to four or five, as a slave was then as necessary as a plow animal is today on a farm. (Note: This fact is obtainable from actual records of slave owners.)

Sweat and grime and splashes of mud had discolored the wearer's uniform, and he was tired and hungry, but here in the Neck were people who knew him and might speak out of turn, so he kept to the cow-paths, and leaving one, he cut across through the timber to the next, and on to another, always out of sight of the main road.

The fugitive ate no food, for he was filled with a strange fullness, and his appetite was gone, but he knew that it was hunger that caused that gnawing pain in his stomach, but he thrust the thought out of his mind, and kept on with the business of surveying the lay of the land, in search of suitable hide-outs.

The section below and along each side of the river was desirable, as there were many outlets for escape in case one had to get on the move in a hurry. He followed the course of the river until he came to the mouth of Big Creek, then he turned up the Creek, north, and came on up through that swamp on up towards Big Creek Church. Here the settlement broadened out, and houses were closer together, so there was danger of his being seen by a ranger out looking for strays, or on the beaten paths might be women and children, or a slave, who would report seeing a bedraggled soldier in a gray uniform, and that would imperil his purpose. So he chose the more rugged terrain and followed the winding creek on up to its source, where it branches out through reedbrakes of a density that would defy most to enter. This was up near the site of the property that Newt had bought from the Huckaby family in Jasper County, and he still owned the land there.

At that time most of the negroes could be trusted implicitly, but due to the fact that they all knew Newt to be a man who would kill a slave for the slightest provocation, they respected him only through fear. He was not afraid to walk boldly into their quarters and demand food, but he needed more than food, and most of the slaves were too stupid to understand the purpose he had in mind. So he starved it out, eating only that which nature provided in the woods, for he was afraid to fire his gun to kill game, which he could have easily roasted, for he knew that the firing of a gun, at a time when guns were silenced, by lack of hunters, there was danger of the report bringing about an investigation, and he might be discovered.

Days later, with face scratches, from which blood had matted the heavy beard, the hunted man wandered across the hills, avoiding the old Paulding Road, and hitting Mason Creek swamp further down below. He had formulated a great plan. He knew that he would eventually come to the plantation of the Knight who owned more slaves than any other planter.

During the long days, and sleepless nights of weary travel, wild ideas invaded his mind, and from these ideas he formed thoughts that grew into fantastic plans for his future.

He tried to shut out of his mind the horribleness of the sight of Morgan lying there, crushing his infant, in a pool of crimson, but the imprint was stamped there, permanently. He turned to more pleasant thoughts and Serena's image flitted before him. He did not blame Serena; strangely as it seemed, thinking back about it all, he could find in his heart for her a kind of pity. He believed that she had been the innocent victim of a scheming seducer in the person of the handsome Morgan. He was glad, now that it was over. He had no regrets. Then he thought of Martha back there with her sorrow, the crying infant, and his own helpless children, and his poor brain reeled and spun with so much suffering, but he kept going until exhaustion finally overtook him, and he dropped down under a mossy tree, in fitful slumber.

The strain of listening had almost split his ear drums. Constantly working his mouth, thinking, spitting cottony saliva, until his throat was smarting and burning and his lips were dry and parched, adding to the discomfort of his burning belly, which had lost its gnawing sensation but had now a hot dry emptiness. The birds and animals scurrying at his approach had startled him, sent cold chills up and down his spine.

He arose and found his aching bones no better, his limbs too weak to carry his now gaunt frame much further, but it was only a few more miles to the plantation, about which centered his wild scheme.

He remembered that there among other old and trusted slaves was a new and strange one, who was reported to be of greater intellect than any of the others in this part of the country.

A new slave brought into the vicinity always created much conversation and interest among all the negroes, and he had heard lengthy discussion among his father's slaves about the great powers and the unusual learning of this wicked "light" woman, who boasted that her father was a noble white man, and from him, she knew things not intended for other negroes to know.

His thoughts were interrupted by a faint stir, a gentle swishing along the path, then the soft hurried tread of bare feet, a few steps from where he had paused to rest. He parted the thick brush and peered out from his place of concealment to see who was passing so near. To his surprise and pleasure, it was a woman and alone. The steps had been light for one so heavy. He had expected her to be slender, but from the long plaited hair, and the pale ginger color of her skin, Newt knew that this was the woman he was seeking, so he carelessly walked out and accosted her with a pleasant "Good Morning!"

"Good mo'nin', Sir," returned the woman. She fumbled in her pocket and drew forth a slip of paper, and presented it to the soldier. He unfolded the paper, and saw that it was a pass. He had guessed right. The paper stated that Rachel was permitted to pass!

Each slave state had rules and regulations designed to hold slaves under control.

After Nat Turner's rebellion, many sections feared like insurrections, and took measures to keep down slave trouble. There was an attempt once to make it a law that not more than five negroes could work in a group, but that was impractical, and was soon discarded, as many planters owned hundreds that cultivated more than one plantation. Here in Jones County, which did not boast such wealth, precautions were also taken, and no slave was permitted to leave the quarters without a written pass. But with fewer slaves in the county, and especially as many were "raised" here from old reliable families, there was no danger of an insurrection, and the pass business was too much trouble to a trusting happy care-free people, and the spoken word of the master was enough to hold most under control, so many were allowed to visit other slaves living on other plantations, and frolic half the night without a pass.

But soon after the Dred Scott decision, propaganda crept into Jones County, and the idea of escaping was presented to the slaves, and the very active underground railroad offering inducement to flight caused a new tightening on the discipline of the "property," as losses in some sections of the South were terrific, due to runaway slaves, so the pass again became an essential.

After the report of such heavy loss, sentinels were placed here and there along the travel routes, and any slave who happened to be traveling, was called upon to produce his pass. If the pass was in order, he was allowed to continue on his journey, otherwise, he was marched right back to his master, and as a rule, got a good flogging. Some of the passes were humorous in composition, and usually the nature of the trip was stated. There is a copy of an old pass that was carried by a negro woman who could not read or write, and therefore had no knowledge of its contents. The pass was granted after she had fought with another slave woman over a male. The obscenity of the rhyme which described the fracas would have brought a blush to the face of any decent Sentry, but the unknowing good woman proudly presented it on several occasions, and was allowed to pass, with pleasure!

So, the pass became an instrument of destiny.

All that Newt had heard about Rachel's prowess was true, and in her, he found a match for his own cunning. First, he bargained with her to supply him with food, which she agreed to do, for a price. So it was arranged between them for her to go to her aged master and tell him that her services were needed on a nearby plantation to help take care of a sick negro.

The good master was more than pleased to grant his servant leave for such a worthy cause and gave her a pass which read:

"To whom it may concern; This yaller woman is privileged to pass at will.

(Signed) *John Knight, Seign.*"

Soon Rachel understood from these meetings with Newt that he was the man who would liberate them when the time came. Rachel was

anxious to help, and every day found her on the path to other negroes'
quarters with information. And from these quarters, word spread by
grapevine, that the time would soon come when all would be free,
regardless of the struggle between the States. There was not a negro in
Jones County that did not know that a white man had run away from
the army, to come back to lead the slaves out of bondage.

So it was that Newt's hiding out became filled with pleasant intrigue.
He was clothed with good clothes, had plenty of fine food and plenty of
sleep, without fear of capture, with these people on guard to protect him.

One day while rambling aimlessly through the woods, Newt
encountered another man by the name of Jasper Collins, who had also
decided to lay down arms and refuse to fight with the South. Together
they talked it over, and Collins was for inviting others to join the three
Knights, and form a band to resist conscription, that was threatening
Jones County.

At that time, with so much propaganda being spread by the abolitionists here in the South, slaves were striking mutiny, refusing to
work or obey the commands of the persons to whom they were committed in the absence of their masters, who were away fighting at the
battlefronts. That added to the scarcity of supplies, for no food was
produced to feed the increasing armies. No cotton grown from which
to clothe our people, so it was necessary for some enactment to free
men from service, who could manage their negroes and provide for the
essentials of war. As a result, there was passed what Mr. Collins termed
"a 20-negro law," whereby a man owning twenty slaves or more, was
permitted to return home, and work his slaves for the benefit of the
Confederate army. Of if a planter owned forty slaves, he could obtain
a discharge for his brother, or could pay a man, otherwise not serving,
to take his command, and he could remain at home to look after his
own interests.

Mr. Collins insisted that it was "a rich man's war, and a poor man's
fight" and therefore he was as much entitled to stay at home as any
other if he so chose, as this is a free country. He failed to see that the
law was passed only for production of the South's needs.

Newt quite agreed with Collins, and together they roamed the woods with Rachel keeping them supplied and in contact with the outside.

Through her it was learned that the sheriff no longer sought Newt, thinking he had returned to duty, and Morgan's murder was forgotten, in the excitement of newer developments.

The next man to join the Knights and Collins was W. W. Sumrall. He also thought that the war was only a scheme to make the rich richer, and he believed that retaining slavery was the primary cause of war. He preferred hiding with his friends to fighting a causeless war.

At about that time, Nat Kilgore and William Fairchilds were appointed to gather supplies from Jones County to send to the fighting fronts. As this was a country that afforded good grazing in winter and summer, there was a bountiful supply of cattle, sheep, and more hogs in the swamps than was necessary to provide our country at home with food. These men made the settlements and asked the co-operation of the families in penning up the stock to be sent to the supply depots, where it would be distributed to the encampments. Some of the people resented this and refused to donate anything, whereas the majority stinted themselves to give to the army.

Those refusing were at once branded "Yankee Sympathizers," and the men in hiding were quick to learn just who these objectors were.

Again the pass came in to play, and a pale ginger woman, with a "hippin'" tied around her head, beat the path into the settlement to get more details to relay to the "liberators."

The party in hiding drew straws to see which would take the pleasure of killing Kilgore and Fairchilds. There was a big clay root, where a big tree had, some time past, been blown up by the roots during a hurricane, and the clay remained intact, filling the gap between the roots. This product of nature afforded an excellent ambush site. The two youngest men were stationed behind the clay root, within easy range of the road over which the food gatherers, as they were called, would travel on their way back to Ellisville.

Newt did not trust the aim of the young men, and just before the time arrived when the ambushed were to pass, he also concealed himself near the spot. The first two shots missed, and before the men could recover from surprise, another shot dropped them both. As there were no witnesses, the double murder became a mystery, and it was a long time before there was a confession as to the actual happening.

Word spread from mouth to mouth among the poorer class of whites that a group of deserters were in hiding. And as gossip spread, along with it came news of atrocities attributed to the Confederate cavalry.

Fine horses disappeared from out of their stables, and who but the Rebels who had demanded the fattest of the land, would steal a horse?

Letters were written to the men at the front, telling them that their families were in danger, that their women were raped, that their homes were destroyed by the Southern cavalry.

Although it did not happen right here in Cracker's Neck, many of the people believed that it was happening elsewhere, and immediately steps were taken to protect the home interest, and those becoming of conscription age were reluctant to leave in the face of such threats to the settlements.

The three leaders rode their horses out of the tall pine timber, down to the broad sandbar on the west side of Leaf River to the edge of the rippling silvery stream. The lacy cypress, festooned with Spanish moss, cast fantastic shapes and weird shadow over the shallow expanse of water, as the moon was riding high in its full glory, across a sky that was without a cloud.

"Better wait here," said Newt, "the moonlight is too bright to ride out into the open." A grunt from his companions was the reply. "We can ride over to the yan side an' wait in that clump o' thicket till the moon goes down." So without further conversation, the three horses hit the water, and as they gained the deepest near the middle of the stream the riders pulled their feet up out of the stirrups, and lifted their legs up clear of the spray, as the horses swam across.

The river was always low in late summer and could be crossed at several points, other than at the ferries.

"They've got word that I am coming, and they have not had time to tell it around, so it is safe to ride right into the Neck," reassured Newt.

"We'll go to my kinsfolk first, and after we've got them to join us, we will recross the river and get Tim." The two companions were encouraged by the leader's confidence. Since they had become deserters, this ingenious person had exhibited the talents necessary to make him a great leader, and as he was in position to lead them safely from one hideout to another, there was little danger of the cavalry ever catching up with them.

Newt knew every pig trail and every foot log from Etahoma, up where Clear Creek joins to form Big Creek, down to its mouth where it flows into Leaf River. From there down the river, clear to Pascagoula, and back up the river to the fork of Bouie, and the mouth of Okatoma, the settlements in Covington County, and the swamp along Currie's Creek, all the country along Tallahala, and the settlements on Rocky were all known to this man whose innate ideas led him to the highest office in Jones County.

The moon went down and the three riders traveled in the darkness that comes just before dawn. Soon they were into the settlement. Leaving his men at a safe distance from the house where he was to go to persuade his kinsman to join them, Newt crept up to the window, and rapped sharply on the shutter. No answer. Another sharp rapping and the loose hanging old wooden shutter groaned and creaked from the pounding.

"Who's there?" finally came the demanding voice from inside.

"Open an' see," replied Newt.

"Oh, I'd reckernize that voice any whar. Jest lif the latch string and come in," his relative invited. And when the fugitive entered, the old man was down on his knees before the fireplace, striking two flint rocks together over a fluff of cotton, trying to spark a light.

"Never mind the light," cautioned Newt. "It seems you're awful keerless, a sleepin' wi' the latch string out, Uncle. Don't you know a raidin' party might come in on you an' kill you abed?" asked Newt.

"Why, what're you a talkin' about? There ain't no sech thing as a raidin' party in these parts! There ain't been a cavalry here except a huntin' you, and' you're gonna git caught and hung! With all yore kin agin you, they'd love to see it! You orter be ashamed to lay out, when there's all o' the decent men o' the name gone. All o' yore cousins, an' most o' them men wi' little chillern. Even yore own brothers, an' here you're a layin' out in cool shades, an' a bein' fed by the niggers. An' now they're a sayin' that you're a goin' to organize an' a gonna start a band to pertect the women an' chillern. Huh! There ain't nothin' here fer the likes o' you to pertect. And them cavalry that'll be a comin' in here after you, will have to eat off'n us too." The old man paused for breath, and Newt, ignoring the outburst, calmly asked,

"Where's Ben?"

"Why, he's abed. Wh—" The sentence was interrupted by Ben himself, who had awakened and walked in.

"Did you want somthin' o' me?" asked Ben.

"Yes. Walk out on the gallery where we can talk."

"There's nothin' to keep you from talkin' right here," said the old man. And as his son and the deserter walked out, he followed, but he did not catch the words.

The next thing he knew, Ben and the outlaw had tied up in a big fight, and in the scuffle, they both rolled out into the yard.

Newt would have killed his kinsman, but his gun was leaning against the side of the house, just out of reach, and to keep from attracting too much attention, he did something that he had never been known to do before. He broke the hold of the young soldier and fled, not because he was afraid to fight, but because he knew that he was in the enemy's camp, and he did not know, since he had met with such a cold reception, whether or not his kinsmen could be trusted to keep this new move secret. In fact, he was sure that the old Uncle would even go so far as to turn him in, and with the thought of capture in his mind, he rushed to his horse and mounted without a word to the two waiting men. However, there was no need for words, for they knew that his mission had failed, and they spurred their horses in pursuit of their leader.

Morning found them in their hideout in "No Man's Land" below the Porter-Welch road, and not too far from the scene of the unsuccessful attempt to recruit a new member of the band. This place was chosen for four good reasons. Newt knew that if a search was instigated, he would be expected to be miles away, and not in the vicinity. Second, he knew that he had once had more friends in this part of the country than in any other neighborhood. The third reason, he felt sure that he could influence some of the younger men to join them. Fourth, he could leave his friends, who knew very little about the territory, here in hiding, while he ventured forth to further the "cause."

He did not have long to wait, as news of his encounter with Ben spread over the settlement.

Quite unexpectedly, they were startled by the sound of the soft tread of footsteps cautiously approaching.

They raised their guns in readiness, should the intruder be an enemy, but the figure of a woman emerged from the thicket. In her hand she carried a note addressed to the leader.

Newt quickly scanned the message, and then passed it over to the others. It was from a cousin, requesting permission to join them. So instructions, along with demands for more supplies, were sent to this young man, who was just old enough to be taken by the Confederate army. He was not a deserter, since he had not been previously in the service.

"The South's Strangest Army," "The Anti-Secessionists," "The Bushwhackers," "The Jayhawkers," "The Guerrillas," and "The Deserters" are some of the most popular titles applied to the Captain Newton Knight Company of Jones County, Mississippi.

Many different and conflicting stories have been told about this unusual organization of men, who were, for the most part, the early settlers of this part of the South. But never the real truth about the company, the men who were members, exactly what part they played in the history of the country, their motives for joining a band that was pledged to kill or be killed. The social status of each has been overlooked, and that for reasons obvious to those who know the story.

Nothing in the history of a county has stirred so much strife, nor created such a sensation as did the organization of the Knight Company.

Families in Jones and adjacent counties are rift until this day as so many were divided in opinion. Many families do, until this day, deny their kin.

Knights deny kinship with Knights; Welches assert that they are not kin to "old Welches," Sumralls say that their name is supposed to be pronounced "Sum-er-*all*" with emphasis on the "all." Some Hollomans spell their names with an "i" instead of an "o," and it becomes "Holliman," and each accuses the other of "having done something" some time or another, hence the changing of the spelling of the name. Walters say that some of the others are pronounced "Waters," or that those "not quite measuring up" are a different set. Many families say that the old muster roll was a forged document, and that their ancestors were mistakenly added, although they were never members of the Knight Company. While the Collins families stand united, and if any person wants to get into a fist fight, just let him insinuate that the Collins fought for any other than the Federal Union, although all the Collins men were not deserters and did not join Captain Knight.

The Davis families declare that they are unrelated, having come originally from different states, to this section.

It is a provable fact that there were names of men entered on Newt's roll who were not actively engaged in the deserter warfare.

Many men joined under pressure, some because they felt that they were right in their convictions, others because they were victims of circumstance, and even many others, because they were the riff-raff of Jones County. It is openly declared that all of these men were of poor pioneer families, toiling in a wilderness with their bare hands, trying to eke out a meager living from the soil, and not slave owners, was the reason this company was organized. Most of the descendants of these soldiers say that the Confederate cavalry was oppressing the women and children.

This writer is not making accusations. The records speak for themselves. That is, the records that have not been burned in the fires of courthouse destruction, which in more than one instance, was designed arson, with record obliteration the objective.

The names on the Knight Company muster roll are accurately copied. Compare these names with the reprinted list of early volunteers from Williamsburg, and it will be noted that many joined by their own volition, and were not drafted, as has generally been supposed, but are the ones who deserted from the army, and turned to Newt Knight for leadership.

It will also be noted that many of these men were from slave-owner families and not at all poor, as records of slave ownership have also been preserved.

Many Knights are listed as having joined their cousin, Newt, but actually, only two did desert the Confederacy.

Here and there, reposing in secluded spots, overgrown by scrub pine, cedar, sassafras, and sedge grass, are the graves of Knights who gave their lives fighting for the Confederacy. Graves in well-kept family cemeteries and old churchyards bear monuments as proof of the valiant fighting Confederate gentlemen who proudly bore the name of Knight. The graves contain the dust of the remains of men who were ashamed of the man who set himself up as a powerful enemy, retarding the progress of our Southern armies, laying waste to the scant provisions, provided at such a sacrifice from our poor source of supply; so ashamed that it is little wonder that all Knights will deny kinship with the infamous Captain!

However, this Knight was descended from the first Knight in Mississippi, therefore he had many cousins by the name.

He was the son of old Albert Knight who was a fine honest man, a prosperous slave owner, and not a poor man, as has so often been stated by many writers.

There has never been found an excuse for this son's strange behavior, but many erroneous tales have been told about his parentage.

He was brought up on his father's plantation, with many slaves, and as there is proof of his early relations and environment, it cannot be said that his was an altrustic nature. Quite the contrary, for he was an oppressor, and with fear and trembling, he was obeyed by his father's slaves. His attitude was probably an acquired trait rather than an inherited characteristic, since his mother was the strange and beautiful Mason Rainey.

That is, Albert Knight married this small Spanish-type lady under the assumption that Mason Rainey was her real name, and all of her legal transactions were carried on under that name. There has been much speculation as to who she really was, because of the conflicting stories that have been told regarding her origin. Actually, her name was Rebecca Griffith.

The story traveled around for years, following Captain Newt's notoriety, that this lovely person was an outcast. And because son Albert had married outside the family's social realm, that he too became ostracised by his family.

At the time the early Knights settled in Mississippi, there were no beaten trails to towns or settlements, and since there were no banks in this part of the country, these people did their banking at a place called St. Martha'sville, near Atlanta, Georgia.

It took four weeks to reach this city, by horse rider, and when a sack of gold was to be deposited, young Albert Knight took the trip.

In the city there was gaiety, and life, and beautiful women. And it was said that from one of these trips, Albert brought home his beautiful wife.

That story is false. There is no record of the exact date that Newt's mother did come to Mississippi, but she came before the beginning of the eighteenth century, along with the first families, as she was an orphan who had fallen in with the Knights, her family all having been wiped out by a plague known as the bloody flux. She and one brother survived the epidemic.

Years afterward, when heirs to an immense fortune were sought, it was definitely learned that the gentle orphan's real name was Rebecca Griffith, and that she was entitled to one half the wealth. But before she could establish her claim, she died, and her descendants made no effort to gain that which was rightfully theirs by right of birth. To have claimed the fortune would have also made it necessary to have claimed kinship with Captain Newt!

Many fancy titles were attached to this stalwart giant of the forests. He was called "Chieftain," "Captain," and "General," by his admirers and subordinates.

His was an imposing figure of arrogance, much of a man, whose skin was as fair as that of his petite mother; his hair was almost a jet black, and curly; his nose was a little crooked, and that was the only imperfection of his countenance. His smile was flashing, and his teeth unusually strong and white, and they gave the impression that he was purposely showing them, so to speak, and the mouth was handsome, though most extraordinary in expression. His lips moved as he thought, and as he was in deep meditation, he unconsciously worked his mouth, made ugly faces, as does a child playing before a mirror, and those strange eyes changed color! His eyes were unforgettable, clear gray, with the coldness of steel, and as sharp as the eyes of a hawk. He stood, barefoot and bareheaded, and as straight as an Indian warrior, to measure six feet and one inch in height, and he weighed a 180 pounds.

Probably Captain Knight's good mother unknowingly aided him in the exploits of his later life, when a human life meant so little to him.

During a fit of temper, when he was a boy, he had murdered one of the slaves on his father's plantation, and that crime was punishable by death. To save her son from punishment, Mason Knight changed his age on the Bible record, and whereas it should have shown that he was born November 10, 1829, the date of his birth appeared 1833. In that way, as a minor, he escaped the penalty, and the atonement was not made for the innocent black one's life.

Later, when he was nineteen years old, he married Serena Turner, and started out to live the good life of a good citizen. He was a smart man, literally and figuratively.

After buying his land at twelve and one-half cents per acre, up in the edge of Jasper County, north of where Soso now is, he built a comfortable log house, as he was a good carpenter, as well as a farmer. This land was up near the old Sixtown settlement and had originally been settled by a family of Daniels, then it had passed into the hands of the

Huckabys, from whom he had purchased it, with the intention of making it his permanent residence.

After fire destroyed his home up there, he was welcomed back to
Mason Creek in Jones County, the little creek that was named for his
mother, as she was the first settler there, and had claimed the little
stream for her very own.

By this time Captain Knight had four children, one girl, Molly, and
the three boys were Mathew, called Mat, and the twins, Thomas and
Billie.

Nearby was the first settlement that occupied the high land overlooking Leaf River. Except for a settlement here and there, all of the
lands of the valley were covered by a dense swamp. Tupelos, cypresses,
oak, and magnolia towered beside the pine, and the heavy-hanging
Spanish moss made darkness out of daylight.

Men were easily lost in this dismal swamp, unless they, like Newt,
knew the trails and bypasses. There were places in this thick swamp
where sunlight could not penetrate the heavy foliage of the trees which
were entwined with jungle vine, where green moss covered the ground,
except where the fern, mushrooms, and lichens abounded. A profusion
of color that lent awe and forlornness to the scene, enveloped in dampness and dark shadow, and a terrible quietness.

The lagoons and hundreds of little lakes were filled with fallen
branches, rotting leaves, old logs, and slithering, slimy, crawling things
that sometimes slipped out of the black waters and hid themselves in
the tall reed cane and marsh grasses that grew luxuriously.

Further up the river, above the Reddoch's Ferry, there was a stony
area, which had been the ancient burial ground of the Mingoes. And
over this grew a thick undergrowth and a tangle of briars, making this
a pleasant den for rattlesnakes.

All these pitfalls were known to the shrewd Captain Knight, and he
was possessed with a keen intuition that steered him clear of danger.

Down below the settlement, the swamp gave way to open fields, and
pioneer residences. Around a few more bends of the river, past broad

white sand bars, and there was another landing, and the settlement of Cracker's Neck.

The first family to settle in that area was named Quaker, and this land, a peninsula, jutting out between Big Creek and Leaf River was known as Quaker's Neck, and much later the spelling was altered, the Quakers had long departed, and it became Cracker's Neck.

In this neighborhood lived many friends of Newton Knight. Here he was always welcome.

Along the Porter-Welch trail that led from Ellisville to the Welch Landing, was another thick swamp which was called "no man's land" because it belonged to no man, unclaimed as a homestead, and was still possessed by the government, under the supervision of the Land Commissioners. It was here in this swamp that the Knight Company was organized, in the fall of 1863.

The time of this organization was exactly twenty months and three days after Williamsburg's mass recruiting incident.

This first organization was not official, just a group of men who met and pledged themselves to defy capture, to kill, or be killed for one another, and for one another's families, if need be. There was no formality. It was only verbal, but was binding.

It was conceded that their leader was to be obeyed in everything he commanded them to do. This, at first, was not agreeable to Mr. Collins, because he had openly left the army and had made no secret of his intention to stay at home with his family, and he did not like this hiding in swamps and moving under cover of darkness.

Finally his argument convinced Newt that if they could secure the cooperation of their kinsmen, that they, with the men from the four families represented, could come out into the open, and defy capture by the Confederate cavalry, when the time came, which he knew was coming, when they would be caught and hung, as that was the penalty for leaving the army.

Some two months later, the group had secured promises of kinsmen here and there in the county, to come in, and legally join. At every opportunity, they rode out of hiding and approached some family that had members serving who wished them back at home. And always the families were lectured on the "Home Defense" idea of remaining in Jones County, and "the 20-negro law" was lambasted on each occasion.

Across the river in Covington County men were solicited, and finally with the addition of T. T. Welch, who was too young to be a regular soldier, and others of the Collins families, the group moved from the lower hideouts on up to the region near Newt's land, in the edge of Jasper County, and there they set up a battery and officially organized.

This was the famous Salsbattery, and it is supposed to be here that "no man's land" existed, but that is where the brilliant tactics were displayed. He knew that it was generally known that he usually stayed down in the "no man's land" of Cracker's Neck, and by creating the illusion that another place existed by the same name, he could confuse the enemy, as he knew also that his desertion was causing many to become wrought up, and not only was he wanted as a deserter; the price was still upon his head for Morgan's murder. He knew that there were hundreds of people who would be happy to aid in his capture.

It was not generally known that the Collins families and Bill Sumrall were members of the band, but now with the Salsbattery organization, these two came boldly forward, and to Jasper Collins, who was a gentleman of the "first water" goes the credit and the honor for an orderly recruit of a company of men which he actually planned to ally with the Union forces.

Had this not been true, Jasper Collins would not have braved the hardships that a hunted man would likely encounter, in trying to make connections with the Union forces in Memphis, Tennessee. The attempt to volunteer his services was, however, futile, and he had no choice but to return to Jones County and be compelled to hide out with the company.

The names that appear on the old muster roll are the names of men who joined, sojourned, left, returned, aided, and befriended the company from time to time, from that first day in July when Mr. Collins and Mr. Knight met in the woods, until even after the surrender!

Most of the names of Jones Countians are kinsmen of the first four men of the organization, either brothers-in-law, brothers, or cousins, so it was more of a family arrangement among the natives who were later joined by outsiders from every section of the state.

* * * *

The following is a list of the names of the company of Newt Knight, of the Free State of Jones County. Organized and equipped at Salsbattery on the 13th day of October, 1863 and commanded by Capt. Knight until the 10th day of September, 1865.

Captain Newt Knight	M. W. Kervin
J. J. Collins, 1st Lt.	J. M. Knight
W. W. Sumrall, 2nd Lt.	T. F. Knight
J. M. Valentine, 1st Sgt.	H. C. Knight
Simon Collins, 2nd Sgt.	B. F. Knight
Alpheus Knight, 1st Corp.	Lazrous Mathews
S. T. Owens, 2nd Corp.	Ausberry McDaniel
Privates: C. F. Prince	C. F. Prince
Tapley Bynum	James Yates
P. M. Bynum	J. J. Valentine
Montgomery Blackwell	Patrick Valentine
J. M. Collins	M. B. Valentine
B. F. Collins	Elijah Welborn
M. C. Collins	R. J. Welch
M. M. Coats	T. T. Welch
S. C. Coleman	W. M. Welch
B. F. Cawley (Corley)	H. R. Welch
R. J. Collins	Younger Welborn
James Ervlen	N. V. Whitehead
J. M. Gunter	W. T. Welborn
Tucker Gregg	T. J. Whitehead
B. H. Hinton	D. W. Whitehead
John Hogan	Joseph Yawn

J. W. Hathorn	Mose Richardson
W. B. Jones	R. H. Valentine
Thomas Yates	Morge Mitchell
Charley Gunter	Jack Smith
Turner Welborn	Jess Smith
John Harper	Jack Arnold
Elisha Wade	Jim Blackledge
John Gunter	Allen Blackledge
Aaron Todd	Jim Tiner
Giles Loftin	Drew Gilbert
Bill Cranford	Archy Walters
Tom Flynt	Guss Lambert
Green Hoskins	Blake Lambert
Scott Bush	Calvin Reeves
Dave Prince	Tom Holloman
Levy Prince	Jim Holloman
John Willis Musgrove	Daniel Wade
Will Laird	Daniel Reddoch
Enoch Davis	Mose Walters
Math Davis	Bill Holifield
Berry Jordan	Bill Elzey
W. P. Turnbow	B. F. Dykes
G. M. Hathorn	D. Pridgen
Jeff Lee	Jack Holifield

As Knight was the first to desert, and as he had shown remarkable ability as a leader, and as he possessed such a thorough knowledge of the lay of the land, from his dodging the law in the swamps, and since he had secured the allegiance of the negroes, he was the man who was chosen as the Captain of the company.

Back there in the neck it was Mr. Collins's eloquent speech to the others that caused them to adopt the following resolution:

"Organize to form a home defense band for resistance to oppression, by assassination, raiding and destruction, and other means to aid the Union, and at the same time save our families from famine."

And it was this man's honesty that influenced the others to come out and organize at Salsbattery, where he became second-in-command to Knight, with Sumrall taking third place as a leader of the company.

His honest intentions thwarted, Mr. Collins, by his own admission, became a ruthless killer, and he was ready to do Knight's bidding.

Knight said of him and Sumrall, "They would stick through thick and thin, and whenever we got into a fight, they could be counted upon to do their part, in the face of any danger."

The news that a deserter band was in hiding in Jones County spread like wildfire, and soon a detachment of Confederate soldiers were sent in to round them up, and take them prisoner.

Alpheus Knight was sent in with the first detachment, as he had been switched to a cavalry division after joining the Coast Guard along with the enthusiastic Jones County group that rushed to Williamsburg.

Soon after he reached the band, which he did secretly, since he did not wish to harm his kinsman, he was by them persuaded to forsake his duty and come in as an officer in the Knight organization.

Up until the Salsbattery proclamation, the deserters kept to their hideouts, or moved secretly over unfrequented trails, or under cover of darkness, and not one dared to fire a gun or blow a horn.

With the new order of things, it would be necessary to have some form of communication, as it was known that they would have to scatter out into small parties of from six to eight, in order to avoid capture. Had they operated as a unit, capture would have been inevitable.

The pickets were men who were stationed to keep watch to ascertain the whereabouts of the cavalry. As soon as it was determined in which direction the cavalry was headed, the picket, who was usually indistinguishable from a black stump, or a clump of brush, and even sometimes from the crotch of a big tree with a commanding view, would immediately sound the warning, and the band would scatter in the opposite direction.

Sometimes it was necessary to ride a horse at a fast run for several miles across the country, in order to spread the alarm in time for the men to seek cover.

It was agreed that no unnecessary killing would be done, and as the choice lay between killing and running, they always ran, unless cornered, then it came to a bitter fight, down to the survival of the fittest.

On that memorable day at Salsbattery, all the men were asked by Knight to carry their hunting horns. It was the custom in the early settlement to use the horn for distress signals, to drive stock, to summons faraway workers to dinner, and every family owned a horn. Many were a work of art, with fine figures carved in an interesting design, with the edges finished in tiny scallops.

Newt's horn was the most unusual horn that was ever cut from the head of a steer.

No matter how black the ox, his horn is usually shaded from black to gray, and from the gray, into a pale smoke, or from the gray to a clear pearl down right at the very tip. But this horn of Newt's was solid black. Its ebony beauty was enhanced by the rasping and sanding he had given it, and it shone with a luster like that of mother-of-pearl.

Just below the tip, a groove was hollowed out to a depth that would carry, looped around it, a fine soft leather string. This string was polished with bee's wax, and worn around the neck of the owner, and he was proud of it, knowing his was the most beautiful horn in the country. It had a mysterious and beautiful tone, unlike any other horn, or perhaps it was Newt's ability to blow upon it that gave it this strange quality. He is said to have been able "to almost make it speak," when he so chose, and the people who knew that sound could always distinguish it from any other.

It was agreed that certain signals were to be blown, and by the number of blasts the different or distant groups of men would know what was meant. Three short blasts meant to come together for further instructions. If one man was the only one within range of the signal, he was to sound off his horn, and that group, or pair, as there were often two operating together, were to sound off their horns, and on down the line in order to reach those stationed at the farthest point, and relayed on to the last picket.

It was agreed that certain signals meant to converge upon the confused cavalrymen, if they were in pairs, or small groups. And often a half dozen mounted soldiers were slain before they knew, or had time to realize that they were ambushed by an unseen enemy.

Their mounts, unless wounded, were appropiated by the bandit gang. If one horse was too badly shot up, or had a broken leg, they promptly killed it and skinned it for the hide, which was tanned for shoe leather.

The approach of the cavalry, in numbers too large to tackle, was to be announced by the old distress signal, and then it was to be every man for himself.

After such encounters, and long after the cavalry had ridden back to the post, there sounded the three blasts from the black horn. The sharp clear notes echoed over the hills, and became lost on the bosom of silence that settled over the hollows.

Alpheus Knight was a young single man, from a highly respected family. He has been called "the trigger man," but in reality, he was sought as a member of the company because of the prestige which he commanded in this part of the woods.

He was a brother-in-law of J. M. Gunter who married his sister, Serena Knight, and it was through his influence that the Gunters came into the organization.

The Gunters were easygoing merry folks, loving a drink, but honest and accommodating before the war, and were very peaceable and good natured. Underlying these fine qualities was a murderous streak, and the second time crossed, the first time having been good-humoredly overlooked, it has always been said that a Gunter would kill as "quick as batting an eye."

Second Corporal Owens was also known as "trigger handy," even before he became a member of the lawless band.

Perhaps there was a reason for his having borne an unsavory reputation.

In the early history of the state, there was a tendency of the people to exclaim, "A chip off the old block," in expressing an opinion of one from a family who had been disgraced for any reason, and relatives were "looked down upon" for the deeds of kinsmen, although they were in no way responsible.

Corp. Owens had a brother, Jack, who had been banished from the country earlier for the murder of Wash Patten.

Differences arising between two men were settled by a duel, each having a witness, or witnesses to go along with him to the designated spot where they were to shoot it out. Such a practice was not uncommon until the close of the eighteenth century, and the victor was not subjected to court trial; the vanquished had died to protect his honor, or the honor of one deserving his sacrifice.

The rule was for the contestants to stand at a certain distance apart, each walk forward towards the other, to meet halfway between the firing lines, on which each was to stand, exchange pistols, step backward, and make ready to fire simultaneously, at a given signal.

The witnesses were to see that the duel was fought fairly, with neither firing before the signal, or one taking any undue advantage of the other. The best marksman won, and the matter was forever settled.

A big water oak with wide-spreading branches was the site chosen for the Owens-Patten duel. They met and went through the preliminaries according to rule, but Owens handed Patten a pistol which failed to shoot, so there he stood before his adversary's fire, defenseless, which act was termed murder.

That incident resulted in a survey of all the dueling pistols and time clocks in the county, and was recorded by the County Board of Police. At that time there were only three clocks registered with the board.

It was a custom then for a man to be "rode out on a rail" or tarred and feathered for dishonorable acts, or deeds of a nature that were termed "a disgrace to decent society."

The sentiment of the people of the county was so against one guilty, he was, by exclusion, forced to seek new territory in which to hide his shame.

There, just below the Reddoch's Ferry, and about fifty yards down along the old Monroe Road, west of Leaf River was where Owens was sent "west" along with the cattle thieves and adulterers, who as a rule became Texans, or Louisianians, as that was the westward route most alluring to these undesirables.

So it was that the Knight Company Owens, disgraced by his kinsman who slew this Patten who was the ancestor of the Wilsons in Jones County was anxious for the dare-devil adventurous life such a position would place him in, and at the same time he would have a chance to do that which was, by opinion, expected of him.

He engaged in all of the roughest and toughest of all the fighting, and did probably as much as did his commanding officer toward rendering death and destruction.

The Gunters and Hintons were kin. And Bill Laird was a member of the Hinton family, so it was a chain of relations, by marriage or intermarriage, that made up the company.

The Turnbows were not Jones Countians, but as Leonard Knight's wife was a Turnbow, they came in by Knight influence. Although Leonard himself was a fine honorable Knight.

It should be made clear, in telling of this great organization, that living in Jones County was not a prerequisite to joining the Knight Company, as any, from any part of the state, and also from outside the state were welcomed in as members. And it was this ruthless band, seeking refuge from other sections that wrought havoc in Jones County. In fact, through Captain Knight's hospitality, this unfortunate county became asylum for all the outlaws, far and near, who wished to be fed while they "lay out."

CHAPTER 8

Men of the Organization

All these men did not come up and join that same day and year, as the record is made to appear, but came in one by one.

Some of the first to come had decided that they were in the wrong company and had left it and gone in with the Union army, as that was entirely possible to do.

The truth of the matter, these men were not fighting for either side, and when many joined, they joined only as protective measures, as it was made to appear that the women and children of the country were suffering from the exploits of the Southern cavalry.

Since most of these men deserted wearing the Confederate uniform, they passed themselves off as being Confederate cavalrymen when they staged raids on farmhouses, confiscating every usable article for the Knight Company. And so it is not at all remarkable that news spread to the soldiers at the fronts, that their families were left destitute by these raids, and they cannot be blamed for being tricked into coming home to take care of their homes and families.

But the sad part is, after they had thrown down their arms and marched in home, they could not stay with their families and provide for them, because that very act brought the cavalry into Jones County by great numbers, forcing the deserters to remain in hiding most of the time, where they became very like a bunch of wild men.

It was known to the Confederate government just which men were deserters, so it was that the families of these men were made to suffer most, in a futile effort to beat them into submission.

The cavalry destroyed everything they could; all that they could not use, they ruthlessly destroyed.

In one particular instance, they piled all the dry fodder which they found stored in a barn out in the open and set it on fire, to keep feed away from the farm animals.

They confiscated all the horses, killed all the chickens, and cut the cloth out of the looms, even before the women could finish the weaving, in a heartless attack upon the little children, as stripping them of clothing was one way to tear the hearts out of the fathers.

Time and time again the order to surrender was presented to the dauntless band, in an effort to stop such useless slaughter and needless pillage of the land, but doggedly the deserters stood their ground, and more and more Confederates were slain in a futile effort to capture the leaders of the band.

The officers were actually sworn in before Vince Collins, and the organization was properly drawn up; in every way except in the manner in which the men were armed, the Knight Company became an army.

The Bynums were good honorable men, and their intention was for the best when they joined the Knight Company.

Newt's old muster roll contains the statement that Tapley Bynum was killed on picket near his home, but it is generally known that Mr. Bynum's wife had a young child, and upon receiving the message, Bynum slipped out and went in home to see his new infant.

While he was in the house, he heard a noise, and stepped out to see what it was, and to his surprise, it was a group of cavalrymen seeking him for desertion. They did not give him a chance to surrender; as soon as they recognized him, they opened fire, and he fell dead in his front yard.

The other Bynum left the company and joined Tisdale's regiment in New Orleans.

The Blackwell brothers did not live in Jones County. They lived in Covington, over in Guinea, a little settlement above where Hot Coffee now is, in the fork of Cohay Creek and Leaf River.

Montgomery Blackwell was a young strip of a boy, not actually old enough to be in the regular army, but he was influenced to join the company, disregarding his young age.

His sweetheart was the daughter of Daniel Knight, who had already gone into the Confederate army with the first volunteers, leaving his family without protection.

On the pretext of visiting the home, Blackwell gained entrance through the daughter, and ransacked the house in search of a gun, ammunition, and any other valuable article that could be used by this unusually equipped army.

The other Collins were known as good citizens. Three of them were captured the same day, and the other escaped and joined Captain Wolfe's company in New Orleans.

Med Coats was also captured in the same round in which the Collins were taken.

Through that same application of kinship, the Corleys were solicited. There were two brothers, one joining Newt, and the other serving in the Confederate army. Their sister was the wife of Newt's brother, Albert, Jr.

The initials preceding Knight names on the roll are not correct, as the Captain listed brothers of his who never thought of leaving the Confederate army, brothers who died fighting for the South. In fact, none of his family joined him except Jesse and Albert, Jr.

Even Ben's name appears on the roll. Because it was near where the company was in hiding, Newt had a hunch that Ben might have been on his way to join him, when he was caught up, and mistakenly hanged.

Green Hoskins was the last of an old family in Cracker's Neck. He was a kinsman of the early Ellzeys, an old bachelor, living alone. No family, and no slaves. But it was his belief that the slaves should be freed, so he went to New Orleans and joined the Yankees, although, for the simple reason that he had spoken against the South, he is listed on the Knight Company muster roll.

The Yates were not Jones Countians, but were from Covington.

Thomas was a member of the band, and served until he was finally caught and hanged, run down by dogs, up near the Knight's Old Water Mill, and James was captured along with the majority of the others.

The Hathorns were not deserters, and they were not Jones Countians. These and other names appear on the roll that Newt kept until his death, for reasons other than service with him.

They are the men who had their names added after the surrender, while Jones Countians struggled for survival under the rule of Newt Knight, during his tenure of office.

These men who did not actually serve, were entitled to favors, if they submitted their names. (They could even vote!) And it was not known by them then that their names would appear publicly on a roll that was preserved by the greatest outlaw that ever roamed the county.

Other men rushed to Newt while he was esteemed a great leader, and submitted their names, under the impression that all men whose names appeared in connection with the Knight Company would be granted a pension for life. And as times were so hard, and there was no money at all, and as long as the pretense would never be brought to light, these good men thought it all right to get all they could out of the government.

The Welch names that appear are not all members of the Knight Company.

Jim Welch did leave the Confederate army, but he went straight to New Orleans and joined the Union there, while his kinsman came in home, dying from body lice and starvation, after the siege of Vicksburg.

There was nothing at all disgraceful about a man dying from body lice, contracted from the trenches. So it is with great pride that people tell about Timothy (long beard), his great service and tragic death.

There was not a place as big as a dime where a louse had not eaten him, and this condition could not be helped under the circumstance, as even kerosene was then practically unknown, and there were no facilities for treatment. And if there had been, none would have been available to the defenders of Vicksburg.

The other Timothy was too young for the service, but he is the Tim that joined Newt, while his sisters' husbands were fighting and dying for the Confederate cause. But Tim was only a lad, and he thought that he was aiding the women and children who were on starvation in the county.

Tucker Gregg was not a Jones Countian. He lived up on the old Military Road that led up the river on the west side, into Smith County. He was later shot and killed on picket along this road in Covington County, just below the southern boundary of Smith.

This road was used frequently by both the deserters and the cavalry on their trail.

The cavalry was made up of men trained by military regulations, and they knew only to proceed orderly, along the main roads. That is where the Knight Company had the advantage, because they knew to keep to the swamps and hideouts. And the cavalry, inexperienced as they were in such warfare, were afraid to venture into the thick reed brakes without knowledge of the number of men or the pitfalls that awaited them.

Judging from the sounds of the horns, and the yelling and cursing, the soldiers were led to believe that there were hundreds, when there would be only a few.

By the time the cavalry had time to call up more reinforcements to tackle the mob, they would have had time to slip out and gain new and secret territory.

Out of shooting range, the clear sharp notes of the black horn were sounded to rally in the strange followers.

Ausberry McDaniel, another Covington Countian, lived up on Cohay Creek. There is not much left of a record of his service with Knight, though evidently he was a highly rated member of the company.

Berry Jordan was not a deserter. It is a provable fact that his wife and the wife of Van McManus lived together so that neither of them would be alone, during the period that both men served in the Confederate army. Yet Berry Jordan's name appears on the Knight Company muster roll!

The same thing happened with Aaron Todd, but he was not one of the company. Many tales have been told about Mr. Todd, who was as fine a man as ever lived in Jones County, and here is the place to clear his name of any connection with the deserters.

He lived on Big Creek and was a neighbor of the early Pinions.

One of his friends was a Confederate soldier by the name of Tom Flynt. Mr. Flynt served until the last year of the war, and then came home on a furlough, as a member of his family was ill. Soon after he came in, he found that many men whom he knew were laying out of service. So he decided that if they could remain, that he should also be permitted to stay at home.

His wife was one of the Pinions, and living with her during his absence was her sister, a spinster.

All went well for a while, with Flynt enjoying his freedom, and fishing to his unmolested satisfaction in Big Creek, nearby. But one day as he sat on the creek bank, he was taken by surprise.

There was a sudden crashing through the brush, and before he could run in hiding, the cavalryman had spied him and was approaching. There was nothing that Flynt could do but throw his gun into the creek, and pretend that he had no reason to be alarmed. But the quick eye of the officer saw the gun as it was tossed into the water, so he knew that this was no innocent fisherman.

The officer was very courteous in demanding the furlough.

Flynt explained that he had come in only because he had sickness in his family, and that the furlough would be found up at the house, as he did not think it advisable to carry it on his person while on his premises. But already other mounted men were riding up in answer to the officer's signal, and a rope was tied about Flynt's neck.

A passing oxcart was commandeered, and Flynt was forced to ride on it to the place of hanging over at the Reddoch Place on Leaf River, where two other men had been caught, and were to be hanged that day. The distance to this place from Big Creek was about six miles, and to the man with the noose about his neck, it seemed that the cart was forever in reaching its destination.

He had hopes that he could obtain clemency from the officer there, Captain Worsham, a Jones Countain whom he knew personally.

Finally the cart arrived.

Worsham was down at a little drain, washing his hands, when the soldiers reached the tree with the victim, but he stood up and commanded the men to go ahead and tie the end of the rope to the limb.

Mr. Flynt was jerked up to a standing position on the cart, as the rope was pulled tighter, and he was unable to attract Worsham's attention, as his voice was cut off by the hangman's noose.

The men were almost in the very act of whipping up the oxen to make them jump, and snatch the footing from under the doomed man, which act would have left him suspended by the neck, as were the two already lifeless ones beside him, when the clatter of horses' feet was heard on the trail.

The speed of the hoof-beats suggested urgency of some manner, so all eyes turned for a moment in the direction of the approaching riders, who turned out to be Flynt's wife and the spinster, the latter frantically waving a piece of paper, which she handed to Captain Worsham.

"Cut him down, men," commanded the Captain, after looking over the paper. "This is the man's furlough, and in order."

"Good ladies, just did get here in time, and I am certainly proud. This is the last hanging I shall ever do, for a man can be mistaken."

Apologies were made, and Flynt returned home with the women.

As soon as the terrible fright was over, although Mr. Flynt was never able to forget, there was much laughing about how the cavalry had been cheated.

The furlough had been faked! It was told over the neighborhood and is still told that Aaron Todd was the friend who faked the furlough, but here is the proof that Todd did not:

In the early settlement on Big Creek, the log church also served as a school building, a crude structure, with split log benches placed on a dirt floor.

The children who attended the school had no desks, and there were no facilities for stowing away a school lunch or other personal belongings. Each child's dinner bucket, or basket, and his vessel of milk was placed beneath his bench until play time.

Aaron Todd placed his dinner each day for five days alongside the dinner of his seat-mate. On the fifth day another older boy carelessly stuck his foot, incased in a rough homemade cowhide shoe, up under the bench to kick over the seat-mate's milk. It was supposed that this was done by the innocent Aaron, and the teacher called him up and punished him wrongfully, with a sound beating.

That was young Todd's last day in school, and he never learned to read or write as long as he lived. So, not being able to write, he could not have faked a furlough for Tom Flynt. Just who did do it is not definitely known, but it could probably be laid to any friend in the neighborhood.

The presence of that honored name on the Knight Company roll is a mystery. It is doubtful if he ever knew it had been placed there.

Many believe that Newt Knight was at times demented and, long after the surrender, placed some of the names on the roll because he remembered them as friends. Or possibly just such a story as the one about the faked furlough reached him, and was accepted by him as a matter of truth, and to honor the hero of such a tale, it was only proper and fitting that his name be placed on the roll with the members of the band that helped to shape Jones County's destiny.

At one time during the war, almost every family on Big Creek, even to the families of the men who were fighting for the Confederacy, looked up to the leader of the band with respect and admiration. He was spoken of as the greatest man that ever lived, because many of these people believed that the Knight Company was fighting our own soldiers to keep them from stealing from the widows and orphans.

Many descendants of these people tell until this day that Newt Knight kept them from starvation, which he did, but nothing is ever mentioned about *how* he acquired help for these families. No praise has been sung by the people of other sections who were robbed that these chosen ones might be fed.

There was a very important reason for the Captain to "stand in" with the citizens of this locality.

If all considered them "friends in need," then no information as to their maneuvers would be given out to the cavalry, and their chances of keeping alive would be greater, and as a result of such strategy, the people along Big Creek and in Cracker's Neck did not suffer as did the people in other parts of the county and state that were overrun by the deserter band, except by the constant and unrelenting harassing of the Confederate cavalry.

Captain Newt's men obeyed him in every respect and carried out his instructions to a letter, fearing death at his hands if he were displeased.

He was the leader, and his intention was to gain the confidence of his adversaries, so he was careful not to incite hatred among the people who were struggling for an existence during the war. On the other hand, he tried to make allies out of the families of the Confederates, and appeared to turn them many favors.

Once when his company was reduced to rags, and their apparel was not presentable, he called together a group of his men and sent them forth to steal. He was not implicit in his instructions and neglected to set forth details, for he felt that some of these had been with him long enough to understand and employ his tactics.

When the detachment rode up to a plantation, they dismounted and entered without ascertaining if the occupants were away. They were not concerned about the attitude of the victims, who were ladies of wide repute, but were concerned only with acquiring the needed material for clothing.

The women had just finished weaving a fine piece of material, which was intended to be made into garments for the children and the half-naked children of the slaves. These ladies feared the very name of Newt Knight, and as soon as they recognized the approaching riders as members of the band, they ran from the house and hid themselves, fearing bodily harm, should the ruffians so choose to inflict it.

The bandits, unopposed, produced their knives, cut the entire piece from the loom, ransacked the house in search of other usables, and departed.

The ladies came from their hiding place, from out in a clump of weeds behind the barn, as soon as the horses' hooves were out of hearing distance, and doggedly set about weaving another piece of material.

The incident was not surprising, for they had heard that the Knight band operated in just such a manner.

The company was in a well protected encampment further down the river, when the thieves returned.

This place was located just across the river, below the Welch Landing, where a deep hollow, through which flowed a clear cold stream of water had cut through the high chalk bluff, and intersected the river.

Up this ravine were high, almost perpendicular bluffs, inaccessible because of the rocky steepness, the tangle of undergrowth, sharp bamboo briars, and jungle vine. Further up the ravine came a sharp turn, and out of the earth roared a big spring, from a dark rocky passage. This passage, like a magic corridor, led to a cave, deep under the hill, large enough to conceal an army and its equipment.

This was known as the "Devil's Den." Here the Knight Company often stayed for days, and sometimes weeks, for with a lookout at the mouth of the stream, they were safe from the cavalry. And at a signal from the picket, the men could place themselves, at such an advantage that they could pick a rider off a horse as often as one approached, as the rider would have to force his mount into the river stream and swim into the entrance to the hollow's stream in order to reach the passage leading into the hideout proper.

Inside this cave, food was cooked, shoes were made, harness mended. And now the task of making new breeches was to begin as soon as the men arrived with the material.

It was certain that they would return, for up until this time, the cavalry's searches were a big joke. So a fat heifer had been confiscated and barbecued for the feast for the returning members.

Newt himself met them near the entrance to the passage, and after looking at the loot, he inquired sharply from whence it came.

The men very truthfully described their exploit, as they felt that they were deserving credit for a job well done, but instead of welcoming them in, the Captain ordered them to go at once and return the cloth, without giving them a moment's rest, or a bite of the heifer.

Quite naturally, the ladies, upon discovering the returning bandits, ran for the hiding place, not knowing what to expect next. They lay still, and quiet for a long time in the Jimsons, for a long time after they knew that the robbers were gone, as they were afraid to venture out.

Finally they returned to the house, and to their surprise, they found a strangely familiar piece of material.

A note was pinned to it, which read:

"With Captain Newton Knight's Compliments."

* * * *

The Big Creek settlement was located advantageously, from a geographical standpoint, lying along the swamp passage from the Salsbattery hideout to the swamp along Leaf River, and it was in this little area that most of the deserter activity took place.

Here were good women who aided the deserters; they were only helping themselves.

At that time there was known a spot described as a "hog calling ground," in open spaces in all swamps where hogs ranged.

The women now, with the men gone, had to ride into the swamps to shell down a little corn, and call up the hogs.

One woman who often went to call up the hogs was a great character by the name of Elly Fair Chain. "Grandma Elly Fair" she was affectionately called in later years by her many friends all over the country.

Elly Fair had fought along beside her husband, until he was killed. She carried ammunition in her checkered apron, and kept handy a fresh load of powder for the nearest man that needed it.

As the guns were fired and emptied in the heat of battle, they were handed to the courageous woman, and she in turn handed them back a freshly loaded weapon.

As far as anyone knows, this was the only woman who actually fought in the Civil War from Jones County, Mississippi.

But when her husband was killed, Elly Fair said farewell to their comrades and came back alone, and on foot, to relatives on Big Creek.

That was just before the big campaign got under way to wipe out the guerrilla band. And at that time the people were looking upon Newt as a great benefactor of the community. So when the tightening rein was thrown about him by the Confederate government, it was brave Elly Fair who took advantage of the excuse to ride into the swamps to call the hogs, in order to warn Newt's men to stay clear of danger.

On one occasion, she ran right smack into a gray uniformed officer, but her quick thinking eased his suspicions immediately.

"Have you seen anything of my stray heifer, sir?" she innocently asked.

When she was answered in the negative, the smart woman declared, "Then I shall turn and ride in another direction, for you'd a noticed a fine one like her."

With that, she wheeled the old mule she was riding and rode in the opposite direction across the swamp to tell the gang that she had just encountered a cavalryman who was out looking for them.

With such a system organized and executed in the settlements where the deserters were usually welcomed, it is easy to understand how they were able to go about freely and apparently unafraid.

It was nothing out of the ordinary for these men to ride into the settlements, conceal their horses, leave a man on picket, while the rest went in and enjoyed the good food that had been prepared for them.

Often it was food that had been taken from some other family, or from the supplies that had been, by Knight, confiscated from our destitute Confederate soldiers.

Many had "no truck" with Newt, or for that matter, with any man that was suspicioned of being a member of his band. These were the good people who were the hardest hit of any, because if they were lucky enough to have anything at all, after dividing with the Food Gatherers, as the men who gathered supplies for the army were called, then the Yankees would surely come to take that, and if they were not directly in the path of the invaders, then Newt's men would swoop down upon them and take the remainder.

Down on Rocky Creek there lived a man named James Oliver Cheek. He is affectionately remembered as "Uncle Pone." He was one of the volunteers from McLemore's Station, and was off to war, leaving his family with a good farm, plenty of livestock, and there should have been no need of his worrying about their welfare. But he could not know what would befall a family that lived beside a public road in a country that was to be overrun by three armies at the same time.

The family lost everything they had in the way of food and property. Every horse was ridden off, every fowl killed, all the cattle and sheep were driven off, as raider after raider came through and helped himself.

The small defenseless children were finally reduced to "pot-likker" cooked from greens, without salt, or seasoning as there was no grease. There was not a goat left for a cup of milk on the premises.

Then one evening, as the sun was setting, a lone billygoat, quivering and frightened, came up to the house. In some miraculous way, the raiders had missed him, and he was the survivor of what had been a big herd.

The children saw him and ran to open the lot gate to let him in. They would have hidden him, but he leaped upon the fence, walked it cautiously. Then from the fence, he leaped upon the lean-to shelter that had sheltered his kindred in the past, and there he stood, rebellious and inattentive, where no amount of coaxing and cajoling could make him change his mind about coming down.

About that time the mother came from the house to assist the little ones in doing something with the stubborn goat, whose value was soaring rapidly, with the knowledge that he was their last animal. Her efforts were also fruitless, and the billy looked away into the distant space, and bleated pathetically.

The family became so engrossed with the task of getting the goat down, they did not see or hear the man on a horse ride up to the gate. And it was not until he spoke and scared them out of their senses that they knew a stranger was sitting there, smiling at them. How long he had been there, they did not know, but he was highly amused at their predicament.

"Madam, I shall be happy to get the goat down for you," he said, as he dismounted and looped his bridle rein over the gate post.

"We'll kill him, and I shall wait for supper."

There was no word of protest. The stranger seemed to know his business and took the situation in hand.

Soon the goat was hanging head down, swung from the "skinnin' pole" by the "gam'lin' stick" placed through the split ligaments of his hocks, and the piteous begging and pleading he did only urged the slaughterer to greater speed in slitting his throat with a sharp knife.

The children covered their eyes in horror and ran at the sight of the fresh blood, but their craving for food soon overcame their sentiment, and they were soon happy to smell the odor of fresh meat cooking in a pot over the fire.

"Now, all that we do not cook and eat tonight, you must hide, for the raiders of the Knight Company will be along and take it from you," advised the stranger.

"You must follow my instructions. Get an old box, large enough to contain the meat, and get together some old rags, so that one searching will think that you have only a rag box under your bed. Wrap the meat carefully, and pile in the old rags up to the top of the box. Then as you and the babies get hungry, you can cook the meat for yourselves."

Together, they hid away the remainder of the goat, and the stranger warmed himself by the fire while the meat tendered in the pot.

Then he dished out portions for the woman and the children, and ate heartily himself. When he had finished, he bowed politely, and let himself out the door.

The mother and her children looked at one another, perplexed at such strange behavior, as they listened to the hoof-beats on the dark road leading away from their place.

"Who was he, Ma?" asked a small boy.

"That we shall never know," she answered, "but he must be one of the Knight Company, and he, himself, must have been a raider, but when he saw that we had nothing left but the goat, his heart must a' failed him."

"Why, Ma?" asked the boy.

"Well, didn't you notice his buttons when the light shone on him here?" she asked, her question intended for a reply to his.

"There were two kinds on his coat. One was a Rebel uniform button, and the other was a Yankee button, so he was neither one.

"His hat was black, and he had on a blue coat and gray breeches. I hear that they wear whatever they can get, if they are Knight Company, so he must a' been one."

She reflected for a moment, "And I guess they'll be back as soon as he gets to their camp and tells them that we've got meat here."

But no one came, and the Cheek family feasted on the goat in peace.

CHAPTER 9

Bold Ventures

As soon as the officers of the company were sworn in, and each had pledged himself to fight and die before surrendering to any man, a boldness took hold of the timid. And with a man already noted for his ingenuity and leadership, the group felt that they were strong enough to defy capture.

There was little fear of the cavalry, because heretofore, the search for the fugitive had been detailed to a few gentlemen who had preferred not to spill the blood of a fellow citizen, and these gentlemen had resorted to methods of capture which had been foiled time and time again, until this thing of eluding the pursuers had become a big joke.

In the bunch were men who were glib of tongue, men who were given to mischievousness and fun.

At first the men in hiding were approached by relatives who insisted that they come out and return to the Confederate army, or at least, to protect the good name of their kinsmen, join the Union forces in an honorable manner.

Three of the first to contact Newt by volunteering to do this service were cousins of the deserter. One of this group was Alpheus Knight. The other two were Dan Thomas Knight and John Knight.

In the organization were big liars who reveled in telling ungodly falsehoods. Of these were men who strived to excel one another in telling big tales of hilarious episodes. In this bunch was one Dicky Knight who was a cousin to the Captain. He was the prize storyteller, and the tales he told kept the men in high spirits.

Reasoning availed relatives nothing, so threats of bodily harm to members of the families of the deserters were relayed to them.

Dicky received word that an aged relative of his was being held hostage awaiting his surrender, and unless he did surrender, the price of his refusal would be the aged one's life.

Dicky pondered this thoughtfully, and apparently made ready to give up and march out into the hands of the waiting cavalry. But suddenly he stopped, and remarked, "Well, at the best, the old man's life won't be but a few days longer, if he dies a natural death, an' mine will be a long life, so jest git 'em word to go ahead an' kill 'im if they like, fer he'll soon die wi' ole age, any how."

A man that came near to topping Dicky's tales was Joe Gunter.

Joe's wife was the sister of Alpheus Knight. Joe was the life of the party, and his bright sayings and antics kept the others in an uproar of mirth, despite adverse circumstances, which were bound to overtake a vagabond army.

Dicky's real name was William Martin. He was of a good family, and soon after joining up with the Knight Company, he saw that he was headed for disgrace, plus disaster, and as he could not go back to the Southern army, he had no choice except to join the Union at New Orleans.

But Joe stayed on with the company until he was eventually captured. He later was liberated by the deserter band when the camp in which he was held prisoner was stormed, in a surprise move by the deserters, but even so he was not alive to see the end of the war. He was slain at the Parker Place where he had sought refuge, up on Tallahala Creek, after an attempted attack upon the supply line of the Confederate encampment at Ellisville.

Mrs. Sally Parker was one of the good women near Ellisville who aided the band, not because of her attitude in regard to secession or slavery, but because Captain Knight was her personal friend. On several occasions, he had done her service.

A short while before the war broke out, he had traveled to Enterprise and had purchased for her two slaves from the market there, and he had delivered them to her at Ellisville.

It was a task, taking time and good weather, to make trips to and from slave markets, as there were no good roads and bridges, and Ellisville was an isolated settlement, as there was no railroad nearer than Waynesboro, which was only a flag-stop. So it was quite expected for Mrs. Parker to prepare a good meal for her friend when he needed one, or provide him with a good bed, if he chose to remain overnight.

Often several of the group were entertained in her home, and she, taking such a view of the situation, felt that she was right in extending this hospitality.

Newt later told that Mrs. Parker and two or three other good women in Jones County secretly prepared big dinners for his men, where they could go in and feast without fear of capture, as it was arranged to send the cavalry in the opposite direction.

There is one story that is authentically supported, that such a feast was held, but there is no other proof of any other help by any other woman except Rachel, the Mulatto, and the help that was rendered by women who were afraid for their lives, should they refuse.

As in the case of any country that is overrun, the controlling power holds sway, and gradually, for a period of a year, the Knight Company ruled Jones County. Those wise enough to extend them favors, or to appear friendly, were the ones who suffered less from the famine that spread over the land.

No doubt loyal Confederates in Jones County suffered more from hunger and privations than did any people in any other part of the state, because of the fact that three armies actually occupied Jones County at the same time! The Union, the Rebel, and the Knight all required food, shoe leather, bedding, ammunition, and transportation.

It took about two years for the information to leak out to all those desiring to come into Jones County, so it was not until 1864 and the early part of 1865 that the band became strong enough in number and equipment to come out openly to fight the other two armies.

The deserters were not fighting for the Union; they were not fighting for the South; they were not fighting "to protect the women" but were fighting for self-preservation, "trying to keep body and soul together."

In fact, the Knight Company hated the Union as much as did any Rebel.

On one occasion, the group headed for Enterprise, after the state's capital had been removed there, in advance of the Union army, upon learning that a host of Yankee prisoners were held at that place. They went with the intention of staging a raid, and liberating the prisoners to a designated group of bloodthirsty ruffians, bent on torture.

These men were so unprincipled and case-hardened, the idea of inflicting slow and horrible death upon the helpless captives was favorably presented, and all joined in eager anticipation.

The plan was thwarted, however, when the band ran directly into a band of Union soldiers, whose objective was to destroy the railroad at Waynesboro.

This was the same Union band that the Captain later described as the band sent into Jones County to recruit them all into the Union army.

It is probably not understandable to many how it was that this party of Union soldiers happened to be waylaid by the Confederate cavalry, but the capture of the entire party cannot be credited to the Rebels.

It must be remembered that several gray uniforms were in possession of the Knight Company, and always, when the role called for a Confederate front, volunteers from the Knight Company, assigned for the part, and dressed for the occasion, could boldly walk right into any encampment. So it was on that morning when the three parties ran together at Rocky Creek.

The very men whom the cavalry were seeking were the gray uniformed men who infiltered and joined in the skirmish, and then before they could be recognized, made a getaway.

Soon hounds were on their trail, and a move such as they contemplated could not be carried out, and Enterprise, for the time, was forgotten.

All was confusion. Dogs running in circles, and barking wildly, as uniformed men were crashing through the thick undergrowth.

A horn blew. The note was long-drawn, clear and sharp; then another horn sounded in another direction, then over the hill, and away from the ghastly scene of battle, out of range of the guns, there came a strange hair-raising, urgent note, the retreat signal of the Black Horn.

The captured and wounded were carried back into Ellisville, the dead were buried, and it was these Union men, coincidently, who gave their lives at Rocky, that saved the lives of their blue-clad fellowmen, safely incarcerated in the Rebel prison at the state's third capital site.

The capital was moved from Jackson to Enterprise, from Enterprise to Meridian, from Meridian back to Jackson. Then from Jackson back to Meridian, from there to Columbus, and from Columbus to Macon, and from there back to Jackson.

Secure in the knowledge that they were well supplied with guns, ammunition, plenty of good food, good horses, and trained by the Captain to avoid traps which would surely be laid for an unsuspecting band, by loyal citizens of the county, the renegade army did not hesitate to divide into groups and openly ride over the country.

After Tap Bynum was killed in his yard, the other Bynum refused to remain with Knight and went into the Union army, joining Tisdale's regiment at New Orleans.

The fact that many men were shot down without trial by Southern officers caused many surviving relatives to become bitter toward their own army. That was exactly what the leader of the band desired.

He could enter these homes, as a friend, and be accepted.

The Knight Company felt that they were numerous to the extent that they should be feared and become too brave in this newfound prestige. They did not take into consideration the fact that other families, in their bereavement realized that if there had never been a Newt Knight, leading a deserter band, there would be no Confederate cavalry, riding up to homes, confiscating property. And these people reacted just the opposite, doubling their efforts in a renewed attempt to help the cavalry catch and hang every deserter.

The result was that no man could trust another. No man's word was accepted. Families were divided. There was brother against brother, and friend against friend. Relations between friends of life long standing were severed, never to be mended.

No matter how remote, or in which part of the county, or whether over in an adjoining county, the guerrilla band was not out of range of some person who would, even if it took walking clear to Ellisville, report their whereabouts, and soon bloodhounds would be on their trail, and a bitter struggle would follow.

A man caught did not have opportunity to stand trial, as he was automatically convicted, as it became the rule to put to death, by hanging, any man who willfully deserted the army. So it is not surprising that these men of the woods, being fully aware of their impending fate, put up such resistance in the face of such great odds.

Some of the Confederate officers were hard and unreasoning, and would not give a man a chance to speak a word in his defense but would immediately snatch him up and hang him to the nearest limb.

But frequently an officer, although his orders were to run down and hang a man, would offer to give him another chance, so it was that many who were listed on the Knight Company muster roll lived to tell the tale.

There has been much speculation as to whether there ever was a Free State of Jones County. There was.

However, the officers, self-appointed, or receiving appointment by their Captain, were on the run at such a rate, they did not have a chance to set up offices, and of course, were rendered inactive by the hot pursuit of the Confederate cavalry.

Nevertheless, the Free State of Jones had long before existed in the hearts and minds of the Knight Company. Their slogan was: "This is a Free State," and from that the county was so named in the organization of the man, Newt Knight, who set himself up as governor of the proposed republic.

Other officers in the "government" were: Jasper Collins, lieutenant governor; Bill Sumrall, sheriff; Meg Walters, deputy sheriff; Med Coats, land surveyor; Alpheus Knight, supervisor; Will Welch, supervisor and tax assessor; Ausberry McDaniel (Covington County) tax collector; and Jim Blackledge and Sim Collins, justices of the peace.

Riles Collins was chosen to write up the Constitution, and as it was a lengthy and tedious process, it was some time before it was ready to be delivered to "Governor" Knight, as he was already popularly addressed, as he was at the time, in hiding over along Leaf River.

All that these men lacked being sworn in as officers of the new government was an opportunity to come out in the open long enough to take the oath of office.

But by this time there was a strong determination to wipe out the bunch feeling having reached a new height, and the number of cavalrymen dispatched into Jones County to carry out the mission had increased to one hundred well-armed and well-mounted men. Soon that number was increased.

It has been said that the reason that the new government was not actually set up was because the war shortly came to an end, but if the record on the muster roll is followed carefully, it will be observed that some of the "officers" were captured in April 1864, a month before the date given of the drawing of the "constitution," which was May 1864.

But with Captain Knight's increased popularity, and with more and more men refusing to go into the Confederate army, the affairs of the county were in a deplorable state.

The following letter will clarify any doubt as to just what the conditions were in Jones County during the absence of the law-abiding citizens.

By permission Mississippi State Department Archives and History
A LETTER FROM JONES COUNTY, COPIED FROM
MISSISSIPPI STATE ARCHIVES, GOVERNOR'S PAPERS,
SERIES E, VOL. 65

Ellisville, Jones County
June 14/64

General C. Clark, Governor of the State of Mississippi

Dear Sir:

I received a commission from your Excellency on the 9th of May to enrole all the citizens of my county between the ages of 17 & 50. I enroled them as soon as I could under the circumstances the Deserters having destroyed the ferries and bridges in this county and the Sense (census) Book having been destroyed I had to pound the county all over without any guide & I have made the enrolement and forward it to the Adjt. General.

It was said by several citizens that the enrolement could not be made. It was said that the deserters would not suffer it tho I passed them unmolested & I wish to call your attention to the Civil officers & this county has more civil officers at present than it ever had at one time—Outside of the Probate Court there is no business done by the Civil authorities. I have noticed that the ablest bodied men holds those offices. We have ten Justices of the Peace, & five Constables & from three to four commissioners in each Police District as commissioners for the (sic) the Destitutes where as one would be sufficient to do the business that is done. All the Civil officers stays at home and attends to there own business and the public business is unobserved. We have not had a Justices Court nor a Circuit Court for this County since the war commenced and if a man is found dead the Civil Authorities pay no more attention to it than if it was a dog & we have been runned over by the deserters but at present they are thinned out so that the Citizens and civil officers could keep them under if they would——

I am over the conscript age not withstanding I have joined a Company in Smith County for the purpose of home protection & I hope I will never be fined as I was some three months ago under the dictates of the deserters. There is at present some twenty deserters in this settlement. The main leaders of the deserters in my settlement is in the woods—

I have taken the liberty to address you a few lines in good faith. Wishing you to excuse all errors and retain the contents as I am in a settlement where I am afraid to speak my sentiments on account of the Deserters.

I remain your friend and humble servant,

B. C. DUCKWORTH

N.B.: When you read these few lines commit the same to the flaims—

B.C.D.

Just before this time, another group of men, living over on the other side of where Laurel now is, decided to organize after deserting. They also lived in a section that offered excellent terrain for hideouts, with creek swamps, through which they could venture out and travel in concealment.

As soon as Knight learned about this other group, he went over and invited them to join in with him. It was very much to his advantage to do so, for they knew more about that part of the country than he did, and especially about Tallahala, on which creek old Ellisville was located. And by having these men join him, he had access to more territory, including Dry Creek.

The Blackledges, Smiths, Walters, and Reeves are the ones that came into the company from that section.

So by this time the leader had become bold in his great power, and the people in the settlements were afraid of the vengeance which would follow, should they make known that the county was completely in the hands of the outlaws.

Old men were sick at the thought of what was going on in the county.

The men who were the civil authorities were members of the deserter band, and by virtue of said offices, they could not be forced into the army by the Confederate government, as civil officers were exempt, although they were known to be secret members of the deserter organization.

It is easy to understand Mr. Duckworth's letter to the governor.

No elections were held whereby these men obtained their "offices."

There is no reason why a court of law should have been held, for out of fear, the families of the fighting Confederates kept quiet, and accepted the consequences, while the families and friends of the Knight Company feasted on the spoils of the land and were content with only the law of the band.

Old Jesse Davis Knight was an uncle of Newt, living down in the Cracker's Neck settlement, and as he was one of the bitter citizens that appealed for help, his family suffered at the hands of the deserters.

It has been said that the names of all of Captain Newt's accomplices were recorded by him, and the duties of his men set forth, just in case he should be killed. It has been said that he had never had more than 125, at any one time, and that they were all good fighting men.

What has been neglected most is the story behind the story of this most unusual organization. All were not men, as several women participated, and several negro slaves aided Newt, secretly, influenced by the "Conjure Woman" as many old slaves termed the Mulatto.

A very useful messenger for the organization was a slave named Joe Hatten, who had been purchased from the Hatten family by the Knights. Joe was personal servant to Captain Knight, and he felt that he was "in the service for his peoples."

One day as he was returning from an errand, he was suddenly caught near the deserter's hideout, up near the Knight's Old Water Mill, by an officer who had hidden his horse behind a clump of undergrowth, and had proceeded on foot.

At the sound of the negro's footsteps crashing through the brush, the soldier quickly stepped behind a big tree that grew beside the path, and as the unsuspecting one darted past, the soldier reached out from his position and grabbed him from behind.

Hatten was so taken by surprise, he could not cry out and was helpless in the hands of his assailant.

A sharp whistle brought two other cavalrymen on the run to assist in marching the captive into the deserted camp of Captain Knight.

The negro was at a loss to explain, and even if he had preferred, he could not have given them any information because he was frightened beyond speech. So a rope was produced and knotted about his neck, and he was led, as a calf to the slaughter, up under a tree with a big overhanging limb. The loose end of the rope was tossed over, and all was ready for the hanging.

"Now, tell us where the Captain is," the soldiers commanded.

There was no reply. Joe rolled his eyes, and his tongue lolled out. He would have spoken, but he was seized with a paralysis caused by the dryness of his lips and tongue, and he could not immediately regain his faculties.

"Give him time," said one, "there is no hurry. We can hold him captive and get all the information we want."

One of the kindlier of the men stepped up, and ran his finger around between the rope and the negro's neck, and was goaded to sport by the thrill of the touch of the pounding jugular vein. It was not his intention to see this poor trembling fellow hanged, but he was enjoying this as would a cat playing with a mouse.

After commanding Joe to sit down, the rope still about his neck, another of the three offered him a chew of sweet Navy. But Joe weakly shook his head. A chew of tobacco would have finished choking him to death! Now was no time to enjoy the sweet pleasures of this life; now was the time to pray, and regaining his speech, he availed himself of the moment's opportunity. He dropped on his knees, and his shaking voice was raised in anguish, as he implored his Maker to grant him deliverance.

The three amused soldiers reverently bowed until it seemed that the negro would be exhausted, and wordless.

He promised the Lord that he would never again serve Captain Knight, if his life could be spared.

"Close your prayer, Joe," commanded one of the soldiers.

"We must go on with the hanging."

The negro begged piteously, but he was yanked to his feet, and again the rope was tossed over the limb.

"Now, Joe, it is now or never. You take us to where the Captain is, or we hang you," said the hangman.

Joe was most anxious to promise anything to get away from this situation.

"You are to take this message to him, and we will follow you. And after you have delivered it to him, you are to return to your master. If we ever catch you away from the plantation again, you are a dead nigger!"

"Yas Suh," replied Joe, as the rope was loosened, and the order to surrender was placed in his hand.

Although the black boy's power of speech had failed him, his benumbed legs were responding to his needs, and he leaped into the brush and was gone before the soldiers could mount and follow in pursuit.

Knowing the country as he did, he had no trouble losing them, as thicket, briar, and quagmire befriended him, as he bounded like a rabbit over the miles that stretched down to where the Captain was waiting at Horse Shoe Lake. He did not pause, but tore through the rough country without stopping until he had this message delivered.

But there was no one near to whom the Captain could surrender, had he been so inclined.

Newt could barely read script, as he had been taught to print, so he worked his mouth, and his eyes gleamed as he deciphered the order to surrender.

The cold blue of his eyes became warm and bright with humor, after the laborious reading. He carefully folded the message, took off his hat, and slipped it under his hat band. Then he let out a hideous laugh, which frightened the already half-frightened-to-death Joe out of his remaining wits, as he lay panting on the ground at the Captain's feet.

He put his hat back on his head at a rakish angle, lifted the horn to his lips, and blew upon it, three short blasts. He sat down on the ground at the foot of the tree and leaned his back against this forest giant, and waited. No sound. All was still as midnight, except for the tinkle of a distant cowbell, and the heavy breathing of Joe, who had fallen into a sound sleep.

In a few minutes, a horse nickered nearby. There was a slight rustle of the dry grass, and a stick broke with a sharp crash.

Single file, from nowhere, appeared six men, with guns drawn, in answer to the Black Horn.

"Gittin' keerless, men. Never step on a dead stick. Shore give you away. Don't let me hear you agin when you come up."

He arose and listened, while they stood motionless.

"Hear the bell? That bell is on the speckled heifer of McAndrews, an' you've jest got time to kill her before them cavalry catch us an' hang us," said Newt, twisting his mouth into a grin.

"Read this 'fore you start."

He took off the black hat and removed the surrender order from his hat band, and handed it to the nearest comrade.

"Now, don't wait to gut her; jest put 'er up on yo' hoss's back, an' you can ride double on down. Can't trust a nigger too fur. He says he didn't, but he mought a' give out some information to them yaller son-of-a-bitches, an' if he did, they'll be a' combin' the woods fer us. So to Honey Island we're headed!"

Another of the men led forth the horses, and all mounted and struck out for this hideout down near where Leaf River and Big Black merge to form the Pascagoula.

This was the hideout that Newt used when he tricked the Union into sending him supplies, including four hundred guns.

He was cunningly deceptive in his tactics, and although he had no intention of joining the Union forces with his band of men, he pretended that the only obstacle was equipment and supplies, in order that they might break through the Confederate lines, but the truth is, there were no Confederate lines in that area at that time, and there was no hindrance had he desired reaching New Orleans.

By the first of April, 1864, news of the daring holdups, and cold-blooded killings had reached a source that demanded action.

That action came in the form of more horsemen than had ever ridden over Jones County before. Such was the number of gray uniformed men, Newt Knight's company was made to appear small and insignificant. These men were here to stay, in compliance with the demands of the law-abiding citizens.

It was then, and then only, that the families of the deserters were so badly mistreated. Then their lot became more unbearable than that of the Confederates who had been robbed and starved out the year previously.

The band broke into small numbers, which scattered out, where they could warn other groups, and in that way, the cavalry was outwitted, never knowing if all the members of the company were hidden in the thick woods, or if it were only a small band.

So unskilled were the soldiers in fighting guerrillas, the Confederates lost heavily, and were as often on the retreat as were the Knight Company.

CHAPTER 10

The Sadness of War

The people of Jones County prayed for peace as the conflict continued on into 1864. Loved ones hoped and prayed for the return of the men who were fighting for the Southern way of life.

Those who were the most heavily burdened were those who had members of their families serving with the Confederacy and other members who refused to fight and had disgraced the family name by joining the deserter band with Newt Knight.

Albert and Jesse were the only brothers of Newt who joined him, and their parents were grieved over the thought of their sons who were known as outlaws, and upon whose heads there was a price.

The older two brothers of the family were killed, together, in a terrible battle near Atlanta, where they were rushed as replacements. They were preparing a breakfast, which was to be the last cooked meal before they were to surge forward in a bold attempt to stem the fury of Sherman's celebrated march.

The Union forces were better equipped than were the Confederates. And, although the regiment, march weary, footsore, and tired, were pausing beneath the cover of a wooded hill for the necessary food, at early dawn, they were within range of the thundering cannon and blasting guns of the enemy.

The approach had been toward the rear of the Confederate lines, under cover of darkness. There was no warning lull; the din of battle beat upon their ears, and then, suddenly and furiously, the Blue line broke through the sagging bloody front, and a new, to this group of replacements, weapon was brought into use by the foe.

The little Gray regiment was wiped out of existence, all captured or killed by the "minnie balls," as this new missile was called, which battered them down with spheres of steel.

John (Wosten) Ellzey came home at the end of the war, to tell how the Knights and Jim Langston were left dead along with countless others, dead and dying on Georgia's gory ground, amid fallen horses, broken wheels, scattered rubbage, and burning wreckage of what had been a proud regiment.

News came, weeks later, of the terrible disaster, to the parents of the fallen Knights, whose gray heads were bowed in grief and shame.

Bravely said old Albert, "Livin' trouble is wors'n' dead, for the dead can be buried, but ah! the livin'! It's the living trouble that's a killing us! We never know when to expect the worst. We know that our son will soon hang by the neck, like the criminal he is" (meaning Newt).

And so, the terrible grief and worry over his family, the group of sons who had chosen such different paths, soon took from the old man the desire to live, as he had been an honorable Jones Countian all of his life. He could not bear the Black Sheep's waywardness, which he felt had heaped disgrace upon him, and the name. Consequently his frail old body was laid to rest beside that of his father in the family graveyard.

Although the negroes were liberated by Abraham Lincoln's Emancipation Proclamation, most remained in servitude until after the last shot was fired in Texas. And it was well that they were near, as it was almost impossible to find anyone to dig a grave. That is, among the people who were not of the deserter families, so the task of burying his master was left to old Jordan, a faithful slave.

Learning of the old man's death, the cavalry kept watch around the home, in hopes that Newt would appear to see his father's burial, for it would be only natural for him to come up for the last rites. But they were disappointed, as there was not a deserter present.

Other old and honorable men were experiencing the same thing that put old Albert Knight in his grave. Yet many were stronger in body and spirit, and determined to live to see the South win the war.

Just over in Covington County lived a handsome young man by the name of Daniel Reddoch. He was an adventurer that fell in with the Knight band, although his kinsmen were all staunch Confederates, and the name of Reddoch tops the list of honorable men of Jones County, but this young one was as wild and daring as they come.

His old grandfather wept for shame when he learned that the boy whom he had reared to be a gentleman had turned outlaw. He impetuously exclaimed, "I have kept him, and I've fed him since he was a babe, and I loved him as mine, but now I would see him starve before I'd give him a bite."

The old man's expression of contempt for the young one was overheard by one not trustworthy, and soon the very words which his grandfather had spoken were relayed to young Daniel.

He was riding through that part of the country soon after, with a gay group of the bunch, when he happened to remember what his grandfather had said. He suddenly reined up his horse and remarked to the others, "My old Grandpa says he'd see me starve before he'd give me a bite. Come! We must have fun. Tonight we dine with him, or he dies! If he refuses to feed us, then we will take him out and kill him."

So they turned their horses in the direction of the old gentleman's house and were soon riding up to the front gate.

It was April, and full spring of the year, but the wet season had brought on a cool snap.

Inside the Reddoch house a bright fire blazed upon the hearth, kindled there to dry out the dampness. Before it sat Uncle Jim, as he was affectionately known. He was old, and alone with his thoughts about the war, and about his son who was wounded yet fighting against his captain's orders.

So engrossed with his thoughts, and also slightly hard of hearing, he paid no attention to the horses' hooves, as the ruffians approached over the soggy ground. He sat with his white head bowed in meditation, and it was after the riders had dismounted and were upon the threshold that he was aware of their presence.

He arose, at once recognizing Daniel, and in his gladness to see the wayward one, he seemed to forget for the moment that this also was a deserter. His being a tolerant and forgiving nature, he welcomed the strangers with a great show of hospitality.

"Daniel, my son, you are welcome," he cried. "Set to the fire, and dry your damp feet, whilst I go summons the cook, for I know you've not had your supper."

It was late, and the slave woman had long before retired to her cabin in the back yard.

All the family were asleep in their beds upstairs, and there was not a stir.

The old man carried a tallow candle, but outside there came a gust of wind, and he was left in the dark. Having walked to the cabin door so many times, he was familiar with the ground, and it was almost as if he knew just how many steps to take to reach Aunt Ceily's door.

Inside the darkened cabin, the sound of even snoring rose and fell. Then a tired groan.

Uncle Jim knocked.

"Ceily! Oh Ceily, up!" he called. "We've got visitors for supper."

No anwser. Another groan, and a big yawn from the other side of the door.

"Ceily!"

"Oh, yas Suh, I'se a comin' Masta," answered the sleepy woman.

When Ceily entered the kitchen, her eyes popped wide with wonder when she saw that the visitors were the outlaws. But not a word, or an ejaculation escaped her black lips. She set about frying ham and eggs, and set it before the men, who laughed and joked as if they were invited guests.

Mr. Reddoch tactfully avoided the subject of war, and the conversation was steered to pleasant subjects.

The hungry men ate hearily of Ceily's good hot food, then pushed back their plates, and arose from the table, following Daniel's example.

"Now, since we have eaten, we must go," said Daniel. "Old Man, your spirit of hospitality has this night saved your life.

"We came here to kill you, but since you gave us the best you had, you shall live—and I shall be back—"

With that they hurried out the door, mounted and rode away, but Daniel did not come back.

The rising waters had cornered in the six deserters on the dry land between the mouth of Cohay and Leaf River, and in that little area they would have stayed, had not a group of Lowry's cavalry happened also to be marooned in the same territory.

At that time a man by the name of Grantham, who lived on the little branch, since known as Grantham's Branch, was a member of the company, and was at home. The mission of alerting Grantham was assigned to young Reddoch. He boldly rode his horse up the Monroe Road to a point some three-quarters of a mile from his grandfather's house, and it was there that he ran into the men who had orders to bring him in, dead or alive.

Daniel raised his gun to shoot, but he was not quick enough on the trigger. The entire party all fired at the same instant, and Daniel fell dead off his horse.

The wounded animal tumbled on top of him, rolled over and was killed also by the cavalry, on the morning of April 15, 1864.

To be exact, the date of Daniel's dishonorable death at the hands of the cavalry, was one year from the date that his grandfather had received the following letter from his son, who fought on, doggedly until the end of the war.

1863

March, 27

Enterprise Hospittle

Dear Father and Mother:

I avale myself of the present opportunity to drop you a few lines to let you know that I have not forgotten you yet. Hoping these few lines may reach you safe and in dew time and find you boath enjoying the best of health.

Dear Father and Mother my jaw is not well yet; it has cured up on the outside but runs on the side, and is still swollen up and pains me a good deal yet. It seems like they intend to keep me in the Hospittle; I have tried to go on several times to the company but they want let me go; I tried to content myself here to stay untill they get ready to send me off; and that may be next week or it may be a month yet. I would like to come home to see youall before

(*page two*)

Farewell for awhile

I go away if I could but I see no chance to do it; and do not want you to grieve after me for I hope the time is soon comeing when we can return to our respective homes and loved ones in peace; and Oh what a happy day that will be for us if we can only live to see it. I saw an old man today on his return from Vicksburg and he told me that we had seven of the Yanky's gunboats hemed up in Deer Creek; and had sent the timber in the river so that they could not get out either way and was likely to take the boats and men and everything that was on them; and he also said they're scurmishing up there every day; that is about all the war news I have; Dear Father assist my folks all you can; give my love to all inquiring friends and receive a good potion for yourselves.

J. O. REDDOCH

* * * *

There were several disadvantages of being cornered on the Covington side of the river.

There were only two crossings on the main travel routes that were ferries, and the Reddoch's Ferry was the most desirable as a crossing, but it was run by Daniel's grandfather, the Reddoch who openly admitted his hatred for the Knight Company.

Mr. Reddoch's house was a big two-story structure which was built on the high ground upon a little creek which flowed beside the public road, and was about 150 yards from the Ferry, which was oxen-powered. And he, being a staunch Confederate, was expected to refuse ferry service to the enemy.

He did not remain on duty all time, as when night came, it was the custom for "honest men to be abed, and rogues on the prowl," but as a convenience to the late traveler, there on either side of the river stood a post, and to it was attached by a leather string, a conch shell, which the traveler, wishing to be ferried across could blow upon, and summons the ferryman.

No amount of signaling would arouse Mr. Reddoch after dark, after it was generally known that the outlaw band was at large, so these members, being cut off from their comrades, were obliged to ford the stream under most unfavorable conditions, even during treacherous flood stage.

It has been the opinion of many that Daniel would have slain his grandfather for this reason, rather than for the reason he stated to the men who dined with him on the night before his death.

Down at the other ferry resistance was not so strong, but then, that was miles below, along the Porter-Welch Road, and would make it necessary to cross and come up through Cracker's Neck, on up through the Hebron settlement to reach the old Knight stomping ground, and aid and information from Rachel and those with whom she had formed an allegiance.

Finally, the band took over the Reddoch's Ferry entirely, and when they saw that such act was to be their undoing, destroyed it completely, and there was no crossing left intact. The dugouts and flatboats were the only means of crossing the river.

Tucker Gregg was the first picket to be shot and killed in the opening campaign of April, and as he was deprived of the opportunity to notify the six men who rode with Daniel, they were not aware of the fact that Lowry's men were scattered to points of advantage all along the west bank of Leaf River.

They got Tucker on the 11th of April, and he had been dead four days before Knight received news of what had happened to him. The company realized that they had made a mistake by staying on that side, but the danger had appeared greater, and they were afraid to take a chance on the other side, knowing full well that swarms of men were awaiting them there.

After the encounter in which Daniel Reddoch was killed, all the others made it down to the Welch Landing through the swamp, except Thomas Yates and the three Whiteheads.

In some miraculous manner they escaped the cavalry who tracked them to the crossing, crossed behind them, and headed on up through Hebron to join another group that had hidden in Mason Creek swamp, near Newt's old home.

The Captain and the Colemans had ventured as near as they thought would be reasonably safe, trying to reach the negroes of the Knight plantation for help, which they were badly in need of, as they had been on the run for many hours, but before they could contact any source, they were hemmed in by another cavalry group, and it seemed that no one of them would escape alive.

There were two Colemans, actively in the company.

Sil was the young one who joined in with the Knight in answer to the call of adventure, not because he was wicked by nature but because the tales of song and dance, and of the care-free daring lives of the men who rode over the hills, filled him with a restless longing, and he found himself wishing to be one of them.

But the other one was the real fighter, bloodthirsty and savage. His name was Nobe Coleman. Had he been more discreet, his life would probably have been saved, as it was not the desire to kill or hang the deserters until after this particular month of April, but he was hot-headed and trigger-fast, and had not the judgment or the winning personality of the other Coleman.

At the time Newt was trying to contact the other men near Mason, Nobe was doing lookout duty. When he heard the cavalry coming, he did not have time to sound the horn to scatter the men from the area, so he impulsively dropped down behind a big log that conveniently offered concealment. He rested his gun-barrel up on the top of the fallen tree, and as the riders passed right before his gunsight, the temptation to shoot was too much. He singlehandedly attacked the party, and was captured after the first Confederate soldier fell off his horse.

He was offered a chance to return to the Confederate army, and for answer he said, "Hell, no. I'll shoot you every one. I'll shoot every chance I get as long as I live."

But he didn't live long. Right there and then, he was swung up to a nearby limb, and his neck was broken.

The company was one more man short when the call of the Black Horn was answered.

The next one caught was poor Sil. He was not given a chance because of the behavior of the other deserter by the same name.

The officers tied a rope around his neck and led him up on the high hill overlooking Mason Creek, to the churchyard there, and strung him to a great oak limb. They left him hanging there, lifeless and cold, and started back towards Ellisville, thinking that they had rounded up all in the vicinity at the present time.

There was a nearer cut-off to the Knight plantation, as one could cross Mason further upstream, on a foot log, without having to cross over the bridge on the long winding trail below.

Ben Knight was at home on a furlough, and carried his credentials in his pocket, on the same afternoon of April 15th. He decided to walk up to visit his relatives in the Knight settlements above Mason near Mt. Olive church before he returned to duty. After the long walk, he used the cut-off path to save time and distance, not aware of the deserters' presence in the neighborhood, nor trying to avoid the cavalry, but as he was off the main road, and crossing the log when they saw him, they thought that he too, was a deserter, trying to escape.

They rushed to him, and without giving him a chance to produce his furlough, looped the rope about his neck and dragged him on up to the churchyard where they had left the body of Sil Coleman.

The dogs bit and tore his legs, as the soldiers dragged him mercilessly by the neck to the place of hanging, which was more than three hundred yards from the creek.

Ben unfortunately bore a strong resemblance to his cousin Newt, and the men, having seen Newt once at a distance, felt sure that they now had the leader of the deserter band. That is why poor Ben was persecuted without mercy, why he was not given a chance to prove his identity.

The hounds continued to bark furiously, and licked the blood from Ben's fresh wounds, as if he were a wounded animal which they would devour.

By the time they reached the appointed tree, Ben was practically dead from the rope having cut and bruised his neck. His eyes had almost popped out of his head, as he lay there, covered with blood and the dirt from being dragged over the ground, yet he held on to consciousness and tried to speak.

He was roughly seized and jerked to a standing position, and as the rope was readjusted, it became loosened until the poor victim managed to murmur, "Water!" His persecutors laughed in his face, but the Captain silenced them and told Ben that he could have a last chance to pray, but his request for water was denied.

Captain Lowry saw that he was almost gone and removed the rope from his neck.

Ben begged the Lord to let water spring up into his grave after his death, as he was not permitted to have a last drink. That was all that he asked.

Then the rope was again placed about his neck, and he was hung to the same limb beside the body of Sil Coleman, who was still hanging limp and lifeless. As he was drawn up, with the noose tightening about his throat, other soldiers ran up and kicked and abused him and spat upon him.

As soon as Ben was dead, other soldiers, by their Captain's orders, cut down his body, and the body of the dead deserter hanging beside him, and threw them onto an oxcart, and drove on up the creek to the house of Serena.

She was back of the house, down at the wash-place in a bend of the creek, and the sound of the battling stick, whipping the dirt out of the clothes, as she wielded it to the block, drowned out the sound of the grinding wheels of the approaching cart, and she did not hear them come up into the lane at the front of the house.

By the time that she discovered that she had visitors, the soldiers had unloaded the two dead men, and were in the act of stretching them out, side by side, on Serena's front porch. When the shocked woman walked around the house, and saw the bodies, the captain bowed politely and announced, "Madam, here is your husband. You will be obliged to bury him."

"My God, Man, that is not my husband," cried Serena. "That is one of the soldiers. That's old Uncle William's boy, Ben, that you've hung by mistake. Ben is only a second cousin to my husband. You have hung the wrong man!"

Then Captain Lowry searched the dead man, and found the furlough in the pocket of his coat.

The cavalrymen were ashy-faced and silent as they looked at one another and then back to the dead Ben on the floor, but it was too late, and the deed could not be undone. So they jumped on their horses and headed for the post at Ellisville, where they were stationed.

No assistance was offered the family. And as Newt was in hiding, and Morgan was dead, old Albert was dead, and all the other men were fighting on the battlefronts, there was nothing Serena could do except summon her small negro, put him bareback astride a mule, and send him to deliver the death message to Ben's aged parents, and his young widow.

The grief-stricken family followed the negro boy back on foot, as their last horse had been confiscated by the deserters.

The mother and wife came crying, and wailing and wringing their hands, as they walked up the dusty road.

As they were passing the old Duckworth place, the mistress of the house was called by her slave women, and in answer to their call, she rushed out to see what was happening to her neighbors. When she learned of the tragedy, and that they were going to claim the body of their dead, she noticed that they had not, in their grief and shock, remembered to bring linens with which to wrap the body for burial.

She called the slave girl, Elsie to go into the house and bring clean white sheets and give them to the distraught mother, who after washing her face, and taking a cool drink which another slave girl brought, started again on the long journey to Serena's house.

The Duckworths went along too, and when they arrived, many other women and children were there, but there were no able-bodied men.

Negroes, wide-eyed and open-mouthed with horror, hovered in little groups about the yard, under the trees, but it was young Taylor, Newt's fifteen-year-old brother who assumed the task of digging the grave for poor Ben. The negroes were too superstitious to be of much assistance, and it took persuasion to get any help out of them.

There was no such thing known then as preserving a body, and burial became necessary before purging from decomposition set in, so Ben was wrapped for immediate burial in the Duckworths' sheets and placed in the crude homemade box which served as a casket that young Taylor and the negroes had made with his grandfather's tools.

Many veracious people were there to witness the miracle for which Ben had prayed, and although it has become a legend that many disbelieve, it must have been a fact.

The Mount Olive graveyard on the high clay hill was the burial site, well-drained and dry in any season, making it a hard task to dig a grave in dry weather, but as soon as the grave was ready to receive the body of the innocent soldier, a clear spring of water bubbled up into it, which could not be dipped dry, so rapidly did it become refilled by the underground stream.

There was no funeral. There was no preacher, but Ben's own old father offered the prayer of supplication, calling upon the Almighty to deliver them from such oppression.

Then the crude box was lowered to become saturated in the cold spring that flows until this day.

CHAPTER 11

The Avengers of Ben Knight

As soon as the darkness permitted, Rachel was on the trail to the appointed place, with news of Ben's death and burial.

When Newt was informed of the sad circumstances leading to his kinsman's hanging, he was determined to rally together his forces and march upon the town of Ellisville, although he knew that such a bold attack might mean suicide. But this thing had come to a pretty pass, when an innocent soldier could not visit his family or friends without being snatched up and hung by the Confederate cavalry.

The attendants to Ben's burial had long departed, and a still sad quietness had settled over the countryside. There was the gentle shrouding of the spring fog to shield the movements of the remaining deserter band.

The black-bearded one stood silent, and as still as the night, working his mouth and contemplating their next move.

From what Rachel had said, the men who had so wrongfully slain poor Ben were out of the country, with tails tucked like dogs who had killed sheep, betraying a great trust. The thought made Newt sick "at his stomach," and he knew that now, there was no turning back. He had promised the ignorant and the innocent that he would bring them peace, yet he had done nothing except congregate a great number of men to be fed.

Stepping out into the open, he lifted the Black Horn to his lips, and the Mulatto who stood near, to do his bidding, shivered, as the notes filled the air with that plaintive urgent sweetness, for which it had become known to every deserter within a radius of miles, for that strange quality of tone had a carrying power that enabled the men to understand for miles around that they were urgently needed.

The three short blasts were at first blown with a tenderness, as would be the tone used to awaken a sleeping child. The three blasts were repeated, this time louder, as if the sleeping one might not have heard the first summons.

Soon the brush was cracking with the stealthy steps of men who were answering their leader's call.

At least a dozen men emerged from the darkness, ready to carry out the oath to do or die.

"Men, listen carefully," commanded Newt, dropping his country vernacular and setting forth the facts in a clear and coherent manner.

"We cannot let Ben's murder, for that is all you could call it, go unavenged. We must leave a few men on the other side of the river for there is still a group of the cavalry there, thinking a bunch of us are still in hiding over there.

"They have no way of knowing that there are none of our band, except the Whiteheads, and I have left them orders to remain in the swamp until all is clear to the Devil's Den. Then they are to proceed there, and lie safely until we return."

So it was that the party who were known as "The Avengers of Ben Knight" set out for Ellisville.

The word had reached Rachel that the same men would return to the swamp again the next day, to hound out and capture the rest of the gang, so Newt decided to beat them at their own game.

He dispatched this party to Rocky Creek, near Ellisville, before the next day's sun was up, and they were waylaying the cavalry, when about fifty of them came riding over the trail, with lusty voices raised in song, as their spirits soared with the rise of the morning's warmth, forgetful of the horrors of yesterday.

All at once, and to the surprise of Lowry and his men, Captain Knight and his deserters rose up out of the creek and started shooting.

The leaders of the march started falling off their horses before it could be determined from which direction the shots were coming.

There were shouts and screams of pain and fright, as horses and riders were piled up along the trail.

The group bringing up the rear turned their horses, and raced back towards the post, as this was no ordinary foe but appeared to be a phantom army, showering them with a barrage of powder and lead.

There were fifteen dead Confederate soldiers, and three fine horses, besides a great number of wounded men and mounts, after the smoke had cleared, following the Rebel retreat.

This April battle at Rocky was the second major engagement in which the company had participated in Jones County.

It was at the time of year when the thoughts of men should have been beautiful; when all nature had responded to the whisper of spring, and there along the swift bubbling little creek, the handiwork of God was manifested in the full glory of the blossoming woodland, where the pink swamp honeysuckle and the white dogwood were by Him arranged, as if by the hand of a meticulous artist, into gorgeous bouquets of pink and white against a background of varying shades of green and gold; where the intrusion of war, or even a symbol of evil was sacrilegious and entirely foreign in that setting of peace and indescribable beauty.

After the battle a stillness settled over the land. The palmetto and green lichen covered ground bore the sign of the trampling of plunging and rearing horses, and in the deep tracks left by the bogging of hooves, muddy water oozed up and was mingled with the blood of man and beast.

Heretofore, there had been no such close call, because after the first interference by the Confederate cavalry, it was agreed that all men would seek first to avoid bloodshed, and would fight only when cornered.

It had not been the intention of the Captain to kill his cousin who was sent to persuade him back into the Confederate army, but when one word brought on another, and the hot blood of the loyal Knight was aroused, and instead of persuading, he threatened, Newt started firing, tearing up the ground at close range, near his kinsman's feet. Had not the bluff of Leaf River afforded shelter, John Knight would have been killed.

But as luck would have it, he saw that his only chance of escape was the river. He threw himself over the steep bluff of the stream and landed with a splash into the dark waters where he was forced to swim for life.

Embarrassed and humiliated, he returned to headquarters and reported that his cousin, whom he was forever disowning, must be caught and hung, as would be the case were he of a less prominent family.

The result of that report was the first encounter, which was very slight, on the very date of the company organization, which was near Smith's store.

The entire company went into hiding, and it was not until November when they decided to move over into Covington County that they were sighted by a mounted officer, as they were crossing an old field near the Levi Valentine old place.

There were a few shots exchanged, with no one killed or wounded. And with the advantageous knowledge of these men of the woods, the cavalry was soon out-distanced.

However, fast horses and bloodhounds aided the soldiers in trailing the deserters into Covington and down the swamp on the opposite side of Leaf to Currie's Creek, where there was considerable shooting and more dodging and running than could be expected from a bunch of hungry, weary men. But it looked as if luck was with the company, as not one man lost his life, whereas a number of the cavalry were wounded by snipers.

Soon tiring of such an unusual engagement, and not being sure how many men were in the Knight Company, the Rebels gave up the fight and returned to Ellisville to administer to their wounded and to secure more aid in the capture, which they felt sure would be accomplished with enough men to surround the group.

But there was no daring holdup, or crime of any kind committed by the company for a length of time, while they were making ready to assert themselves. And apparently they were forgotten by the citizens who were relieved that their government had sent in the cavalry to aid them.

With Jasper Collins desiring to call himself a Union man when he was on maneuvers with the band, Union songs were adopted. The entire group raised their voices in song as they rode along through comparatively safe territory.

"John Brown's body lies a moulderin' in the grave," rang over the countryside. And Rebel field workers' ears picked up the Yankee tunes, and righteous indignation filled the people.

"Righteous people, working for a great cause, while a worthless band roams the woods, livin' off'n' the fat o' the land," complained old Davis Knight.

"Soon, we won't have a hog left to kill. They keep missin', one, or two at a time, an' it ain't no trouble to figger out where they're a goin'."

At the end of the month, the party rode across the river, crossing at the Welch Landing into Jones County and taking to Big Creek swamp, up to the fork of the old trail leading to Indian Springs, and by way of the old Jesse Jones house, across the reedbrake from whence Rocky Creek heads, and crossing the deep hollows, they came to an open meadow, over which had grown a luxurious growth of hay, now piled high in stacks, as there had been no cattle to consume it.

The canter of feet beat a sharp thud, a kind of vibrating, hollow sound, as they entered this quiet glade.

They stopped and listened.

"Spooky, sorta," said Newt. "Hit's jest too quiet."

"No. Hit's jest natural," replied one of the Jones brothers. "This here is jest peculiar kinda country. List'n! You hear that silvery tinkling trickle, like water rushing over a rock?"

"Uh huh," nodded the skeptic one.

"Well, hit is a rock, and I'll be blamed, if I don't b'lieve that dad-blasted rock don't run clean under this whole hay field! Listen!"

He wheeled his horse, and ran him across the meadow to the opposite side, next to a thicket, and back.

Reining up to rejoin the others, he asked, "Didn't youall hear something that you never heard before?"

The others nodded in apprehensive silence.

"Well, if hit ain't a big rock that spreads out over acres, it's ha'nted ground. My old Uncle has told a many ya tale about runaway slaves, a runnin' neckid up through that water, so as not to leave tracks fer a hound to follow."

The Captain thought this last remark over, turning it over in his mind, he placed it in an appropriate niche for future reference.

"Marching Through Georgia," was struck up by the band, singing to reassure themselves that they were not afraid of the strange quietness, as they cantered over the "haunted ground," but Newt did not join in the song.

The remark of Jones persisted in slipping out of the place where he had tucked it, and already he was twisting and working his mouth with a plan that was shaping, whereby he could use that piece of information.

To himself, he said, "That's what we'll do, when we git in a big tight. We'll take to the middle o' the streams."

To the others, he said aloud, "Let's git out of here, an' ride over an' make the acquaintance of some a the men who're a trying to come in from 'tother side a Tallahala."

"Ya ain't in no hurry to leave on account a' that peculiar ground back yander, air you?" asked one of the men.

"No, I ain't superstitious," denied the Captain, "but any time it is too quiet, is the time to 'spect trouble."

He spat out his tobacco, moistened his lips. His eyes became set and motionless, almost opaque in color, as he worked his mouth, deep in thought.

The others respected the mood; by his countenance they understood, and fell silent, slowing their horses to a walk.

Those cold eyes looked straight ahead. Again he spat, and cleared his throat.

"Hit was quiet like that, back there on the 16th. (I've jotted down the date, fer them dates torment the hell outa' me) when I lost my cousins and Thom Yates to them polished button bastards—" He paused, and wet his lips with his evil tongue. "They had no business a hangin' the Whiteheads like they did. It was just because Dan was named White-head that they killed him like they did." He shook his head sadly, and continued, "If I hadn't a left them over there in the swamp, while we went off avengin' Ben, we could a helped 'em, but we can't all stay together, all the time. Hit'd be suicide, if we didn't have sense enough to scatter."

All listened attentively, but no comment was offered. They knew that the Captain was working himself into conversation, which he seldom did, unless one of his talkative moods hit him.

"I'll never forget the day that small Dan wandered up to me, an' I told 'im he wasn't old enough to be a member, but if'n he was hungry, to fall in, an' follow to the camp, an' he'd always be fed. Well, he started following at the wrong time, that morning after they got Daniel Red-doch, and we pushed out from the other side of Leaf, to run into the bunch that hung Ben, thinkin' he was me."

The horses were reined to a sudden stop. The men stiffened in their saddles, listening.

The laconic drawl of the speaker became hushed.

The sound that had alerted them was a tap, tapping like that of a cobbler's hammer, which in the imagination of the men, swelled into a booming like the sounds made by a chopping axe in a quiet forest.

The knowledge that death lurked in every shadow along every trail, kept the men on edge, and even the tapping of a woodpecker foraging for worms embedded in a dead tree chilled the marrow of their bones and impulsively brought their guns into position.

"Dad blasted woodpecker! I figured that was all to start with, but we can't ride into a trap," said Newt.

"Let's turn an' ride right back the same way we've come. We will do better to go back to thicker swamps and prepare ourselves better. We don't have enough men, nor enough horses together to stand up to 'em yet."

Note: There is a record showing that twenty-one horses were taken by the deserters from the Confederate cavalry near Reddoch's Ferry, and Newt made the statement on the record that the Confederates were taken prisoner by twelve of his men. He further states that these prisoners were by him paroled November 1864.

The men did not need to hear any more of the story of young Dan Whitehead. All were familiar with the details of that horrible episode, which occurred the day following the tragic death of Ben Knight.

The Whiteheads were cousins of Newt, men who came from an honorable Jones County family, and those old enough went first to Williamsburg and joined the Confederate army, were later persuaded to leave the army and return to join the "Defense of Jones County." With them came other Whiteheads who were Covington Countians.

When the two older ones came home, they found that there was only one survivor, and he was their young brother, Dan, who was too young to volunteer.

Their home had been destroyed in their absence, and Dan had become a wanderer, emaciated and weak from starvation, and with no place to lay his head, unless he were invited in by a kindly neighbor.

Captain Knight took in all the stragglers, and observing the slender boy's condition, he was filled with pity, so Dan was invited into the company, not as a member but in order that he might be fed in the Knight camps.

So, small Dan was happy to tag along, following along from the Covington side of Leaf River, where he had encountered the Knight on the day of Daniel Reddoch's death.

He was trying to make his way to the hideout down below the ferry, on that fateful morning when the stream was swollen by the recent rains, and as there was no ferry at the Reddoch Landing, the band were fording the treacherous stream, a few hundred yards below.

The footpath cut down through the steep bank, and it was along this secluded path that Dan and the party were ambushed by a group of Rebels, the very same group who had killed Daniel the day before.

There before the youth's amazed eyes, a bloody battle was taking place, and he was helpless to aid his friends, but disregarding the danger, he plunged into the river and was making an effort to swim to the opposite shore, where he could hit the swamps and get help from Newt's men, in hiding over there.

Sighting the lad swimming across, one of the soldiers took aim at the boy's head, but missed, as the water swept him downward, and the load of shot tore away his right shoulder, and his blood reddened the muddy water of the stream. However, the coldness numbed him, and he felt no pain, but shock at the realization that he was rendered almost helpless in the dangerous river filled him with panic, and he almost drowned from fright, went under, bobbed to the surface, again was swept down under by the swift current, to come up against the bank under a clump of willows.

The fragile pale limbs, and the tender green leaves protected from view the blond head of Dan, which was easily mistaken for a mass of foam which drifted down, denoting that the river was still on the rise.

As far as the cavalry knew, another member was taken out of the Knight Company.

But Dan clung tightly for a few minutes, trying to get his bearings and catch a breathing spell before he determined to carry out his mission. Then he pulled himself out by the strength of the left arm and set out at a lope, up the high bluff and into the swamp.

Behind him was left a trail of blood, splotching the glossy leaves with crimson. The trail was taken up by eager dogs, and Dan, too weak from the loss of blood could run no further, was overtaken by the cavalry, who were waiting at the Jones County line, having routed out the men the youth was seeking.

The other deserters made a getaway, but Dan was brought to the Reddoch's Gap where he came face to face with his brother, who had also been caught, and was awaiting a hanging along with Thomas Yates.

The men were strung up to "the hangman's limb," and the beardless youth was hung beside his unfortunate brother, without their knowledge of the other brother's death back there on the other side of the river, where he had been shot to death.

N. V. Whitehead was on picket, and was taken by surprise, so he had no time to sound his horn to warn his comrades before he was shot down at his post. That was the last of the Whitehead family in Jones County.

The Valentines named on the roll did not desert the Confederate army, along with the Welborns and Jones family, but neither were they old line Jones Countians, but lived in or near Jasper County, and were neighbors of Newt when he had lived there shortly after his marriage, but many by the same name did live in Jones County.

The Welborns were all captured except Elisha, and he ran away from the Knight Company and joined Wolfe in New Orleans.

The Welches were also captured on the same date that the Welborns were taken in, on the 25th of April, 1864.

CHAPTER 12

Preparation

The members who remained in the company were of one accord; they must prepare to withstand the strengthening of the Confederate forces, and there was only one way. They must slip out of hearing and out of sight for a length of time. "Out of sight, out of mind," and in that way they could plan attacks which would surprise the enemy, since they had, heretofore, been more on the run than in the fight.

So, being acquainted with the terrain, these members made their way back across Leaf River, keeping to the swamps clear down to the forks of Bouie and Terrible creeks, as that territory also afforded excellent hideouts.

From the date of the first Tallahala interference, there is no record of actual warfare between either group, Union or Confederate, and there were the months of January, February, and March of 1864, in which the company made elaborate preparations to take over Jones County.

Keeping out of sight of the Confederates as much as possible, these men were, during these months, receiving aid from the Union. Aid in the form of ammunition and guns delivered to Honey Island, where they were transported upstream by flatboat, and cached away in the Devil's Den.

There was a fine shipment of double barrel shotguns, and with Captain Knight's original ideas put to work, the men were soon busy creating for these guns more powerful ammunition than had been used before.

They ran rifle balls in bullet moulds. The gunbarrels were loaded with thirty-six of these bullets, with a heavy charge of powder behind them.

When this heavy charge of shot was fired into a group of the Confederate cavalry, armed only with the ordinary weapons of the day, they were forced to retreat with great losses.

There was the problem of food.

The number of men had, during these few months of unmolested quiet, increased to a multitude, and all had been promised ample provisions.

Men tiring of the conflict, and hearing that fighting was a matter of choice, were coming in by swarms.

Even the very men who had been sent into the swamps to persuade the Captain to give up his stand were joining him!

The Southern armies were becoming more depleted by the loss of men, and the replacement material could come only from the men, old, maimed, and unable to fight, and the young boys who were anxious to make the sacrifice.

So in Jones County, men who had earlier in the war remained at home were shouldering their guns and marching away to join in the struggle. That left the rest of the people unprotected and defenseless, and at the mercy of the Knight Company.

Down in Cracker's Neck Davis Knight left his family to look after their own interest as best they could. A wife with small children at her knees, and a few negro slaves, who were faithful at their work in the fields, trying hard to produce enough to keep them all alive.

Even so, they were half starving because their animals were going so rapidly, there were none left to kill, and by night, rogues carried away the bread corn and swiped the chickens off the roosts, until there were no hens left to lay eggs.

One morning when the family had been without breakfast, early in the spring of the year, they were huddled on the porch in the warm sun, waiting for the negroes to return from hunting rabbits for food, when they were startled by the approach of riders.

Getting up from her chair, the mother shaded her eyes from the sun and peered from beneath the shadow of her hand, trying to make out the features of one of the riders.

At first she thought it could be her husband returning, and her heart beat wildly in happy anticipation. But no, it could not be him! Yet there was something strangely familiar about the rider in the lead. The way he tilted his head, as if to balance himself in the saddle, the way he hunched up his shoulders.

Nearer and nearer they came. Right up into the lane. Three were strangers, men that Sarah Ann Knight had never seen before, and she was acquainted with most of Jones County's people, but the man in the lead—! "Why, that is Alpheus!" she exclaimed.

But what would Alpheus be doing here with a party of strangers when he was supposed to be with the Confederate cavalry?

Three months before, he had come in to her house, as her house was the only home he had, and he had announced that his intention was to try to locate Newt's hideouts.

The parents of Alpheus were dead, and as he was a relative, and unmarried, he was invited to make his home with this family of Knight. Here he was the same as a member of the family and was loved by Sarah Ann as if he had been her own son.

She was proud of him in the gray uniform when he had come in on this mission of seeking Newt a few months before and had expressed her appreciation of him by doing him little services, such as preparing for him his favorite dishes. That was before they had become so destitute.

The visit was pleasurable and short, too short. He was leaving, with Sarah Ann kissing him and wishing him luck.

Now, the return was so different from the departure!

Alpheus did not come inside the front gate. He did not raise his eyes to look in her direction, nor did he make any attempt to come near this good woman who had proved to be his best friend. Instead, he disregarded her presence and shouted in a loud voice, "Just go right into the lot, men, and start yokin' up the oxen."

He did not even speak to the children, who were running up to him, expecting an affectionate pat on the head.

He sullenly followed the other men into the barn lot where they were rustling the oxen out to the two wagons.

There was a double-pen log barn, with a lean-to shelter, under which were the hayracks, made from perpendicular poles, where the thin animals could nibble the straw through the cracks.

Sarah Ann had decided that it would be unwise to let them graze away from her sight, as they too would surely take missing, now that the milk cows were going, one by one. So she had stood them up for protection, and they were always in the barn, all eight of them, when not in use by the field hands. There were two yoke to each wagon.

"Now, what does this mean?" she asked Alpheus.

"I am a' borrowin' the teams fer a few days," he replied, without meeting her eyes.

Sarah Ann was beginning to tremble. She knew the truth. She knew that he had become a member of the deserter band, and now he was here robbing her in broad daylight!

"Alpheus, after I've mothered you, and you've lived here in my house, how could you?" The tears were coming, but she choked them back. She would not give him the satisfaction of seeing her cry.

He stood up straight, and unhunched his frail shoulders.

"But I am not going to take off and keep your teams. I'm just goin' to use 'em to haul some corn," he replied, looking at her for the first time, but he quickly turned in the opposite direction, avoiding her questions.

She persisted, "You know as well as I do that there is no corn in these parts to haul, so where do you think you are going to haul corn?"

"That is a military secret," he replied, and a hint of a smile flickered across his gaunt face, softening the corners of his hard mouth.

Sarah Ann shivered, although the morning sun had warmed up the earth. She bit her lower lip, and blinked hard, to keep back the tears, so she could look at the men, trying to remember if she had ever seen anyone whom they resembled. But she could not remember any family in the county with whom they might be connected, or related, judging from their looks, and manners.

Then she looked again at Alpheus. She had thought of him as being slim and "snipy," like a bird, a water fowl with sharp features, a timid bird that needed extra care and feed.

Now, she, even though shocked at his behavior, thought of him as needing, even more than ever, good food and a warm bed. In her heart she pitied him, but in her anger, she resolved to show him no mercy. Once the tears were under control, she let out on him a rain of abuse.

"I know what you're a doin'. You don't have to tell. You're a' plannin' on raidin' an' pillage!" she stormed. "Now tell me, what would you do if the cavalry waylaid you, which I hope and pray they will?"

"Oh, that would be simple," he answered, tauntingly. "I'd circle the oxen around the wagons, and get behind them for cover, and I'd kill the last one of them."

To the men he commanded, "Hurry. We've got to make connections with the other four wagons that the boys have gathered up."

"I know what you're a goin' to do. You're goin' to get our last oxen killed. That's what! Then I don't know what we're to do for bread. Oh, Lord, please spare the oxen! You've taken everything we had, and now you'd take the last!" she cried.

Alpheus paid her no mind, but hurried his men.

They were driving away. Sarah Ann followed them out of the lot, wringing her hands.

After them, she called, "Alpheus, the Chufeur patch, and the goobers that were planted down yonder in the lower field for the hogs to fatten on, do you remember?"

He dropped his head, and meekly answered, "Yes."

"Well, I turned in the hogs, and they've all been killed in the field, drug over the rows, and weren't even scalded, but have been skinned like a yearlin', and hog hides are hung up and drying on bushes and fences, and I'm without meat. Did you have anything to do with that?"

He did not answer.

"Answer me. 'Yes or no,'" she demanded.

He focused his eyes on the toe of his boot, and hesitantly replied, "Maybe some of our men did, for they try to make it mighty hard on the people who are agin the Knight Company."

Sarah Ann was left open-mouthed by his ill-concealed threat, which was her answer. She watched him turn and gallop off to overtake the men with the wagons and teams. She wished with all her heart that there could be some way in which she could contact the Confederate cavalry and inform them of the newest developments, but there was no one to send, no one to apprehend the group of men who rode along beside six wagons to Paulding to attack the supply depot there.

In some manner Captain Knight had learned that a big shipment of supplies was stored in a warehouse there and was awaiting distribution to the Confederate troops. He also knew that these supplies were under a small guard, as most of the Rebels were in the fight.

As they were nearing the outskirts of the town of Paulding, the oxen were halted, and the wagons were hidden. Leaving the oxen tied, the Captain and two or three of the fastest shooting, hardest riding of the company, boldly entered the town.

They hitched their horses to the hitching rail, in front of the saloon, and walked in like regular customers.

The Captain ordered a round of drinks at the bar, which they gulped down. Then aside to the saloon keeper, the Captain said, "I'm bringing in a party of men who will be stationed in your town. And they are not to have any whiskey until their business is finished. If one man, just one man in the bunch gets one drop of whiskey from you until I give the order, I will shoot your brains out."

"Yes Sir," was the eager answer, when the mild mannered bartender realized that Newt Knight, in person, was standing there looking a hole straight through him. The cold killer expression of those colorless eyes filled him with a vague uneasiness which haunted him for days, but the request was obeyed, and the men remained sober.

Under cover of darkness, the fifteen men, besides the extra six drivers, slipped into Paulding and surrounded the depot.

The guards were captured with little resistance after they saw that the odds were against them, but the defiant officer in charge refused to surrender the keys.

The Captain walked up to him and demanded that he unlock the door and help them load their wagons. The officer flatly refused, and was promptly shot down.

"Bring an axe out of one of the wagons and we'll cut a hole in the side of the building," ordered Newt.

Soon the wagons were loaded.

An Irish family, not participating in the war, were on starvation, and just as the wagons were being loaded, this family drove up, and the Captain gave them some of the corn.

The pink streaks of dawn were lightening up the blackness of the eastern horizon, before the last of the supplies were hauled out of the warehouse, over the body of the Confederate guard, which lay cold and stiff on the platform before the locked door, which he had protected with his life. There was no interference, and the loaded wagons creaked out of town unhindered by any man.

Years later, long after the war was over, the Captain told newspaper reporters and magazine writers that he had been accused of taking many things in that daring raid, but it was only corn for himself and his army that he took, along with a few suttler things!

But here is proof that something besides corn was taken on that raid. The following paragraph is taken from an old letter that a Confederate soldier mailed to his family on Leaf River. The faded address on the envelope is: Reddoch, Miss.

March, 1864
Somewhere between Enterprise and Mobile

We had waited as long as we could to get the supplies before we set out on the long march. Many were heart sick when we learned that the Deserters had captured the shoes, as most were barefooted. Our only food to take on the march is a little parched corn; we had to start as it was looking like snow but we have stoped to rest a little before we go on. Some of the men are leaving blood in there tracks.

(*name*)

NOTE: The signature is withheld because the letter was copied without permission of the owner.

Freak weather often hits this part of the South. In late February the weather will warm up, and the sap will rise, the buds will swell, and the mayhaw will blossom out, and the birds will begin to pair off.

Then suddenly black clouds will gather, and roll out of the North.

The cattle will come lowing and seeking shelter, and the worst wintertime weather will slip up, unexpectedly, and cover the South, spewing up the ground with ice, which is often followed by a light snow that kills the budded trees.

The morning after the raid, as if in answer to Sarah Ann Knight's prayer, such luck was to befall the Knight Company.

Caught up in the ball woods away from shelter, the men were compelled to rough it like animals. But with dogged determination, they finally made it in to a hideout where the ill-gotten gains could be stored.

Two weeks later, in the early hours of the morning, just before day, Sarah Ann was awakened by the sound of grinding wheels, and the unmistakable squeak of the ox-bows.

The ice had melted, and the roads were a slush down into the Neck. As the sound came nearer, Sarah Ann got up and placed a candle in the window. Then she laid another piece of wood and a stick of kindling upon the coals in the fireplace for added light, but she did not venture out.

"If that *is* Alpheus coming back, he'll come in when he's put up the oxen," she said aloud, hoping that it was he.

But Alpheus did not come in to face his friend.

She waited, and all became quiet except for the bumping of the oxen's horns against the hayrack's poles.

Soon the gray streaks of morning appeared, and Sarah Ann was out in the early light to see if all the animals had been returned.

They were all there, standing hunkered under the shelter, gaunt from starvation, and weak and weary from the long trip, worsened by the weather. But the knowledge that they were alive gladdened the woman's heart.

She looked into the wagon beds, and there, clinging to the cracks in the flooring, were a few corn silks, but there was not a grain left to show that bushels and bushels of corn had been hauled.

There was a slight stir in the hayloft.

Sarah Ann peeped in, and there sprawled in a sleep of exhaustion lay Alpheus. He opened his eyes and smiled at his friend.

"Why didn't you come in and go to bed, like you always did?" she asked kindly.

"I didn't feel that I had a right," he replied, honestly.

"Did you get the corn?" she asked.

"Yes," came the answer.

"Well, what did you do with it? You shorely didn't give any to the oxen, er they'd not be so hollow. They look like they've been gutted."

"We gave it all away to families who are in need of bread," he answered.

At that very moment there was not a piece of bread in Sarah Ann's house, but she proudly squared her shoulders, and walked rapidly into her kitchen where she started a warm fire for her children.

To herself she said, "Well, at least we shall starve honorably. I couldn't eat stolen bread, anyway."

* * * *

Over in the eastern part of Jones County, another group of men organized and rebelled against the Confederacy, and these men were actually laying out of the war because they were of the opinion that it was a rich man's scheme to hold his slaves and let the poorer men do the fighting.

They were not willing to leave any one man at home, and the 20-negro law became a hated thought, because the rich could avoid military service by its enactment.

These men could have been excused, perhaps, had they not joined Newt Knight. When they all came in with him, the number to be fed was seventy-five, and that was every day, besides the numbers who were constantly visiting in the camps and plundering the country.

There was the Hawkins Water Mill bunch from up in Smith County, and the followers of the Reverend Augey, from up in Lauderdale County, and other stragglers who came in and out of Jones County, at will.

The men coming in from the eastern section were: Jack Arnold, Gus Lambert, Albert Blackledge, Jack Smith, Jeff Lee, Tom Holloman, R. C. Reeves, Mose Walters, Warren Walters, Blake Lambert, Jim Tiner, Jim Blackledge, Jess Smith, Morgan Mitchell, Jim Lee, Calvin Reeves, W. T. Temple, and Dan Pitts.

(Since it is a provable fact that names appear on the Captain's muster roll, of men who did not actually serve with him, it is presumed, and has been claimed, that some of these men entered his company for espionage purposes, and it is a pity that it is not known just which of these men were responsible for the final defeat of the organization.)

The Confederate officers were informed of all the hideouts, and with the exception of the three months of preparation, the deserters were never given a moment's respite, until the band was entirely wiped out.

When the eastern group joined Knight, they brought with them information that he did not have, of a hideout equal to the Devil's Den.

This location was behind a big bluff on Mill Creek, in the edge of the swamp. It was thickly swamped on each side, with a heavy dam and a big pond out in front, and near the water was a big hole under the bluff, large enough to accommodate seventy-five or a hundred men.

In this hideout under the bluff were beds, and a place to cook and eat. They could remain in this place indefinitely, in rainy or bad weather.

Although this place was known to the officers of the cavalry, they would not attempt to enter it, because it was so located that a few men could slaughter an entire regiment without losing a man.

This was one of the most desirable storage places the company had, as food was the first requirement, and with the increasing numbers coming in as members, the raids were intensified.

That is what caused all Jones County to hate the guerrilla band; not because they were slackers, refusing to fight for their country, but because of the menial tactics employed for self-preservation.

Not only did they steal horses and provender, but they waylaid ammunition wagons as supplies were sent over land. As soon as they learned that supplies were coming through the locality, they would place themselves at an advantage and would pounce down, like vultures, on the unsuspecting drivers and take what they had.

Usually, the driver was left dead beside the road, the wagons burned, and the oxen slaughtered for food.

The oxen also provided the Knight Company with material for shoes. A hide was never left on a dead animal, but was removed from those slaughtered and preserved by a crude tanning process.

An ordinary hole of stagnant water of the proper depth was easily converted into a tanning vat, and the walnut hulls supplied them with the necessary tannic acid.

So, with Newt's skill, a fine piece of leather was produced, which was softened and made pliable by the application of tallow, which was scraped with knives and worked into the hides.

The company kept divided into small groups, unless they were bent on mischief that required a number, and operated as single units, with not more than six or eight in the party.

Every account of their activity is limited to a small band. In fact, most of the men whose names appear on the roll were simply deserters, in hiding, and did not wish to interfere with, or to be interfered with by, anyone choosing to live a free life unattached to any group.

On one occasion, when, according to the Captain's own words, they were to hold up an ammunition train, he could secure only a small number to tackle the Rebels. He took the few who were game and stationed them at strategic points in the woods and near the trail over which the wagons would pass.

As soon as the wagons were entering the thickest part of the swamp, through which the trail led, it was arranged to set off a big blast of powder, away to the right, and before the explosion had died down, to set off another to the left, and then even another, up ahead, and in front, and another, simultaneously, behind the wagon train. Then before the drivers could recover from the surprise, the toughest of the men were to ride out from cover of the timber, shooting wildly and blowing furiously on their horns, which each carried, as if summoning to the attack an entire army.

The drivers threw up their hands and surrendered.

The bandits rushed the wagons, while the leaders disarmed the drivers and took over the teams.

Left bound and gagged beside the road, the victims realized, to their chagrin, that the holdup was accomplished by less than a dozen men.

That single raid yielded enough powder and lead to stock the hideouts for the duration of the war.

The guns were the articles most needed. The company had repeatedly raided homes in search of firearms.

Once the Captain sent a courier to the Union post at New Orleans, with a request for four hundred rifles, on the promise that he would join the Union army, if from them he could obtain enough war material to protect his men through the Confederate lines. That promise was not made with any such intentions, but the Union fell for the scheme and promptly sent the rifles, which were captured by the Rebels.

However, such cunning deceptions were responsible for Newt's standing in with the Union government and was what caused him to receive the provost marshall appointment for Jones County.

Many people actually believed that he was a Union man.

His own personal weapon he cherished as long as he lived. He kept the wooden stock oiled, and there was not a weather-crack in the fine old wood. The steel was polished until it shone like a new gun. It was a double-barrel twelve gauge shotgun, muzzle loading, with twin hammers, and nipples for the percussion caps, and a slender polished ramrod down beneath the barrels.

He fondly called his gun "Ole Sal," and she was his constant companion.

From the name of his old gun, the idea was presented to him for the very suitable name for the organization, "Salsbattery."

Few men were possessed with such keen imagination as was this Guerrilla King. Although he was not formally educated, he was endowed with a marvelous gift of knowledge.

CHAPTER 13

Captain Knight's Strategy

Some of the officers of the Confederate army from Jones County, assigned to the deserter chase, were Captain Worsham, Captain McGilberry, and Captain McLemore. These officers knew more about the swamps in the county, and more about how to proceed with the undertaking of capturing the Knight Company, than did the officers sent in here from other parts of the South.

There was Captain Gillis and his company, Miller's cavalry, Col. Lowry's company, Forrest's cavalry, and Lieutenant Wilson's infantry.

After the big battle on Rocky Creek, Wilson's men and volunteers, upon discovering that the impostors' uniforms were not measuring up to specifications, and noting the horns, which were a dead giveaway, did not relent the chase, and from that day forward, until the end of the year, the Knight Company was in for a continuous fight, or inevitable capture.

Realizing this, the Captain of the Knight Company sought first to kill the Jones County officers, as it was by them, and through their knowledge, that the other officers were led into the swamps and hideouts.

Headquarters were at Ellisville, and as a special courtesy, the officers were invited to occupy the Deason home.

McLemore was a guest there, where the men, after hard days in the woods, trailing the deserter band, could come in to hot food, a warm hearth, and a good feather bed.

McLemore was a hot-headed young fellow, who took the task upon himself, against the advice of close friends, to go into the neighborhoods where the deserter captain had friends and endeavor to learn from them things necessary to aid the Confederate cavalry's campaign.

He was warned that he was treading on dangerous ground but he refused to heed the warning.

Now that the conflict of the county officials at Ellisville was over, or, as a matter of fact, lay smouldering silently, for the time being, the Confederate headquarters, recruiting station, and the general activities of the people were carried on as in the manner of any other typical Southern town.

But McLemore had plans of his own. He went from Ellisville to the old recruiting station which he had opened on Big Creek in the old log house, and not too far from the old Pinion post office, and directly along the established travel route of the Knight Company. The one most frequently used by them when they came over from the Covington County side of Leaf by way of the Welch Landing, and headed on up through Cracker's Neck and hit into Big Creek swamp below the old burying ground and on up to the Salsbattery camp.

With Captain McLemore were several old men who were too feeble to serve in the regular army. These men were sent by him on the pretext of making a survey of the beef cattle and hogs, obtainable over the county, whereby they could gather other information.

Soon it was known at Ellisville just which families were giving aid and comfort to the deserters.

On the other hand, Captain Knight was fully informed of McLemore's tactics.

"His is the first name I've got carved on my gunbarrel," angrily commented Newt. "I have sent him word that I will tolerate no meddlin', but if meddlin' is what he wants to do, then I can stop that."

He stroked his gun stock fondly, as he twisted his mouth and sank his teeth into his lower lip.

That very night a small band slipped into Ellisville, with the intention of apprehending McLemore on the trail. But instead of taking the route he usually followed, the young Captain returned to Ellisville by the upper road, over Buffalo Hill, and the plot to kill him just before he gained the town failed.

But Newt's obstinacy knew no bounds, and when the time passed and the expected riders did not appear along the trail, he beckoned his men to follow, for he knew that he had missed his victim by taking the lower road.

The three men approached the Deason house, and outside the fence that inclosed the grounds, they paused in whispered conversation.

"We had better not lift the latch on the gate, for in so doing we might be discovered. There might be the clink of metal, or the screeching of a hinge," said one. "We shall scale the fence, and creep up to the window."

There they had a good view into the room occupied by Rebel officers. The dark silhouettes of the three moved cautiously into obscurity, fearing the light from the window, so against the outside wall they stood, immovable and breathless, waiting.

It had been a wet dreary day, and on the hearth a bright fire blazed. Before it were boots, caps and coats drying. The officers had eaten a good supper, and were conversing in pleasant relaxation.

Outside the three men huddled closer as one whispered,

"Which one is McLemore? He looked different when I saw him last," as Newt pointed in toward the smooth haired young officer.

"That's him all right. The one sittin' with his back toward us," answered another.

"Which of you wants the honor?" asked Captain Knight.

Neither answered.

From his pocket Newt drew a piece of broom straw. He fumbled in the dark, then held out to the two others his damp hand, which was faintly visible from the window's light.

"The man who gets the shortest straw shoots," he whispered.

The straws were drawn, but for some reason, the Captain did not trust the aim of the man who did draw the shortest straw, so he remarked, "I have waited a long time for this, so it would only be fair to me to just drop the straw, an' let me shoot his brains out."

The other two crept back to their mounts, and sat astride them, holding the Captain's horse by the reins, with his saddle stirrup turned toward the building, in order that he would lose no time in making a getaway.

Knight would have followed his usual procedure of shooting a man in the back, but another man, a stranger whom he had no desire to kill, was in the way, and there was no way to get a good aim on McLemore's head without also hitting the stranger.

As silent as a cat, he crept around the building, keeping his body close against the wall, until he reached the front porch. He pulled himself stealthily up over the banisters, without making a sound, and felt his way along to the darkened door. He tried the latch. Gently, it gave. He turned himself in, inch by inch without letting a hinge creak.

Once inside he froze to the wall of the deserted hall, and before there was a sound to warn the men who were laughing and talking, Newt stood in the doorway leading into the room, his aim on McLemore.

Some of the men said later that Newt stood there in the doorway, like a figure stepping out from a hideous nightmare, working his mouth, and before a gun could be reached, there came a terrible blast, and a fog of gun smoke filled the room.

McLemore half stood, clasped his hand to his heart, and screamed, "Help me!" He never knew who shot him or what happened.

The other officers rushed out of the house, some without shoes or hats, but before they could mount their horses and give pursuit, the murderer and his henchmen were well on their way to a hideout.

McLemore crumpled forward into a pool of blood, hot dead. In the confusion which followed such a brazen deed, the blood was allowed to remain too long on the floor where it became cold and set, before there was any attempt to remove it.

The superstitious claimed that it could never be removed because it was spilled by a man whose spirit was to live forever. The stain remained there on that old heart flooring for years and years, despite the fact that hours were spent through the years in a vain effort to remove the trace of McLemore's tragic death.

Servants scrubbed the wood thin with sandstone rocks, and apparently the job was well done until there would come a wet, rainy spell, and then the blood-stain would again rise like grease to the surface.

Many generations later, the spot was covered by a heavy coat of paint, and it is no longer visible, but the story still goes that the house is haunted.

When the hands of the clock reach the hour, 11 PM on the date of McLemore's death, the door to the doorway in which Newt Knight stood, swings open and promptly closes, as if by an unseen hand.

After McLemore's murder, the cavalry sent for more bloodhounds, as that was about the surest way to track down the Knight Company. There were more than a hundred bloodhounds brought into Jones County and delivered to Ellisville from other sections of the country, as feeling ran higher with news of Knight's atrocities.

Ellisville was seething with excitement, as the wagon trains lumbered in bearing such unusual and spectacular freight. The people had never before witnessed such a sight. Never had there been in this part of the country such dogs as were arriving, escorted by soldiers displaying all of the pomp and splendor of the Confederate army. Soldiers riding beautiful horses, decked out in fancy tassels, beside the army mules, hitched to the wagons laden with dog crates. Never had the people of the town experienced the excitement created by the howls, the yelping, the whimpering, that came from a hundred cooped up and restless canines! Each trying to express his emotions as an individual, each seeming to realize that he was important and was therefore deserving attention.

The dogs were beautiful. Their dark red coats glistened and shone from brushing, yet to many they appeared funny-looking, with their short legs supporting long bodies, and with their long velvety ears almost touching the ground.

It was the nose which counted, and these dogs had "trained noses," long and keen, and were supposed to be able to pick up a track hours after the quarry had passed.

In every garden in the country there grew herbs for seasoning, as every family prepared meats for the table at home. In the corners, or planted along beside a row of pansies and candytuft, there grew in the old paled-in gardens, beds of mint, garlic, clumps of sage, which had to be handled carefully, lest it crumple up and die, should a pregnant woman, or a woman during her "period" touch it. And there were a variety of peppers, peppers to be pickled, to be eaten fresh and green along with other summer vegetables, and all that was not used in that way was allowed to remain in the garden to ripen into brilliant reds, with various degrees of hotness.

The long pods were a beautiful scarlet just before frost, and were fairly smoking with heat, to be used in souse-meat and sausages.

Beside every kitchen fireplace, or out on the porches hung strings of these red peppers, dried and ready to be pulverized for seasoning.

On the big plantation that lay up on the high ground between Leaf River and Mason Creek, the preparation was the same, except the planting was more extensive. For years preceding the Civil War, ample provision was made for a multitude of people, slave people, by the good planter.

Each family was permitted to own personal property, a cow to milk, and was permitted to kill and cure meat for the tables in the quarters.

But now, with the master dead, and most of his family, there was no one to hold together these people, and the slaves who had not been given to relatives of the old man lived almost as a free people in the quarters where once old Jim's word was law.

The big house was crumbling, and the grounds were growing up with weeds, and behind the house on a hillside above a spring, there were many vacant cabins.

Rachel and her children remained. Accustomed as they had become to big gardens, when there were many mouths to be fed, a surplus was grown.

Rachel harvested the surplus, and she and her children hung long strings of red peppers about the doorway, giving it an air of festivity.

The Knight Company, realizing that their chances of being caught were increasing, with an army accompanied by bloodhounds, knew that something would have to be done to save them.

The Captain had a plan. He knew of one woman to whom he could go for advice. He sought Rachel in the dilapidated quarters.

Rachel had told tales of having helped slaves escape by the "underground railroad," and somewhere, in the back of Newt's mind, there lurked a faint recollection that he had heard her tell of helping to keep dogs off the trail of the fugitives.

Believing fully that the Captain's intention of organizing a band was to free the people, Rachel trusted him implicitly, and her exultation was evidenced by her eagerness to aid him. Her slick tongue clattered away, without fear of divulging secrets which she had kept from other men, out of fear of harm to her race.

It was not necessary to keep secrets from this great benefactor. All her knowledge was at his disposal, and if there could have been any other way in which she could have aided his men, she would have been happy in making the sacrifice, even if that sacrifice had meant giving her life.

The Captain had never been foolish enough to go, in person, to Rachel, as he knew that he would be expected to go near his old home, but he had waited while others of his men had crept into her quarters, under the cover of darkness and had given her the signal that he was near.

The call of a whip-poor-will brought the woman to her feet, and soon she was swiftly on the way to the appointed place, in answer to the Captain's request.

From late autumn until spring, the call of a whip-poor-will would have been unnatural, and would have excited suspicion, but the ginger colored woman was wise enough to foresee that, and so, the in-between months slipped by with many numerous hoot-owl cries.

No matter how late at night, or how bad the weather, rainy, or bitter cold, a "Who who who cooks f'r yu *All?*" brought Rachel out into the night.

So it was on the night after the Captain had heard that many dogs were coming into Jones County to catch him. There was no light, not even a flickering star, and all was pitch dark in the woods, but the woman knew that the call was urgent, so she quickly ran over the familiar path, unafraid in her great anxiety. The call had been repeated, three times in succession, and that meant that she must hurry.

"Did you tell me once, woman, that you knew how to keep dogs off the trail?" Newt asked, as she rushed up, breathless from speeding over the ground between this meeting place and her cabin.

"Give her time to catch her breath," demanded one of the men.

"Yes, Sir," her bosom heaved with labored breathing, "they's lots a' ways to choke a dog 'sides on butter!" replied Rachel.

The Captain's men laughed at the woman's pert reply.

"So you'd catch 'em an' choke 'em," they laughed, making a great joke of the Captain's belief in this strange half-breed.

A grunt from the leader silenced them, and they were all attention.

"Go ahead," Newt commanded.

"Well there's ways to do eny thing you wants," began Rachel, "they're things a houn' dog jes cain't stand. Pole cat musk, red pepper, an' it helps to wipe the bottoms o' yo shoes on garlic. Garlic confuses 'em, but pepper is what stops 'em. They cain't smell fer coughing and sneezin' when a handful o' red pepper, powdered fine, is dropped behind you in yore tracks."

"How much pepper can you git?" asked Newt.

Rachel scratched her head, and turned the thought in her mind.

"Well," she answered, "there's several long dry strands a' hangin' in the old Jim house, that wuz never used atter he died, but hit ain't lost hits strength yet, and' on down three cabin below, on the gallery, there's more, an' some gourds full that wuz never strung. An' I never did git all that that wuz left in the garden rows, an' hit's not hurt, 'sides what's in my house, an' what's in the Big House, where yore ole Aunt is too feeble to know er keer what she's got. I'll git you that, too, Sir," she promised.

It was arranged that a single call was to be the signal.

"Don't you be trust'n' too fer, these owls," warned Rachel.

"If'n them cavalry had a' ben a' list'n' tonight—," she paused, "why, eny fool could a' tole that warn't no owl!" exclaimed Rachel, shivering, not from the cold, but with the fear of what would happen should they all be caught.

Early morning found the hearth in Rachel's house covered by a thick layer of red peppers, drying and being readied for powder. All morning long she kept drying and powdering pepper, powdering it in the ancient pestle.

That morning the Captain did not blow upon the black horn, and he forbade any man to blow a single note.

"We must lay low, an' let things cool off," he warned.

But he sent the men, singly, back to three neighborhoods in quest of red pepper, and an order for a large supply was left with their women folk. Soon the women who were friendly with the Knight Company were equipping their men with the fiery stuff that would stall off a hound.

In Rachel's cabin, before the hearth, squatting, were three children. A hungry-eyed, lanky white boy, with sandy hair, straight, and close-cropped and clean.

An even lankier and taller black girl, with soft black eyes that were sad and expressionless. And the third child was a delicate-featured little white girl of about eight, who appeared not to belong with these strange people. A beautiful child, but she was also at the task of turning peppers. Her fair face was reddened by the heat from the hearth, as she worked, but all day long, she assisted her Mulatto mother, pausing only, to wipe the tears, and smother a sneeze which this pepper toasting job brought on.

Now and then the monotony was broken by the appearance of a black grinning face at the window.

"Go on 'bout yo business, nigger," Rachel would command, "an' keep yo big mouf shut," which admonition was entirely unnecessary.

The Captain was informed that McGilberry was in command of an entire army of trained hounds, at least fifty, and possibly more. So he gave instructions to his men to try to kill off a dog every time they could get a shot at one, as killing off the dogs became more important than killing off the Rebels.

"But kill every man that attempts to corner you. Be it your own brother, or your closest neighbor. The color of his uniform makes no difference, blue or gray, or homespun. Hit's the color uv his eyes you're to be lookin' fer," instructed Knight. "Divide, and scatter!"

"Two more names are yet carved on my gunbarrel, an' I've got to work 'em off. Me an' ole Sal is out fer McGilberry and Worsham. I hate to kill old Worsham, but he's got to have it."

He wheeled his horse and was gone.

It was breaking day, and the earth was wet with the dew, but the hour of the day was never taken into consideration when it became necessary to get a message across the country.

The Captain was beginning to lose faith in the ability of his men, and he trusted no man any more, as he felt that he had been careless in letting his men in for trouble on the Covington side of Leaf, and now, with the latest developments, he was not sure that any of the men, away from the hideouts, and without benefit of his leadership, could meet the situation.

It had bothered the Captain's conscience that he had left some of his very best friends up in the edge of Jasper County, with only three pickets. He worked his mouth and licked his lips, perplexed that it could have happened.

Salsbattery was located in one of the most desirable sections, and he had stationed R. H. Valentine on picket near the Knight's Old Water Mill in Jones County, and up above Salsbattery, in a thicket, guarding the approaches to the swamps, he had stationed J. M. Collins and James Ewelen, to keep a lookout for the rest of the detachment.

By smart maneuvering, the Lowry Company had moved in from each direction and had captured the pickets, simultaneously, before they could warn their comrades by blowing upon their horns.

There was a pretty hot battle for a few minutes, and then a mad scramble for cover, when Elisha Welborn and R. J. Collins bolted for the reedbrake and made a swift escape. Together, the two made their way to New Orleans and enlisted in Wolfe's regiment.

Seeing that they were greatly outnumbered and were in for a sure death by hanging, the remaining came out with hands raised in surrender. That incident practically took the Collins men out of the war, as half their number were captured, along with all the Welches who participated in the guerrilla war, and also all of the Valentines, except one. M. M. Coats and two of the Welborns were also taken in as captives on that same day, April 25, 1864.

The Captain resolved to take revenge on the Confederate cavalry, following this wholesale capture of his men.

This daybreak mission was to warn the few remaining that they must stick closer together, and fight until death, with never a thought of surrender.

Banded together in the cause of their self-asserted freedom, freedom from either army, this group of blood-thirsty men set out for Ellisville, by the lower road, and it was again at Rocky Creek that the cavalry was openly attacked, taken entirely by surprise.

Lowry knew that the surface was just beginning to crack, and he wished to get the situation under control and be about the business of fighting the Yankees instead of loafing here in Jones County, waiting most of the time for the Knight Company to come out and offer battle.

The Confederate soldiers were riding along in high spirits, when suddenly, up out of the creek, arose a host of men shooting down horses and riders, before the Rebels knew what was happening.

There was a place where the water was about shoulder-deep, and the rocky bottom slanted into sandy shallows. Old fallen logs jutted up here and there out of the water, offering excellent camouflage.

Taking advantage of the natural barriers, Knight and his men hid in the stream, where after getting in a good sure shot, a man could duck down behind a log, or duck beneath the water and save his own life.

Without a single loss to themselves, the company killed and wounded many of Lowry's men, and three of their finest horses.

Thinking that they were outnumbered, and unable to ascertain how many men were hidden beneath the cover of the bank of the stream, the cavalry retreated hastily, and returned to Ellisville to rally more horsemen.

After the battle was over, the women and children who lived near came up to salvage the dead horses.

Many families were happy over the prospect of eating a steak from a slain horse, while others sought only to gather the hides for leather, and the fat to cook up into soap, as there were no provisions made for civilians, and the populace was entirely without shoes and soap.

The Knight Company did not follow the retreating soldiers into Ellisville, but dripping, they emerged out of the creek and followed its course on up to a point near the old Wheeler settlement, where they felt that they would be safe enough to build a fire to dry out their garments.

When the new detachment of soldiers reached the scene of the battle, there was not a man there, except the slain Confederates, who were buried on the site.

There were the remains of the horses, which had been haggled in a ghastly manner, to be burned, because the cavalry begrudged even a dead and decomposing horse to an enemy of the South, and these unfortunates who were gathering the hideous remnants of battle were possibly members of families who were with the deserters.

Before their clothing had time to dry, a picket sounded a horn, a faint signal, which was to warn the men around the fire that the enemy was coming, but at a considerable distance.

The camp was broken, and the fire extinguished by Knight's men throwing the burning wood into the stream, where there would be no smouldering remains to bear evidence of their presence in the vicinity.

They were on the run again. This time, they completely outwitted the cavalry, by taking to the reedbrake near the Jones House, waiting until the coast was clear before they proceeded on up to the Salsbattery hideout.

The Jones House was a long low log structure that nestled against a wooded hill, along an infrequented path. In front of it was a level patch that bordered the stream which trickled over the strange rock formation, that had mystified men for ages. There was not a more picturesque or peaceful habitation than this in Jones County. Yet the men did not tarry, for the enemy was not far away.

Riding past the Jones House, they spurred their horses, and were soon ascending the high ground, which is Pleasant Ridge.

From this high point, their eyes commanded a broad view of the outlying lands, shrouded in a blue haze that appeared to be smoke settlings, or a misty rain while the sun is almost shining. Behind them were the lowlands and gently rolling hills and the hollows that separated the two great ridges, the highland of Covington, known as "Nigger Ridge," and this fertile plateau, over which, in time past, had roamed countless herds of buffalo, stalked by Indian hunters. In front of them were other small creeks and the marshy lowland, overgrown by laurel bushes. In the late afternoon, it became, by tricks of light, a broad and mysterious purple valley, a fairyland out of which arose a painted steepness, where the underbrush, the gentle knolls, dotted with a riot of color, blended into the background of tall timber, which was etched in mystic blackness against the azure horizon.

(*On this spot, Laurel, Miss., was much later established.*)

To the right of them was Ellisville, just over, and beyond Buffalo Hill, where legend tells us that these animals by the name maintained a sleeping ground, bedded down beneath the scrubby slash, whose short needles growing from low-hanging branches provided them with shelter from the weather. Where ancient skulls scattered about attest to furious battles fought for herd supremacy by great and vicious bulls, long extinct. But the hill has always been a Jones County landmark.

To the left of them the ridge continued, broadening into the country that was fast becoming known as "No Man's Land."

Not far up the ridge lived the Corleys (Cawley). One brother was a Confederate soldier, while the other had sent word that he was ready to come in with the Knight Company.

"If he's a' aimin' on joinin' us, his folks will know about it, and mought be, we orter ride up that way an' find out. Might be we'd run right into a good cooked meal," said the leader.

So they headed their horses in that direction.

Newt's brother Albert was in the group, and his wife was a sister of the Corleys, so it was agreed that Albert should ride up first and find out if they were welcome.

They were. When they left that part of the country, they had established another place where a saddle-worn deserter, sick or in need, could find shelter and protection, and a place where they could all get a good meal, provided they brought along the provisions.

This place also became known to the Rebel officers who were trailing the Captain, as information leaked rapidly, through unexpected sources.

So it is not surprising that after a few days Captain Worsham was leading a small party of soldiers up the Ridge over Buffalo Hill from the post, in search of the elusive leader of the band.

The Corleys were noncommittal and refused to answer the Confederate officer when he asked them if any of the Knight Company had passed that way.

The fresh hoof-prints, and the sign that hitched animals had pawed impatiently in the lane, bore out Worsham's suspicions that this family had had recent visitors, so he ignored their protests and directed his men to search the surrounding woodlands.

However, they soon returned to the lane to report that there was no evidence of anyone in hiding in the thickets.

Worsham was not entirely satisfied and decided before leaving to take one last look for himself.

The house was erected on a high knoll, facing a deep hollow. The top of the knoll was in cultivation, a little patch about the house and barn, from which there led a path to the wooded pastureland, cut by gullies, and sloped steeply down towards the hollow.

The pasture was overgrown by sparse shoemake, sweetcedar weed, bitter-tops, and here and there clumps of briars, not thick enough to afford concealment.

Separating the lot from the patch was a rail fence, with the gateway a barred gap. The posts were square-hewed, heavy heart pine, the tops of which were smooth, and adequate shelves for placing the milk peggin, out of reach of the dogs and cats, while the milk hand separated the cows and calves.

Worsham walked to the gap on the high open knoll, and stood there, resting his hand upon the smooth shelf-like surface of the gate-post.

Unconsciously, he thrust his thumb upward, his attention centered on the rough terrain below. His sharp eyes scanned the gullies, and one by one, he carefully examined the clumps of brush, but there was no sign of a human figure.

Just as Worsham was beginning to think that they had followed a false lead, there was a shot fired at close range from the wooded slope in front of him. He spun around, shocked and giddy. He knew that he had been shot at. The hand that rested on top of the post was numbed and feelingless, and there was a tingling in his shoulder. He looked at his hand, and to his horror, the thumb was missing! Torn entirely off.

A few hundred yards off down the hollow, there came the long, drawn-out note of the black horn. There was no mistaking it. Further over the ridge there came an answering horn, and then another, and another.

The soldiers were confused, and although Captain Worsham insisted that he was not hurt, he was bleeding to death, there before their surprised eyes. A tournequet was fashioned, and he was placed upon his horse and started for Ellisville, leaving the outlaws to their mischief and pleasure.

After that, Worsham hated Newt Knight with a passion, especially after hearing that the sly Captain had purposely taken his thumb for a target, while lying flat on his belly in the weeds.

The hopes of capturing Knight alive seemed to be out of the question, and Worsham soon gave up.

CHAPTER 14

Many Fronts

The cavalry in Ellisville received a tip that the entire party was down in the "no man's land" along the Porter-Welch Road.

All except a small detachment which remained at the post, and another party under Captain McGilberry, went from Ellisville into that area and instigated a search.

But McGilberry was a brilliant officer, and he had a hunch that the tip might have been to throw them off track, so it was to the "no man's land" of Salsbattery that he headed, where he had more specific information regarding a camping place. A place up near the Jasper County line, where two small branches merge, and the land that lies in the fork is known as "Panther Fork," a territory of impassable bogs.

In this fork was placed a watchman, while the weary men of the Knight Company were about the preparation of food, up further in the density of the forest.

When the watchman was first aware of the fact that an officer was coming in after them with hounds, his first impulse was to blow upon his horn, but on second thought, he decided it best to run ahead into the camp and tell the men what he had seen.

From the barking of so many dogs the hunted men knew that they were completely surrounded, and many were frightened and began to pray.

The encouraged dogs, thrilled over the hot scent of the quarry and the delicious odors from the cooking, were coming faster and faster.

The tramp of horses' hooves, many horses, was heard above the din of the hounds.

The men were helpless.

"My God! What shall we do to be saved?" cried several.

Strong men wept, and those that did not weep were white and shaken.

"Be calm," commanded the Captain.

"Follow me. Act as if you are not afraid. Don't shoot a dog. We must make it out of here and hit over into Etahoma swamp."

He led the way, and after him ran men in a stream, trying to outdistance the barking dogs. How they would have enjoyed killing them! But they knew that the soldiers were not far behind.

The food was forgotten, left to burn over the coals of the deserted camp fire.

Etahoma swamp was at least a mile over across numerous steep hills and deep hollows, and the deserters would have to cross the road that led over Panther Branch.

McGilberry thought that the men would try to escape down the stream, as they had done before, so he had the road completely blocked by soldiers, anticipating capture of the entire group.

But Captain Knight led his men, at tall speed, up the smaller stream and crossed that prong of the branch and on up the deep hollow, and made it up to the road on the hill.

As they breathlessly scaled the hill, the cavalry, about fifty or sixty in number, and accompanied by as many dogs, were almost upon them; but they were almost to the swamp by this time, and safety. They kept running.

The cavalry split up into two groups and separated in a maneuver to surround the fleeing men, but Knight did not slack his pace until he finally made it to Clear Creek swamp, where it became necessary to cross on logs, as there was no bridge.

As the last man of the party stepped upon the logs, he turned and walked backward, sprinkling a quantity of red pepper to stall the hounds.

He sprinkled the ends of the logs, and carefully sifted the powder into the tracks of the men who had crossed before him.

Then he joined the others, up ahead.

Just as they all reached the other side, the first hounds, those in the lead, were at the end of the crossing, but the pepper turned them back. Coughing and sneezing, the agonized creatures rubbed their muzzles in the dirt, in a frantic effort to rid themselves of the pepper burns. The first ones seemed reluctant to take up the trail.

One by one the best dogs were led to the logs, but neither would they make an attempt to cross.

Knight had once again outmaneuvered McGilberry!

"His name is on ole Sal's muzzle twice now," grinned the Captain. "I'll kill 'im, shore," he said. "I could a' killed him today, but 'twarn't the time, but hit's not too fer off."

He smiled and twisted his lips, as he polished his gun in the protected hideout.

Just how close the time was, he did not know, because Newt Knight was beginning to see that he stood to be the loser, and he did not wish to cause good men to die needlessly.

In his heart he had wanted to kill Worsham, but when he had the opportunity, he could not bring himself to take it. Just as he was now wanting to kill McGilberry, and he knew that he would, eventually. For one thing, he had promised his men that he would, and he had always kept his word with them. Now, he knew that he would have to carry out his threat, although it might have to be carried out in the same way that he had stopped McLemore. And it would, in the face of all this new development, with an entire army stationed in Ellisville, be extremely difficult for him to get within shooting range, without risking his own life or the life of an accomplice.

After all the big encounters, he became less and less talkative.

His mouth twisted and worked almost incessantly, while he sat apart and made plans for their future.

"We'll need to contact the women, an' have plenty a' pepper handy from now on," he remarked. "We can't afford to be without it, since we know that it will work."

"You'd prefer to run, then, than stand and fight?" asked one of his men.

"Lord, yes," he replied. "Unless some man has done enough to you, don't ever kill 'im."

The others were amazed. It was so unnatural for their leader to make such a statement. They knew better than to say so, but they thought that he was beginning to weaken.

Captain Knight would not have admitted it, but he was afraid to go near Ellisville, and if he had any way to recall it, he would not have boasted that "this is a free country," where a man did not have to abide by any other man's choice. He was secretly sorry that he had attempted to set up a republic within a state, with himself as the highest official, or rather, as a monarch, which thought had invaded his mind, back there when he was raiding the supply lines, unhampered by the law, or any man outside the law.

"Free State of Jones," he mused.

"Why, I have only the freedom of the air I breathe. I do not have the freedom of a slave, for a slave can lie down and sleep, unless his belly pinches to keep him awake," he bitterly remarked to Alpheus.

There was no reply.

The Captain sat, deep in meditation. "I am a slave," thought he, "a slave to this curse that hangs over me. This thing that I cannot put behind me, these wild imaginations; these people that I have promised to set free."

Newt had always kept his word, and he had repeatedly told Rachel what to tell her people.

Now, he was beginning to realize that if the South should win the war, which at that time, it looked very likely, with England aiding in every possible way, that his promises had been so foolish. He wondered what he would do, here among these innocent ignorant people who were helping to feed him and his men. He could not betray their confidence.

Deep within him, he felt a sense of guilt, because, in the beginning, he had sought only a means to an end, and what the outcome of the war should be had made him no difference.

Now, his was a changed attitude, and he was wishing, although half afraid to admit it to himself, that the North would win and all people could be free.

With the country gutted and torn by the internal conflict, this fantastic idealist foresaw that slavery was a hindrance to progress; that while part of the nation's people were free, others were in bondage, was inhuman and intolerable.

He had feasted while these faithful ones had starved!

Every conquest makes a bold man bolder, and with the miraculous working pepper trick, another party of the Knight Company taunted small groups of cavalry into giving chase through impossible country.

One day about fifteen riders cantered up the lane to a house on a hill, the home of a deserter, who was by them known to be a member of the Knight Clan, and demanded that the good wife tell them where her husband was in hiding.

"I don't know where they are," she answered, innocently.

"Oh, yes, you do know, and we have come to stay until you decide to tell us," stated the leader.

"No. I can't tell you," she insisted.

There were rude, uncouth men in the Southern army, as well as in any other army, and the wearing of a Confederate uniform did not convert such a specimen into a gentleman.

When the women of the deserters were approached, they were shown little respect by some of the soldiers and were subjected to insults and insinuating remarks.

As a rule, when the cavalry approached a house in search of the men, the women refused to come out, barring their doors, and not interfering with the pilfering and plundering they did about the place. In some neighborhoods, the situation became almost unbearable.

The woman started to walk into her house but was stopped by the soldiers who demanded that she wait and talk with them.

"But I don't know where my husband is. I told you the truth in the first place."

"Liar! Liar!" the soldiers cried.

The woman became very angry, and frightened.

"I said I didn't know where he is, but I guess I could find out for you."

A hunting horn hung from a peg on the rustic porch, within her reach. She snatched it from its peg and blew upon it.

The men sat their horses and watched in surprise.

Down behind the house was a long hollow, and from the far end of the hollow, a horn answered.

The cavalry picked up their horses with their spurs and were preparing to give chase down in the direction of the sound of the horn, but before they could turn in the lane, another horn, from over the hill beyond, and at a great distance, but clearly distinguishable, answered. Then another, in an opposite direction spread the alarm, and another, and yet another, until it seemed that the hornblowers were in position to trap the Rebels in the lane.

There was no way of knowing how many deserters were near, or how well fortified they were, so the fifteen men raced out of the lane and went for help.

The woman's intention was to call the men to her assistance, as she felt that they were numerous enough to wipe out this small party of insolent soldiers, but instead of coming near the house, they banded together, and made for the Salsbattery camp, where they would be safer when other soldiers would be surely coming.

They did not have long to wait. The very next day, armed with the information that the deserters were up in the northern part of the county, or possibly, up in Jasper, McGilberry moved in with more dogs than had ever participated in a manhunt before, determined to do that which had never been done before, enter Salsbattery!

Near the camp lived a family by the name of Dulancy. The Dulancys were neutral, not preferring to have anything to do with the conflict and not taking any part in the war between the states.

Members of the Knight Company could go into Aunt Sallie Dulancy's house and have a meal cooked, and by the same token, any Confederate officer, or man of the common ranks, was also welcome to drop in for a meal.

Aunt Sallie was not called upon to make a distinction, simply because she was a resident of Jones County.

The morning that McGilberry and his men rode up to Salsbattery, the Knight Company was camped along Horse Creek, in a little fork, where the branch runs south, and there in comparative safety, the Captain decided to leave them and pay the Dulancys a visit.

The Dulancys' house was located along a trail that led around a small clearing, and on down by way of a big spring that was near the camp, where there was fresh water.

The moist earth was suited to the growth of big timber, and here beside the spring, and on the steep treacherous bluff overlooking it, grew tremendous oaks, under which there sprang up a growth of bamboo briars, and reedcane.

At the beginning of the hunt, McGilberry divided his men and dogs, sending one party down one side of the prong of the branch, and another party down the other side, in order that there could be no crossings, and fouling up the hounds with red pepper. If there could be a possibility of hemming all the men on one side of the creek, it would be an easy matter for the other party to cross over and aid in the final capture.

Another party, very small, he kept with him, and taking the lead, he followed the trail that led around Dulancy's rail fence.

When the Captain heard the dogs barking, he looked out, and saw the group, with McGilberry riding abreast, almost at the point where a foot path ran down the bluff through the reed cane and briars to the spring where his men were stationed.

With the agility of a jungle animal, Knight sprang out the door, and hit out for the camp, trying to reach it ahead of McGilberry by cutting across the clearing, out in the broad open, over about a two-hundred-yard stretch of plowed ground.

He was immediately sighted, and the attention of the party was focused upon the runner. Guns were thrown up, and there was a boom! boom! as shots rang out, and bullets whizzed around the Captain's head. Two holes, cut by bullets, through his hat almost got him.

Another marksman shot his shot-bag strap in half, but he kept running. Then just before he reached the bluff, he stumbled and fell to his knees, as another soldier's bullet found its mark.

Firing ceased, and the Captain lay still on the edge of the bluff. Horses were running towards the spot, and the party thought that they had ended the Deserter War by killing the leader.

Suddenly, as if by magic, the Captain disappeared before their eyes, down the bluff, rolling over and over, and out of range of their guns, for it was impossible to see through the thick undergrowth where he had disappeared. They could not hear a sound, or see a man, but several shots were fired at random, into the brush.

By that time, the dogs were upon the camp. There was repeated firing and sudden yelps.

The party of Rebels sat their horses, awaiting the arrival of the men who were scaling the banks of the little stream, not daring to enter "the lion's den," as many called it, without enough men to take the deserters.

Captain McGilberry could not sit still, knowing that these fine dogs were being killed as rapidly as they entered, so he rushed his horse, and was in the act of descending the bluff, at the same time shouting, "Quit killing my dogs."

The words died on his lips. His horse reared and plunged, as brave Captain McGilberry fell off.

Men were crashing and thrashing about in the brush, shouting and screaming. Other men were leaping off horses. Horses, riderless, were flying away from the scene. The roar of guns down in the bottom did not cease.

As McGilberry was seen about to enter the camp, Newt Knight laid the barrel of his gun up against the trunk of a big oak, for steady aim. The target was the daring one's head.

"Truce!" came the cry from the bluff, when comrades saw their leader lying on the ground, helpless, and dying, and with no reinforcements near enough to step in and halt the slaughter.

"Truce!" came the answering shout, from the jungle-like bottom.

Taking advantage of the situation, most of the Knight Company fled, while Captain Knight and his most trusted officers came boldly up the bluff, and joined the few men who were their known enemies.

McGilberry was begging for water.

One of Knight's men brought a hat full from the cold spring, and kneeling, passed it to the wounded man's lips. The remainder that was left in the hat, he dashed over his head and face.

They were now of equal number, the dying Confederate captain and four soldiers who remained with him, and of the other side, Captain Knight and his four devout followers.

Knight was slightly bent, and was hugging his belly with his left arm, while in the other, he was carrying his gun, but not at a firing angle.

"Make a litter, men," commanded Knight, taking the situation in hand. "We'll git him up to Dulancy's house and lay him on a bed."

It was then that it was noticed that McGilberry's brains were running out of the hole in his head.

"Don't shoot me again," he begged, in delirium, as one of Knight's men stuck his finger into the gunshot hole to keep it closed.

He walked along beside the litter, still holding in the brains with his finger, as the others gently bore McGilberry's body up the rugged trail to Dulancy's house, and left him in Aunt Sallie's care.

All night long he breathed, and talked, never ceasing, about the small insignificant things of life, until just before dawn, and then he became silent and still, and life was no more.

But the man who had desired to see him die was not there!

* * * *

"What is all that blood doin' runnin' down yore britches leg?" asked one of the Knight men, when they had regained the bottoms, after leaving the foe dying on neutral ground.

"Jest deep bamboo gashes, I reckon," replied Newt.

He was still hugging his belly.

"Them gunshot holes jest went through my coat in two er three places. Not hurt."

"Go git my hoss, an' lead him to me," he commanded.

When the horse was led up, the Captain was staggering, and too weak to mount.

"Too much excitement fer one day," he commented, as his friends assisted him. "I'll make it all right."

He led the way, out through the familiar paths, and on down into the Leaf River settlement, although at times, he appeared to be asleep, and would reel and almost fall off his horse.

Near the old plantation, he halted and said to his men, who pulled up their mounts beside him, "Now two uv you ride on down about Eastabucha, an' fetch the doc. Fetch him, if you have to fetch him in cold."

When the men reached the old doctor's home, they were informed that it was too late, and that he was too old to go away from home in the night.

"We didn't ask you the time o' night," answered one of the men, "an' we didn't ask yore age."

When the aged doctor saw the glint of their guns, pointed threateningly towards his middle, he went immediately with them, not knowing who was the patient, or into what part of the country he was being escorted.

He did know that he was being brought up the river, and over a round-about route, until he came to a ferry landing. He was not sure, as he had been led in one direction, and then in another, without benefit of light of the moon, and now judging from the high bluffs of the river, he suspected that this was the Reddoch's Ferry, but there was no attempt of a crossing made by his guides.

They had been coming all the way up on the east side of the river. By the stars, he could tell that much. Then suddenly these strangers headed their horses in a more easterly direction, up through an old sand field, then northward, up into a wooded thicket.

A faint light shone through the cracks of an old dirt and straw chimney, and from beneath the door, but there was not a window, or if there was one, it was boarded up. There was not a sound.

There had once been a fence around this deserted house, from which the light glowed like that from many fireflies, but the fence had so long ago rotted away, until all that was left was the big posts to which it had been built. An old run-down settlement.

These posts, outlined by the crack of light, were used as hitching posts by the newcomers.

It was well on toward daybreak, for the cocks were crowing as they were passing through the last settlement.

A sharp rap. A soft footstep. No other sound, except the sounds of the night and the breathing of the three men standing on the threshold. The katydid's singing, and the sad, sighing sounds of the mourning pines. No one spoke.

Finally the door opened inward, and a woman stood silent, holding it ajar for the doctor and his two companions to enter.

At first the doctor thought that the woman holding the candle was a white woman. In the soft dim light, her face appeared very white, and very beautiful, and her eyes were not the eyes of any slave woman he had ever before seen.

His attention fell next upon the figure of the tall rawboned man, lying on a straw mattress in a corner of the one-room cabin. A man, pale from the loss of blood, pale brow, sunken eyes, strange and wild, and white lips that moved and twisted spasmodically. A black beard covered the rest of his face, and his hair hung to his shoulders, in soft black curls that would have been the envy of any woman.

The doctor swiftly went down on his knees to examine the patient.

"What's wrong here, now?" he asked, matter-of-factly, as if this was an ordinary call, and an ordinary patient.

"Jest some deep gashes I got in a little skirmish, yesterday, Doc," answered Newt, weakly.

"Um, I see. Let's take a look," said the doctor.

The woman had lighted another candle and handed it to one of the men, while with the other hand she punched up the fire for added light from the hearth. As she came forward, holding her candle near her face, the doctor saw that she was a pale ginger Mulatto.

"My God, man, your entrails have been shot out!" exclaimed the doctor. "Your belly is shot full of holes! How did you manage to keep your guts in?" he asked in alarm.

"Oh, I jest held 'em in, wi' my free arm," answered the bearded one.

"The main gash that has bled you down is the biggest job," said the doctor, taking out of his satchel a soft puffy cube of a white substance, about a quarter of an inch in dimensions, and this he laid in the palm of his hand. With the other he took a small penknife and sliced the cube. "Here, swallow this morphine. It'll help some."

"Huh, don't need nothin'. 'Tain't mor'n a briar scratch," came the reply, but obligingly he opened his mouth and took the dose from the outstretched hand.

"Some of these are surface wounds, and some of the bullets are too deep to progue out, so you'll have to tote a load of lead the rest of your life, Captain Knight," announced the doctor.

"You recognize me?" asked Newt in surprise.

"Why, shore, anybody would know Newt Knight, any other normal man would be dead," replied the doctor.

"Well, hit's all right fer you to know me tonight, er is it this mornin'?—but as soon as you ride away from this place, you are not to remember that you have ever seen me, or this place, to any person."

The doctor parted his lips to speak, but the look of those terrible eyes glaring steadily into his, caused him to wince and close his mouth tightly.

"You love your life?" asked the Captain.

"Yes, sir," came the prompt reply.

There was no further conversation.

"Keep yourself easy," said the doctor, as he was snapping together the catch on his satchel.

The woman held out her hand, and the doctor dropped a handful of the cubes into it.

"Thank you, doctor," murmured the man on the pallet.

He withdrew from beneath the bedding a small leather pouch, with a draw-string closing, and he reached up and dropped it into the doctor's coat pocket.

The contents opened wide the doctor's eyes, when he emptied out the little bag the next morning. Pure gold! More than he had earned in a year. No wonder it had felt so heavy!

There never was a word of this mentioned to any person, friend, or foe, and even the Captain himself would deny it and say that he was only scratched by a bamboo, but he suffered from that old wound as long as he lived, especially during his last days.

CHAPTER 15

The Captain's Decision

There were many days that followed the doctor's visit that found the Captain unable to lead his men. Without him, they were at a loss to know what to do. And as the hideouts were guarded by swarms of soldiers, the little scattered groups of the Knight Company were compelled to keep to the brush and sneak out only when the coast was clear, and make it to some friend's house for food.

Then it was not infrequent that hounds would soon strike the trail, and men would be riding over the ground in search of the fugitives.

The Captain was grieved to learn of the sad plight of these men who had joined him, believing that they were fighting for a great man who stood for a great cause. He could not reach them to give them advice, now that he was wounded and past getting around, and it was too far to some of the neighborhoods, where some of the families resided, to send his servants. Besides, Rachel was the only one of them who knew enough to get by, and he could not take a chance on sending her past the cavalry, who were guarding every road.

He did not have a chance to record the death of four of his men, who were run down by dogs over on Dry Creek, up near the Errata settlement, because, in hiding as he was, he did not have an opportunity to contact the only person who knew where the roll was kept.

But much later, he wrote a little account of what had happened to Jack Smith, Jesse Smith, Jack Arnold, and Morge Mitchell.

When they were caught, the four protested, saying they were innocent, but their plea was disregarded, and with ropes around their necks, the Smiths and Arnold were led on up to Errata and hanged without trial.

Mitchell had the rope around his neck, also, but a strange thing happened.

When he was asked the meaning of a white feather that was adorning his hat, he would not reply.

The truth of the matter was, that feather represented a lot of idle time that the wearer had had on his hands, and to while away the hours, he had played with the feather and had stuck the quill under his hatband for no reason at all. And he was not aware of the fact that it stood out so prominently.

When he noticed his captor's curiosity, he thought to stall them off by pretending that the white feather bore some significance.

His three comrades, they left dangling by the neck from the scaffold, but they decided to carry Mitchell into headquarters, where he could be questioned.

He was relieved that he had another chance, and went, rejoicing, but his pleasure was soon outlived. And after a few pointed questions by the officers at Ellisville, the noose was again placed about his neck, and he too was hanged.

The smaller the group, the better the chance of survival.

Cut off as they were the men were starving, as the food they had stored was out of reach or had been captured by the Confederates.

Many left this part of the country, and made their way to other parts of the state, and the others operated as quietly as possible, after McGilberry's death.

The people over the county would have been overjoyed to have known what a tough existence these men lived, but so loyal were the friends of the Knight Company, they would have died before they would have revealed the real conditions, so few knew that hunger drove the men who were in hiding almost insane.

It was May, and the algae was green on the ponds, and along the shallow edges of the streams. The green flies were beginning to buzz and hover over the stinking mud, where tadpoles and crawfish were dying, as the hot sun started drying out the earth and receding the water in the stagnant waterholes.

Tom Flynt and a party of the company were passing through the old lagoon where there had been, several days before, an encounter with the Rebels, and as they had not eaten for days, one man remarked, "I am hungry enough to eat a dead horse."

At that moment, they were rounding the edge of a shallow pond, where a mortally wounded horse had staggered into the water and died. Lying, broadside, his head was submerged, and the water came well up over his sides, and was almost up over his exposed hindquarter.

The water had dried down, and lowered in the pond, a few inches since the horse was killed, and there was pond scum settled upon his haunch, in a band of foamy, whitish lather, streaked with green.

The flies were swarming over the portion that extended up out of the water, but the men waded in, and took a look to see if he could be salvaged for food.

Maggots were working in that side, as the hot sun had aided decomposition, and overhead, like black birds, high above them, a few buzzards were soaring, waiting until the stench was right, before they flew into the lofty roosts to notify all the scavengers that the carcass was ready, and then they would all come circling, and flapping, with a noisy whir of wings, to light on the old dead snags that rose up out of the lagoon.

Flynt did not wade in, but he stood on an old chunk, up off the boggy ground, and watched the others. He could observe the condition of the animal that his men were about to claim for food, and something inside him turned over and filled his stomach with nausea. The sweat stood out in big drops on his face, and a faintness overcame him.

"Men, that horse is fit only for the buzzards; come on, and let them have him. We can't eat carrion."

He turned away from the revolting scene and walked a few paces away, to drier ground. But his weak stomach overcame his resolution to give no show of weakness.

He said later that he "puked like a dog," but the men would not come on and leave the animal to those who had first claim.

Instead they waded on in deeper, until the green water came almost up to their waists, and with a mighty effort they turned the animal over. The underside had lain against the cool bottom of the pond, and was protected from the blow-flies and the sun, by the water. That hindquarter had been perfectly preserved. And when Flynt looked again, the men were raking off the scum and the mud from the horse's haunch with their hands, and getting ready to skin the hide off that part.

Flynt returned to his vomiting. When he had heaved until he could heave no more, he ventured another look to see how the men were progressing.

This time they had their knives out, and had cut out huge chunks of red steak, and were wading out with the meat, ready to roast.

Flynt returned to his vomiting.

Nearby, there were the signs that showed that a basket-maker, recently, had passed that way. There were a few long white oak splints left scattered around among the chips, and the limbs, where he had gathered the material for cotton-baskets. There was still the scent of new wood.

The men gathered these shavings and chips to start a fire, while the others had sliced thin the steak in order to cook it rapidly by holding it on a long sharpened stick over the fire.

The odor of the sizzling meat, and the sharp fragrant smell of the burning wood, was soon tickling Flynt's nostrils, and his sickness subsided. Gradually, he felt a great desire for food coming upon him, and that desire expanded into a ravenous appetite.

The hungry men could not wait for the meat to cool to eat it, and were burning their fingers, trying to pull off bits, which they blew their breath upon, trying to cool it enough to put it in their mouths.

That was enough to convince Flynt that dead horse was exactly what he had an appetite for, so he pitched in with the others and ate heartily.

After eating their fill, they set out merrily, on the way to try to contact their Captain and decide what was best to do.

"We are not beaten, but it is best to lay quiet, for awhile. If any man wants to slip in home, it is a big chance to take, but you might be able to slip in, and help your women and children with the crops in the field, if you'll keep somebody on the watch, so you can hit for the swamps when they come after you," Newt said to them.

But that advice was not taken by many. Two or three men did manage to make their way in home, but there was not a chance for them to do any work, because their homes and farms were searched every few days, in spite of the rumors that reached Ellisville that all of the men were gone from the state or had escaped and joined the Union army.

There were no more daring raids, where there had been robbery and murder in every section, before the Confederate troops came in to break it up.

There is no record of any activity, not a single battle, on the Captain's muster roll, from the last day of April until December, which shows that there was an intervention of peace, for a space of six months, in 1864, while the Captain was recuperating from his battle wounds.

That is, there was peace from the Conferedate cavalry, and peace for the loyal citizen of the county, now that they felt that they were free from the fear of the bandits, as it was believed that the Knight Company had been conquered.

Many thought that there was no need for the cavalry to remain in Jones County and were not too well pleased that they loafed here, having a big time and riding over the country and pestering the daylights out of the widows of those men who had gone with Knight.

Other citizens, upon hearing that these poor women were given no peace, were sorry for them, and protested the treatment that the innocent families, who could not help the situation in which they were placed, were receiving at the hands of the cavalry.

It was not uncommon for deeds of pure deviltry to be inflicted upon some woman who was striving to hold home together.

All the people were reduced to poverty, and the only brooms were those wrung from the sedge grass. The long straws were stripped of chaff, by the whetting motion of a knife. The cleansed ends of the straw were bound by a broom-string, hand-spun, and twisted by the women. Near the brush of the straw, the string was secured by a loop, and the loose end of the long string, wound round and round, like the stripes around a stick of candy, and the end was fastened at the "hand" (the end).

With a shuck mop to first scrub the floors clean and white, it was an easy matter to keep them spotlessly swept with these straw brooms.

The Confederate soldiers delighted in setting this straw on fire, destroying the only brooms the women had.

They did the feathers which the women had picked from the geese and ducks in the same way, or would gleefully open a bag and let the feathers fly away in a high wind, in an effort to deprive them of beds and pillows. And finally, there were not even enough shucks left in the cribs to fill the scrub mops.

The cavalry knew every man who was a deserter, or was friendly to the deserters, and as a reprisal, these harassing Rebels would perform atrocities unmentionable.

Over in the eastern part of the county, the other side of Tallahala, there had been little interference with the families of the men who were reported as deserters, but with this new war being waged on the families, no community was overlooked. There was no direct evidence that men from that side were contributing to Knight, except the hide-out under the bluff. That was enough. The cavalry bore down on that section in great numbers.

One night, a number, possibly a hundred (one excited child claimed that there were five hundred) rode into that section to give the people a taste of what they had given the people down in Cracker's Neck, up on Big Creek, and up in the Salsbattery country.

They knew that some of the Blackledge and Walters men were on the list, so they chose the home of one of these of which to make an example.

There were many shade trees in the lane. The open ground in front of a home, outside a fenced-in yard, was called "the lane," although it was not bounded by fences, but was, as a rule, a place used to hitch horses, a place usually provided with a "salt lick" where the cattle and goats would come up, late evenings, as the enclosed grounds were planted with shrubs and flowers.

Many people would not permit horses to be tied to the shade trees but established permanent hitching posts, with convenient mounting blocks, in the lane.

Realizing this, the Confederate cavalry tried to ruin the shade trees by tying two or three horses to each little tree, splitting off and breaking the limbs. They also hitched to every available post and to the fence, until horses were hitched all over the place, for the night. They kept coming and tethering their horses until there was not a space left to stand another one.

Then the pilfering was begun.

The corn-cribs were filled with corn and fodder, so the soldiers went in and piled out every ear of corn and every bundle of fodder before the animals, where all that was not eaten would be trampled and destroyed.

Then they went into the chicken yard and caught every hen on the place and brought them squawking out into the lane, where they killed and cleaned them all, leaving the feathers there among the destroyed corn.

The lady of the house barred herself in, with her little children, and refused to come out, although she knew what they were doing.

Taking the chickens was not enough. They went to the smokehouse, and cut down every piece of cured meat and carried it out into the lane also. There, they cut it into big chunks and wallowed it into the dirt, and let the horse trample upon it where it would not be usable.

All night they stayed in the lane and kept a big fire going, and all night long they kept up a roar of laughter and song, driving the good woman inside to distraction, but she would not come out and protest, afraid that the mad men, as she supposed them to be, would do her and her babies bodily harm.

When morning finally came, the men and the horses were still in the lane. But about sunup, they decided that they had done enough at one place and started mounting and riding away.

Through a crack in the door, the woman and children watched them, until it seemed that their getting away was taking them forever, so anxious was she to have them gone.

As the last horses were leaving, she heard a commotion going on in her lot, and dared to peep out and see what it was.

It was a lagging Rebel, out running the last mare on the place, with a bridle to catch her and lead her away.

This act was too much for the woman. Forgetting her fears, she ran out and grabbed a fence-rail, and rushed right up and knocked the man down. She ran the mare off in the opposite direction, as the soldier got up, embarrassed and brushing off the dirt. He mounted his own horse and followed the others.

After they were gone, the larger children went out where the big party had taken place and tried to rake up some of the wasted corn. There were about five barrels that had not been eaten by the horses but was rendered unfit for bread by the tromping of many feet. And there was not a fowl left to eat the waste. All that the family had to live on was gone.

That is just one instance of how these people were treated. It happened to every family, until finally it got to the point that the men in hiding could endure it no longer.

"This is a Free State," vehemently declared Captain Knight. "All we have to do is go out in the open and tell every Rebel and every Yankee to step to hell!"

"But we tried that, and you had to bring in all the dogs and Rebels in upon us, by killing off the men you hated," put in Alpheus.

"But we didn't have a thing to back us up. We were ready, but we were not organized, and I'll admit we went at it a little hasty, a' settin' up without a drawn up proper consitution," answered Newt.

"Where's the proper constitution now?" asked Jim Gunter.

"It's ready, and has been ready since the battle at Salsbattery, but it couldn't reach me, over here on Leaf River," answered the Captain.

"All we do now is go in and be duly sworn in. Scatter, men, and notify every group that we are ready to rally our forces, an' drive the drunk devils out of the country!"

There was not a word mentioned about the Captain's old wound, as he had given strict orders that it was never to be mentioned among them.

"It would do too many too much good," he admonished, "and as long as they think they are scrapping a super-human, the better chance I'll have."

A rider was dispatched down into Perry County, where a small group were lying out, the Hintons and Kervins.

At that time there was no Forrest County, and adjoining Covington on the south was Perry County, which afforded, by being a thinly settled, open range country, excellent hideouts, where it was thought that the cavalry would not be informed of their whereabouts.

But just as the messenger was entering the timberland, he was sighted by a settler, who promptly reported the presence of a strange horse and rider in the vicinity, and by the time the party was reached, a group of Ellisville's soldiers were also on the lookout.

There was a run-in, and a fast getaway by the deserters, on this occasion, with M. W. Kervin coming in badly wounded.

That little skirmish sent hordes of men into that area, instead of up into the Leaf River and Big Creek settlements. The settlements where the Knight Company were welcomed with wide open arms by the majority of the people, people who had been treated worse than the people of any overrun country in history, by a group of Confederate men, who in their lust for vengeance had thrown to the winds the principles of civilized gentlemen.

For six months, the people had suffered at their hands, and now they would welcome anything to be rid of such malicious mischief-makers.

"The Free State," became the propaganda cry, in this new, all-out move by the deserters, as had been the 20-negro law and the "Home Defense," the cry in the first mass effort to alienate the people from their duty.

"The Free State of Jones, wtih Captain Knight for Governor," were the words expressing the sentiment of at least half the people, as half the people, seeing the needless (apparently needless) destruction of property, were in favor of getting Jones County out of the conflict.

Newt Knight seemed to be the only man with a plan, offering possibilities, in the midst of chaos, for the people to get a breathing spell.

The new effort began on the 1st day of December, 1864.

The negroes were jubilant. Already free by the Emancipation Proclamation, they were held in bondage, and with starvation facing the South, the negro was the hungriest creature on the face of the earth.

In this little isolated, very much in the spotlight, area of a few hundred miles, many people were conscientious in their belief that this marvelous man could actually set up a republic within the state!

"The Free State of Jones" became the battle cry and the watchword. More men deserted and came in, replacing those who had been killed, hung, and captured.

More negroes joined in the struggle, and a few Yankees were smuggled in. In fact, every man, except the old and enfeebled Confederate men, whose families, sons, and son-in-laws were fighting on other fronts, were the only ones in Jones County who did not fall in with the deserters' plan to set up an independent neutral government here in Jones County. And they were so few, and defenseless, they could not resist the opposition, even with the devout and faithful wives of the absent fighting Rebels keeping the cavalry informed of every move the deserters were making to overthrow Jones County's way of life.

The deserters rode up to the houses of these old men, and in many instances, beat them into promises of not revealing any information.

The Confederate cavalry, right to the minute in the retaliation, caught up old men and young boys who were known to be friendly with Knight and held them prisoners, extorting information from them by threat of hanging.

So it was in Jones County. No one giving, and no one taking, but it was a struggle waged very like the old game "tug o' war," with each side pulling with all might, trying to find the weak link in the chain, whereby there would come a break, and one side would be declared the winner.

After the little group was routed from Perry County, they made their way on up Leaf River swamp to the hideout in the Devil's Den, and there they entered, where they could treat Kervin's wounds.

Although this place was large enough to accommodate a large company, and was most inaccessible, it was decided by the Captain that they were to split their forces, and at least half of them travel up through the Neck for a ways, and then strike into Big Creek swamp and make their way into the almost impossible swamps around Salsbattery.

The time it took to rally the men, re-equip, and stock their bags with grub, took three weeks, after the Captain made the decision to do or die, for the "Free State of Jones."

CHAPTER 16

December Battles

Weeks passed, and there was no sign of the deserters.

The Christmas season was approaching, with the war still raging between the North and South.

Not many men would be home for the holidays.

Those who were absent from Jones County could not obtain furloughs.

And Southerners from other sections, assigned to the task of tracking down Knight and his clan, could not return to their homes, for their orders were to remain at Ellisville until the last deserter had been caught and hung.

So it was a sad Christmas for all, with the young soldiers homesick, nothing to do, and no entertainment provided.

Each day was the same. Groups were sent out from the post on a search, but the report at headquarters was always the same.

"No activity," in answer to the question, "Did you get any information?"

The reports from the neighborhoods were the same. "Nobody has seen them pass."

The cavalry traveled in groups of from fifteen to twenty, as it was unsafe for a half-dozen men to ride over the strange country, especially since the information had been sent into Ellisville, that a big campaign was brewing, that Knight was planning a new move. That the company was increasing in men and equipment to the extent that they were getting in position to capture the entire outfit at Ellisville, which was greatly exaggerated, but that was one of the Captain's shrewd policies.

He managed to appear to command ten times as many men as he actually did, and this was the reason he managed to survive the many battles in which they participated, with only a handful of daring men to do his bidding.

A restless adventurous group of young soldiers rode out of Ellisville, and headed north, over Buffalo Hill, and on up the Ridge Road, past the Corley place, and on up into the broad high country, where the Knight Company might be found, or at least, some information of them.

This thing was too quiet. It was known at headquarters that the company still existed, and were finally back in possession of their old hideouts, but no one would venture a word about what they were doing, or when they had been seen.

There had been no robberies, or acts of violence, so it was supposed that they were just "lying out," keeping out of sight, since that little upsurge, on the 10th of the month, when they had been put to flight down in Perry County.

Said one of the soldiers, "If they can't start some excitement, we can. There's no use riding up this way without doing a thing, or getting into anything except a whiskey jug! Let's ask some of these backwoods folks up here to give us a dance."

All agreed that a good frolic would break the monotony, so they were soon up at the Levi Valentine Place, not too far from the Captain's land.

There were several young ladies in the settlement, and the cavalry-men were anxious to make their acquaintance.

At first Mr. Valentine declined, and the young soldiers were very disappointed. (They knew that the Valentines had been in the Knight Company, but they did not distrust the old man.)

It was not far on up the country to where the deserters were in hid-ing, while making preparations to renew their activity, at the time the soldiers were asking for the dance from the Valentines.

After they had mounted and ridden back to the post, word was sent to Newt that they had been there.

"By all means, give them a party," was the Captain's answer. "But I would also like an invitation."

The next time the soldiers were through the neighborhood, they were cordially invited to stop in with the Valentines.

The subject was brought up about the dance, and Mrs. Valentine announced to the young Captain that they had reconsidered and would be happy to stage the frolic in their honor, and would invite all the young ladies in the neighborhood.

She told them that they could bring their own musicians, as most of the men who were good fiddlers were away at war.

All was arranged for the young Confederates to be slaughtered.

On the appointed night, the Knight Company were concealed near the house, and were watching when the Rebels placed their guards outside.

Young and carefree as they were, the soldiers did not forget precaution.

Captain Knight had been earlier to the home, in person, to make the final arrangements, in order that no one of the family, or any of the young ladies would be shot, when he rushed in with his men.

He left instructions that after the first shot, all in the house were to run out the back door, as they would be shooting down soldiers who would be running out the front door, trying to reach their horses.

Indian fashion, the scouts of the Knight Company crept upon two of the Rebel guards, about the time the dance got under way in the house, but the third sentinel saw the men slipping up on the house, and he started firing wildly.

The firing brought out a rush of soldiers, on the run out the front door, where they were shot down like rats running out of a hole.

According to plan, the women ran out the back door, followed by the old man, who was exempt from the war because of his age.

The soldiers kept pouring out of the house, shooting into the dark. Coming out of the bright light, they were at first, blinded, and unable to see, but a load of shot found its mark in the person of John Parker, who was killed on the spot.

Parker was the only man that Knight lost in the hot little shooting scrape.

The small group of merrymakers, thinking they were in for a big battle, and not being able to shoot accurately in the dark, ran for their horses, carrying along with them wounded soldiers, who were thrown over their horses' backs.

One Confederate soldier was left dead at the steps in the frontyard, and another one was dying, and by morning he was lying cold and stiff beside his fallen comrade.

The Valentines did not know what to do about the dead soldiers, and were anxious to have them off their hands, so it was decided that a small boy and his sister, who had been one of the hostesses for the dance the night before, should carry the bodies to Ellisville in an oxcart, where they were delivered by the accommodating youngsters to the Confederate post.

But Captain Knight knew that he was in for it now, after such a bold attack, so he scattered his men back towards the Big Creek swamp.

Taking with him Alpheus, who was his best marksman, he left for Cracker's Neck settlement, where Alpheus was to be married.

It had been proven that the hounds were not as valuable as had at first been supposed, and after the first two or three manhunts, the women who had been friendly with Knight started putting out poison for the dogs.

The cavalry's hounds had been kept in a half-starved condition, in order to make them more anxious to hunt, as a well-fed animal would prefer to sleep, so it was an easy matter to induce the dogs to eat anything.

Powdered glass was put in food, along with strychnine, and soon dogs were found dead all over the woods.

It was getting colder, as winter advanced, and it looked like snow by Christmas, but weather did not mean a thing to the hardy woodsmen of the Knight Company.

"We won't have a big weddin' on account uv it might get out, an' the Rebels would be a' tryin' to attend," remarked the Captain, "but you can go ahead an' get married, an' all have a big time.

"Some of us will keep watch, so if any of the soldiers come, we can let you know in time."

The plans were all laid for the wedding, and not very secret. In fact, everyone in Cracker's Neck knew about Alpheus' approaching marriage.

It was generally understood that most of the men were in the Salsbattery area following the dance that turned into a battle, and with men stationed at the Reddoch's Ferry, and others holding the fort at the Devil's Den, there were not more than ten of the company at liberty to attend the wedding.

A Confederate widow living in the vicinity could not resist the temptation to inform the cavalry of the wedding plans, and let them have the same advantage over the company as the company had had over them at the Valentine Place a few nights before.

She was one of those good women who hated any enemy of the South.

The woman's husband had been killed on a distant battlefront, and with the slaves doing very much as they pleased, with no one at home to hold them under control, all had left her except one negro woman, who had been her faithful cook for years.

Many of the males did nothing except hunt and fish and roam the woods, pretending to be out looking for strays, animals which they without their owner's knowledge had driven off to the Knight Company, and the missing animals that provided the excuse had long before been slaughtered for the deserter army.

"Cover the coals with ashes, pull back the spider, hang up the kettle, and go, Gal, with this message. Take this note to the cavalry down by Ellisville, and don't you stop to eat or sleep until you have it delivered into the hand of the Captain, and you are back to me."

The black woman took the note from her mistress, and set out on foot for headquarters, but she did not obey her mistress in detail, although she did not stop to eat or sleep.

She did stop long enough to deliver a message of her own to Captain Knight, by way of a pale ginger-colored woman, who had been a regular visitor to a sick old negro nearby.

The message read: "Vis'ters cumin frum Ellis Vil fer wed'n."

That was all the Captain needed to know, but he could not believe there was too much danger of the cavalry slipping in upon them.

On the night of the wedding, there was laughter, and gaiety, and warmth in the house, but Captain Knight had a premonition that all was not well, and he got up and paced the floor at intervals, he worked his mouth, and sunk his teeth into his lower lip.

Alpheus, accustomed as he was to these little mannerisms, knew that his cousin was worried.

Several times Newt left the gay party, and sauntered out into the dark, listening.

All was as still as death. There had been a big freeze, and the ground had not thawed in three days, due to the heavy clouds. Then the clouds had cleared away, and the skies were blue and cold.

The frost had fallen and blanketed the earth in white, which gave it the appearance of being covered with snow.

The stillness was broken by a gentle stir. The bowed down grasses and vegetation trembled. The stir was soon whipped into a breeze, icy and penetrating, as if it were coming straight from the North Pole.

The wind had risen, and it whistled and moaned as it shook the icicle-laden branches of the bare trees, and swept around the corners of buildings.

Outside, the tall man hunched his shoulders against the wind, wondered if it were really the wind that he was hearing. It sounded more like an animal caught in a snare, or a human in distress, a sad lamenting wail that lost its strength of voice, as if suppressed by the tightening of fingers about its throat.

"Whatever it is, unless it is the wind, must be a' sufferin' somethin' awful," said the Captain almost aloud to himself.

"I'd better do the watchin' myself, for I don't know of a man left alone, down there by himself, but what wouldn't get the creeps."

Inside, the fires were burning brightly, and there was not a care. All was music, and feasting and dancing, as the friends celebrated the wedding, but the scene did not lift the Captain's spirits.

"I will keep watch down by the river crossing, the rest of the night," he announced to the others. "This wind is getting rougher by the minute."

"But you will freeze to death down there in the swamp on a night like this," said one of the women.

"Oh, I will keep walking, and if there is any danger, everybody scatter," said Newt.

"But there won't be any danger?" anxiously asked Alpheus' bride.

"No. He will remain here with you, but I may need some of the fellows to go on up Big Creek to the camp there, before day," answered Newt, stilling her fears by his quiet complacency.

He moved toward the door, but was recalled for another glass of wine.

"I never drink when I have work to do," he replied courteously, and bowed himself out and disappeared into the bitter night.

The ferry had been destroyed earlier in the year, but the deserter inactivity had permitted the rebuilding of another one, which had been in use only a few weeks when the new forces took over, in a second attempt to control Jones County, but it was immediately destroyed in November, with the Captain's determination to take over the Confederacy.

Every bridge and ferry was destroyed by the deserters, as that was one of the best ways to slow down their adversaries, when it came to getting away from trouble in a hurry.

Nevertheless, it was very possible for an army to cross without benefit of ferry at the Welch Landing, and the Captain, although very sure that a big manhunt was going on for them, up towards Salsbattery, felt an uneasiness that there might be an attempt to slip in upon his little wedding party from the west, and so he decided to watch that possibility.

In the thick swamp, the wind was partially cut off from the watchman, but overhead, it swept through the timber-tops, creaking and groaning, as bare branches were swaying and rubbing together.

He walked beneath the tumult in the treetops, and on to the river's bank.

The gurgling and swishing of the water as it flowed swiftly by was mingled with the sounds of the night, but the lone vigilante kept up his uneasy pacing, paying no heed to these strange and weird noises.

A half mile upstream he walked, above the crossing, and then retracing his steps back to the crossing, and then a half mile below, and back to the beginning.

His feet became numb, but he could not stop. Had to keep moving to keep from freezing to death. All night long he kept up the watch, while the others, a half mile away, were enjoying his protection.

Just after daylight, there were still red streaks in the east, and the sun would rise, and perhaps warm up the swamp a little, the cold man was thinking.

The night had been rough, but better than clouding up on a frost, which would, in three days, bring on a rain to add to the misery of the men in the swamps.

"We must keep outsmarting them, and try to lose as few men as possible," the Captain's lips were forming the words, but they made no sound. He licked them, and his wet tongue warmed them with the warmth from within him.

When he opened his mouth, his breath became smoke in the icy air of the early morning, reminding him of how badly in need he was of a warm fire.

Then fancy carried him back to the times he had sat with Serena by a warm fire in his home, good beds where he could lie down in comfort and peace and listen to the wind howl, on nights like this one had been.

He wondered if he could ever again find peace and warmth. He doubted it, but there was no turning back.

The road by which he had entered was closed, barred by the many deeds and words of impetuousness and hate. He was trembling, but he assured himself that it was from the cold that he was shivering.

About the time he had decided that there was to be no interference with the wedding, as the sun was peeping up, red and cold, and another day had come, he was startled by the sound for which he had been straining his ears all night. This time, there was no mistaking it.

The wind had receded; and there was an icy stir, followed by an occasional blast from the north. It came during the lull between the puffs. That rattle!

The Captain knew that it was someone crossing on a flat (flatboat) a few hundred yards away. He could tell by the rattle of the chains.

Crouching behind trees, he made his way up nearer the river crossing, for a view of the trespassers.

There in plain sight were at least a hundred horsemen stomping on the flat. No other sound except the clacking of hooves on the timbers, the squeak of saddle leather, and the rattle of chain. There was no conversation among the riders. They meant business! That was evident.

The Captain could not run, for fear the icy ground, and the frozen twigs would crack and snap under his feet, and excite the suspicions of the cavalry, so he had to take considerable time getting out of earshot, before he could sprint over the distance that separated him from his friends who were depending on him.

When he gained the house, the wedding party was just sitting down to breakfast. The table was beautifully laden with food, pies and cakes of all kinds.

"You're just in time," cried the lady of the house. "Sit down and eat."

"I've no appetite," replied the Captain. "A big fight is coming!"

Alpheus and the other men jumped to their feet, anxious to receive their orders.

A cup of hot coffee was placed in the Captain's hand, and a piece of pie was urged upon him, which he finally took and ate along with the gulps of hot coffee.

"We've got to get out of here," he told them. "At least a hundred soldiers are marching on this house, right now! Get the women out, and send them in the opposite direction," he commanded.

But in the confusion, the women were frightened and would not leave the house.

Alpheus' bride clung to him. Minutes were flying, and the riders were drawing nearer.

The Captain knew that it was needless to try to do anything except make a getaway.

To the men, he said, "All of you head on up into Big Creek swamp and try to reach the others. Alpheus and I will try to get the women out of the way before they get here."

One of the women had a small baby in her arms.

"Run!" commanded the Captain, as they rushed out of the house, and made for a path that led in a direction which he thought would take them out of the cavalry's way, a dim road that was seldom traveled.

The woman carrying the child was beginning to lag behind.

"I can't keep up with this baby to carry," she said.

So Newt turned back, and reached for the infant. "I'll carry your baby, mam."

"And I'll carry your gun," said she.

He stooped, and lifted the baby from her arms. "Nobody carries my gun," he answered.

Faster and faster they ran until they had gone a distance of about two hundred yards from the house, and then suddenly, the Captain stopped and listened.

The others paused and held their breath.

The Captain handed the child back to its mother.

"Here. I am going to have to use my gun. Take your baby. That's them. Coming right at us!"

There was not time left in which to flee in another direction.

Then the clatter of hooves brought out of the brush a bunch of frightened colts, wild creatures. Something had stampeded them, and when they ran right into the path of new fear, the presence of humans, they snorted, and leaped into the thicket, and went crashing through the frozen woods, with manes and tails in the air.

All breathed a sigh of relief—then suddenly guns were firing.

Right behind the colts were about twenty soldiers, and when they saw the two men they were out to get, they opened fire.

A big gray-clad Captain was riding right toward Captain Knight, trying to run his horse over him. He must have intended to try to capture the deserter alive, because he was not making an effort to shoot him, which he could have done.

Knight raised his gun and shot the Rebel out of his saddle.

Another shot felled another soldier.

"Fall into the brush, ladies!" shouted Newt, as he threw himself into a thicket.

Seeing that they were without a chance of survival, he remembered his old trick.

"Attention! Battalion! Rally on the right! Forward!" he yelled, as if commanding a number of hidden soldiers.

From his place of concealment behind a big fire-blackened stump, Alpheus had the advantage, as his sure aim directed his shots to tumble off soldier after soldier.

The Confederates were confused, and were surprised at the number of shots coming from the two directions.

Again the Captain yelled, "Attention! Forward march!"

Already the writhing horses, and dead men had piled up before the remaining soldiers, who were shooting wildly into the brush, without damage to anyone.

They wished to avoid killing the women and the child, and although they would have braved the "unseen army," they were forced to retreat and try to rejoin the other group of the cavalry who had marched upon the deserted house in which the wedding had taken place.

Every inch of the territory in the neighborhood of Cracker's Neck was searched, in a vain effort to find some sign of the Captain's where-abouts. But the old fields, overgrown with high grasses and weeds, untended for lack of men to till the soil, gave them no clues, and neither did the old bays and flats near the "no man's land" where the thick swamp was frequented.

While the woods were combed in a fruitless search, the Captain and his men were making their way across the country, in an effort to rally enough men with arms to defend the hideouts.

Past experience had taught them that they must remain near the source of supply, lest they be cut off and forced to disband, as had been the case back in April, when they had no choice but to accept the condition of "every man for himself."

Things were looking up. These men, sent in here to capture them, had no knowledge of the woods, or how to deal with men who were as much at home in the swamps, as were the wild creatures.

Many old men were dead, or abed from sickness and malnutrition, and many more young boys had gone with the conscription, designed to provide more troops, so there was less and less opposition from within the county's boundaries.

That was encouraging to the Captain, and his wild dreams were soon to materialize, when he would, in truth, and in fact, be the governor of the Free State of Jones.

On up in the swamp the party made their way until it was decided that they split and at least half of them cut across the hills and enter Leaf River settlement above the Reddoch's Ferry.

The others would make their way on up to the Salsbattery country, with the assurance that enough men were on their way downstream to make it to the hideout before the Rebels could finish up the business of tracking down the bridegroom.

But this time, the Knight Company had not reckoned with these determined soldiers, who had come in to wipe out the last man, or break up any such scheme as they might have concocted to avoid serving their country in its darkest days of bitter struggle.

A handful of soldiers were left to scour the countryside in the Cracker's Neck settlement, and a much larger detachment was dispatched up the river from the Welch crossing, while even another party was sent up the Big Creek swamp, right on the heels of the escaped wedding party.

The date was December 28, 1864.

In each detachment of soldiers, there were enough men to greatly outnumber the small groups of the Knight Company.

By the time Captain Knight's Leaf River objective was reached, they found the Rebel cavalry already there and waiting for them at the Gunter Place, which was not right near the River but was near enough to be designated as a part of the settlement.

There was a heavy barrage of shot from each side, and a scamper for the swamps, by the Knight men, but the Lowry Company was too quick for them.

Gunter himself, who was leading the group, was caught alive, and the Confederates took great delight in hanging him by the neck there in the swamp that day.

Seventeen others threw up their hands and marched out, and were carried, captives, into Ellisville, while two or three escaped, and made their way on up the river towards the country that was least likely to be searched that day.

At the same hour that the encounter was taking place over on Leaf River, the Big Creek encampment was attacked by that group of the cavalry, which had trailed them to that hideout. There it took place! All the rest of that day, the battle raged, with the creek separating the two groups of bloodthirsty men.

The Knight Company, only a handful, took heavy toll of men and animals, killing a horse as often as they could.

Finally, the tide turned, and the Rebels had them hemmed in, in an old lagoon, where the ice had not melted all day. The old ponds bore a shield of ice, where the thick growth of the timber had prevented the sun's warmth from thawing out the bitter cold.

It was coming night again, and the Knight Company was thankful for the cover of darkness in which to escape.

Men were wounded and dead on each side of the little creek. Here and there, big horses, still wearing bridle and saddle, were stretched out dead.

As Captain Knight ran through the frozen woods, he stumbled over an obstacle. He thought it was a chunk until his foot felt the soft belly of the dying man.

The man moaned, and Knight heard a faint word, "water," or he thought that was the word. In the early darkness men and horses were crashing and thrashing about in the brush, but Knight paused, and looked down at the dying Rebel.

"Oh, damn you! I never could refuse a man," he exclaimed.

He ran back a few paces, disregarding the danger of capture, to a frozen pond, took the heel of his boot, and broke through the thin ice. He took off his hat and crushed in the crown, making a deep impression in the thick felt. He scooped pond water up into the hat's cup, and rushed back to the dying man, whom others would have regarded as an enemy.

He knelt beside him there in the darkness and bent to find his mouth, "Here, drink, Old Boy, I am afraid this will be your last one."

He gently laid the bloody head back on the ground, after the wounded man had swallowed, then he stood up and knocked the flecks of ice from his hat's crown, jerked it down upon his head, and continued on the run. He never knew who the man was, or whatever became of him.

By the time they had gathered up their forces, after the two last fights, they were so few, it was impossible for Newt to convince them that they had a chance. All were ready to lay down and quit.

But the four strongest of argument, the four leaders were still alive, unhurt, and they would not give in, but insisted that the Free State of Jones was not an impossibility.

"We will put out the word that we are in 'no man's land,' below, and head on up towards Salsbattery," said the Captain. "There we can have food brought to us, where we can rest and get our plans laid. More men will come to us, and we will gather strength.

"The Rebels think they've about wiped us out with so many killed and captured," Newt continued.

Then, reflecting, he said, "I guess they'll hang them too, poor fellows!"

He shook his head sadly, and twisted his mouth.

All were grim-faced and silent.

Then came the worst weather the South had ever had, with rain that turned into sleet, and the slush froze on the ground, to be topped off by a big snow.

The men in hiding would have starved if it had not been for the wild game that came near their encampment.

Rabbits and blackbirds became their meat.

"Well," remarked the Captain cheerfully, "when we have bad weather, we have not the cavalry. They have to sit in around the fire, so we are not the ones to complain."

But this respite was not to last forever. The days would warm up, and the stiff north wind would dry off the trails, and the cavalry would be after them again. The Captain knew this, but he did not expect it so soon.

Captain Gillis's Company came in on the hideout quite unexpectedly, on January the 10th, 1865, and the men were not ready to put up a fight, but there was a little battle in which several of the Knight Company were wounded, including S. G. Owens.

The Confederate cavalry lost six of their men in the battle, which was to be the last one, as most of the men were incapacitated by wounds, and the hardships that they had been compelled to endure.

The celebrated governor found that his men had dwindled until there were too few to carry on further, so he commanded the remaining ones to flee for their lives, and to remain in hiding or join the Union army.

That was the day they disbanded, never to roam the hills of Jones County again, as a guerrilla band. They had been beaten, at last.

There was not much effort put forth in the search for the remaining half-dozen, because it was believed by the Rebels that the Captain was dead.

The Confederates had reason to believe that he had lost his life, back in April, when the streams were swollen by the spring rains. Yet they knew that some great leader was in command, but they had not been able to get a recognizable glimpse of the Captain, since he walked out in the open, during the truce at the Dulancy place, when Captain McGilberry was killed.

It was generally supposed that the man who escaped, by slipping his hand through the handcuff, and jumped into the river was Captain Knight, but there was no way of knowing.

The banks were searched, both sides, up and down the swamp, by torchlight, but there never was a trace of the escaped man found. It was decided that it would have been impossible for him to have swum the stream, without someone on the other side seeing him, so thick were the soldiers in the swamp.

But that was just another of the Captain's brilliant tricks, and it was by sheer trickery that he lived through such hectic days.

He knew every bluff, and every clay-root, and, no doubt, every cypress knee in Leaf River swamp, so it was an easy matter for him to come up under the bluff of the river, keeping under the water as much as possible, until he was far enough downstream to make a break for the Devil's Den.

Tales the men told were conflicting, and very confusing.

One soldier would tell that he was sure that he had encountered him in one part of the country, while another would assert that he had seen him in another part, the very same day!

CHAPTER 17

The Last Year of the War

Rachel and her children were still occupying the cabin that had been assigned to them when they first arrived at the Knight Plantation. They were all that were left of a great number of slaves, who had once lived in this expansive slave quarter.

A slave quarter that had, in reality, been a little village, where there had been laid the foundation for Christian citizenship, where the black primitive people had been taught by old Jim that negro and white could live side by side, in peace and happiness, without either trodding over the rights of the other, as long as each remembered the teachings of the Bible.

But old Jim was dead. His remains lay in the same burial ground with those of his beloved master, his mistress, and the father of Captain Knight, who 'twas said died from grief and shame. There in the row of other slaves, and other white people, long before departed. Now, there was no one to reproach Rachel.

Another white child lay in the cradle, rocked by the foot of the woman who was to shape the destiny of a strange people.

There were no excuses offered; there were none to make.

War always brings on an extra crop of babies, and Rachel simply had another baby.

Other negro women were also having babies.

In families where there had never been a "light" one, families who were proud of their purity of race, funny-looking, green-eyed Mulattoes were springing up.

White men's children were soon to play in the yards of negro women, with little black half-brothers and half-sisters. The aftermath of war; the pity of an overrun country.

That was all there was to say in answer to the question, "How did this happen?"

Where, in the beginning there had been only one mixed people, one family, Rachel and hers, there were many in Jones County.

From the last deserter battle on the 10th of January, there were four more months of the War Between the States, in which the Captain was forced to remain in hiding. It was no trouble to keep out of reach of the Confederates, because those last four months were the hardest of the entire war for the South.

The cavalry at Ellisville was called out for more important duty than the rounding up of the last deserters. And the town and the county were without soldiers.

Nevertheless, the fugitive kept to the old deserted plantation where his father had been born. From that place he could sneak out and visit his wife and children without fear of capture.

Yet there was one fear that hounded him from which there was no escape, the fear of public opinion.

He had failed entirely to set up the republic which he had promised, and he had become the laughingstock of the county.

He was disowned by his kinsmen, and the friends he had once had, gave him a cold reception. Many would be pleased to know that he really was dead!

During the last four years, many things had happened in this part of Jones County. Where there had been fine homes of his kindred, there was now ruin and desolation. The houses had been burned on three plantations, and the orchards and gardens were overgrown with briars and weeds. The Captain's parents were gone, most of his brothers were dead, and those who lived turned him away. He had become a stranger to his own children.

After the surrender, the bedraggled Confederates marched in home. Those that were able made it in on foot. Others died by the wayside.

The wounded, starved, sick, and beaten finally came back to the place where they had left families and friends.

Many failed to make it back and lie buried on distant soil, as was the case of Peyton Graves, who fought through, managing to keep body and soul together. But on the way home, there was no food, except that provided by nature.

The blackberry vines were loaded heavy with fruit, and the wounded soldier, hobbling back to Jones County on a crippled leg from Mobile paused along the way to eat the berries, which contributed to his stomach ailment. But there was nothing else to eat.

He was found dying, by the side of the road, when a passerby came along and carried him back to Mobile, where he was buried.

Those that came back learned from their families that a man named Knight had forever ruined the good name of Jones County. They could not bring themselves to use the term "The Free State of Jones County." In their opinion, it was a disgrace to the Confederacy, a disgrace to the men who had given their lives fighting for a great cause.

So bitter were they, it was resolved that they should band together and by petition change the name of Jones County.

In honor of the president of the Confederacy, the county was to bear his name. And in their opinion Ellisville was a name that should never be mentioned, due to the fact that when the call for volunteers came up, the old residents who had established the town there were deprived of the privilege to contribute their part to the cause of the Confederacy and had been compelled to shamefacedly cross Leaf River and join along with the Covington Countians. So Ellisville should be erased from the map in an effort to obliterate the disgrace which that very name would call to mind, throughout the South.

Leesburg was the name that was chosen for the first incorporation in Jones County, in honor of General Lee.

The following is a list of the signers of the petition to change the name of Ellisville and Jones County:

J. M. Bayliss

W. M. Bayliss

Hugh Gellender

J. W. Grayson

Henry Gardner

J. E. Walters

R. Jenkins

Charles Williams

Angus McGilvery

M. W. Slaten

Danuel McArthur

Enoch Walters

W. M. Wood

Willis Windham

Robert Windham

John Knight

B. C. Duckworth

W. H. Turner

R. Safford

A. Simmons

W. Duckworth

Edmond Dossett

Abner Dossett

H. D. Dossett

John Byruns

W. M. Byruns

W. M. Bryuns, Sr.

S. H. Smith

J. A. Fairchilds

Willis Dickson

Henry Parker

E. M. Duvall

W. W. Shows

James Cooper

Hiram Cooper

Allen Smith

D. C. Smith

John Smith

M. F. Smith

J. Y. Gardner

D. Melvin

James Melvin

M. A. Melvin

Robert Jordan

P. C. Jordan

J. G. Williams

Bradford Shows

A. Gaddie

F. M. McDaniel

C. C. McDaniel

George Davis

John Ferguson, Jr.

M. Ferguson

B. F. Barrett

Jeff Musgrove

Robert Cooper

T. C. Bryant

Ruben Creel

J. B. Reeves

Sam Trest

N. Y. McGill

A. G. Welborn

E. C. Welborn

W. M. Gore

A. P. McGill

Daniel McGill

W. B. Shows

W. J. Shows

J. L. Shows

J. P. Shows

John Fergurson

A. B. Jordan

W. M. Grayson

John Walters

Elliot Stewart

Sam Walters

John W. Harvy

Allen Gunter

Thomas Walters

W. M. Dement

Eligah Powell

Robert Fairchild

A. T. Dossett

James McGill

James Gaskin

J. H. Overstreet

James Gunter

R. J. Craven

Arch Patterson

Berry Smith

W. M. Temple

Sam Prince

W. M. P. Tisdale

Elijah Tisdale

Wes Tisdale

J. A. Tisdale

John Overstreet

A. N. Drennan

Simpson Bruce

S. N. McManus

* * * *

After legal adoption, all business, county and municipal, was transacted under the new names which had been chosen, Leesburg, Mississippi, and Jefferson Davis County, Mississippi, which was all well and good until the beaten citizens were confronted with another problem which had not been anticipated. But they kept the two new names for a period of two years.

The end of the war had not freed them from strife. The Union was in command of Jones County!

There followed twelve long years of domination by the abominable rule of a few, who sought to "add insult to injury," and in 1868, the original names of Ellisville and Jones County were restored by legislative act, and the populace had no choice in the matter; but they had no choice in many matters!

Tennessee was the only Southern state that would accept the 14th Amendment, so in 1867, Congress, by the Reconstruction Act, began at the beginning, as though the war had just ended. It proclaimed martial law throughout the South, which was divided into five military districts.

To escape from martial law, the states must reconstruct according to Congressional plan.

All persons, without regard to race or color, who had not taken a part in the rebellion were registered by the commander as voters.

Those men of the Knight Company in Jones County, and even those who were residents of other counties, came forward as the qualified electors, along with every negro!

It was not only in Jones County but in all the other counties of the state, which explains how Mississippi came under "negro rule."

Mississippi was also forced to accept the 15th Amendment.

The law disfranchised most all the leading white men of the South, and placed the ballot in the hand of the negro, in every section, and the carpetbag rule existed until 1877.

CHAPTER 18

The Carpetbag Rule of Jones County

The people reacted in various, and unexpected ways, as the news of the Provost Marshall appointment spread over the settlements. To most, that was a bitter pill to swallow! While the followers of Captain Newton Knight, those who had been lucky enough to escape death by hanging or being shot by the Confederate cavalry, were highly elated over the appointment.

Men who had never been members of his guerrilla band came up and informed him that they had stood stoutly behind him but were hustled off to the Rebel army without a chance to contact and join him.

Many sought to have their names added to his muster roll, and the families of the deserters flocked to him.

This new position in which the Union placed him elevated him above any civil officer, and, in fact, all civil offices came under his controlling power. Actually, he was the governor of the Free State of Jones, and his friends preferred to call him that.

When word spread that the returning soldiers and their families were to bow in respect to the hated leader of the deserters, that he, Captain Knight, was to hold the whip-hand over Jones County, excitement reached a high pitch.

The beaten Southerners swore to kill him, by means fair or foul, and the friends of the outlaw decided to protect him, even if it caused a massacre of the entire county.

So both sides were set to await developments on his first day in Ellisville.

There was a hurried whispered consultation (couldn't be told exactly on which side of the fence a man was) among the loyal citizens, and by grapevine, the news of the plans went from one to another, until the population understood that they were not to make a move of any kind, or incite trouble, but were to simply ignore the guests and behave as if nothing out of the ordinary was happening, or about to happen, and just wait and see what would result.

So the town appeared on a Saturday afternoon, as usual to the visitors, as it had back when all were fellow-citizens and friends.

The activity was greater, more people in town on that day, as has always been the custom of little Southern country towns.

The wagons were standing with tongues let down, while the oxen nibbled on the short grass, not far away, further down the street.

The heavy yokes creaked as they moved slowly their massive necks, trying to forage an extra cud. Except for an occasional look down in that direction, owners left them unattended.

There were horses at the watering trough, there were horses standing tied to the hitching posts. Spirited horses nickered, and lazy ones lifted their heads, pricking up their ears at the approach of these horses, bearing the mischief-bent riders, but there was no sign of recognition by any of the town's inhabitants.

The McManus store was crowded with the usual Saturday traders and loafers.

The negroes, newly freed, were at a loss to know what to do with themselves, but there they were! Decked out in the best they had, and putting on an air of importance. Many of the old and faithful sadly shook their heads and were anxious to greet an ex-master or mistress, as the war had nothing to do, whatsoever, with the relationship that had formerly existed. And this newfound importance was manifested only by the young negroes, and a few arrogant ones of poor standing. These stood about, grinning broadly. And whereas, on Saturdays before, the negroes did not crowd the street, now, without supervision, they could not plan out work to do, and most would not work if they could, there was plenty of time to loaf.

But at the sight of the company, displaying the best in fine horses, good saddles and bridles, flashing pistols, and shining spurs, the negroes were excited into a state of jubilancy, exceeding that of the gay friends of the Knight Company. The grins became broader, song, and laughter, and cheers broke out from the congregation.

A pistol shot rang out. A wild whoop followed, and then more whoops and shots.

The grins vanished, and so did most of the negroes.

Why shouldn't these men take over the town? Did not the town belong to them? Their leader was the only authority to obey, and certainly he had no objection to a little Saturday afternoon celebration in his honor! This was all innocent fun, and the guns were brought along, just in case there should be some objection!

Whiskey bottle corks popped, as the drink was opened and passed.

More pistol shots and loud laughter.

John Willis Musgrove waved his whiskey bottle by the neck and announced the bright idea, "Le's ride into the courthouse and take over the sheriff's office."

All laughed uproariously at the suggestion, so down the street they went to the courthouse, where county officials were winding up the week's work.

The riders did not dismount, but six men were chosen to ride their horses right up the steps, and enter the office, just for a joke on the town!

There was a man early in the settlement whose name was John Musgrove. And the John Willis Musgrove, Private, Captain Newton Knight's company, was the eldest son. Mr. Musgrove, in order not to show favoritism, named each of the other five sons John, for himself also. There was John Willis, John Mathew, John Richard, John Jefferson, and even the two daughters were given his name. They were John Margaret, and John Clare Ann.

But the muster roll shows that John Willis was the only one of the family to desert and join Newt. But after Newt became the great man, the other brothers rode before him. They were the ones who were chosen to ride into the courthouse.

In that day and time, all buildings were well built out of heavy substantial material. The courthouse was built out of all heart timber, placed high off the ground on heavy sills. The hallway was open through the entire length of the building, with the offices opening off to either side. At either end of the wide hallway were steps of thick heart plank.

John Willis led the parade right up to the steps and, amid curses and whoops, began spurring his horse, which was reluctant to mount and enter.

The others followed suit, and the blood spurted from the sides of the rearing and plunging horses, but their masters urged them with the spurs, until they jumped over the steps and clomped right into the offices.

The occupants sought refuge under tables, or jumped out windows and ran for safety.

Soon the Musgrove brothers had the courthouse in possession. Through the hall they raced, the snorting horses' hooves clattering through the building; out the back they went, leaping over the steps like mad Indians. Round and round the building they ran, the horses blowing and snorting in fright. Back to the front steps. More spurring and cursing, and again the horses obeyed, and the performance was repeated until the horses were exhausted and the riders were finished with the show.

It was so much fun, it was agreed that every Saturday they would come back and ride through the courthouse.

There was no criticism. It was accepted.

Between the courthouse and the inn was the McManus store, also built high off the ground. McManus was a shrewd merchant, and in his store he had finery that could not be purchased nearer than Mobile.

His was the first glass showcase in Jones County. In it were contained ladies' beautiful, be-plumed, be-flowered, and beribboned hats.

The brass-tack heads shone on the counter, four of them placed along the edge of the counter at the half-yard, the quarter, and the three-quarter yard marks, for measuring cloth, lace, and ribbon. From this old system of measuring came the old saying, "getting down to brass tacks" (meaning specifically), and Mr. McManus could be specific!

He was very proud of his business, and he was one of Ellisville's best liked citizens. He was accommodating, friendly, and a perfect gentleman.

Whether Rich McManus had a "past" or not, was not even debated, and he had become an unquestionable accepted resident, having married the daughter of the town's doctor.

The doctor was also the keeper of the inn, and his office was located in the inn, which was the only place of lodging for transients in Ellisville, or there about, where food and shelter could be obtained during court sessions.

Here, all were treated alike, all taken in, whether handyman, dude, or dunce. That is, the bill-of-fare, the price of lodging was the same for all, for being a public place, all ate together at the long tables.

The inn became famous for its fine food, which was prepared by three or four negro women, who had been trained by the lady of the house, who saw to it that the tables were beautifully laden with fine old Southern dishes.

By Southern foods, one means hot biscuit, golden fried chicken piled high on hot platters, a bowl of creamed chicken gravy, to be eaten over steamed rice; at least a half dozen varieties of fresh grown vegetables, crowder peas, okra, fried squash, butter beans, roast'n'ears, sliced onions, and cool salted slices of cucumber. (Tomatoes were then unheard of in Jones County, and the first plants were cultivated as an ornament, under the belief that the fruit was a species of "love apple" and was thought to be poisonous.)

The desserts! Never, in any part of the world were desserts so elaborately prepared as in the South, where the humble pumpkin and the sweet potato are dressed up to make Sunday pies on a week day! And the egg custard, shaky, and golden in a crisp brown shell graces the table along with all the fresh fruit cobblers, topped off with whipped cream. Pots of black coffee!

Above all this, the punka, attached to a beam of the ceiling, creaked and groaned, as a breath of air was stirred, and the flies were shooed by its perpetual motion.

On a low, three-legged stool, towards a corner of the room, sat a little black "punka boy," faithfully pulling the string that kept up that motion.

It was Saturday again, and all was quiet and peaceable over the town.

At the inn, dessert was being served to the guests who were all making merry over the joke that was to be played on the Musgrove brothers, when they returned to again ride through the courthouse.

* * * *

THE EGG CUSTARD RECIPE

Use only salt to taste in the flour for the crust. A lump of butter or lard the size of two eggs, kneaded into the flour with enough cold water to make a piece of dough large enough to cover the chosen pie plate. Roll thin, place over the rim of the plate, and make a design with a fork, using the tines, in the edge of the crust to fasten it to the plate.

For a 10-inch custard, have beaten only enough to blend the yolks with the whites (not to a froth) three eggs. Mix 1 cup sugar with two level tablespoons flour and blend with the eggs until smooth. Add a dash of nutmeg, two pinches of salt and a teaspoon of butter. Add, gradually and stir in two cups of scalded sweet milk.

Pour the mixture over a spoon held four or five inches above the crust, so that the custard will spread and fill the pan without tearing a hole in the unbaked crust.

Cook slowly in the oven until the custard becomes firm and shaky.

* * * *

It was planned to have the building deserted, which had already been done, and all was in readiness to give the frolicsome lads a big surprise. Great care had been exercised in bolting all the doors from the inside!

But some tattletale had let the cat out of the bag!

Evidently, the riders had some information that their big joke was going to backfire.

Soon the noonday quiet was broken by the sound of horses' hooves. They were coming! After a little, the sound of a horn! (Newt still proudly carried the black horn.) The horn again! Then pistol shots!

It was a hot day, and the horses were lathered from hard riding, and the riders were sweaty and dusty, but all were in a jovial mood when they rode into the town.

Instead of going about the courthouse, as had been expected, the riders talked for a few minutes and then wheeled their horses and rode up to McManus's store.

This building was erected upon a much higher foundation than was the courthouse, and no amount of spurring or beating would induce the horses to attempt to scale the high platform across the front of the store.

Finally, John Willis's horse gave a mighty bound and gained the entrance.

The shoppers had fled and were by that time hidden beneath the floor of the building.

Other than faces behind parted curtains at windows, it appeared that nobody was observing the incident, as the streets were deserted.

There was a big crash. The glass showcase! An angry shout. The sound of a shot. And then it seemed that the building was being demolished, judging from the noise that came from within the store.

A few yards down the street, men rushed out onto the inn veranda, to see the commotion.

What they did see, after a minute's wait, was John Willis's horse, riderless, leaping off the platform.

In another second, Rich McManus appeared at the door, holding John Willis by the nape of the neck, marching him right up to the edge of the platform.

Guns were pulled by the companions, but Rich was not afraid, for he was shielded by his victim, and he knew that they would not shoot John Willis.

"Put up your guns, and I'll let him go, unharmed," he commanded. So the guns were holstered, and two or three dashed off to head the frightened horse, which was badly cut and bleeding from the broken glass case.

Rich spurt out a mouthful of tobacco juice and slowly and deliberately, carefully aimed his big foot in the proper direction to the end of the spine, just below, and exactly right, to kick John Willis out into the middle of the street.

There was loud laughter. But the laughing suddenly stopped.

As John Willis was getting to his feet, bleeding and filthy, he noticed an old ex-slave named Houston, who was approaching with a basket of freshly laundered clothes balanced upon his head.

Old Houston was not aware of what was happening and was minding his own business, but as there was no one else on whom John Willis could vent his rage, he jerked out a long knife and lunged into the unsuspecting negro and stabbed him in the neck, leaving the knife buried to the hilt in his jugular vein.

Although he was dying, Houston ran up onto the veranda steps and fell, as he gave a mighty heave.

The kind old doctor, his wife, and many other white friends rushed to try to aid the faithful fallen one, but he was beyond assistance. He was dead.

All the attention was upon this scene on the inn veranda, and nobody scarcely noticed John Willis as he sauntered off down the street in the opposite direction, as he, presumably, was unarmed. His knife was still in the negro's neck, and Rich McManus had his gun.

Mr. John Bunkley was coming into town. He got off his wagon, and started down the street towards the store. He had gone only a few steps from his wagon when he met John Willis.

Mr. Bunkley said, "Howdy do," very pleasantly.

For answer, John Willis produced another knife and sailed into Mr. Bunkley. Before anyone could reach them to interfere, Bunkley was slashed to shreds.

Ellisville had never witnessed such crime before, and the whole town went wild.

The wounded man was removed to the veranda, where the doctor closed his wounds and administered to him.

Feeling ran high, and there were threats of lynching, so John Willis was thrown in jail, and justice was done, but before daybreak the next morning, Captain Knight and his men had staged a jailbreak, and John Willis was free.

Thus justice was meted out during Captain Newt's tenure of office.

After the kicking episode, the town waited with bated breath, expecting the worst to come. But always there has been some bad man, bad enough, or bold enough, or wise enough to outsmart and subdue the worst man. So it was told that John Willis Musgrove had met his match in the person of Rich McManus.

The tale was circulated that Mr. McManus was also a fugitive from justice. Whether or not this was true, it caused the Knight Company to form a new respect for him, and after hearing that he came to Ellisville, the town without a railroad, in order to escape punishment for having slain a dozen slaves that had struck mutiny in his father's winery, back in the country from whence he came, it was understandable that he had the guts to kick John Willis.

Thereafter, Knight was seldom accompanied by the Musgroves, but when they were along all kept peaceable.

Years later, when Laurel was beginning to sprout into a town, the Musgroves set forth to halt the progress, and it was near the Matty Bush place that John Jefferson was slain in the ruckus with a Mr. Wilse and a Mr. Cally.

John Willis was also in the scrape, but after Wilse had knocked John Mat down with a "scant'lin'," Cally shot him through the mouth, and he lay dead, there on Laurel's new street, while John Willis sent for one of the negroes on their place to drive over a wagon on which to haul in the body.

After that, John Willis left Jones County, but he is remembered as one of the most loyal of the deserter band and also as the best fiddler that ever fiddled in the hideouts.

The other brothers became good citizens and were good neighbors.

They were all converted and became Christians, and ministers of the Gospel.

CHAPTER 19

Reconstruction

It has always been the rule, in time of war, for a few to "live off the fat o' land," and so was the case in Jones County. Amid the desolation of ruin, and ravage of starvation, a few apparently prospered, and a quantity of gold was cached away. In a few of the homes, there was still to be found elegance of living, as the inhabitants were usually warned of the approach of raiding Yankees, and prized household possessions were carefully hidden.

One family in Ellisville managed to save their belongings by possessing the knowledge of an old gully, where a series of sinkholes had started a landslide, and the caved out area had become large and treacherous to a horse rider. Down in the bottom of this gully was dry sand, and fallen pine straw. Although it was in open view of the trail, it provided a perfect place of concealment.

Just ahead of the invaders, the feather beds and pillows, the china and silver, and personal finery of members of the household was carried down to this old gully and buried beneath the dry sand, and more dry pine straw was gathered from the hillsides and deposited carefully in a natural like manner over the surface.

Since there were no tracks or traces of disturbance, the pilferers rode by, on the trail above, followed by scouts of the Knight Company, with neither party giving more than a downward glance in passing.

On the other hand, families were made destitute, and in the face of starvation, widows and orphans were compelled to cast aside pride and class distinction in order to gain assistance from the hardy peasantry, who seemed able to cope with the situation.

The day of governesses and private tutors was forever past. Soon the children of the upper class were associating with those of the more rugged citizens, who were formerly treated with polite disdain.

It is safe to say that the invasion of the North gave the South a half-century setback, socially, economically, and educationally, most especially educationally. And from this conflict there can never be complete recovery.

As people became more and more wrought up over the carpetbag rule in the South, hatred for Captain Knight increased.

He became wary as a cat, and perhaps that is the reason he lived to be an old and repentant man. Soon he came to distrust his friends, and members of his old Company who had stuck beside him through thick and thin turned him the cold shoulder. He sensed the change, and of them he also became suspicious.

His mouth twitched and worked, in keeping with his moods, until the handsomeness began to disappear, and in the place of the ready smile, was a smirk that added to the cruelness of his cold gaze. Newt always looked one in the eye for a second, before shifting his eyes, as if seeking out a hidden enemy. Then he would dart another sharp quick look, before resuming, or beginning a conversation. Always on the alert! Those eyes remained with the man who looked into them. In them there was a compelling fascination, of a strangeness that made an impression on the subconscious mind that time did not erase.

Now, as the Captain entered Ellisville, he rode with caution, for he knew that enemies were out to get him.

"Old Fox," was a suitable name, and that he was called, for with his knowledge of danger, it seemed that uncommon cunningness was at his command.

He was able to see through a pretended friendship. And on an occasion several years after the surrender, as he was in town, he chanced to meet two old friends who were glad to see him.

The welcome was too warm! They were too anxious to solicit his confidence and overdid the flattery.

After hearty greetings, they brought up the subject of old times, and the days when he was the great leader of the band. They reminded him that he was still, although unpopular with the families of the Confederates, the greatest man in the state. That he was spoken of as the slyest man that ever attempted to outwit the cavalry. They mentioned the narrow escapes he had had, and how he had shot his way out, when the odds were against him. And in truth there never was a better marksman than Newt Knight!

Finally, the friends came around to the point and proposed a scheme to get their intended victim out of town and away to a nearby swamp.

They told him that they would greatly enjoy having him take along his gun, conceal himself in a thicket, and let them from a distance observe the technique he had used in slaughtering his pursuers when he became cornered and had no alternative.

The Captain concealed his suspicions and obligingly went along pleasantly conversing, as they walked the open road, leading out of the town. From the open road, they were soon to enter a dim trail, which they traversed to another path. They left the path, and the three walked out into the thick brush.

One of the friends asked Knight to back himself into the bushes, leaving only his chest and head exposed, raise his gun up in a firing position, and pose for a picture to be taken.

The other friend stepped up and asked Newt for his gun, "So that you can make a break, and run through the brush, as if getting away," he explained.

But Newt replied, "No. I'll give my gun to no man, but I'll give you both barrels if you don't leave here, and leave here fast!" Quicker than lightning, he had his aim on both men, who raised high their hands, and started backing off, protesting that this was a mistake; that they were innocent of any wrong intentions.

Newt said one word, "Run!" And as they turned to run, hands still upraised, a mighty blast from the old gun tore up the ground at their feet.

These two men were forever afraid of Newt, and kept out of his sight after this plan to murder him fell through.

But other men had plans also to kill him.

It was known, and well understood, that if this man were openly slain, the Federal government would take action, since he was an officer. Or a few of his old gang who remained faithful would retaliate, so it was safer to plan to ensnare him in such a manner as to make the evidence appear that the act was self-defense, an accident, or possibly suicide.

However, after the first attempt, Newt became even more careful and suspicious.

He cautioned his family not to trust any person. He taught his children that any person who seemed overly friendly was an enemy. He told them not to ever let any man hug them, or pat their backs, that such an outward show of good fellowship was deceit in disguise.

Captain Knight was also a Federal Revenue Collector, but it was not this job that caused men to become his enemies.

On an occasion shortly after the picture-making incident, he was on his way to Jackson to attend to business, which was not unusual, and was waylaid at Newton, Mississippi, by six men who had planned to take his life.

It was known, generally, that he was often in Jackson for two or three weeks at a time, and that he went and came by way of this little town.

While Knight was waiting for the train, he overheard one man say to another, "That's him! Let's go let the others know that we have spotted him, and get several together to help, and we will kill him, this time, and it cannot be proven who did it."

Newt did not so much as bat an eye. He pretended not to have heard, and as soon as the men had rounded the corner of the station, he darted out onto the cotton platform and hid behind bales of cotton to wait for the train to pull in.

Soon his adversaries reappeared.

From this vantage point, Newt could observe them searching for him, and when they were convinced that he had given them the slip, they sauntered upon the very platform, and leaned against bales of cotton very near where he crouched, scarcely breathing. There, he heard every word they said. They talked about him, and his agility in making a getaway, and about how they would like to get their hands on him and place a rope about his neck!

Presently, the train arrived, and the men who would kill him, were between him and the coach. So for a minute, he experienced the fright of a hunted animal. He could not remain under the cotton bales, and if he made for the train, he would be shot! But the excitement of the approaching train gave him cover, for it attracted the attention of the six men, and Newt slipped from the platform, and made a dive for the moving train as it pulled away from the station. Just as he gained the caboose, he thought he heard one say, "Missed him again, but we'll get 'im on the return."

The Captain stood bareheaded, and gaily waved his black hat, as the train rounded a bend and disappeared from sight.

When Newt got to Jackson, he went to the governor and told him of the experience. The governor immediately formed a plan:

"We will trick them when you go back," he said. "You must be well armed, and on guard to defend yourself. You must change your appearance, so that you will not be easily recognized. You must shave off your full beard, and have your hair cut, and you must wear different clothes."

So when the business in Jackson was completed, Newt went about the business of changing his appearance.

Several days later, when the train arrived in Newton, a dude stepped off, wearing a new and shiny pistol in an elaborate holster. His hat was a soft dull gray, and he wore it handsomely, set back from his forehead. His shirt was a "store bought," finely tucked down the front. His boots were shined, and he looked not at all like a hunted man, or the man who had leaped upon a moving train, wearing a big black hat, two weeks before!

When he reached home, his own children did not recognize him and could not, at first, believe that this handsome stranger was their father.

Now, as the Captain had assumed an air of aloofness, and scarcely spoke to the remnant of his old cronies, they too became less ardent, and not realizing that it was the strain which public opinion was having upon their old leader, they thought that he had some personal grudge and wished to separate himself from them.

When he went into Ellisville, he was not accompanied by the gay and noisy band but went alone.

There was not much left for him to do.

Most of the old slaves, although free to go and come, preferred to remain with their former owners.

There were not so many arrogant and disrespectful negroes in this part of the country, as there were in other sections, because most of the population of black people were born here, or were brought here by people moving in and were reared by good families.

At last, free! The good misguided, misinformed negroes thought that all they had to do was walk out and claim a parcel of land, settle there, and be the owner.

Abolitionist propaganda had worked them up to a stage of expectancy, and they were waiting for the Union to buy them a fat horse. Many expected two fat horses, and a carriage, fine clothes, and to be set up equal with the white masters.

A slave girl, Elsie Duckworth, aged sixteen, upon being told that she was free, rushed out of the quarters on her master's plantation. She ran like a wild animal that had been released from its cage. Over the hills and fields she ran, across woodlands and stream, with the one thought prevailing, Free! Free!

A song rang from her lips, a wordless song, a song that only a negro woman can sing. A low sweet hum, that rises to a strange falsetto, followed by treble notes, musical and wild.

Exhausted, Elsie returned to the orchard of her ex-master, and with a grubbing hoe, removed sprouts which grew from the base of the trunks of his apple and peach trees.

These she gathered up in her arms, climbed over the rail fence, and there on a woodland slant, she decided to plant an orchard. Elsie's orchard! With the endless song of happiness continued, as she carefully spaded the ground and set out her little trees, she did not realize that this ground could never be hers, as it was part of the master's plantation.

Such pathos was not uncommon. Always seeking something better, these people, unused to shifting for themselves, became more and more distressed, as the clothing which they wore away from the master's homes became more and more ragged. From ragged, it came to tatters, and they were unable to hide the nakedness of their empty bellies.

The roads were a dust-bed in dry weather, a slew of thick mud after a rain. But the negroes, barefoot, winter and summer mushed through the hot dust, or the icy mud, in search of food or a place to lay their heads.

Mercifully, the South, with its long growing season, provided food, such as it was. In the spring, there were berries growing wild and of many varieties, the huckleberry, the blackberry, dewberry, mulberry, and gooseberry, and as spring opened into summer the negroes ate every maypop (fruit of the passion flower). Then autumn came, with wild grapes and muscadines and wild nuts. The chinquapin, chestnuts, and walnuts peppered the hillsides. The persimmons, bright with the first frost, became ripe and luscious. So all, though hungry most of the time, managed to survive.

There were loads of household goods drawn by ox wagons over the trails, the personal belongings of displaced persons, in search of new homes after the war. Many people left Jones County immediately after the surrender.

An old letter says in part:

"Here we are, set up in our new home, and we are making a good start. I have thirty young turkeys, and we have a nice garden, and good neighbors. The people here seem just like the people in Cracker's Neck.

"We could be happy here but for one thing. My father's old slaves have found out where I am, and they have followed me here. They think we could keep them, but we can't, they are a pitiful sight. Him and her, grown man and woman and they act like the five little ones they have hungry, and she is a lookin' agin. There bodys are fat enough but they are neckid, and I don't know what is to become of them. I dont want this one to be born here in or crib. We have to let them sleep on the fodder as we have no other place."

The letter makes no further mention of the unfortunate black family, and the subject is abruptly changed to inquire about the whereabouts of other people.

After it began to dawn on these people that their livelihood depended upon their labors, and that they would not receive any assistance from any other people than "their white folks" in the South, many were willing to work, but there was nothing with which to pay them for their services! So, an old bone, to boil as seasoning with a pot of greens, became pay for a day's labor in the fields.

The joy of living ebbed from the blacks. No longer did they sing as they worked. A saddened mother coined the words for a prayer, and her little ones, often gathered together, from other plantations miles away, where they had been sold or exchanged, joined her in repeating the words. A low sad mumble swelled into wails of lamentation, as all labored together for their bread.

Some, in the fall of the year, stripped sugar cane, worked at the molasses mills at feeding the cane into the huge rollers that squeezed the juice which poured into wooden barrels. The rollers were set in motion by oxen power, as these patient beasts of burden plodded round and round in the beaten circle, keeping the juice running. Endless toil! Forever it seemed! There would never again be a time to sing, a time to shout, or a time to frolic and dance till the break of dawn!

The Southerners could barely feed themselves, let alone assume the burden of their ex-slaves, and the North did not want them! So they became, and have been to this day, a people dependent upon the friendship and help of their white friends, because they are not yet able to cope with this thing called "civilization," as a race, as civilization is a thing new and strange to their natural instincts, so they plod, as oxen to the mill, patient and enduring, and for this faithfulness they are being rewarded here in the South, as the people are forgetting how short the time has been since these people, nameless, whose parentage was as varied and uncertain as that of the beasts of the forests, whose ancestors boiled and ate their sons, came to America. And are permitting them to establish themselves, as they are fitted, as individuals, in positions of trust and responsibility.

The negro race in the South fully understands the attitude of their friends, and are encouraged by the increasing respect that is being shown them and are making an earnest endeavor to measure up to the standards of an enlightened people, but as a people of pure race.

They understand perfectly that there must be two races, a black and a white, for a mixed race will always be a people without "place."

Captain Newton Knight foresaw this in the year 1884, when he made the most sensational sacrifice in history, in a vain effort to eradicate a mixed-blooded race in Jones County!

* * * *

Men who had been in the company of Knight joined the Ku Klux Klan, which shows that their purpose in fighting against the Confederacy was not for emancipation of slavery. However, the purpose of the Klan organization was not altogether a plan to control the negro, but was for a means of combating other anti-Southern activity.

A white man was not exempt because he was a white man, if he had a beating coming to him, and here in Jones County, the negro problem was really no problem at all, as he has always been the scapegoat for some wicked white man.

There is no man that has not some good mixed in with the bad, and it cannot be said that Newt Knight was altogether bad.

Although he was radical in his viewpoint, he still held on to a few of the principles instilled by his progenitors, for on occasion he exhibited chivalry expected of a Southern gentleman.

After he became so unpopular in Ellisville, after he had suffered the indignity of Rachel's trial and was occupying the position of a social outcast, he performed an act of chivalry that should, in all fairness, be mentioned here:

The carpetbaggers had imported some strange negroes into Jones County to propagate the "Freedman's Bureau" and the "Loyal League," and of these, a tool was made, to test the attitude of the white population, as the North, even at that early period, advocated social equality and attempted to inflict preposterous insult upon a helpless and injured people.

Before the Ku Klux Klan could take the situation in hand, many atrocities had been committed.

These imports were dressed in the finest of clothes, and they preened and paraded like peacocks on the street. Of course, the citizens understood what it was all about and ignored the act. But one big African refused to be ignored. He paraded and strutted in his fine black mohair suit, a silk waistcoat, from which dangled an enormous gold watch-chain. He doffed his high silk hat to the ladies as they passed, but they looked straight ahead, and paid no more attention than if he had been a post standing there.

So finally, he mounted the steps and loitered about the door of McManus's store until a lady shopper came out with her child in her arms and also carrying a bundle.

Then the black stepped forward and planted his foot firmly on the hem of her skirt (the style had changed from the hoop to a full flounce, with a dip, suggesting a train in back). The skirt swept the floor of the platform, as the lady had no free hand to gently lift it clear, and seeing this, he stood there, like a statue.

"Will you step off my dress, please?" she asked.

The black did not answer, and neither did he move. He pretended to be unaware of the fact that he was hindering her progress.

She raised her voice, and demanded, "Get off my dress!"

Again, he ignored her and looked in the opposite direction, as if intently engrossed with something across the street. He did not move.

Just as the distressed lady was about to cry out for help, there was a sudden commotion, as Newt Knight darted like a flash, from out of space it appeared, and landed squarely behind the negro on the platform.

Before he had time to move, Newt let him have a mighty wallop with his fist, on which he wore a pair of brass knux (knuckles) to the base of his skull, which was enough to have killed a white man. The negro landed, unconscious, in the middle of the dusty street, his bloody face plowing into the ground.

The lady did not have a chance to express her gratitude; the Captain was gone, suddenly and unseen, as he had come. But this lady of the gentry passed the word around that her hero was the man who was regarded as "a negro lover" and the most contemptible man in Mississippi!

Born out of this incident was a new respect for Newt Knight. Perhaps that one gallant act kept him from being tarred and feathered by the Ku Klux Klan, for that deed alone shed light on how he stood on the "negro rule."

At that time our state government was practically run by negroes, placed there by the carpetbaggers and dishonest politicians bent on holding the South in ruin and disgrace.

Newt Knight was by no means the "lowest" man in Mississippi, for during the Ames Administration, we had nine negro senators, fifty-five negro members of the House, our lieutenant governor was a negro, our state superintendent of education, and the secretary of state, the commissioners of agriculture and immigration, were all negroes, having been elevated to these various offices by shrewd and unscrupulous white men who were behind the Freedman's Bureau and the Loyal League. Most of these negro officials could not even read and write, and the affairs drifted into a deplorable state and remained so until after Governor Stone became Mississippi's highest executive.

Then these organizations were curbed, and gradually the state started the snail pace of progress out from under her yoke of oppression.

It was in disillusionment and humility that the negroes turned to their former white friends for comfort and help.

Esther Barnes was a slave woman who was freed with her brood of hungry children, and her descendants say that she and her family would have perished from starvation had not her ex-master divided his scarce bread with them. That is just one case. It happened all over the South.

Earlier than most ex-slaves, Rachel realized that her only hope, now that her master and mistress were dead, and she was free, would be to find one member of the Old Family who would accept her and hers as hands on a farm. But she knew that they all hated her for having befriended the deserters, and she knew that in their hearts, they could have no love for her, because she had refused to be disciplined and had become a strumpet.

Finally, she decided to take her children and try to locate with Newt, as a share-cropper on his land, up near Salsbattery, where he had returned to make his home. And it was he who took her in.

It was agreeable with Newt's wife to have a woman to help with the household tasks, the washing and the ironing, and the cooking. And Rachel was well trained, having learned much from the aristocratic Georgia family to whom she had belonged before she came to the old Knight household, where she learned much more. And she was polite and respectful.

But Serena was unaware of what went on with Rachel and the army under Newt. Had she known, she would never have consented to Rachel's moving in to become a tenant.

Serena Knight reared her children well, prepared a good table, and with the exception of that little affair with Morgan, had always been true to her husband.

Newt forgave her for that, and she, in turn, forgave him for all the deeds that he had done, deeds that would have wrung the hearts of most women.

Now that the tide was slowly turning, and her husband was at home, little things kept coming up that irked Serena, things small and of no consequence.

For instance, Rachel was stealing the affections of her children by little courtesies, sweet talk, and favors of every kind, and they were staying around Rachel's house more than their mother liked.

Newt had a fondness for apples, and a fondness for planting apple trees. They grew, not only in a well laid out orchard, but in every conceivable spot. As shade trees, ornamenting the yards of his tenants, and in the fence corners. The hills were fragrant with apple blossom in spring, and with the fruit in autumn.

Near Rachel's house, which was a full quarter of a mile from his own residence, there grew a big gnarled apple tree, which he had planted there before the war. Its age seemed to lend enchantment to its beauty in blossom time, and its shade was most appreciated in summer.

Under this tree was a rustic bench, and it was here that the "hair dressin'" of Rachel's family took place, during the long summer months.

Rosette and Rachel decided that they would also wrap the hair of Serena's children.

The children, unwilling to protest any demand of Rachel, who had won them over and had them completely under her influence, submitted to the negro hair fashion. To them, it was a big joke.

But when they returned home with their blond hair twisted up in unsightly wrapped tufts, tied with many colored string, it was the last straw with their mother!

"Why, that hussy is trying to make negroes out of our children!" she exclaimed.

"Oh, I guess it was all done in play," answered Newt.

But Serena disregarded his opinion and rushed down upon Rachel and angrily ordered her to let that be the last time.

Serena's anger only encouraged Rachel, as she was filled with a streak of maliciousness, and as she knew that she could always "square" Newt, there was no reason why she should not enjoy tormenting his wife.

The hair wrapping continued, every time the children played near Rachel's house, and with it, the unhappiness in Newt's house grew.

Then tragedy drew the family closer. One of the twins was burned to death, a horrible death, and as it was the first occurrence among their children, it hurt deeply.

High up on the hill above Newt's house was an old cemetery, forlorn and unattended. Here were the graves of the people who were drowned when their oxen had leaped off the ferry into the raging waters of Leaf, as they attempted to cross during flood stage.

The people were on their way to visit the Daniels who lived up there before Newt, possibly kin, so their five bodies were taken from the river and carried on up to their destination, where they were buried side by side, in a row.

In this cemetery were the graves of two of Newt's ex-guerrillas, who had been hanged nearby.

A few feet away from the graves of the deserters, were the graves of six Confederate soldiers who had been killed in a battle which had occurred at Newt's old barn.

Little Billie was laid to rest here beside this strange assortment of dead. And Newt's family walked back to their home in sadness.

After that Rachel was kinder and tried to lighten the burden of her landlady.

All was forgiven, and Serena was convinced that she had been mistaken about Rachel and repented her accusations. Peace and harmony existed between the two families, and the past was forgotten.

Chapter 20

Discord

After the war was over, and normalcy had returned, the Knight Company was disbanded, and men went back to their homes to take up where they had left off, and were making an effort to live peaceably, as far as possible.

Many of these were never seen by the general public, and as this was a secret organization, many served without their own families' knowledge.

It seems that the leader of the band was the only one that stood to bear the blame. He and a few of the others had made no secret of the fact that they were deserters. It was convenient to let him bear the blame, although, three or four men who had been with him remained faithful to the end.

Their friendship did not lighten his burden, and gradually, Newt realized that he was losing his prestige.

Quietly, and gracefully, he withdrew from public duty, and as he was seldom invited to take part in the affairs of the community, he spent more and more time at home.

His was the finest land in this part of the country, and with time on his hands, he worked hard at improving it.

When he had first returned to the lands where he had settled after his marriage, there was already a prolific orchard, an enriched garden spot, and all of the barn was still usable.

The ashes of the old house were so ideally located until it would have been impossible to have chosen a more desirable spot, so he cleared away the site for a new foundation and set this new house upon the old ashes.

It stood high above a deep hollow, through which trickled a little stream. From the house there led a path down to a clear cold spring that poured out of the hillside and fed the stream.

The house was plain and unpretentious, though well built, with a big fireplace of rock taking up one end of the big living room. The kitchen was built off away from the house, with a sheltered walkway connecting it to the big house. The kitchen also had a big open fireplace at one end.

Above the mantles were gunracks holding firearms. Even the kitchen bore the emblem of protection. Hung on pegs at either side of the fireplace were pots and pans and strings of red pepper, strings of vari-colored popcorn, and a string of lucky charms!

Newt was superstitious, and with the coming of Rachel, he was induced to believe more and more in sorcery, since Rachel practiced witchcraft.

Rachel was the first "conjure woman" in Jones County, and many people paid her to keep evil from their doors.

There were signs about Newt's premises that denoted this weird characteristic, despite Serena's protests (another thing that irked her with Rachel). Above his gate posts, atop a high pole was a good-luck charm, whittled from cedar, a pinwheel, which he called a "windmill," as it spun and twirled in the breeze.

A picket fence encircled the yard, protecting it. The palings were sharpened at the tops and were five feet high and closely spaced.

In the yard were flowers of all the old varieties, the pink burr rose, bachelor buttons, and prince's feathers, and the edge of the high front porch was bordered by four-o-clocks, which were drenched by the waste water, after one took a drink from the old gourd dipper, out of the brass-hooped cedar bucket that set on the watershelf.

On the porch were homemade hickory chairs, with cowhide bottoms, hides that had been tanned with the hair left on. These were shaded by a sweet honeysuckle vine, and a climbing red seven-sister, which grew up over the end of the gallery.

Here was evidence of peace and happiness. And Newt's family were happy here, for he was a good father to his children. He was never cross or unkind, and now that he was at home, he seemed more devoted to them than he had ever been before.

Yet there was a dread premonition hanging over him, and he could not be happy. He was given to changing moods, and from a great show of pleasure in romping with daughter Molly, or the other twin, he would suddenly become sad and morose and would drift into a silence from which he could not be removed.

These silences grew upon him, and unless he was directing the negroes at their work in the fields, he would wander off alone.

His family spared him questions, and his wife seemed to understand that a man as great as hers would be expected to isolate himself during these thinking periods.

He would shoulder his old gun and go off down the path towards the spring, as if looking for wild game, and spend the day alone, brooding. What his thoughts were will never be known.

Before night, he always came in, and in he stayed, until the next morning, with windows and doors barred and the latch-string pulled inside.

Perhaps he tried to shut out the ghosts of the many men he had slain!

He had acted as if he expected a sudden presence since the day he slew Morgan and had kept his eyes open and his ears attentive.

It has been said by men who tried that it was impossible to sneak up on Newt Knight, and that no one ever was permitted to walk up behind his back, as he would always manage to keep his guests in front of him.

As night drew near, he would saunter out and lean on the old picket gate and look long and hard down the road, as if attempting to discern a movement of a stealthy human figure among the deepening shadows. Always on the alert. Always casting furtive glances, to the right, to the left, and behind him as he walked, working his mouth, and starting at sudden noises.

The sound of the martin gourds bumping together in the wind filled him with panic, and the barking of his old dog made him apprehensive.

His family became accustomed to his moods, and when he sat with his gun across his knees before the fire, they thought nothing unusual. He seldom talked to them, but that did not seem strange to them, as all great men are reserved, to an extent. When he did speak, they heeded his words, and whatever he said to them became law!

The tenants on his plantation obeyed him and granted his every wish.

To them, he was a god. Was it not he who had taken in Rachel and her hungry brood when they had been turned out on the mercies of the world after the surrender? Was it not he who had, with his own hands, grabbled a few sweet potatoes from his own patch to feed the little black scrawny Rosette and the three "white negroes" belonging to Rachel? Did he not let them sleep in the old bullet-riddled barn under the leaky roof, until he could build, with his own hands, a shelter of split cypress boards, that did not leak, over a house for them to live in? It was their house!

These favors were full payment for all that Rachel had suffered at the hands of the wicked followers of Captain Knight.

She absolved him of all blame, as she understood only too well that had she been less solicitous to aid the deserters, she would not have been subjugated to the sensuous demands of unchastity.

But Rachel's forgiveness did not ease Newt's conscience.

He felt that he was entirely responsible for the existence of little Fan, the white child born to Rachel, whose face was fair, whose hair hung in soft brown curls to her shoulders. Because he knew that it was he who had detained Rachel to satisfy the evil pleasures of his men, when she had come to their hideouts to bring food, or powdered red pepper for the cavalry's hounds. So it was up to him now to make some atonement.

There existed between Newt and Rachel a common bond of sympathy.

She worked here and there, wherever she could get a day's work to do, when she was not busy on Newt's place. And from other negroes with whom she came in contact, she kept posted as to what the white people said and thought about her benefactor.

These things she told him, and with his information of more gossip, he became even more aloof.

The boy Jeff was a good sized plowboy, almost grown now, and with the undernourished long-legged Rosette, and the plump little Georgianne for hoe-help, Rachel was equipped with the help to grow a good crop. And Fan was getting big enough to keep the little ones that kept popping up at Rachel's house.

Rachel had no husband, but then, no husband was necessary, and was hardly expected, as it was commonly known that Rachel was an undesirable, having mixed-blood children at the time she was sold into Mississippi.

All three, Rosette, Georgianne, and Jeff were slave-born, and it was the custom for slave women to bear children of different fathers. And quite the exception for children to all have the same father, although children of a wedded mother.

Just because of the fact that Rachel was freed was no earthly reason why she should cease child-bearing. So, no explanation of the free-born was forthcoming.

In fact, Rachel had never been called upon, except on one occasion, to explain her circumstance.

That was at the time when Jones Countians were so bitter towards Newt, after he became the Provost Marshall. And to accuse a man of mixing the blood of the races was the most detrimental testimony that could be offered. Nothing worse could be said of a man. And as it was known that this Mulatto had been his accomplice and was then living on his plantation, it was rumored that the Captain was the father of Fan.

So each time the tale was repeated, it was elaborated upon, and finally it grew to such proportions until it resulted in Rachel being arrested and carried into Ellisville for trial.

At the trial, the very pointed question was asked by the Prosecution, "Who is the father of your child?"

But Rachel was smart, and her answer was anything except to the point. She replied, "When a rabbit is thrown into a briar patch, she cannot know which briar pricked."

So, with no further statement from Rachel, and as there was no substantial evidence or testimony, the case was dismissed.

(The record of that court procedure was destroyed in Ellisville's courthouse fire.) However the story kept traveling, and it is believed until this day that Fan was Newt's daughter, but in view of other facts, that could not be true.

Rachel's answer was the truest one that could have been given, for in reality, at the time of Fan's conception, Rachel was a victim of circumstances, and it would be impossible to say just which of the 125 men was the father of the "white negro."

There was no discussion among Rachel's children regarding their color. They were just another negro family, with some "dark" and the others "light'"cause they had a white grandfather. That was reason enough.

And, although Georgianne and Fan were able to pass as full white, with their beautiful eyes and soft olive skin and light brown hair, they were negroes because they were only three-quarter white, so they were reared along with the "dark" ones, according to the old traditions and customs of an enslaved people.

Rosette's hair was not only black and kinky. It was short and wiry and had to be "wrapped" as it was too stubborn to wear in pigtails.

Rosette's father was a full-blooded, blue-gummed African, and his daughter bore no resemblance to her Mulatto mother, but from him she inherited her negroid characteristics, in fine detail, even to that little odor peculiar to the full-blooded black race.

It was quite natural, she being older, to give attention to her younger sisters' personal needs. She checked off their hair into many little sections, caught it up in tufts, and wrapped 'round and 'round each tuft with twine string, just as she wore her own.

By the time they became covered with the thick dust from the fields of Newt's farm, where they hoed and picked cotton, the two white daughters were a sad sight.

Their brother Jeff was a handsome boy, almost as white as any member of his landlord's family, but he too was just another negro, and he "stayed in a negro's place," remembered always to enter by the back door.

But peace was short lived, and Serena's life became miserable, with Newt staying down by the spring, day after day.

At first she thought that he was silently grieving over their lost child, but now he scarcely spoke to her, and when he did, it was some word of reproach.

More and more superstitious he became, and he was forever having business at Rachel's house, because she had led him to believe that she was "a seventh child, born with a veil," and had the gift of strange and unnatural powers because of this fact.

She kept a pot of coffee on the coals on her hearth, that she might have ready grounds for the cup, when her landlord came to have her peer into the future and predict his fate.

When Newt drank from the cup, he handed it back to Rachel, with always the same question, "How am I to die? Are my enemies near me now? What will become of my family?" were some of the ones he asked her over and over.

"Oh, your enemies will never ketch up wi' you," Rachel comforted. "You trusted me whilst you wuz hid out, an' you're yet alive," she boasted.

"Jest trust me now, an' do what I say, an' you can be spared. I will prepare a magic potion that will keep harm off'n you," she told him. "An' your fambly an' my fambly shall be as close as one. I shall see that all is well."

As he would start to leave, she would call him back and ask him to sip from the cup again. Then she would roll her green eyes mysteriously, look long into the cup, and then shake her head.

"Bad, too bad!" she would exclaim. Then she would proceed to caution Newt to watch his wife, tell him that his wife was unfaithful and that great trouble was in store.

Then Newt would hurry away and hide near his house and watch for some imaginary lover to approach for a clandestine visit with his poor innocent wife.

This jealousy was fed by Rachel's predictions, and that carried him more often to her house for advice and comfort in his imagined troubles.

As soon as he left out, other men crept in, for other purposes, and other children were born to Rachel.

There was Floyd, Henchie, Stewart, and Martha Ann, all born under the name Knight, because that was the name that their mother bore.

It has been said that they were the children of Newt, but that is not true, as Newt was visiting with Rachel for other reasons and did not have issue by her of any child.

It was thought, even by his good wife, that he was guilty of carrying on a liaison with the green-eyed Mulatto, but of that he was innocent, and it is doubtful if ever he thought of such a thing.

CHAPTER 21

The Unhappiness of Serena

Serena knew that over the beaten paths from the main road, men rode to Rachel's house.

The mounts of white men stood hitched for hours to the picket fence in front of her house.

Of this Serena demanded an explanation. When her husband had no answer, and refused to reply to her questioning, she became furious and stomped and fumed. But he remained uncommunicative.

"Do you 'spose they're here to hire 'em off?" she demanded.

No answer.

"Then, you're not to put up with that. Lettin' 'em pole off to some other field to work, an' come back to us to be fed," she stormed.

"That's a sorry nigger bunch. I want you to run 'em off the place. A trouble-maker, that's what she is. Her and her fortune-telling! Bah! A stink stirrer!" snorted Serena, as she snatched an empty coffee cup off the table, lifted the pot, and poured in a few drops of the black ground-thickened liquid.

She turned the cup round and round in the palm of her hand, gave its contents a gentle slosh, and held it mockingly, up to the light. She rolled her eyes, mimicking Rachel, and blew her breath into the cup.

"I see—" she began, and stopped short, and gave Newt a look of utter disgust and contempt.

"Why, you're not that crazy, tho people are a' sayin' you're crazy; you know that that slut can no more tell fortunes than I can," said Serena, through her tightly drawn lips.

Angrily, she dashed the cup against the rock of the kitchen fireplace, spattering it into pieces.

There was no comment.

Newt did not move, or look up. He sat silent and motionless, gazing into the fire. Then he started moving and twisting his lips.

Serena rushed out of the room.

That scene ended to begin another, and another, with Serena finally accusing Newt of "keeping" Rachel.

There was no reply.

But early mornings by the time light broke in the east, Newt was up and preparing to leave, in order to escape the constant nagging. Always with him he carried his trusty gun.

Rachel and her family were fully aware of the state of affairs in Newt's house, and they avoided Serena as much as possible, so she was left very much alone with her hatred and jealousy.

The friends she had once had forsook her now, and she had no one in whom she could confide. "Why?" she asked herself. Why was it that once they were leaders in their community, and now they were avoided and left out of things? She wracked her brain for a reason. Why did no one come to visit, as of old?

Finally she came to the conclusion that it was because of her husband. She remembered some of the things that people had said the morning they opened the new school.

Every two or three miles apart there was a white family who had children in need of schooling.

Included were the children of two or three of the men who had been secret members of Newt's band when he had deserted the Confederacy. These men came to Newt, and he was instrumental in the organization of the new school.

They selected a teacher, who was to "board about" and receive ten dollars per month as his salary.

The term, boarding about, meant that he was to sojourn in the home of each patron for a given time, in order that his expense would not be a burden on any but would be equally borne by all.

On the morning of the school opening, the children came to enroll and begin classes, and most were accompanied by their parents.

All unexpected, there appeared Rachel's children to be enrolled also! The audience was thunderstruck for a few minutes, and there was started a buzz of whispered conversation.

The teacher jumped upon the rostrum and angrily shouted, "What is this? I thought you hired me here to teach a white school! I refuse to teach negroes! I resign!"

Other men arose, and in plain solemn words asked Rachel's children why they had come.

They replied simply that their mother had sent them.

Then one of the trustees got up on the rostrum to make a speech. He began by first ordering the mixed-blooded children to return to their mother and tell her that white schools did not accept negro students.

Then he assured the schoolmaster that he would have no trouble with similar occurrence. So the excitement was soon over, and school was begun.

But it lasted only one day. Shortly after dark that night, the country was weirdly lighted, and the beauty of the majestic pines stood out in bold relief, on the hill by the light of the burning schoolhouse.

"How did it happen? Who did it?" were unanswered questions.

It was at once said that Newt set it because he wished the negroes to have equal opportunity. Others said that Rachel, angry over the refusal to let her children enter, set it. And even another said that, secretly, under cover of the evening's shadows, Rachel had called on two white men who were the fathers of her children and had threatened to expose them if they did not burn the school, as her two were half-brothers to theirs, and therefore should have equal rights. And to silence Rachel, the men gladly complied with her wishes.

But poor Newt bore the blame.

Already he was burdened with the fear of losing his wife. Serena was becoming more difficult to live with, and now she was giving him his choice of sending away Rachel and her family, or she, the mother of his children, would be forced to leave. The breach was widening.

Newt knew that there was no place for Rachel to go. And he knew that he was the cause of some of Rachel's children being in the world, not because he was their father but because he had compelled Rachel to satisfy the lust of some of the lawless band under his command. And besides, Rachel's negroes were good field hands, and she was able to support them from the abundant crops which they grew. He was also profiting from their labors, as one-half of what they made belonged to him, and his plantation was expanding under their management and labors.

Divorce was most uncommon in that day, and he could not believe that Serena would make good her threat to break up their home and leave him.

So he did precisely what he always did. He worked his mouth, he jumped at sudden noises, he maintained a stony silence, and he came in before good dark and shut himself in, away from the lurking ghosts of the past.

But one morning, Serena kissed her children before they were awake and left them to whatever fate was likely to befall motherless waifs. Because now the green demon had taken her affairs completely in hand, and she was leaving.

She crept out of the house with a few personal belongings, and slipped down the road, to where there was a bypath that led through the heavily wooded timberland. Through blinding tears, she stumbled onto the path, unmindful of the dew from the wet weeds and grass that drabbled her skirts.

Where?

She had no idea. Just away from the terrible suspicion that was gnawing her heart; away from the half-breed who was holding her and her family under her evil thumb by the power of black magic! Serena could have killed Newt for being such a fool!

Wild morning glories lifted beautiful trumpets of color to greet the day! Here along the path, they grew profusely, twining and intertwining from grass to bush, from bush to tree, and were, in places, connected across the path by silvery spiderwebs, hanging with drops that glistened like diamonds in the early light.

Serena walked right into these and, without seeing their beauty, carelessly brushed the wetness from her face, for her grief had made her insensible to the exotic charms of nature.

Onward, onward she went, not knowing to whom she would go, or where she might find peace. She walked as one in a trance, not realizing how far. She knew only that the settlements of Big Creek and Cracker's Neck lay southward, in the direction that she was walking, and in those settlements were other people, happy people, and with them, any of them, she would be away from this terrible aloneness.

The sun rose and warmed the day, but Serena kept walking.

The path led down toward a little creek, that was overgrown by briars and bamboo, but there was no turning back.

It had been reported that panthers had, in the spring of the year, been seen in this area, but Serena was not afraid. She pushed through the tangle, and made her way downward to the foot-log that was the only crossing.

Just as she stepped down off the log on the other side, a gun fired at close range. The report was so near, so sudden and unexpected, poor Serena's heart almost stopped from shock.

Out of the thick bamboo stepped Newt. Although they had barely spoken at home for weeks, they were here alone in the woods, and the silence was awkward. So Serena spoke.

"Why, why," she stammered, "did you shoot?"

He replied in even tones, "I shot at a jaybird and—missed."

She knew that he was lying. She saw it on his face, saw murder in his strange cold eyes, that met and held hers. He had looked like that through the open window, just before Morgan fell face first in a pool of blood. She would always remember that look! And she knew that he had followed her here to kill her.

Later, he admitted that a low-hanging branch had caught the hammer of his gun, as he had raised it to shoot her, and in that way, his aim was knocked off, and she was accidentally spared.

He did not ask her about her intentions of leaving him. He roughly seized her and turned her around in the path and ordered her to return ahead of him to their home.

From then on, she remembered the look in his eyes when they had stood facing each other back there in the woods, and she knew that she could never leave him without him taking her life.

As there was no alternative, poor Serena committed herself to a life in which she had no plan and did Newt's bidding without complaint.

As time moved on, the children of Captain Knight, those born before the war, became quite grown up.

Their mother had taught them at home, and not only had they grown in stature but intellectually, as well.

Miss Molly became the favorite of her father. It was she who cheered him when all the world seemed against him. It was she who gave him the little attentions that endeared her to him. He was proud of her beauty, and it grieved him sorely to think that she was doomed socially.

Molly was of medium height, statuesque as a queen. Her hair was soft and shining, and she wore it lifted high above the pleasing soft-ness of her beautiful white neck, and piled high on the top of her well-shaped head. Tiny ringlets in bangs accented her even brows and the sweep of her long dark lashes, over eyes that were a true violet. They were like her mother's eyes, except Molly could not remember the same twinkle, for Serena's eyes were sad.

She bore only a slight resemblance to her father, but in her was his determination, and like him, she was hasty and often unwise in her judgment.

But Molly was a lady, in every respect. (Had she been a foundling, with an environment among more fortunate people, her life would have been so different.) She was dainty in her habits, and her manners were impeccable.

Often at dusk, she would walk out to the gate with her father, and they would talk about their circumstance. Molly would giggle and say that she preferred living unmolested, to themselves. But deep inside she burned with an uncontrollable resentment.

Molly was not a tomboy, yet she played with the others at boy's games. Playing ball with her brothers and Rachel's children, in order for them to have a number required for the game was the only reason Molly had for playing at all.

Serena watched them at play and ridiculed her daughter for indulging in this innocent pastime.

Even she did not know what was going on with Molly, who would have preferred to join other young people in the fun and frolic that was popular in that day.

Molly loved to dance, and gay house parties were staged in good homes here and there over the settlements, where the young ones danced until morning. But Molly was not invited.

The family of Newt Knight still attended church, and they sat apart from the others. Not by choice.

Other ladies ignored Molly and Serena, and they, in turn, sought no recognition.

Hoop skirts were the fashion of the day.

A part of the bringing up of a little girl was to teach her that strict attention must be paid one's garments.

Any female on whom there was "talk" was to be avoided as a thing untouchable. And the skirt of one chaste must not, in any way, come in contact with that of the unchaste.

Attached at the tiny waist line was a ribbon that reached to the hoop, on which it was securely fastened on the right side. This arrangement gave the wearer control of the hoop, without attracting attention, as it was gently tilted by a tug at the ribbon, in passing others, becoming seated in a carriage, or in avoiding contact with undesirables.

As Molly sedately walked down the aisle of the church, she was conscious of many ladies tugging at their hoop-ribbons.

She was sure that this meant only that she was shunned because she was the daughter of the notorious Captain, so she proudly thrust her nose in the air and continued on her way to her regular seat, where she sat, obviously heedless of public opinion.

Secretly, this was too much for poor Molly, who was guilty of no wrong, but instead of breaking her spirit, there arose within her an indignation which impelled her to action.

Molly knew that as far as looks were concerned, she was envied by other belles, so she determined, as a reprisal, to cast her charms, and wreck the happiness of her persecutors by stealing their beaux.

CHAPTER 22

Shunned by Society

The people of the Cracker's Neck settlement were a gay carefree bunch, believing in fun and pastime, so it was frequently that big frolics were held in the homes of the families of that section, who had once recognized Captain Newt.

But since all this "negro talk," his family was omitted from the invitation list, and the church was about the only place that was open to Miss Molly.

However, she had a cousin, by the same name, who still dropped by Newt's house occasionally, and it was he who offered Molly an opportunity to attend one of these affairs.

At the homes where the functions were held, the young men of the household cut and piled wood high on the scaffolds in the chimney corner, just outside and beneath the window. And much more was cut and wheelbarrowed up to the front porch, where it was stacked in preparation for the big dance.

Always the preparation was the same as that made in advance of a big snow, because the fire would be kept blazing all night.

Armloads of split "fat lightered" kindling was cut and brought in along with "lightered knots" to mend the flame for added light.

There was preparation among the ladies of the home also, for the guests must be served. Many would arrive before supper, sometime during the afternoon of the day before the event, and there was much cooking to be done.

Molasses taffy was made and pulled by buttered hands (to keep the candy from sticking) into long slender brittle sticks, for the "candy breaking."

Peanuts were washed and dried to be parched or boiled in salted water, to be eaten before the fire.

For days, the meal bran had been saved from sifting the meal, to scatter on the plank floors, to make them "slick" for the dancers' feet.

The old fiddlers were all invited, and each fiddler, in turn, invited a "straw-beater" to accompany the banjos.

By midday on the date of the big dance, groups of young people, lads in Sunday best, and pretty girls, "a' sittin' side-saddles" were riding from distant settlements. From Ellisville, from down about the Seminary, from Sullivan's Hollow, out about Williamsburg, and from up above where Soso now is, to be there by nightfall, or before, for the big occasion.

Corn was already in the troughs for the visitors' horses, shucked days ahead by the farm boys, and everything and everybody was "in tune."

There was also great preparation at Newt's house, for Molly was invited!

She did not bother to tell her parents by whom she had been invited. The fact that she was going was enough!

Rachel had been summoned to assist, which she did, with deft hands.

Rachel liked to boast that she had been a lady's maid before she came to the Knights.

Molly's side-saddle was brought out and shined, and her horse was brushed and curried by the faithful Jeff.

Georgianne was a paid servant in the house, and she had been marvelously taught by Rachel.

The younger negroes brought green oak limbs to burn into red coals for Georgianne to have handy to heat the flat irons to iron the petticoats that her mistress would wear to the dance.

She starched the bottom layers of the skirts until they were stiff enough to stand alone on the floor after they had been ironed.

The sweet scorched cedar and melting bee's wax filled the room with a wonderful aroma, imparting a faint sweetness to the garments, as Georgianne rubbed the hot iron, first over the piece of bee's wax, to make it smooth and then over the fresh green cedar leaves, placed over the "ironin' rag" at the end of the board. There must be no trace of a spot on the dainty garments! And no Chinese was as flawless as Georgianne.

The other four or five petticoats were dainty and flimsy, and were worn as ornamentation and fashion rather than as a necessity.

When her escort arrived, Molly was waiting in high spirits. This was her big chance to get even with the girls who had shunned her back at old Mount Olive. This was her chance to meet the men she wished to ensnare with her radiant beauty!

Many admiring eyes watched her as she rode away. Although Rachel and her quadroon daughters hated Serena, they loved Miss Molly, and they were happy because she was happy.

It was early fall. Cotton was opening in the fields, and the fodder had been pulled. Drying bundles, tied to the bare cornstalks, rustled in the night wind. The sweet odor of autumn filled the air. Outside the zigzag rail fencerow by which the road led, the purple asters and the goldenrod waved.

As Molly passed, she felt that they were waving to her. Funny that she had never noticed their personalities before! But they were gay! The whole world was gay and bright! And there was the brilliant red of the shoemake, almost black in the early dusk, nodding!

Molly had never felt like this before.

The conversation of the two riders was light and gay, as gay as the wild flowers, which they were passing, as they rode along in the waning light.

Presently, the house came into view. The bright fire burning upon the hearth threw long rosy panels of light out through the open doors and windows. Across them flitted the shadows of the dancers inside. Gay laughter was mingled with the strains of the fiddle.

Molly's heart beat faster. Her gay patter ceased.

The dark bulk of horses loomed before them as they rode up into the lane. Some so tired from hard riding, they were content to stand still and motionless, while others pawed. And nearby in the lane, a horse who would rub off his bridle was hitched to a swinging limb.

"I had a piece a' pie, I had a piece a' pudd'n', but I gave it all away fer tuh see Sally Good'n'," sang a young blade, in a high ringing voice, to the accompaniment of the fiddles.

That one was a favorite, and so was the "Old Cacklin' Hen," and "No Hell in Georgia," and "Cotton Eye Joe."

Inside, amid the gaiety, a group was forming into positions as an old quadrille tune was struck up by the musicians.

Breathless with eager suspense, and a sensation akin to fear, Molly entered the open door. An uneasy tightness seized her throat at the recollection of the tilted hoops that swept aside the skirts of haughty ladies, before her presence, back there once at a concert at Mount Olive, and a flood of color rushed to her cheeks.

This would be different, she thought, surely here among many strangers, she would be cordially accepted.

But poor Molly! As she entered, many faces were turned in her direction, and a hush fell upon the room.

Molly was introduced to several of the young men nearest the door, and before the introductions were over, ladies were whispering.

The room was too warm, as it was not yet cool enough for a big fire, but Molly and her cousin joined a group of older people before the hearth.

Beads of perspiration stood out on the foreheads of dancers and fiddlers. The dancing stopped. Of course, thought Molly, it was only the heat. Too warm for dancing.

But nearby two young women were talking quite audibly.

"I will not get on the floor, if she does," said one.

The other replied, "No. Lest we be classed as she. 'Birds of a feather, flock together' is a true saying, and we'll not be flocking."

They couldn't be talking about me, Molly thought. So she brushed her uneasiness aside, and flashed her beautiful smile, as her partner swept her out on the floor.

Molly danced in a state of happy abandon. Forgotten was the unpleasant past. Forgotten were the family troubles at home. Forgotten were the mixed-people, who were neither white nor negro, back there on her father's farm.

The word was passed from one to another that the young woman who was gaining all the attention and the admiration of the men was Captain Newt Knight's daughter.

Molly was having such a wonderful time, she paid no attention to the other girls leaving the floor, one by one, until only she and two others were taking part in the evening's pleasure. The last two were escorted from the floor. Then Molly's partner drew her aside.

Beside him, she stood radiant and beautiful, near a group of other girls who were sitting out the dance. It must surely have been maliciousness that caused one girl to say to another, "Negro blood. I thought everyone here knew that Newt Knight's daughter is part negro."

"Oh, you must be mistaken," said her friend, "they say the daughters of him who are part negro are much prettier than this one."

"You can't be sure which is which," replied the first girl, "for they are all one family living up there together—"

Molly could not help hearing what was said.

She touched the young man's arm with one hand, the other she clasped over her heart, and together they rushed out of the room into the cool darkness outside.

Perhaps he had heard too. No word was spoken. Her heart was pounding loudly as she stood very near, so near, a damp wisp of her fragrantly scented hair brushed his cheek.

He drew her beneath the clump of myrtle trees, where there was a low-limbed cedar sheilding them from view.

Molly's hurt turned into a bitterness which filled her with a recklessness that she had never known. She leaned nearer, her soft body touching his, determined to ensnare men by the age-old method, and there alone in the dark, sheltered by the cold stars of the heavens, she melted into his arms. His lips sought hers.

Another girl's young man had succumbed to the wiles of the Tempter, intoxicated by the atmosphere of the night, which was heavy-laden with the scent of horses, saddle-leather, smoke from wood fires, and the new-mown hay in the barn, mingled with the freshness of the dainty Molly. He could not resist her closeness, and . . . Molly was launched out upon a career of prostitution.

Other men took Molly for other walks, and she felt that this was vengeance wrought upon the hated females of her acquaintance.

Now that she had taken the fatal step, Molly knew that she would never be alone. She knew that men would ride over the trails seeking her.

What other women said, or thought, made no difference now. And she returned to her father's house, a changed and bitter woman.

But she was too fond of her father to add her grievances to his, for she knew that he was staggering under the heaviest load that a man ever carried. It was all unraveling to her now.

She could understand his strange silences. She knew that he was burdened by many cares which he had kept secret in order to spare her and his other children.

She knew that her mother no longer loved her father, as a result of the friction over Rachel's family, and she knew that Serena's accusations were false and unfounded. So she decided to stick to Newt, through thick and thin, because he was the only friend she had in the world.

CHAPTER 23

Molly's Marriage

The tranquility of the Knight plantation was frequently broken by the unannounced arrival of one of Molly's many suitors. Her popularity was established. Many called at the house, but many others waited at a distance for Molly to slip away from the house and meet them without her father's knowledge.

But Newt's sharp eyes had detected the change in his daughter. He knew all along what was going on, but no mention escaped his lips. No word of reproach. No questions.

Rachel had foreseen Molly's future as a harlot and had warned Newt that his beautiful daughter was destined to become a brazen hussy, unless he provided her with a husband.

The box of Lily White, beside the decanter of Attar of Roses, on Molly's dressingtable, was a constant reminder that the owner was becoming worldly and sophisticated, but Serena kept her tongue.

She did not blame her daughter, since this was the only way she could be associated with young men, as they were an ostracised family. What young man with any self-respect would be seen in public with the daughter of Newt?

Serena could not forget Molly's swollen eyes and tear-stained face when she had returned from the dance.

Rachel's family whispered. They seemed to know what it was all about but were tactful in Molly's dejected presence, and "made strange" that all was not well.

Together, in their own house, they rejoiced over Molly's sad plight.

Rachel took the floor.

"My chillurn, wait an' see! I'll bring 'em down, one by one. They, who've set they selves above us. They who've tried to move us off the land. They who've been so high an' mighty has come low. Jest wait an' watch, an' I'll brew a potion that'll place 'em in my han'!"

Rachel stood, feet apart, hands placed on her widening hips. Her teeth gleamed white as she smiled wickedly.

"My chillurn, list'n! There's potions to make a man do anything you wants. Come close."

They obeyed and drew their chairs in a close circle about the speaker, so as not to miss her whispered plans.

The black daughter sat between the two white daughters, and the white negro dropped down beside the fireplace, on the floor. He drew his knees up under his chin and hugged them with his long strong arms, listening to this strange mother.

The other children, varying in color, from pure black to almost pure white, lay about on pallets asleep.

The plot was laid.

The next evening as Rachel was brewing the coffee, a familiar foot-fall was heard on her gallery.

Rachel's little negroes ran to welcome the Captain in. But he sat himself down on the porch, as it was warm inside.

Soon Rachel joined him, bringing him a cup to drink and holding in her other hand the fortune cup.

According to plan, she foretold sorrow.

"No good news?" asked the Captain.

"Oh, it won't be you, but you will hear uv a death," warned Rachel.

Sometimes it seemed that Newt entirely disbelieved her. This was one of the times.

He got up, and abruptly changed the subject.

"Git that earliest cotton picked out, 'fore you begin on the next cut, an' see to it that the chillern don't put in trash with the cotton," he instructed.

"Yas Sir," she replied.

"It's a' comin' night, so I'll git along," he said, and started at a brisk walk, so as not to be caught out after dark.

Just as he gained the opening between the trees in the lane, a screech owl sent shivers up and down his spine with that eerie foreboding voice that has always been an omen of bad luck. Newt hastened his steps, and was soon inside with his old gun across his knees.

There was nothing to fear. He knew that it was just a superstition, but, "That owl! Rise the hair on yore back," he said, shivering.

"We'll hear o' somebody's bad luck," remarked Serena. "And they say if one hollers three times in your yard, there'll be a death in the family."

The owl moved from his perch in the oak in the lane to the apple tree in the yard.

There were three distressing wails.

Newt got up and cracked the door and put out his old gunbarrel and shot into the apple tree.

The owl became silent.

It was not long before a rider was dismounting at the picket gate. He brought news that one of Newt's brothers was dead.

This was the only brother that had associated with Newt, in any way, since he deserted the Confederacy. The two who had been members of his band were killed, one by hanging, two others had lost their lives fighting for the Confederacy, and the others had disowned him and had fled the country in embarrassment.

There were cousins here and there in the country that refused to claim kin with the man who was looked down upon as a black-hearted bandit.

His nieces were cautioned never to speak to him in public and were told to deny kinship with his family.

So many vile things were said of Newt, even his own brothers were led to believe that the governor of the Free State of Jones was banished because he was guilty of mixing the blood of the races.

Yet this messenger came in the hour of death, and the family of Newt were requested to attend the funeral.

First, Rachel's uncanny prediction, then the screech owl, strengthened the family's belief in the supernatural.

Embalming was almost unheard of in that day. There were no under-takers or florists. So funerals were sad, and burial was crude, with usually the casket homemade. And the only flowers were those old-fashioned bouquets brought by the good women from their gardens, to lay on the new mound.

The body was brought to the cemetery on an oxcart, where neighbors lent a hand when it came to lowering the box into the open ground.

It had been years since Newt had seen Martha, the sister whom he had widowed by slaying her husband, Morgan, the Smithy. But she was there at the funeral of their brother.

When she saw Newt, she ran to him, and embraced him there, pub-licly, but all the others of the kin ignored him and his family.

In Molly's arms she carried a huge bouquet of Cape Jasmines (garde-nias) to place on her Uncle's grave. She stood quietly, with head bowed, unaware that many eyes were watching her.

The neighborhood turned out for the burying, back then, as a last respect to the dead.

After she had deposited the flowers, and all were leaving the grave-side, an old woman walked up to Molly, and with close scrutiny, she looked at her from under the ruffled edge of a black bonnet.

"So ye're Newt Knight's daughter?" she asked.

Molly nodded.

"Why, you're as white as anybody," remarked the woman. Molly did not reply. She understood that she was mistaken for one of Rachel's daughters.

She brushed the old lady aside, and rushed from the cemetery, her face crimson. She mounted her horse ahead of the rest of the family and rode back up to her home in the "no man's land" of Salsbattery.

Here, she could give to her emotions and cry as hard as she pleased.

When her father arrived, Molly decided to tell him about this terri-ble thing that was happening to her everywhere she went. She told him that she could no longer bear the insults of the people who believed that Rachel's white daughters were her half-sisters, and she vowed to never again leave the plantation.

He could not comfort her.

No other member of the family spoke, but the others of the family understood.

Crestfallen, the two brothers walked out of the house, together, without a word.

Rachel and Georgianne stood silent and respectful, awaiting Serena's orders to begin supper.

Behind her back, in the kitchen, they gleefully hugged each other.

Newt walked up to the wall and lifted his gun from the rack. His head soon disappeared, as he followed the path down by the spring. He rubbed the barrel of his gun with gentle strokes. He could usually find comfort in the touch of it. He worked his mouth, but his thoughts would shape no plan.

Finally, it occurred to him to consult Rachel and leave it up to her to find a way out of this terrible dilemma.

The idea of running away from the country presented itself, but he felt that he could not run away and leave behind him the family of Rachel, people as white as he was, as to the color of their skins, and a people innocent of any wrongdoing.

He knew that they were dependent upon him for a place to live, as no other white family would tolerate a mixed people. And beneath this reasoning there lay upon his conscience a sense of guilt, when memory carried him back to those nights of entertainment, back there with his men, in the hideouts.

Orgies, ghastly in obscenity, where Rachel and another black slave woman writhed and twisted their naked bodies in eerie dances, to the applause of the deserters. Where fiddling and dancing went on for hours, undisturbed, back there in the Devil's Den, where there was feasting, drinking, and pleasure. Where booze-crazed, prurient, sex-mad men indulged in fornication and evil pleasures of a hideous nature.

More than one man joined the organization of the Knight Company, and upon learning that revolting conditions prevailed, quickly left it and returned to the Confederate army, or joined the Union at New Orleans.

Night drove Newt in, with an even more befuddled mind. He could not sleep, and lack of sleep further incapacitated his overburdened brain.

Serena felt that he was losing his mind, and, although disgusted with him, and her life, her among negroes, she felt a pang of pity for him, as she watched him tremble when he lifted his cup to his lips. The way he continuously worked his mouth, as he sat with his old gun across his lap.

Up early, before the sun was up the next morning, he was on the path to Rachel's house. With Rachel's family, he felt free to talk, which he seldom did at home.

He knew all the details of Rachel's past life, as she had given them, and he believed her. He believed her story that she had been sold away from a rich plantation in Georgia in order to cover the disgrace of the family to whom she had belonged, as her white children, Georgianne and Jeff, were the offspring of an only son, a handsome blond young man.

"So they are not negro," thought Newt, speaking aloud, "but are white, with no 'place.'"

He compared these people with his own unfortunate children, and he wondered what the future held in store for them.

All day he stayed at Rachel's house, and by the time he beat dark in home, a vague plan, instigated by the ingenious Mulatto, was shaping in the back of his mind.

He was, at first, shocked by his own thoughts, but he was becoming rational, and to him the preposterous ideas were becoming logical. But of them he made no mention. He was leaving the details to Rachel, for she had promised to handle the situation in a way that would work out for the good of both families. Hers and his.

Perhaps the constant fear of ambush, and death, and the fear of the future of his children had weakened his mind. Or perhaps the constant and timely predictions of Rachel had cast him under the spell of black magic. He was afraid of he knew not what. And as he could keep his children no longer innocent of the consequences of his past, which he had endeavored to do, in many ways, he decided to abide by Rachel's wisdom.

There were many angles to be considered. There was young Tom, fair and handsome and a born gentleman. Respectful of his father's wishes, he had always obeyed him and had accepted the fact that "they were not wanted" by the general public.

Tom was kept under the powers of Newt and Rachel, being told that they were poor, too poor to provide him with clothing, other than that made from the loom at home, and as money was not given him, the youth did not attempt to go abroad in search of pleasure. He and his brother Mat were brought up in ignorance of the outside world.

They grew up simply, on the farm, working along beside Rachel's family and tolerating them because they were tenants on their father's farm, and by his will. However, they both had a certain respect for Jeff, because he was good and honest in his dealings and was nice to them.

Having no other boys to play with, and with whom to associate, and it being customary for white children to play with negro children on the place, Tom and his brother occasionally played with Jeff and the younger negroes, but Tom did not place himself as an equal with them, and they were made to understand that he was superior to them.

The attitude of his mother caused Tom to have little or no use for Rachel and her two white daughters, but he accepted little favors from them and in return treated them with kindness.

Going to mill was a "must," and the two brothers took it, turn about, with Mat going one week, and Tom going the next.

It was several miles from Newt's place to the Knight's Old Water Mill where the neighborhood grinding was done.

After supper, it was a fireside job to shell a "millin' a' bread corn" after it had been shucked in the cribs, on the night before the grinding day. The children joined in, and soon the task was finished, and the meal sacks tied and ready to be laid across the horse's back the next morning.

Rachel followed the same custom at her house, and as had always been the case, one of the boys would ride by and carry along her sack on the same trip.

One afternoon before it was Tom's day to go to mill, Georgianne came up and reminded him that her mother would also like to send "a turn o' corn."

He replied that they would, as usual, be glad to carry it for them.

Georgianne loitered around, not ready, it seemed, to leave. It was some time before she got up the courage to begin a conversation.

"Mr. Tom, don't you sometimes have a long wait, before your turn comes at the mill?" she asked, by way of beginning.

"Yes, there are sometimes a good many ahead, and I have to wait to get mine ground, as it is quite a ways to go," he replied.

"Then," said she, "I guess you sometimes git mighty hungry, with having to miss your dinner?"

"Well, yes, sometimes," he answered civilly.

"Tomorrow, when you come by to get our corn, I'll have you a little snack prepared," she promised.

"Now, that would be mighty nice," said Tom.

Georgianne left, and he soon forgot all about the promise.

But the next morning early, when Tom stopped by, Jeff was on hand to hoist up the heavy sack of corn onto the horse's back.

Georgianne came up behind him, with a piece of cake wrapped carefully for his lunch.

Tom thanked her and placed it in his pocket.

"Now, that is most unusual," said Tom, to himself. "They have never done that before. Must be a' fixin' to ask me to do 'em a favor, or somethin', cause, for sure, they know that I don't like them any better than they do me, which is mighty little." And with these thoughts running through his mind, as he jogged along, he was suddenly surprised to see Fan, the other white daughter, step out into the road, away from Rachel's house, and out of sight of her brothers and sisters.

"Oh, stop a minute, Mr. Tom," she cried, "I must tell you something! Don't eat that cake my sister gave you, whatever you do, not if you want to keep your right mind. All day, Ma and Georgianne have plotted against you, an' Ma brewed the potion, an' they've got it in the cake fer you to eat, an', an'—" she paused for breath, "you'll be under the spell, if you eat that potion."

"Thank you, Fan, I'll not eat it," he replied and smiled at the serious-faced girl.

He rode on down the road, amused, and somewhat puzzled.

"Now, that's just like a nigger," he said to himself. "Crazy thing, but they are all superstitious. They've got Pa believing in that stuff. Potion! Pshaw! There couldn't be nothin' to put me under a spell, but thanks to Fan, I'll not eat the stuff."

He was crossing a little creek, where a swift stream ran under a rustic bridge. He stopped and took the piece of cake from his pocket and threw it into the water. He watched it whirl around and be swept downward by the current.

"Well, that's the last of the potion," he laughed to himself. "Why Pa wants to keep foolin' with them niggers, I can't see. He b'lieves everything old Rachel tells him. And, honest to goodness, I do believe if it weren't for me to keep the niggers in their place, he'd let them come right in, an' run over mother.

"Mat is too timid and innocent to know how to handle 'em. And they're smart ones! It's that white blood in 'em that makes 'em smart. But as long as there is a drop a' nigger blood in one, he's still a nigger," ran Tom's thoughts, as he rode on to the mill.

It was late Indian summer, but there were a few days of hot weather, like mid-summer, and the sun shone hot and bright. The sky was blue and unclouded.

Much work was done during these pre-winter days, and the Captain, his sons, and the tenants were all tired when night came.

After supper, the house was warm inside, and Newt did a thing most unusual. He asked Georgianne to bring a quilt and fold it into a pallet at the end of the front porch, where there was a cooling breeze, before she washed the supper dishes. He turned a chair down, with the front edge of the seat resting on the floor and the legs turned upward. The chair, in that position, made a backrest, and with the quilt pulled up over the slats in the chairback, Newt had a comfortable place in which to relax.

Tom brought out himself a quilt and likewise made himself a pallet at the other end of the porch.

They lay there a long time, and rested, and watched the full moon.

"Well, it won't rain fer a few days, yet," remarked Newt, "and we're about through. We're about to get the crops in. Jest a few more days' pretty weather, an' we'll be through."

Clouds were beginning to drift, now and then, between them and the moon.

A whip-poor-will hollered in an oak down the lane. All was quiet and peaceful, with only faint night sounds, and a tinkling of the tiny bell on the old nanny, as she licked the salt-block in the lane.

Presently, Georgianne came out, and started on her way home for the night.

Others of the family came out, and got a last drink from the cedar bucket on the watershelf, and went to bed.

Finally, there was only the man and the boy, alone on the porch. All was quiet.

"Pa, hadn't we ought to get up an' go to bed?" asked Tom, yawning.

Newt did not reply. He lay very still and quiet, and Tom thought he had gone to sleep. After a long silence, he said, "Son, there is something I want to talk to you about," but he did not get up off his pallet.

Tom got up and moved closer, as his father had spoken in a confidential tone.

"I have been a thinkin' what's to become of youall," he paused, and Tom was filled with wonder.

Tom asked, "What, Pa?"

"Oh, I have thought and thought about what would become of you, an' I've thought about what was to become of old Rachel's children, since they are not negroes—," he paused again, and Tom put in, "But they are niggers, Pa, and superstitious, an'—"

"No," interrupted Newt, "they are not negro, therefore they can never marry negroes, because they have in them better blood than a common nigger. Their father was white, and Rachel, herself, is only part negro, so they are almost white people, yet they cannot have the privileges of white people, because of that little streak of negro blood." He said no more.

Tom did not answer but waited for his father to finish.

Newt cleared his throat and started again.

"I have been a' thinkin' the way you children are a bein' treated, by other folks, that you can't marry either, because nobody would have you," he paused again, and cleared his throat, unnecessarily.

"We are a people up here to ourselves, and nobody wants us. I don't know why, but they don't." His voice trembled.

Tom was awed beyond speech. His father had never spoken to him privately on the matter of their banishment from society.

"I have been a thinkin' that the negro blood could be bred out o' Rachel's family. A white man could marry one of Rachel's daughters, and there would be only one more generation to carry the stain of negro blood—," again he paused, and before he could begin, Tom interrupted his thoughts with, "I wonder what white man you think would have one of them yaller niggers?"

"I was a comin' to that," replied Newt. "I was a thinkin' as it is impossible for Molly to ever marry a decent white man, that she could marry Jeff, and you and Mat could marry the other two. Mat could take Fan, and you could take Georgianne."

Newt had risen to his feet and was picking up the chair, as nonchalantly as if he had been discussing the weather.

Tom was too stunned for a moment to say anything; his voice seemed to stick to his throat. The strength to stand left his legs, and he leaned against the gallery post for support.

"Pa, you've gone crazy. As crazy as a bat," he answered, weakly. "Surely, you in your right mind, wouldn't ask your own flesh and blood—"

Newt towered above him, "But I tell you, these people are not negro, but are white like you."

Anger got the best of Tom, and he was ready for a scrap.

"You, and your damned niggers!" he stormed. "You can't make me marry a damned negro!"

Newt swung the hickory chair.

Tom dodged, and came up under the chair, to knock it against the wall with such force as to shatter it. They tangled, and rolled over to the edge of the porch, which was about four feet from the ground, with Newt apparently having the advantage. Newt's arms and legs were longer, but Tom was a vicious fighter, once his gentle nature was aroused, and he fought from savage rage.

As Newt sought to roll him off the porch, Tom purposely rolled off suddenly, pulling his father on top of him. In doing that he got him further from his gun.

They lay there, panting like two animals. Neither would release his hold.

Finally, Newt asked his son to let him up.

Tom held on for a minute, contemplating his father's next move. Instinctively, he knew that once up, his father would kill him, but he released his hold, and as he did, Newt whistled for his bull dog.

By that time, the family was awakened and ran out to see what the ruckus was about.

The dog made a dive for Tom, but Tom was trying to gain the picket fence and was almost in the act of scaling the palings, so the dog did not get a good hold, but tore Tom's pants leg off.

"You, son-of-a-bitch! Gol durn ye!" shouted Tom to the dog.

Newt rushed for his gun.

"You can't cuss me, damn you. I'll blow your head off!" cried Newt, thinking his son meant him, instead of the dog.

By that time, Tom had gone over the pickets, at the place where the gourd vines grew thick and rank, and next to them was a weed-grown plot that had once been a fertile garden, so the vegetation, together with the clouds flitting over the moon, gave him cover.

Tom did not tarry. He sneaked through the weeds, on to the cotton rows, and there, half crawling to keep out of sight, he wondered why he had ever been afraid.

Tom had always been afraid of the dark and had never, that he could remember of, ventured out alone in the night. Now, the darkness became his friend, shielding him from the wrath of the madman, who was out with shotgun and blazing torch, seeking to kill him.

At a safe distance, up in the field, Tom stopped crawling beneath the cotton stalks, and stood up to see if he had been discovered.

He could make out the figure of his father, carrying the light high in his hand, lowering it, now and then, to look under the house, under the pomegranate's low-hanging branches, behind the big Cape Jasmine in the corner of the yard, and finally, the torch seemed to be bobbing along, in the opposite direction, up towards old Rachel's house.

Tom stood there a long time, indecisive and shaking, although the night was warm. He was cold, yet sweat was oozing from his pores.

A few yards up to his left was the old graveyard, where his twin brother was buried.

Tom cast his eyes in that direction, and found himself wishing that he too were there, at rest beneath the cedars that sheltered the graves. The hot tears streamed down his cheeks.

He turned his steps back across the high level, to within a few yards of the old Huckaby house. There, he turned right, and headed out of the field to a thicket that jutted out into the fenced-in land.

He stopped here and rested awhile, not knowing what to do or where to go. But there was one thing certain, he would never return to his home and submit to the demands of his father.

Tom had never prayed, and he was at a loss for words, but there in the dark thicket, he dropped down on his knees and prayed his first prayer for Divine guidance. How long he stayed there, and just what he asked for, he could not remember, but evidently his prayer was answered.

He got up and felt an impulse to climb over the split rail fence and hit the old cavalry trail. The trail that was beaten out in a deep rut, where horses, bearing riders of three different armies, had repeatedly trod the earth, cutting down the red clay, and forming banks on either side. He followed this trail to a path that was familiar.

The Welborns were still friendly, and remembering this, Tom went to them for food and shelter. There he was welcome. There the young ladies of the household treated him royally.

They made him new clothes, as he had brought none with him, and soon he was attending church services with them.

After a few weeks of living with the Welborn family, Tom found himself in love with one of the daughters, whom he later married.

In many ways, Newt was good to his family.

He had let each boy have a cotton patch of his own, that year. But poor Tom had been forced to run away in self-defense, and leave his cotton, white and full in the field.

It happened that his patch was a good distance from the house, so he decided to arm himself with an old pistol, and sneak in from the back side of the field, and gather his cotton. He planned to shoot first, and kill his father, if he came near, and offered to harm him, or tried to make him return to marry the quadroon daughter of Rachel.

One day as Tom was busy picking his cotton, he happened to look up, and saw his father approaching.

"He is coming, now to kill me," thought Tom. "I shall be ready." So he touched his gun in his blouse, as if to make sure that it was still there. His body had warmed the steel, and he had become accustomed to its feel against his body. It was right there, and ready, but in his eagerness to be first on the trigger, Tom could not wait.

He removed it carefully, and held it concealed behind his cotton sack, as he watched the slouched figure of the man, whom he had sworn to hate, pick a fluffy boll here and there, with one hand.

After he had more than he could hold in one hand, he transferred the fluffs to the crook of his elbow, where he held his arm against his bosom.

"He carries a gun concealed there," said Tom, "but that is all right. I, too, have a gun." And he made a motion to stroke the weapon to reassure himself, and found that he was shaking, and his heart was beating rapidly and loudly. So loudly, Tom felt that it could be heard.

Newt kept picking a handful here and there, unhurriedly, as he gradually came up to within speaking distance of his son.

"I see you're a' pickin' your cotton, Son," said Newt, pleasantly, as if Tom had left the house only that morning to pick cotton.

"Yes Sir," replied Tom.

Newt kept picking.

"I hear as how you're a' seen at meetin' wi' the Welborn gal," said Newt.

"Yes Sir," answered Tom.

His father waited for him to add words to the conversation, but Tom was silent, thinking he was being tricked, as no gun was in evidence.

"Well, go ahead and marry her, Son, if she'll have you, and I'll build you a house here on the place."

"Thank you Sir," replied Tom.

Neither spoke another word, and Tom gathered his cotton with no objection from his father, but the offer to build him a house had made no difference in the attitude of the boy, for he had severed relations with his father, and he had no intention of ever becoming friendly with him again, as long as he lived.

Away from his home and family, Tom found a new life of happiness that he had thought impossible on earth. He was content to bask in this new warmth, and forget his bitter past.

He knew not what was taking place back there with his people. And it was little he cared, until the news reached him of the fate of his sister and brother. He would have preferred to hear of their deaths! Then he blamed himself for not staying, and protecting them, but it was too late!

With Serena afraid to cross Newt, since she knew that he was anxious for an excuse to kill her, she made no verbal objection to his preposterous scheme, and with Tom, the obstacle removed, there was no interference with the plan of Rachel and Newt to have their children intermarry.

There was no further mention in Serena's presence, and she thought that her husband had been driven to insanity, especially since he had sicked the bull dog on his own son, and had stalked him with a gun to shoot him, but she was helpless, and afraid. And she hoped that this was just another of his wild obsessions that would soon pass, and he would return to normalcy. But poor Serena's hopes were in vain.

October's bright blue days brought cool nights, and the month of November came with a cold snap that sent the wild geese over by droves, southward, to the winter feeding grounds in the marshes and lagoons along the Gulf of Mexico.

As they were passing over the year before, a young bird gave out, and dropped from flight, and joined the tame geese on the plantation. He became tame and ate corn with the tame flock around Rachel's door.

During the summer he had padded along, and pulled the blades of grass from among the young cotton plants, like any ordinary goose.

He had not forgotten! The cries of the wild ones stirred in him the memory of the past, and he craned his neck, and cocked his head and listened; he looked skyward toward the black line of little specks that was moving in a V formation. The cries came nearer, and he spread his wings, grown strong and black, and rose to join the flight.

"A wild gander again," said Molly, as she watched him leave as suddenly as he had come.

"I wish I could do that," thought she, "and leave behind me forever, No Man's Land, all of its unhappiness, and all of its people."

Jeff came around the house with a wheelbarrow load of fire wood, which he proceeded to lift off, and lay, by pieces on his strong arms to take inside and lay upon the hearth.

Night was coming on, and the air was chilly.

"Heavy frost, tonight," remarked the Captain. "Did you hear them geese?"

"Yes Sir, that was the second flight to go over, an' ole Abe went with 'em!" replied Jeff.

"Pshaw! And ole Abe went! That just goes to show that you can't change that which is natural. Abe knew that he belonged wi' the flock, an' he knew that he warn't no cotton patch goose. Funny, but everything knows his place," said Newt.

"After you've laid on the fire, Jeff, set down an' warm yourself," invited Newt.

Jeff obeyed in silence. He knew that he was being detained for a reason, but he had no idea what it was. His landlord was ready with conversation, here of late, and often talked with him, more than he ever had. Almost as if he were a member of the family.

Newt sat before the fire, while Jeff chose the chair over in the corner, as a negro has always sat in the chair nearest the corner, before a white man's fire.

Jeff watched as Newt gazed strangely into the fire, his mouth moving into a freakish shape, and he knew that he was deep in thought.

They were alone together, and after a moment's hesitation, Newt came to the point, and started, "Jeff, you are almost a white man. You are as white as anybody. You could pass for a full white man anywhere, so I have decided that you shall be treated so in my house. From now on, you are to enter by the front door."

"Yes, Sir," replied Jeff.

"Your white sisters may also enter by the front door."

"Yes, sir," was the only reply.

"You may go. That is all," said the Captain, curtly.

Jeff got up from his chair, and from habit, started to depart by the back door, then he paused, turned on his heel, and walked out the front door.

Autumn in the hill lands of Mississippi surpassed the beauty of the fresh fragrant spring. The paintbrush of nature colored the landscape with a riot of exciting shades. The shumake shone brilliantly, like red fruit at a distance in the sun. While the leaves from other trees flitted through the air like red and gold birds, alighting upon a brown carpet. The tall grasses, bowed with the weight of brown seed, humbled down by the frost which had heightened the brilliance of the purple wild mulberry. The green pine plumes glistened and shone richly black against the wintry skies.

Squirrels chattered in the hickory and beeches, and the acorns fell among the dead dry leaves, like a peppering of pebbles.

The potatoes were dug and banked for the winter, and the blue sugar-cane was stripped in the fields, and the cattle were turned in to fatten on the waste from the harvest.

Coveys of quail soared over the fields in search of grain, and the turtle doves followed the cattle by droves.

The hunting season was on, and the Captain stayed away from the house during the daylight hours.

When he came in home, Jeff was on hand to take the game bag, which he carried into the kitchen, where Fan had now joined Georgianne as helper.

It happened that every time Jeff came into the kitchen, the Captain detained him, in order that Molly might observe him, and become accustomed to his presence. Now, they were sitting across the table from each other, drinking coffee, as two white men would.

But Newt would not sit at Rachel's table, and he made it plain to his wife when she objected to his having Jeff sit at their table, that these three, the boy and his two sisters, were unfortunate white people.

The murderous look he gave her silenced her, and although she would not seat herself with them, she made no objection to anything that her husband chose to do or say.

Gradually, Molly found herself agreeing with her father, because Jeff's manners, now that he was losing some of his inferiority complex, were gentlemanly, and he was intelligent, and very personable.

He was as handsome as any white man Molly had ever seen. His features were not negroid, and his eyes were clear, wide open, honest in expression, and were a beautiful shade of blue. His hair was a light sandy color, and very straight and fine textured.

"It's just a shame," thought Molly, "that he has negro blood in his veins." And soon she found herself pitying this young man, whose misery must be equal to hers.

Soon the leaves were all off the trees, and winter, heavy with black rain clouds, was upon the settlement. Cold winds and wet weather kept the family indoors, where carding, spinning, and quilting was done, as a necessity, and as a pastime, by the women.

Georgianne and Fan were in the house every day, helping, and every day were becoming more as girls of the same family. They joined in the conversation, and helped to pass off the bleak days.

Nothing was ever said about their color, or their station in life. They were becoming accepted, much to the satisfaction of their mother, and much to Serena's chagrin.

Where there was joy in other homes, in anticipation of the Christmas season, which was rapidly approaching, there was melancholy in the house of Newt.

Tom was gone from them forever. And although Serena was happy to know that he had escaped a fate, which would have been worse than hers, she missed him at home. She knew that he would have stood firmly with her, and together, they might have prevented Newt's taking in the mixed-bloods as equals.

Alone, poor Serena was helpless.

On Christmas Eve, 1884, there came a blanket of snow, changing the countryside into a glistening white fairyland. Icicles hung to the bare limbs of the trees, and their beauty was enhanced by the towering frozen pines. Snow was as welcome as Santa Claus, and the children, so seldom able to see a snow this far South, made snow men and rolled snowballs.

Inside the Knight home, the fire logs burned brightly, replenished often by the faithful Jeff. Red berries, holly, mistletoe, and bouquets made by Rachel's family adorned the rooms.

Half the cedar sprays, with their tiny leaves, were dipped into a thin flour paste, and dried, and then arranged among the sprigs of green cedar to form a Christmas bouquet.

The odor of good Christmas cooking drifted from the kitchen, where Georgianne and Fan were preparing wild roast turkey, with plenty of "cush."

The cushion was prepared from cornbread crumbs, which had been softened with the broth from the fowl, and to which had been added onions and other seasoning. There were also the other choice meats and delicacies in season, and in the kitchen there was merry making among the young women and Mat.

But in the house, the Captain sat sad and silent before the fire. Serena sat opposite him, at the other side of the fireplace, knitting. She was also silent, but her silence was not unusual, for Serena never knew when to speak, and if she did, she expected for answer, that glowering look from her husband.

He sat with his hat on his head. He usually wore it inside the house. Finally, he arose from his chair, removed his hat, and stood before his wife, his back towards the fire.

"I have made the decision," he announced. "This is Molly's and Mat's wedding day."

Serena opened her mouth, but no word would come. She clasped her hand to her breast, as the color drained from her face.

He spread his hands, palms upward, and outward, as if to hold out to someone else, the burden that had lain within him.

"That is the only thing that can be done," he said. "Molly can never marry any other white man, and her children will not be, ah, negro—," he did not finish.

Serena's knitting fell to the floor, unnoticed, as she jumped up and rushed into the kitchen, where her children were.

Before she could gather strength, and gain control of her voice, Newt burst in behind her. He seized her roughly by the wrist, with fingers having the grip of steel.

All in the kitchen were amazed and shocked at the sudden intrusion of Newt standing there, crushing Serena's frail arm. A pin dropping would have sounded like a crash, so still was the kitchen.

"We were a talkin' about you a marryin', Molly," explained Newt "an yore Ma is sorta cut down about it."

"But I didn't know I was a marryin', Pa!" exclaimed Molly, in surprise.

"Yes. It is arranged. This Christmas," replied her father, "Today!"

So many strange things had happened, and this strange man who was her father, was capable of anything. So Molly was not too surprised to hear that he had spoken to some young man about marrying her. And she knew that whatever he willed, would be done. There was no use for her to ask questions, or raise objections.

And true to his promise to wipe out a mixed race in Jones County, Newt Knight began by sacrificing his own son, and his only daughter.

There, up in the hills bordering Jones County, Jeff, the mixed-blood son of Rachel the Mulatto, became the husband of Molly, the full white daughter of Serena and Newt.

And Fan, the white skinned girl born to Rachel, who was conceived at the time when Rachel lived as an harlot with the men of the deserter band, became the wife of the full white son, Mat, in a double wedding ceremony, performed on that horrible Christmas Eve, not by their choice, but because they would have been murdered by the madman, if his request had been denied.

When Tom learned that his sister and his brother had been forced to become legally united in marriage with the son and daughter of a Mulatto, he became distraught with grief. He did not blame them, because he knew what had happened, how it had all come about. And he remembered how his father would have killed him if he had not escaped.

The person that he did blame was Rachel.

CHAPTER 24

Tom's Marriage

Tom would have run away to escape the embarrassment which this most unusual development was causing him. He would have liked to leave far, far behind him, the people who knew about his family. He felt that the sister and the brother with whom he had been reared, were no longer his, that they too, had become negroes, and he set his heart against them, resolving to disown them forever.

He did not blame them when he learned of their marriage, but since they were setting up homes with their spouses, he knew that they were not trying to run away from their father's choice.

He was so much in love with the girl who was the daughter of these people who had become as parents to him, he could not bear the thought of asking her to marry him. He could not bring disgrace upon them, and he knew that the only way out would be for him to slip away, to a strange land, among strangers. Yet he could not bring himself to part with his sweetheart, without telling her why he was leaving.

When he mentioned going away where he was not known, she offered to marry him and go with him to a new country.

They were immediately married, and he went at once to the Land Office at Paulding and applied for a tract of land for a homestead.

Together, they went miles above the settlements where they were known, to this land that was a wilderness. This was good land, and once cleared, it would be a good farm, and there they would find new friends and live the good life.

As other pioneers before them had done, they built a good house and were becoming established and acquainted.

Then quite unexpectedly, Tom received a message from home.

After Molly and Jeff had built a house, and moved to themselves, and after Mat and Fan were set up to housekeeping, there was no one left at Newt's house except Georgianne with Serena.

With Tom out of the way, Georgianne, disappointed because she had failed to ensnare him, and angry because his mother constantly reminded her that she was a negro, and should remember a negro's place, spitefully decided to charm the captain.

And, with the aid of Rachel, soon the fair Georgianne became his mistress.

He was very flattered to have the young woman flutter about him, and wait upon him, hand and foot, as he was fast becoming an old man.

Still, he had respect enough for Serena not to keep another woman in his house. So he built Georgianne a house near the house of Rachel.

Serena informed Georgianne immediately that her services were no longer needed, that Rachel could come in whenever someone was needed to help with the work, but Georgianne refused to be dismissed. Every day found her in the kitchen, pampering the Captain.

Serena became so angry because of this, she refused to speak to her husband, which pleased him well enough. He did not speak to her.

Rachel took the cup. She looked long and searchingly into the dregs.

"My daughter, you are so unwise. You must get the Captain's wife out of the way, before she gets you out of the way, because trouble shows in the cup."

She shook her head, and her golden earrings jingled. "Ah, poison," she whispered. "I see a poison death, but I can't see to make out the face of the poisoned one," said Rachel.

She lifted the pot from the coals and poured a few more drops of the coffee into the cup, trying to capture the vision of the face of the poison victim.

There were several unsuccessful attempts, and Rachel gave up.

Georgianne pondered this, and by morning she had formed an evil plan. She was afraid to wait, for she was sure that Rachel had foreseen her death in the cup, and she knew that Serena, who was fully aware of her power over Newt, hated her enough to poison her.

The quadroon and the wife of the Captain were not speaking.

She waited until Serena took her noonday nap, and while she lay sleeping, Georgianne crept in with an axe.

She had planned to tell Newt that his house had been robbed, and the robber had slain his wife. No one would know. There would be no witnesses.

She stood there, motionless, and watched her victim breathe evenly, in restful sleep. Slowly, and deliberately, she inched up the axe, as she moved on tiptoe nearer the bed, until the axe was poised in the right position for a death blow to the head of the sleeping woman.

Behind her, Rachel screamed, and Georgianne, taken by surprise, whirled around without striking.

Serena bounded up, awake, and Georgianne rushed her with the drawn axe, but Rachel was quick to wrest it from her hands.

Something had prompted Rachel to follow her daughter, because the premonition of evil had hung over her, and she knew that all was not well. She knew that Georgianne was mean and unmanageable, with a will of her own. She would not listen to Rachel, and the Mulatto was afraid for Serena's life.

Serena saw that Rachel had saved her life, and while life existed within her, she knew that she must get away.

The message to Tom informed him that his mother had been driven from home by the quadroon, and that she was on her way to live with him.

Later, Captain Newt sent Serena word that he would send away the negroes on his place, if she would return to him, but she did not trust his word, and she knew that the promise was a scheme to get her back.

All this, Tom and his wife were keeping a close secret from their neighbors, and they spread the news around that his mother was coming for a visit.

It was the custom back then for neighbors to help one another. And Tom wished to clear the land, so he invited seventeen families to come for the log-rolling dinner.

His wife and his mother made big preparations for the occassion, working late at night, carding the bats, and getting ready for the quilting.

Whenever log-rollings were held, the women went along, as the quilting bee was a social event, where they laughed and talked, as they busied their needles, quilting out two or three quilts for the hostess, or for a family that had had a burn. And at noon, when the men came in to eat, there was frolic and fun and feasting.

It usually took the greater part of a week to cook up for the log-rolling dinner, and Tom took great care, he being a newcomer to the neighborhood, and wishing to make a good impression, to provide the best of everything for the dinner at his house.

His mother and his wife were both good cooks, and they determined to set a table that would be the envy of the other ladies, and one that would receive praise from the men, so they baked and worked at the task for days before the date that was set for the log-rolling.

The butchering that Tom did gave them even more work to be done, but they wanted the best of fresh beef and tender hams.

By the time the morning arrived of the big day, there was little else to do, except to add the final touches.

The quilting frames had been suspended from the beams of the ceiling by the stout cords, and the first quilt-top and lining had been whipped in, with the softly carded bats laid between, and the chairs had been placed around for the ladies, and every little detail attended to.

Serena and Mary were dressed for company, in their neatest calico, and Tom was very proud of his women, and was most anxious to have his neighbors come to eat his food.

The hour arrived. It began to look like the people were a little late.

Mary and Serena were becoming a little nervous.

A man came up on horseback, and was welcomed in. But with him was no wife. He made an excuse for his wife's failure to come, which caused no great concern, because out of the seventeen, surely, there would be more women than could find room around the quilt to have room to quilt!

Soon another man came up in an oxcart. No woman was with him. He also had an excuse for not bringing his wife. Then the third man arrived, but with him was no wife.

No one else came.

Poor Tom quickly suspicioned the reason his invitations had been rejected, and was overwhelmed by the piteous expression on his dear wife's face, when she realized that, as his wife, she was doomed to share the fate of the unwanted.

The story of the Knights had followed them here, and Tom was expected to be like his father. Therefore, the people felt that they could not afford to associate with these people, who had come from a family that were mingled with negroes.

The three men worked as hard and as faithfully, as if a dozen others were there, and gave Tom a good day's work in the clearing.

Serena stepped out in the yard and looked towards the sun. Then she carefully placed her right foot in the shadow of her head.

"When you can step on your shadow, its dinner time," she announced to Mary. "Blow the dinner horn."

When the men came in to dinner, neither of the women showed signs of disappointment or sadness, and Mary smiled bravely, as she waited table and carried on pleasant conversation.

But after the day was done, and the men had departed, and the three of them were alone, it was Tom who was the more downcast, because he felt that he had brought this terrible thing upon one so young and innocent. Poor Mary! Why did he ever bring disgrace upon this lovely girl, who could have married a man with a good name to offer? He reproached himself, but she would not let him bear the blame. She rushed to him, and threw her arms about his neck.

"I am not sorry," she insisted. "I asked you to marry me, and bring me away from where you were known, but we just didn't go far enough. We shall move, go to other parts, if you like, or we shall stay here, and stick together. And we shall trust in the Lord, and we shall prosper," said she, trying to console him.

"Oh, the awfulness of it all," wailed poor Tom. "Just three men and nary a woman, out of seventeen families invited! We don't have enough friends to bury us!"

But brave Mary would not have it so.

Dusk was upon them. Tom and the sorrowful women carried out whole pies, cakes, and big platters of meat to the rail fence, and while he called up his hogs to throw the food to them, Mary, with a wooden tray balanced upon the fence, wept silently. Not because of hurt pride but because she was so sorry for poor Tom.

She wiped her eyes on her apron, and lifted her head, determined to help him live down the name that had followed him like the shadow of a ghost.

The courageous spirit of Mary goaded Tom to greater efforts, and despite the attitude of their neighbors, they were beginning to get a good start.

People, seeing their determination, were soon sorry that they had mistreated them, in their hour of need.

But poor Mary's frail body could not withstand the heartache, the toil, and the hardships this life of loneliness in a wilderness afforded her, and after two short years, she died, leaving an infant daughter.

This was too much for the young husband, and weaker men would have given up, but Tom became more religious, and his faith lifted him up from the depths of despair. Left with the young child, he resolved, for her sake, to carry on and prove to the people that he was a real man.

His wife's family came to his rescue, and to be in the same house, where she could take care of her orphaned niece, Sarah, the sister of Mary, became Tom's wife.

What people said or thought made no difference to her, and with her courage and help, Tom prospered and became respected by all those who knew him.

The trials and hardships that he went through were known to no man. It seemed that disaster hounded him wherever he went, but patiently, he trudged along, doing the things he thought were right.

The biggest problem he had to confront him was his mother. What to do about Serena, since she had become his responsibility, tormented him day and night, because they were of such different views.

It was only natural that Serena loved her daughter, Molly, and her son, Mat, so she could not help being concerned about their welfare. While on the other hand, Tom blamed them for continuing to live with their mixed-blood mates whom his father had chosen, and had forced them to marry, and he set his heart against them, refusing to speak to them, or to even mention their names, except on the occasion when he lectured his mother.

"Now, Mother," he said to her, "you know you are welcome to live with me in my house, because I love you, and I cannot stand by and let you be murdered by that hussy, which I know would happen to you, because now, you would not have old Rachel there to protect you."

"But I must go back up there to see my grandchildren, for Molly's children are mine, and Molly is still my own, and as near to me as you are," retorted Serena.

"Mother, you may go, if that is what you wish, but you are going to have to choose between me and Molly," Tom replied. "I have never spoken to her, although she is my full-blood sister, and I have never set foot in her house, since she has had one, and I shall never, as long as I live, for I am a white man, and I am living like a white man."

"Molly is not a negro, and neither are her children negroes," answered Serena, hotly.

"Well, you may do as you please," said Tom, "but there is one thing certain, you cannot go back up there, and associate with them, and then come back to me. You may get together your belongings, and if you had rather live among negroes than to live with me, I shall carry you back, but remember, it is for always."

So, Serena cast her lot with Molly, going to live in Jeff's house.

The face of the poisoned one in the cup proved to be Rachel. She evidently failed to predict her own future.

Suddenly, death was upon her, and at the early age of forty, Rachel left behind her a strange people, whose lives were a turmoil of hate, and fear, and humility. A people without "place," a people not belonging to either race.

Little ones, not old enough to look after themselves, but the three grown sisters, the two white, and the other black, took on the responsibility of rearing them.

Especially did Georgianne take an interest in her half-brothers and half-sisters. And it was Georgianne who always told them, "You are not negroes, so do not associate with them. If you must marry, then marry a white person, so that your children can be taken into the schools and churches."

She counseled them as to their rightful place, and told them to be always anxious to gain the favor of white people, to invite white people into their homes, but never, on any occasion, try to visit a white man in his home. "Let them come to you," she advised. And she, likewise, abided by this sound judgement and wisdom.

Like Rachel, Georgianne possessed a strange and relentless power over men, and after Rachel's death, she stepped into her mother's role. And men rode over the trails to Georgianne's house.

To Georgianne were born children who were white and beautiful. Children who called themselves Knight but who, actually, did not have one drop of Knight blood in them. But since their mother was liberated by the Knight family, they had no choice except to bear that name, as they were without benefit of one provided by a legal father, as Georgianne never had a husband and lived to a ripe old age without changing her slave name.

The descendants of Rachel were never quite sure how she got the poison dose.

Many thought that Georgianne poisoned her own mother, while others thought that Serena mixed the dose for Georgianne, and Rachel got it by mistake, while others thought that Rachel partook of her own concoction, while brewing a magic potion, and was accidentally poisoned.

Despite her evil cunning, there were some good characteristics about the Mulatto. It was she, with the Captain's help, who taught her family to work and earn an honest living. It was she who taught them that they must become a respected people, and try to find "place."

Tom thought that he had turned his back upon his mother. He thought that he could forget her, now that she was living in Jeff's house, with full knowledge that he was one-quarter negro, but when Serena came back, Tom relented, and welcomed her home.

From the conversations with his mother, he learned that she had been trying to help Molly to rear and educate her children as Christian white people, but her plans were shattered upon learning that Molly had not become Christian, as she supposed, and there had been a disagreement between them that was not altogether pleasant. And to avoid bitter conflict, Serena was back at Tom's house seeking shelter.

Piece by piece, Tom got the story of Molly's life up there in "No Man's Land."

Serena had insisted that they, she and Molly, go to church and carry Molly's four children, which Molly agreed to do.

When they entered the church, on that Sunday morning, everyone turned to stare, because in that part of the country, strangers were unusual.

Molly was not known to many of her neighbors, as she had kept out of sight after her marriage, but some of the older ones recognized Serena. There was nudging and whispering among the members of the congregation, while the pastor read his text.

When he had finished, and before the newcomers were hardly settled in their seats, one of the deacons arose and asked for the floor, which request was granted.

He cleared his throat, vehemently, and began, "Uh, I wish to say we have with us some people, er some people," he stammered, "Uh, that have not been a' comin' here, and I er wish to say that this is a white church for white people, and no niggers allowed."

He did not finish, and he did not have a chance.

Serena rose to her feet, "If you're a meanin' us," shouted Serena, "I'll have you understand, sir, that we are as white as you are!" She clenched her fists, and the color rushed to her face. Her voice trembled, "I have as much right here, in this house, as you have!"

Her argument was interrupted with, "People who live with negroes are no more than negroes, an' what you say about bein' white is true, but what about them chillern, there?"

"Molly's children are not negroes," replied Serena.

"Then, they are not the children of the white negro?"

Serena did not answer. She was lifting one of Molly's small pretty ones off the bench, and Molly was getting up, and getting out, with the little one in her arms. The bigger ones followed, wide-eyed, and astonished, too young to understand, and failing entirely to comprehend the meaning of their beautiful mother's bitter tears.

Serena told the story to Tom, her anger mounting with the details of that last effort to gain admittance into a white congregation, in that part of the country.

Her own tears flowed freely, as she related to her son the sadness and grief of his sister.

"And I stood up, and told him that Molly's children are not negro," repeated Serena.

"Mother, I would not have had you stand up and say that for fifty dollars," said Tom.

"But, it is a fact. They are not one bit negro," insisted his tearful mother.

"I know that as well as you do," he replied, softly, "and other people also know that, or at least, they think that, for it is common talk, that marriage has not changed my sister."

Serena then knew that the information had leaked out and had reached Tom, that his sister was continuing to live the life of a strumpet.

Having Jeff for a husband had not prevented her from having the men of her earlier acquaintance call upon her. And her children were not the children of her quadroon husband but were the children of different white men.

Although the first four children of Molly bore the name Knight, they were not Knights. Her first son was a handsome man of pure white blood, whose father was a counterfeiter, and as soon as he was old enough to learn the story of his origin, left this part of the country, and later married a white woman, and his family, bearing the name of Knight, are entirely white, with no trace of negro blood. The other three also married white people, and theirs are of the pure white race.

All Molly's children were brought up with the knowledge that they were white, and were educated in their own private school and abroad, and they all married other white people, and it is doubtful if Molly had but one son by Jeff, and he was Otho, whose characteristics are to an extent, negroid.

Although Otho has lived apart from negroes, and has never sent his children to a negro school or church, they are not acceptable as white people, because they are, if Jeff *was* their grandfather, one-sixteenth negro.

These unfortunate people should bear the name of their Georgia ancestor, the man who begot Jeff, because they are not entitled to bear the name Knight, by right of birth.

As Tom went his way, he lived a good life, with the exception of hating the negro race. He hated any person whom he so much as even suspicioned was not entirely white, and would never consent to any one of Molly's or Mat's children entering his house, which on more than one occasion, they attempted to do, because of their grandmother.

Tom's refusal to let Molly's family visit Serena caused her to leave him a second time, to return to her old home, up in the Salsbattery country, as she was gradually dying from cancer.

Mat lived up there with Fan, the quadroon sister of Jeff, until after six children had been born to them. He seemed to be satisfied, and worked with his family, with apparently no thought of their "place."

One day when Tom was at work in his fields, he saw his brother coming to him. They had not spoken since Mat had married Fan, and had seen each other from a distance, only. And then Tom had turned and walked in the opposite direction, pretending he had not seen Mat.

Now he knew that something was wrong. Why would Mat come to him, unless perhaps to tell him that his mother was dead?

So, expecting such a message, Tom went forward to meet his brother.

Grown men seldom weep as Mat was weeping. He could not immediately tell Tom what was the trouble. Sobbing brokenly, he fell at his brother's feet, prostrate with grief.

Tom tried to help him to his feet, begging him to quiet down, and tell him what had happened. Finally, Mat became subdued, and implored Tom for help.

"What kind of help do you need?" asked Tom.

"I have just had an awakening," answered Mat. "I have just come to realize what I have done. I am guilty of the greatest sin a man ever committed, by bringing into the world a family that is part negro. I never thought, after I took Fan, that my children would show a trace of negro blood, because she didn't. But as they get older, it is plain to see, and I am the cause!" he cried wringing his hands and weeping even harder. "I wish I could die and get out of it all."

"That wouldn't help. You could a done like I did, Mat. I would a stood and died, before I'd a been forced into a thing like that to please a crazy man. You could a' run away, like I did."

"But I was afraid then," wailed Mat. "I wish I had died when I was born—this is killing me!"

"You just as well stop that carryin' on then, an' do something about it," Tom advised.

"You can't undo what you've done, but you don't have to keep on living up there with that woman, an' keep a' bringin' more children into the world, which of course, you'll do, if you stay with her.

"I'll help you on one condition, and that is, if you'll promise never to go back, or never to go inside that house again, as long as you live. I will take you in with me, although I am ashamed of you, and I will help you to get a divorce, and then I will help you to find a white woman that you can marry.

"With leaving your folks plenty to go upon, they can live without you, and you can become a white man again."

Mat agreed to do anything his brother asked of him, and steps were immediately taken to free Mat from his quadroon wife.

But when a lawyer was consulted, it was found that no divorce could be granted him, because, under the law, he had never been legally married, as it is against Mississippi law to marry a person that is negro, or a person with negro blood. And any person who has as much as one eighth negro blood, must pass as a negro. Therefore, since there had been no legal marriage, there could be no legal divorce, and Mat found himself free.

Soon he married a white woman by the name of Francis Smith, and together, they started out trying to make amends for the mistake of Mat's boyhood.

The people born of Mat and Fan are the only Knights with any part negro blood, and they all left the country and went where they were not known, and married white, in order to reduce it to one sixteenth in their children.

There were many other negroes, besides Rachel, former slaves of the old Knight family, who bear the name, and some of them are intermarried with Mulattoes of the Musgrove and Ducksworth negroes, but there are no mixed people living today, who have in them Knight blood.

CHAPTER 25

The Captain's Last Days

One by one, as they grew old enough to leave the high fertile plain on which they lived, the mixed people and the white people with whom they were related slipped away into obscurity. Other states became their homes, and they never returned openly to Jones County.

Once the son of Jeff and Molly (Jeff was not his real father, but because he was brought up in Jeff's house, he was presumed to be negro) and his wife, a white stranger, wrote a postal card home, announcing that they would be in for a visit on a certain day and hour.

The card was read at the post office at Soso, Mississippi, and when the time of arrival was at hand, the train was met, en masse, and riled citizens ordered the conductor not to put off any travelers. So after a long journey home to visit his mother, the young man was not allowed to see her, but was transported out of the country, because he was supposedly part negro, and would have, therefore, been guilty of a crime, by having married outside his race.

Finally, there remained only a few people, over whom an old man reigned, as a king, over his subjects, up there in the "No Man's Land" of Civil War fame. An old man, with a warped and twisted mind, a man who was almost wild in his habits, living in the woods by day, and always looking and listening for a hidden foe. A man who made weird faces by working and twisting his mouth.

When night came, he was indoors, and always with him were a strange group of people. People who felt that it was their responsibility to look after the "Captain," as they fondly addressed him.

He was waited upon, hand and foot, and his least wish was granted by the dusky daughters of Georgianne. And by the offspring of Rachel, who were a mixed race, with apparently more negro blood than white, because the sons of Rachel had not been careful in choosing wives.

With having accomplished his purpose in getting Fan married, and Jeff married, the Captain cared little about what became of the rest. He did not mind two or three of his old cronies visiting with Georgianne whenever they chose, and he was not concerned about the number or the type of children born to her.

Banished from society, and with no true friend left in the world, Newt turned more talkative. And great tales he told these people about his exploits during his reign as governor of The Free State of Jones. Great tales of daring and cunning, back when he was leader of the deserter band, back in the days when a man's life was no more than the life of a dog. Back when bloodhounds trailed the scent of men, and led them into encounters that resulted in terrible and violent death.

These people believed his every word, and many pretended that they, also, were his people, to other negroes, as it was a great privilege to have even known, and associated with so great a man, let alone, be his kinsman! negroes, not related to any Knight ex-slave assumed the name Knight.

Many of these were sired by the mill hands from the Panther Branch mill, and the Price mill, up above the old Sixtown settlement, and there was no accounting for their color.

Whether or not Newt had any intimate relations with Georgianne in his later life is not known, but presumably, he did not, since he never permitted her to live in his house, not even after Serena's death.

During Serena's last days with the cancer, it was Newt and Georgianne who brought her back to her old home, where she had reared her children, and nursed her as if she had been a child.

Old Georgianne was sad and repentant and begged Serena's forgiveness. And before Serena asked to be carried back to Tom's house to draw her last breath, she had made peace with Georgianne, and the gentle care and kind words of the quadroon soothed and quieted her troubled spirit.

She also forgave Newt, before her death, for all of his wrongs.

It was Tom who buried her, in a churchyard, where she was not excluded by the other white people, for in death, she was Serena, the faithful, the mistreated, and abused mother of a full white gentleman.

Out of respect to Tom, his father's name was never mentioned. And pleased as he was to avoid talking about the past, he could not muster the courage to speak to him.

In Tom's heart, there was no love. The memory of that night when he had run away occasionally stabbed him like a poisoned fang, and quickly, he brushed the thought from his mind.

Keeping his promise never to go back, Tom was not in close contact with what went on up there, after his mother's death, but from reports that occasionally reached him, he knew that his father was reaping a bitter harvest from the seed that he had sown.

The men that once had been his friends were all gone, now, to other states, or dead. Most of them were dead.

The swamps beckoned to him, and the old man entered the dismal fastnesses, to be alone with his thoughts. Over the old beaten paths he trudged, until exhaustion halted him, and he would sit down upon a moss-covered fallen log to rest his creaking old bones.

The gun across his knees kept him steady company and was all the company that he desired, with the exception of a worn and dirty piece of paper.

Often he went into the secluded spot where he kept this piece of paper hidden, in a hollow log, known only to him. This paper bore the names of the men who had served under him, when he had held the upper hand of Jones Countains.

Upon hearing of the death of one of these loyal followers, Newt would arise and take his gun down from the gun rack, working his mouth and casting suspicious glances in all directions, as if to see if there was a possibility of his being followed. Then he would proceed, leisurely, and carelessly, toward the path that led down by the spring, mentioning to whoever happened to be with him at the time of his departure,

"Well, I must go and pay my respects to the dead."

So, off into the swamp's concealment he went, and when he reached the log in which he kept the old muster roll, he gently, even with a touch of reverence, withdrew it from its hiding place, and sat himself down on the log, carefully and painstakingly reading over the list of names, until he came to the name of the recently deceased, then he would place a mark beside that name, which signified that homage had been duly paid.

One by one, the marks were placed, and finally, the Captain felt that he was coming to the end of his road.

Although he had money, money that he had gleaned from the carpetbag regime, Newt made a pretense of being a very poor man.

His buggy was shabby, and his striped-legged mule was shaggy and unfit for much except buggying, but he called forth the grandson of Rachel one morning and instructed him to hitch up.

"I've got business to 'tend to, Boy, so git me off."

He had casual acquaintances here and there, and a few folks that he called "friends," because he had peddled a few fruit trees over the settlements before he came to this station in life, and those he had sold, and those who had taken the time to talk with him, were those he remembered. But to them he could not go, because this was a very personal matter, and he must find someone whom he could trust to carry out his instructions.

It was a bleak cold February day, and the road down into the Cracker's Neck settlement was slushy. The old mule's legs were muddy, up to his haunches, where he had sloshed through, bearing his master on this unusual mission.

His destination was the home of a cousin. A man who had long before denied kinship with the man who was banished to the negroes.

But when the creaking old buggy stopped, this Knight walked out and inquired of Newt what he would have on such a day.

Seeing his gaunt old frame, stooped with age, and shivering in the near freezing weather, he invited him to get out and come in to the fire and warm himself.

"I have come to make a request o' you," said Newt.

"And what will that be, that you want?" asked the cousin.

"Well, the time is a' drawin' near, an' I'll be a needin' ye to see to my burial."

"Oh, Pshaw! You got to die first, an' ye'll be here 'til the jedgement, an' then ye'll be to run down wi' bloodhounds," answered the cousin, jokingly.

"I am not a jokin', this time. I want you to list'n keerful, an' bury me like I say—" he paused, and blew his nose, which was in the very act of dripping—"I have nobody to see to it that I am put away like I want, an' I knew you'd do it."

He blew his nose again.

"Now, how is it you want?" asked the cousin. "Of course, that's the last thing you kin do fer a man, so I'll do it fer you, Newt."

"Wal, jest see to it that my coffin lid is not nailed down. Jest lay the lid down, lightly like, an' leave me be."

"Now, is there any further instructions as to how ye want to be put?" asked the cousin.

"Yes. You can be lookin' out good timber to build my box. See that it is plenty long, an' have the sides twelve inches high."

"Why, twelve inches won't be deep enough for the box, Newt, but if it's twelve inches that you want, that's how deep it will be," replied his cousin.

Those instructions completed the business, and Newt got back into his buggy and rode back up the way from which he had come.

With the final arrangements made with a man who had always kept his word, there was nothing more to do, except to return to his people, the only people he had in the world, who cared enough to give him decent burial, and await the time when the markings beside the names on the Knight Company muster roll would be complete, with the exception of one—his own.

"There will be no one," he mused, "to put the mark beside my name."

"Come, Chillern, an' le's clean off the graveyard. Hits growed up scan'lus, wi' the late rains a drenchin' the sage grass and bitter weeds. And out o' respect to them dead, we orter hoe er off clean."

The boys and girls of Rachel's sons immediately pulled the hoes out from under the house at the end of the gallery and set out across the broad level, up towards the burial ground, in obedience to the Captain's wish.

He arrived shortly behind them, breathing evenly, as he was strong-winded, even up in the last decade preceding the century mark, which he had hoped to attain.

His hair hung now, down to his shoulders, in a snowy mass of white curls, not a black hair was on his head. But even so, he did not look his age. He was slightly stooped, and time and toil had knotted up the big blue veins and the sinews that stood out on the backs of his big hands.

He wore his own natural teeth, and his eyes were without glasses, still sharp and clear, and capable of that strange killer expression, familiarly known back in his more active days.

He walked without benefit of cane, and he liked to "cut the buck" to amuse the young ones. With feigned gaiety, he passed between the two big lightered posts that were the gateway into the plot, which was staved in.

"If I'd a brought along a tool, I'd a worked some too," he announced.

"You?" queried a young woman.

"Why, shore. I feel up to dancin' a jig, er takin' a jug," he retorted.

He walked up to Rachel's grave, and leaned there upon a stick that he had picked up, looking thoughtfully down at the mound.

"Old Rachel," he said, aloud. "Many a time she's fed me, and many a time my entire Company would a starved, if it hadn't a' been fer old faithful Rachel.

"I'd just as soon be laid here, beside her as anywhere."

He turned, and stepped away from the grave, to a small straight cedar, a few feet away.

"I guess this place, here with this little cedar at the head of my grave would make me a good enough restin' place," he said, talking to himself.

The young woman ceased her work, and observed that he was trimming up the little cedar with his knife.

A few days after that, in passing the cemetery, it was noticed that this particular cedar was dying! The negroes thought that such an occurrence bore some significance and were reluctant to pass after that.

It was strange that this man who was not sick should be picking out a place to be buried. Surely he could not be sick, because he never missed a day taking down his old gun and walking into the woods, where he remained later and later in the evenings, even until pitch dark drove him in.

There was a mossy glen, off the beaten path, into which, now, a dim trail was beaten. This trail was made by the feet of the Captain.

Other trees, majestic and beautiful, reared lofty heads toward the sky, but one mightier than all the rest stood alone in the middle of this haven of solitude and peace. A long-strawed yellow pine, straight and towering, as a monarch, above the timber of stunted growth.

The dim trail led directly to this spot, but here it did not stop. Around and around the pine, encircling it, as if the feet of many children had beaten bare the earth, in playing a game. The trail was endless. The scaley bark of the tree was scrubbed slick, as if hogs had scratched and rubbed their lousy backs against the tree.

All this was the sign the Captain had made, in his last days of life. The pine drew him there, like a magnet, and he could not bring himself to leave it. Whatever power that tree held over him, he could not explain, but in his lonely days of ostracism, he found a kind of solace there, in nature's realm.

He worked his mouth, he fondled his gun, he got up, and he sat down. He got up again, and he walked around the tree, seating himself down, and leaning his back against the trunk.

All day long, in any kind of weather, these movements were repeated, thousands of times, until repetition wore away the vegetation, and there was not a sprig of grass left.

Here, undisturbed, he had time to ponder the past, and the memory of many events crowded upon him.

He wrung his hands and beat upon his breast, but he could not shut out of his mind the horrible picture of that double wedding on a white Christmas, 1884, try as he might.

Remembering that there were many people of mixed-blood in Jones County, people who were not Knights, he felt that his inhuman sacrifice had been in vain.

He was not to know that in future years his purpose was to be accomplished, when the grandson of Molly would stand trial on a charge of miscegenation. He was not to know, that a man, then unborn, named Davis Knight, who was not a Knight by right of birth but was a Knight by right of a slave-name, inherited, would be on trial in the courts of Mississippi, where the Supreme Court would rule in his favor, and declare him a white man! Had he known these things, perhaps he would have been less bitter.

The terror on the faces of men, with ropes knotted about their necks, as they were suspended from limbs, raced through his distorted mind. The cries of starving children, the sound of many horns, echoed through his being—and he walked around the pine, working his mouth, and shaking his long white hair.

Creeks running red with the blood of friends and kinsmen, Jones Countians, as well as that of other Confederates, passed before his eyes. He closed them tightly.

The baying of hounds, the sound of fiddling, the beat of many horses' hooves, the patter of rain on the roof, aroused him, but it was not rain on the roof, for he was only sheltered by the timber.

"Must be a goin' crazy," he said aloud. "Better git to the house, the rain is a mendin'."

The rain had washed clean the earth, and morning came, sun-drenched and fair. The air was crisp and fresh, and exhilarating, but it did not lift the spirits of the old man who sat huddled before the embers of an early fire.

The old rocker, homemade, creaked, as he rocked to and fro, meditating. He lived entirely in the past, as it was in past memories that he drew consolation. Sometimes he could almost feel the touch of his mother's hand, could almost hear his father's voice, and then that voice became confused with many voices. The melodious voices of field hands, singing and swaying in rhythm, to ancient tunes, as they bent over baskets of cotton, baskets, handwoven from white-oak splints. The odor of the new wood was still fresh in his nostrils.

Glancing up above the whitewashed fireplace, his eyes fell upon the black horn. The leather string was looped over the peg, and the beauty of its contours stirred in him a pride, as the pride that comes from the possession of a precious jewel, as he gazed upon its pearl like surface, dangling there.

Then he recalled the men, long dead, who had rallied to its clear notes, when he had summoned them from the hills and the hollows.

Pleasant memories were giving way to memories that were haunting him, and he shook himself, and stood up, tottering a little, as he reached for the black horn. He took it down from its peg, fondled it, like a kitten, in his arms, and then replaced it upon its peg.

He walked out into the brilliant sunshine, and from the steps of his porch, he surveyed the lands about him, the great trees that had sheltered his little children from the heat in summer, when they had played beneath the great branches.

"They are all gone now, though, the children, an' I am here, alone," he said to himself.

He walked on down the path to Georgianne's house, where he would find companionship and hospitality. His step was slow, and he poked along, with his hand involuntarily going down to rest on the lower portion of his abdomen, as he often did.

Seeing him coming down the path, Georgianne walked out on her front gallery to greet him.

"Mornin', Captain. How're you a feelin' this mornin'?"

"I never felt better in my life," he replied. "I feel jest like dancin' a jig," and with that he leaned the whittled stick, which he had been using for a cane, up against her door-facing, and went into a dance.

The young women of Georgianne's household, hearing him, also came out, clapping their hands, as he "picked 'em up, an' put 'em down."

Clapping and laughing at the Captain's antics, they encouraged him on, but suddenly he stopped, and breathed deeply.

Not realizing that anything was wrong, the girls kept up the rhythm, but the grin on the Captain's face changed to an expressionless mask. The mouth refused to work. The lips were tightly compressed, and the unseeing eyes were motionless, not a quiver of an eyelash. He toppled forward, and was caught in the arms of Georgianne.

The sudden weight against her forced her backward, but the quick-thinking onlookers came to her aid, and the dead body of the Captain was gently laid down on the edge of the gallery.

Georgianne seated herself beside him, flat on the floor, and drew his head upon her lap. Her plump old hands smoothed his brow, while the girls brought wet towels, she leaned over him, listening, trying to hear a last word, from the forever silenced lips, but no word came.

It was February again. The flowering shrubs in the yard were budded out, and the scent of spring was in the air, quite a contrast with the February a year before.

The striped legged mule to the old buggy was soon on the road to Cracker's Neck. This time, the driver was a negro, going to deliver the message to Clean Neck George Knight, as he was the good man who had promised to carry out the wishes of a man who was to die friendless and alone.

There were so many Knights, bearing old family names, they were distinguished by nick names. There was "Hayseed George" and "Clean Neck George," and the Jims were likewise nicknamed, "Water Mill Jim" and "Dry Jim," in order that there would be no confusion.

So it was that Mr. Clean Neck George and a Mr. Edd Williams went up to Newt's house to attend to his burial. They found him there, surrounded by Mulattoes, and Quadroons, and Octoroons of varying shades, from blond to light chocolate.

They were a people respectful, tiptoeing in and out, offering assistance, and demonstrating a willingness to do everything in their power.

The Captain was "laid out." Nickles weighted his eyelids, lest those strange eyes remain open, and staring in death. His white hair framed a face, weather-beaten and tanned by exposure. The hands were folded across his breast, stiff and cold beneath the sheet that gently covered him. A new pair of high-top black vici kid shoes were on his feet.

"We been a waitin' fer Mr. Tom to come claim his body," said an old darkey. "We 'lowed as how he would be the one to bury him, to suit hissef, him the only son, but it looks lak he's not a comin'."

"When did you send the word?" asked Mr. Williams.

"Soon as we knowed he wuz dead," was the answer.

"Well, then," said Mr. Knight, "we'll just start on the coffin, and get it ready, for he might not be a comin'."

Tom had no intention of claiming his father's body. When he received the message, he bowed his head, experiencing a strange emotion, which was part relief, and part grief. He was relieved that it was all over. This life of hate, of shame, of persecution, which he had been forced to endure, because he was the unfortunate offspring of the Captain.

"One can bury the dead, and in a sense, bury the past," thought Tom, "but as long as there is a living reminder, the past cannot be buried. I am glad that he has gone on, but I shall keep my word. I said I would never go back up there among them niggers, and I'll not break it now."

Tom thought about all the newspaper articles, and all the magazine clippings that he had collected, where reporters gave elaborate accounts of this unusual man, so he got them all out, and read, and re-read them.

The emphatic denial that his father had ever been a soldier of the Confederacy, and the assertion that he had always been a Union man, fighting for the Union, that many writers chose to portray as a fact, gave Tom food for thought.

He thought that if what his father had told newspaper reporters was true, that then, he could be partially excused for the havoc he had wrought in Jones County.

With these thoughts in mind, he planned to write a story of his father, which would place him in a more favorable light, but he did not know enough about his father, or his father's people to write an accurate account. So he fell upon the plan of contacting the descendants of the men who had been members of his father's old Company, and they, quite naturally, wished to cover the black past of their ancestors. That was all the material that poor Tom could gather, and that is the story that has been handed to writers, over and over again.

The old clock on the mantle ticked away the hours. There was not another sound. There was not another white man there except the two, Mr. Clean Neck George and Mr. Williams, on the premises.

The hammers were silenced when the last tack was driven in the coffin. The material of the covering was black sateen, stretched tightly over the box. The store-bought handles were screwed in, and fastened into the wood. The lid was smoothly covered, and the inside of the box was carefully padded, and the body of the Captain had been gently laid.

The toes of the new shoes had stuck up above the rim of the coffin, as the twelve inches were too shallow, but the splicing to give the sides the right height was cleverly hidden.

No Tom.

"Well, we can't wait much longer," said the white men.

"Since he has been here all this time with you folks, and his own does not come, then you are the ones to say where to bury him."

There was a long silence. Then the young woman who had watched the Captain trim the cedar, came timidly forward.

"He picked a place, when we wuz a hoein' off the graveyard. He wanted, he said, to be laid wi' that little cedar at the head a' his grave, but hit's died since—" she explained.

A small group were dispatched to the old burial site to dig a grave for the Captain, on the spot of the dead cedar, and his body immediately followed.

Behind it were all ages and sizes and colors of people, those who inhabited the highlands of that famous region, where many have sought without success the true story of their origin.

The two white men took charge, and the sateen-covered casket was placed inside a box of heavier timbers. The black smooth lid was laid down carefully, contained within the moulded edge of the coffin's rim, that was designed to hold the unnailed lid in place. Then the heavy lid of the rough box was placed on, and there was not a nail used!

Mr. Williams was an uneducated country preacher, and a Godly man. He stepped forward, bareheaded, and lifted upward both hands.

"Les' sing a hymn," he commanded.

No more beautiful song service was ever rendered, as singing is the greatest natural gift of the negro. Voices were raised, softly and sweetly in reverence, as they sang "Nearer, My God to Thee."

The tiny ones, not knowing the words, "carried the tune," and all that time Mr. Williams stood there, hands upraised.

There was silence, as all the heads were bowed, but there were no tears, no flowers, just bare reality. The prayer was said, and the thudding of clay upon the unnailed lid sounded hollow, and eerie there in that remote and forsaken land.

The striped-legged mule fidgeted, and the wheels of the old buggy were moving a little, first backward, and then forward, just over, and outside the fence.

On the buggy seat sat old Georgianne, sad-faced and dry-eyed.

Her hair was as white as new-fallen snow, and her old wrinkled face appeared even whiter, as she sat there, her body swaying with the movements of the buggy.

The late sun's rays glinted on the golden circlets in her ears, as she sadly shook her head.

The rest were leaving.

"Git up, Critter," she slapped the lines, and clucked to the old mule, "it's a gittin' late."